Managing Adaptability, Intervention, and People in Enterprise Information Systems

Madjid Tavana
La Salle University, USA

Information Science
REFERENCE

Senior Editorial Director: Kristin Klinger
Director of Book Publications: Julia Mosemann
Editorial Director: Lindsay Johnston
Acquisitions Editor: Erika Carter
Development Editor: Michael Killian
Production Editor: Sean Woznicki
Typesetters: Deanna Jo Zombro, Jennifer Romanchak, Natalie Pronio
Print Coordinator: Jamie Snavely
Cover Design: Nick Newcomer

Published in the United States of America by
Information Science Reference (an imprint of IGI Global)
701 E. Chocolate Avenue
Hershey PA 17033
Tel: 717-533-8845
Fax: 717-533-8661
E-mail: cust@igi-global.com
Web site: http://www.igi-global.com

Library of Congress Cataloging-in-Publication Data
Managing adaptability, intervention and people in enterprise information systems / Madjid Tavana, editor.
p. cm.
Includes bibliographical references and index.
Summary: "This book highlights ongoing issues in three areas having implications for EIS: adaptability, intervention, and people, discussing the role of change management, conversion management, readiness management, knowledge management, e-business management, people management, and stakeholder management for a competitive advantage in EIS"--Provided by publisher.
ISBN 978-1-60960-529-2 (hbk.) -- ISBN 978-1-60960-530-8 (ebook) 1. Management information systems. I. Tavana, Madjid, 1957-
HD30.213.M348 2011
658.4'038011--dc23
2011017289

British Cataloguing in Publication Data
A Cataloguing in Publication record for this book is available from the British Library.

Table of Contents

Detailed Table of Contents

This chapter reflects on ongoing research in SMEs in the manufacturing and service sectors. It contrasts different approaches to the issue of preparedness from an organizational and social perspective, in two cases where new enterprise-wide business processes were implemented and integrated in different settings. In both cases, the emergence of new systems presented a huge challenge to companies hard-pressed to marshal the resources to mount effective change and implementation projects on this scale. The cases presented enable a comparison of different strategies used, one firm responding to organic growth, and the other to rapid industry-driven change. The chapter focuses not on the implementations per se, but instead on the issue of preparedness for change. The chapter concludes by drawing out general lessons concerning how to support and maintain organizational preparedness for enterprise wide change in different industry settings.

This article describes a complex adaptive system (CAS)-based enterprise knowledge-sharing (KnS) model. The CAS-based enterprise KnS model consists of a CAS-based KnS framework and a multi-agent simulation model. Enterprise knowledge sharing is modeled as the emergent behavior of knowledge workers interacting with the KnS environment and other knowledge workers. The CAS-based enterprise KnS model is developed to aid knowledge management (KM) leadership and other KnS researchers in gaining an enhanced understanding of KnS behavior and its influences. A premise of this research is that a better understanding of KnS influences can result in enhanced decision-making of KnS interventions that can result in improvements in KnS behavior.

This chapter presents a study conducted with several Chief Information Officers from large Iberian companies with the purpose of identifying and characterizing the roles played by IS and the motivations currently behind their adoption. The findings of this study reveal the reasons why IS and technologies are being adopted by Iberian companies are evolving and that, while the adoption of certain types of systems such as Enterprise Resource Planning systems is now consolidated, the adoption of other systems like Business Intelligence is expected to increase significantly in the near future.

Preface

MANAGING ENTERPRISE INFORMATION SYSTEMS FOR COMPETITIVE ADVANTAGE

Enterprise Information Systems (EIS) provide a technology platform that enable organizations to integrate and coordinate their business processes. They provide a single system that is central to the organization and ensure that information can be shared across all functional levels and management hierarchies (Wikipedia).

As a business management system, EIS seek to combine all aspects of the organization. EIS facilitate enterprise-wide integrated Information Systems (ISs) covering all functional areas of the organization and perform core organizational activities. EIS differ from conventional IS packages known as legacy systems; legacy IS are highly resistant to modification and evolution, whereas EIS are auto-transactional and self-assisting.

In today's business environment, EIS are critical to organizations. Business practices are constantly changing, and it is new Information Technologies that can provide competitive advantage. As systems are repeatedly modified over time, EIS evolution becomes more complicated. Businesses today must deal with new materials, growing competition, and increasing customer expectations. EIS must efficiently synchronize demand, supply, and productions, support quality, reduce costs in the supply chain network, provide reliable delivery and better service to customers, diminish inventory to a minimum, et cetera. EIS allow for integration of heterogeneous applications, protocols, and formats.

EIS form the backbone of an organization; therefore, organizational changes affect the enterprise system model when modifications have to be made. For this reason, business needs an infrastructure that supports change. Adaptive systems are necessary to enable the core business to cope with unforeseen circumstances. Adaptability enables EIS to follow changes that occur along the system's lifetime.

The terminology on adaptability is inconsistent. Flexibility, agility, and adaptability are often used interchangeably in practice; although, what follows is one understanding of a distinction. Within flexibility, the range of possible alternatives is considered fixed, that is, considered as being anticipated and pre-installed at the point of initial investment. The system can easily adapt within this range. In contrast, adaptable systems are not limited to a fixed problem set. Adaptable systems are highly self-organized, therefore, capable of creating a solution from within the system to adapt properly. Agility is considered dynamic context-specific, aggressive change; it is the ability to rapidly respond to an external and unexpected even. Agility is mainly seen in a business or process context emphasizing fast and efficient behavior.

Another distinction views flexibility as understood by three aspects: anticipation, agility, and adaptability. Combining these aspects for managing Information Technology (IT) in a changing and uncertain environment presumably would improve flexibility. Anticipation balances *planning* for expected change with *preparing* for unexpected change. An example of anticipation is aligning IT strategy with business strategy. The ability to anticipate provides the opportunity to plan and then prepare. Agility is the capability to respond quickly to environmental change. Agile managers plan for both the known and the unknown, acting versus reacting to respond quickly and effectively to both anticipated and unanticipated business changes. Adaptability is the capability of the organization to self-learn and self-organize based on previous experience. Adapting emphasizes the ability to maintain the status quo despite internal or external change. When combined, these three aspects form an IT flexibility framework that operates in a continuous cycle: anticipation occurs first; then, over time, situations change requiring agility, that is, the capability to respond quickly to the environmental changes; after responding to the changes, adaptability occurs; then, the cycle starts over beginning the anticipation stage again.

From a research point of view, adaptable systems represent the ideal final condition reflecting unlimited problem space. Therefore, understanding the constructs that underlie adaptable behavior and transferring these constructs to IS is essential. To measure the relation of IT adaptability and its impact on the organization, research suggests considering two important aspects: the organizational dimensions and the technical system that supports or hinders adaptability in these areas. Researchers propose that business system adaptability is quantifiable and recommend a measurement approach based on two dimensions: systems-based and business-use. The system-based dimension measures the inherent ability of a system's technical architecture to respond to change, while the business-use dimension measures the circumstances of usage of each system within the business. Each dimension includes several patterns or characteristics for adaptability. This measurement approach for assessing and evaluating adaptability is one contribution to a growing need to manage change.

Managing adaptability in EIS is a challenging task. It requires identification of factors that affect adaptability and how these factors affect adaptability, as well as understanding of the opportunities for and threats hindering successful adaptability. It requires understanding of the interventions that lead to change as well as an understanding of the role that people play in the change process. The next section highlights ongoing issues with implications for EIS and its management. We discuss the role of change management, conversion management, readiness management, knowledge management, e-business management, people management, and stakeholder management for competitive advantage in EIS.

CHANGE MANAGEMENT

In order to be effective, an EIS needs to be flexible. In addition to the extent of flexibility, the type of flexibility that is built into an EIS impacts system performance, in particular regarding the degree to which the system can be changed after its implementation. Few researchers today, if any, would consider EIS flexibility explicitly as a factor of EIS design and development decisions; rather such decisions tend to be dominated by short-term political considerations. Several researchers have investigated factors influencing EIS flexibility. One proposed model provides a general way of thinking about flexibility of an EIS to support a given business process. The model relates business process characteristics (uncertainty, variability, and time-criticality) with two basic types of EIS flexibility: built-in flexibility to use the EIS and flexibility to change the EIS; the model serves as a guideline for the evaluation and management of EIS flexibility.

Another model provides an EIS planning model for building flexibility and success that considers a volatile environment and the possibilities for leveraging the user's cognitive capabilities. The model specifies EIS success and organizational flexibility as dependent variables, and EIS flexibility as the means to achieve EIS success and organizational flexibility. User involvement in EIS planning is considered as an antecedent variable. The model designates EIS maturity, business strategies, user expectations, user perceived personal usefulness, and user internal flexibility as control variables. Study findings indicate that EIS success and organizational flexibility could be achieved through EIS flexibility, which could be generated by involving users in EIS planning.

Technology is a dynamic result of the interaction process between people and organizations. EIS adaptation can be viewed as the process by which staff members try to maximize an application's fit, thus enhancing their satisfaction with EIS. But fit for the uses of the same application system is not stable, because many organizations face ever-changing environments. Therefore, a dynamic and continuous view of the EIS fit is more appropriate for EIS effectiveness today. An understanding of the relationship among cognitive factors, EIS flexibility, and adaptation activities considering the temporal dimensions of adoption, implementation, and post-implementation is essential. This points to the importance of managing different levels of cognitive factors of EIS staff members, and the need to understand how these cognitive factors will change in each EIS life-cycle stage.

CONVERSION MANAGEMENT

The EIS conversion is not just a technical change; it is an organizational change that involves technology and people. Traditionally, little attention is given to the human aspects of EIS conversion. There are generally two types of managers involved in an EIS conversion project, those representing the human side and those representing the technology side of the organization. The two sides need to be in constant communication with each other, like two parents. Parents at odds in a child-rearing decision need not involve the child. Parents must make decisions as 'one parental unit,' privately; the two managers would be wise to do the same. Both managers need to point out why there is a need for change; both parties must have a desire to support change; people must receive sufficient technical training from the IS side; and the people side needs to reinforce the need for change in order to keep the team 'on board' and make the conversion successful.

Business process re-engineering (BPR) is also often used to bring technological change to organizations. The EIS conversion with BPR requires a cultural shift. Employee empowerment, leadership, teamwork, and entrepreneurship are important ingredients of this strategy. Small to medium-sized companies with decent infrastructure and knowledgeable EIS staff are better positioned to re-engineer than many of their competitors because of the lack of bureaucratic nonsense and the presence of a team-based orientation. Combine lack of technical expertise with a poor infrastructure, and a disaster is eminent.

Good top-down communication, top-management commitment, and enthusiasm from the owner or managers are crucial for the success of BPR. A more flexible structure is able to better adapt to changing customer needs and BPR. Availability of financial resources, strong managerial skills, and long-term strategic planning can also contribute to successful BPR. A good EIS infrastructure can promote successful BPR; a bad EIS infrastructure can inhibit it. A cohesive EIS infrastructure eliminates time and distance for process integration. Usually in small and medium-sized companies the decision to re-engineer comes from a position of strength; whereas, it is implied that large companies may only re-engineer when they have to.

An ongoing goal for most organizations is to grow. This is especially true for small and medium sized enterprises. As the target market for a business grows, more comprehensive EIS is needed. A number of exciting opportunities exist for business owners and managers in this position. Where there is a threat, there is an opportunity. Managers must continuously learn, seeking consultants, if necessary, to learn about what EIS solutions exist for them. Learning more about technology is the first step to achieving a competitive advantage. Because of today's economic climate, smaller companies need to make more innovative use of EIS. Business owners usually compete on price, differentiation, or both. No matter what, innovative thinking is the key to a successful change. It is surprising how the same companies that employ this strategic thinking for their marketing and business relationships often fall short when it comes to EIS innovative thinking.

In managing conversion, it is important to consider all feasible and available technical options. If there are more than one feasible option, then cost, time, and risk analysis could be used to determine the best fit. In addition, it is imperative that the conversion itself is carried out with both managers representing the human side and the technology side of the organization.

READINESS MANAGEMENT

As EIS become more deeply integrated with business and play a vital role in modern organizations, a critical question emerges: is the organization ready for EIS? This leads to an EIS implementation problem in need of address – how to prepare an enterprise with organizational and social infrastructure for technical innovations. Researchers have proposed methods to overcome this problem. Qualitative methods to analyze enterprise preparedness have been suggested. One such approach considers a rational approach consisting of two parts: preparing the people and preparing the technical system. Preparing the people involves gaining support from future users of the system, training them on the technical aspects of the system, and educating them about job and process changes after implementation. Preparing the technical system involves converting data from the legacy systems into required formats the EIS software. Quantitative methods to obtain evidence of an organization's readiness have been developed. One proposed approach includes the concepts of organizational culture, user empowerment, and change management to develop an organizational readiness benchmark for EIS readiness. Yet other researchers provide methodological frameworks for examining and improving organizational readiness for EIS implementation. A proposed architectural framework extends organizational readiness analysis from a technical project towards organizational awareness. The focus onto organizational and cultural dimensions allows for an examination of structure, stakeholders, responsibilities, activities, and norms for EIS implementation; different levels of readiness requirements from perspectives of technical systems, business processes, and organizational culture in terms of norms can be classified.

The ongoing research in this area of organizational readiness highlights the need for organization proper predisposition before adopting an EIS. Clearly, there is a need to assess preparedness for change of business environment when designing enterprise systems.

KNOWLEDGE MANAGEMENT

In a highly dynamic environment, enterprises increasingly recognize that knowledge management is one of the most important factors contributing to business success. There are two types of important assets in an enterprise: physical assets and knowledge assets; the integration of the two is required for competitive advantage. It is essential for enterprises to refresh their EIS and integrate knowledge management function. EIS with knowledge management capacity can be more responsive to changes in the global environment.

Knowledge is a mix of experience, values, contextual information, and insight that provides a framework for evaluating and incorporating new experiences and information. Knowledge management is the organizational process for acquiring, organizing, and communicating both explicit and tacit knowledge, allowing users to employ knowledge to be more effective and productive. Knowledge management systems are Information Systems designed to collect, code, integrate, disseminate, and facilitate organizational knowledge. One of the challenges of knowledge management is that of getting people to share their knowledge. Knowledge-sharing is the process of exchanging knowledge among organizational members. An enhanced understanding of knowledge-sharing behavior and its influences would aid knowledge management leadership in their management efforts.

It is conceivable that any model of knowledge-sharing include a complex adaptive system perspective. A complex adaptive system is a system that emerges over time into a coherent form, and adapts and organizes itself without any singular entity deliberately managing or controlling it. Complex adaptive systems are composed of interacting agents which respond to stimuli and stimulus-response behavior that can be defined in terms of rules. Agents adapt by changing their rules as experience accumulates and can be aggregated into meta-agents whose behavior may be emergent. Viewing business systems from a complex adaptive system perspective, the organization can better assess their flexibility and adaptability and evaluate their architecture. Enhanced flexibility, adaptability, and reusability of these systems can strengthen the ability of an enterprise to evolve and survive in the marketplace.

E-BUSINESS MANAGEMENT

Today's EIS managers face tremendous challenges given the increasing complexity of Internet and Web technologies and their rapid evolution. Within their enterprise information and technology architecture, they seek optimal utilization of their existing IS for business performance while ensuring integration of the latest Internet and Web technologies. At the same time, they must meet the expectations of business managers who must keep up with the changing competitive environment and customer needs by creating and sustaining innovative business value propositions. Customer-oriented e-business solutions provide a means to deal with the complexity of the latest technologies while ensuring their rapid adoption and adaptation. There is an increasing greater need to integrate across extended value chains. Realigning product and service platforms into e-business solution architectures can better address the needs of improved integration and inter-operability.

In addition to enabling the technology, a better understanding of organizational cultural issues and their strategic implications is critical to the implementation of e-business technology architectures. E-business technologies cannot be effective if implemented without regard to vital aspects related to organization, culture, strategy and management of the enterprise – aspects critical for enterprise agility and adaptability. Researchers describe seven challenges related to organizational cultural aspects of the enterprise with strategic implications that e-business implementations encounter: strategic, control, organizational cultural, knowledge, economic, structural, and management challenges. Technology managers are encouraged to take a holistic approach to designing inter-and intra-organizational systems with consideration not only for the technological design but also for the design of non-technical enablers of these systems in order to successfully manage these challenges.

PEOPLE MANAGEMENT

EIS and people are inextricable. EIS are the outcome of human design and implementation and their benefit arises due to their efficacy through their application by humans. Therefore, EIS require both efficacious design and implementation by people and use by people. This relationship is foremost in the implementation and application of EIS. EIS are a source of competitive advantage at the functional level as firms may compete due to a lower cost of production or through innovative products or both. This is relevant to all firms. It is especially relevant for service firms, especially firms that provide information on complex products to consumers and also use information and communication technologies to provide services.

Information and communications systems and technologies have increased in importance for organizations at a functional and business level, that is support and operational level respectively, and also at a strategic corporate level. Many of these focused on task automation and transaction processing to obtain economies and reduce costs. Of course, the motivation for implementing EIS varies widely between them depending on the aim and the level in the organization, that is at an operational, support, or strategic level. The type of system may also be to support management, assist in knowledge management, or improve performance and may be based on internal or external information. They may also be associated with Internet technologies such as in business-to-business and business-to-customer marketing and customer relationship management.

The main reasons for introducing EIS are to improve the quality of products and customer service, as well as differentiating from competitors at the product factor and service factor levels, to improve business processes, to increase productivity, and to reduce costs. They are also implemented to increase knowledge flows, improve internal and external communication, and in formulating strategy in terms of markets, industries, and countries.

Essentially, EIS aim to obtain and store proprietary information on internal processes, on the external market, and on customers. They allow people to retrieve and disseminate this information and convert it into knowledge so as to increase organization learning through knowledge sharing or assist in the planning processes and resource management.

In the engineering language of business processes people are considered as merely service providers, and their role is not considered as central as the processes themselves. However, people interact and cooperate in EIS and are central to an organization's processes. The origins of this perspective may be traced to EIS. This evolved into process-oriented approach consisting of user tasks, that require a people input, and automatic procedures, that do not require people input.

When people are part of the process, they are service providers according to the orchestration-oriented approach. This considers people as generators of a process, such that, an instruction from one person to another consists of different though sequential processes. This assumes that the processes are distinct and most people interactions are cooperative. This cooperation may be considered as conversations.

One approach to this integration is the People-Oriented Business Process Notation (POBN) and when conversations and processes are integrated it is referred to as a conversation-oriented perspective. This differs from the orchestration-oriented perspective that follows a centralized approach whereby individual interactions are not explicit in the process.

There are three elements to a conversation. These are the type of interaction, the direction of the interaction, and the process initiated. In a conversation there is interaction between people. That is one person communicates with another and it is the content of the content that elicits a response. The object of the intended communication is the business content. It is important that the communication clearly specifies its purpose. Assuming there is a request initiated by one person the responder may accept, not accept, or request clarification. This is the interaction between people to initiate a business process. Therefore, the conversation-oriented perspective places great emphasis on the participation and cooperation of users in intra-organization business process.

STAKEHOLDER MANAGEMENT

Managing and designing EIS requires the management and inclusion of stakeholders in the process. People are central to the efficient and efficacious design, implementation, and functioning of systems, and thereby, users play an important role in ensuring the quality and user satisfaction and ultimately user acceptance of a system. However, with the increase in external system design, such as standard packages and outsourcing, it is difficult to incorporate users into the design. That means that stakeholders in system design may be from within the organization, and more often from different departments in the same organization leading to different perspectives of users, and also from outside the organization. This diverse group of stakeholder, may include external stakeholders such as suppliers, customers, and sometimes regulatory authorities and government. Especially in virtual firms, outsourced activities must be included in the systems design. The exclusion of some or all stakeholders in the design and implementation of a system may lead to resistance on the part of some or all.

The project manager must determine the relevant stakeholders and categorize and rank these in order of importance. Their management is central to the management of the project. These stakeholders have a role in the decision of system functionality and output. Of course, consensus is not always possible, and that means that despite inclusion, some stakeholders may oppose it. However, in the instance where stakeholders are not included in the design of an IS, the users react differently. Designers and users may have different a priori expectations. The a posteriori reaction may be acceptance, adaption, or not acceptance. Therefore, the probability of acceptance is higher when stakeholders are included in the design and implementation. Stakeholders also have the opportunity to influence the design, and designers must accept this intrusion. An argument could be made then that ISs are not merely technical systems. They are socio-technical systems involving social factors, power through hierarchy, and politics through alliances that are part of the dynamics of any group.

Stakeholders in EIS project are individuals and groups within departments in a firm, as well as entire departments, or indeed the firm at the business, functional, and corporate levels, who have the capacity to influence or be influenced by the proposed system. These stakeholders may have a common understanding or diverse reaction of the efficacy of an IS. It is unusual to have such common understanding, so it more likely to be influenced conflicting arguments.

Of course, influence may be a perception that is realized or not, depending on power and politics. Furthermore, the stakeholders opinions may be merely perceptions and may also be subjective, and when objective may be biased based on personal, group, or organizational objectives. This depends on the management of the consultative process.

The stages of stakeholder management are to determine the stakeholders, determine the stages of their involvement and their roles and objectives and their degree of involvement, classify their relevant importance and proceed with a design and implementation plan. The order of these varies depending on complexity of the project, requirements of the project and the power of the individuals and groups who are considered the stakeholders.

To determine stakeholders, the project managers must decide as to who could affect the design and implementation of an EIS and who could be affected by such a system. In effect, this is subjective. The methods used to determine the relevant stakeholders. It could be based on generic groups such as managers, administrators, or suppliers, among others. This could be adapted to include more specific relevant sub-groups within the various generic stakeholder groups depending on the industry. Another approach is to ascertain the most relevant groups based on specific questions, such as, who the users of the system, the users of the output, the managers that make decisions based on the output, or those that are would affected by the system. The questions are different for each project and industry and firm. The stakeholders may be different using this approach although there should be a significant overlap. Another alternative approach is based on the network of relations within and between organizations. This network based model allows the entire stakeholders to be considered as a complex interacting group and that this is evolving. That is unlike the other approaches that are static there is a dynamic and temporal aspect to this approach.

An EIS project has stages, such as design, implementation, use, and disuse. Some of these stages are sequential, parallel, and may be repeated through the temporal continuation of the system. And it this temporal aspect that suggests that the stakeholders may be different as the project continues and the when the system is implemented and evolves. As the project evolves, the influence and importance of stakeholders may also evolve. And, of course, the actions of stakeholders may evolve in terms of their involvement depending on the significance to them at the various stages of the project.

It is also important to establish boundaries for stakeholders. Otherwise their inclusion could be interpreted as intrusion. This is where the stakeholders have a representative role or an influencing role. Furthermore, the role of the stakeholder may evolve as the stages of the project evolve. A stakeholder may be a designer and a user simultaneously during the project or at different stages. The possible roles of a stakeholder range from owner, project manager, user, developer, decision maker, or passive involver.

In terms of interest, it is essential that the stakeholders be determined based on their interests in the project. When the stakeholders, their roles and their interests of stakeholders are determined they should be associated with objects and interests.

The objects and issues within an EIS project are scope of the system, that is, the aim and advantages of a system, business model or business processes, functioning enterprise, the inputs and outputs of the system, system model or human interaction, technology, configuration or compatibility, and the project performance and cost. These issues have different importance or interest depending on the stakeholders and their specific roles. This also determines the level of motivation at the various stages, the priorities, and reaction to the issues. Of course, some stakeholders' interests may not be realistic or realizable within the scope of the project.

It is possible to outline the interest of stakeholders and include those that the system allows for the realization of objectives, has a positive return on investment, improves business processes, provides quality information, has easy functionality, performs, as well as that the project is completed on schedule. Assessing the relative importance of stakeholders is a more dynamic process than a static process as their importance may evolve with the project and their interest and power.

There are obviously conflicting roles and levels of stakeholders in terms of interests and motivation, power, and stage of the project. These stakeholders must be managed to ensure the progress of the project. This may include informing the stakeholder without further influence on their part, consulting with the stakeholders, involving stakeholders and allowing them influence, collaborating and allowing co responsibility for the project, and empowering the stakeholders such that they are responsible for one or more objects of the project.

The final stage having determined the status of stakeholders is to develop a stakeholder management plan specifying the appropriate type and level of communication and interaction with stakeholders based on their roles, interests, and salience. This should be continuously reviewed to incorporate the dynamics of the project, due to internal and external factors, and also to calibrate the demands of the project and the inclusion of other stakeholders that may not have been considered in previous stages of the project. There are inter-stakeholder dynamics also, and a review could equilibrate their interventions, where necessary.

In developing and implementing ISs and technologies it is obvious that people are central to their design, implementation, and use. The design process is most important and therefore, involving stakeholders in the process leads to a more efficacious system provided that the roles and the power of the stakeholders are balanced and managed to ensure that conflicts between individuals and groups, and between various functions and operations. It is also important to determine in the design the aim of an IS either as a process support, as a source of information and data or as a strategic and resource management. At the implementation stage it is important to avoid resistance to implementers from managers and end-users of systems and technologies. This is only partly accomplished at the stakeholder involvement stage. Finally, it is important to have integrated enterprise-wide systems that allow a firm to harness the proprietary information and knowledge within an organization and to have communications and data flows both within and between departments at the functional level, or business units at the business, and finally, with the corporate level.

CONCLUSION

Companies today are immersed in highly competitive world-wide markets that are continuously changing. As a consequence, companies must evolve introducing strategic and structural changes as a response to the external forces of the environment. Ongoing research on EIS is vital to provide insights into the challenges, issues, and solutions related to management of various aspects of EIS. A recurring theme threads through the EIS issues highlighted above: business/IT fusion. The message – business and IT "working as one" is essential to achieve business breakthrough performance and competitive edge in EIS.

IN THIS BOOK

Ruey-Shun Chen, Chia-Ming Sun, Marilyn Helms, and Wen-Jang Jih in Chapter 1, *Factors Influencing Information System Flexibility: An Interpretive Flexibility Perspective*, provide a model of IS flexibility that encompasses all stages of the IS life cycle. The model posits that cognitive factors from both IS staff and users are important for leveraging IS flexibility with adaptation activities. The study uses an interpretative flexibility perspective and distinguishes between flexibility to use and flexibility to change. The authors present propositions hypothesizing the relationship among cognitive factors, IS flexibility and adaptation activities considering the temporal dimensions of adoption, implementation and post-implementation.

Lorraine Warren and Ted Fuller, in Chapter 2, *Contrasting Approaches to Preparedness: A Reflection on Two Case Studies*, present two contrasting approaches to the issues of preparedness for enterprise-wide change in small organizations. These contrasting approaches point to the need for different enterprise design. In the *step change* scenario, a robust platform that integrates and supports the needs of the company over the years in what is expected to be a relatively stable environment is required; in the more *just in time* scenario, the design must accommodate a constant state of preparedness that results in the partial construction of new systems aging the potential existence of developing project that may or may not be realized.

Cynthia Small and Andrew Sage, in Chapter 3, *A Complex Systems-Based Enterprise Knowledge Sharing Model*, describe a complex adaptive systems (CAS)-based enterprise knowledge sharing (KnS) model. The authors show that the CAS-based enterprise KnS model and methodology provides knowledge management (KM) leadership with an enhanced understanding of KnS behavior and KnS influences. The KnS behaviors incorporated in the enterprise KnS model are defined by types of knowledge (tacit and explicit) and ontological dimension (individual, group, and organization). KnS influences included are the enterprise KnS environment, KnS behavior of other knowledge workers, and attributes of the knowledge workers.

Kari Smolander and Matti Rossi, in Chapter 4, *Conflicts, Compromises, and Political Decisions Methodological Challenges of Enterprise-wide E-Business Architecture Creation*, focus on the creation of e-business architecture and observes that the architecture emerges through somewhat unintentional actions obliged by the situation and its constraints, conflicts, compromises, and political decisions. Based on observations at an international Information Communications Technology (ICT) company, the authors argue that organizational problems as the major problems to be solved when creating an e-business or enterprise architecture.

Efrem Mallach, in Chapter 5, *Information System Conversion Strategies: A Unified View*, propose a step-by-step method for IS conversion. Mallach points out the importance of paying equal attention to both the technical and human sides of ISs. The author categorizes five components of ISs as hardware, software, data, procedures, and people. Mallach also discusses several conversion methods including: direct cutover (i.e. plunge) conversion, pilot conversion, phased (i.e. modular) conversion, and parallel conversion.

Sajda Qureshil, Mehruz Kamal, and Peter Wolcott, in Chapter 6, In *Information Technology Interventions for Growth and Competitiveness in Micro-Enterprises*, identify the following challenges facing micro-enterprises: affordability, awareness of IT, infrastructure, private versus government sectors, and management's capacity. They show how micro-enterprises can adopt IT to achieve competitiveness. They propose IT Therapy for helping micro-enterprises develop tailored IT solutions for their needs. They study seven micro-enterprises and argue that without IT Therapy, the owners of these businesses might not have figured out how to best use their newly awarded gifts. They proposed a model of micro-enterprise growth based on the resource-based perspective and the focus-dominance model, both of which were employed in this study. All micro-enterprises studied were actively seeking to adopt new IT to help achieve a competitive advantage. In most or all cases this involved launching, or improving upon, a website.

Jeffrey Chang, Margi Levy, and Philip Powell in Chapter 7, *Small Firm Process Re-Engineering Success*, discuss IS conversion with BPR in small to medium sized enterprises (SMEs) versus BPR in large corporations. They study eight Taiwanese case studies and explore issues contributing to the successful process re-engineering in small firms. They propose a framework that is comprised of four components:

culture, structure, resources, and technology. They outline factors for success or failure, depending on how the four components are understood. Some of the major factors affecting a successful BPR are innovation, employee empowerment, top management commitment, and strategic perspective. Usually the re-engineering decision in SMEs comes from a position of strength; whereas, it is implied that large companies may only re-engineer when they 'have to.'

Albert Boonstra, in Chapter 8, *Aligning Systems, Structures, and People: Managing stakeholders in Enterprise Information Systems Projects*, focuses on managing stakeholders in EIS. He argues that stakeholder management should go beyond the conventional user participation and management involvement since all stakeholders have a genuine interest in the successful implementation of the system. Boonstra proposes to use several methods from the organizational management field for the successful implementation of EIS.

Giorgio Bruno, in Chapter 9, *People-Oriented Business Processes*, considers the role of user participation in business processes. He argues that current approaches do not put emphasis on user participation in business processes and lack the capability to represent user interactions. Bruno shows that human work is a cooperative process and the cooperation between coworkers generally takes place through structured interactions called conversation. He proposes conversation-oriented perspective to effectively integrate business processes with conversations.

João Varajão, Antonio Trigo, and João Barroso, in Chapter 10, *Enterprise Information Systems Adoption in Iberian Large Companies: Motivations and Trends*, discuss the importance of IS and technologies in organizations and the motives for their adoption. They carry out a study with the participation of several chief information officers to identify and characterize the motivations behind the adoption of Information Technologies in large Iberian companies. Their study reveals that while some technologies such as Enterprise Resource Planning systems are now consolidated, other technologies such as Business Intelligence systems should increase significantly in the near future.

Kathryn A. Szabat
La Salle University, USA

Aidan O'Connor
Ecole Supérieure de Commerce Et Management, France

Madjid Tavana
La Salle University, USA

Section 1
Managing Adaptability

Chapter 1
Factors Influencing Information System Flexibility:
An Interpretive Flexibility Perspective

Ruey-Shun Chen
China University of Technology, Taiwan

Chia-Ming Sun
National Yunlin University of Science & Technology, Taiwan

Marilyn M. Helms
Dalton State College, USA

Wen-Jang (Kenny) Jih
Middle Tennessee State University, USA

ABSTRACT

Information System (IS) flexibility has been regarded as an important indicator of information technology success. This article provides a model of IS flexibility encompassing all stages of IS implementation and usage. The model considers the cognitive factors from IS staff and users as important leveraging IS flexibility with adaptation activities. A review of constructs extending from the interpretive flexibility perspective in the literature is used to identify these cognitive factors. By hypothesizing the relationships among these cognitive factors, IS flexibility, and adaptation activities several propositions are identified. Empirical testing is then warranted to refute or validate the propositions.

DOI: 10.4018/978-1-60960-529-2.ch001

INTRODUCTION

Enhancing information system flexibility with flexible information technology infrastructure and adaptable application systems has been a critical issue for IS managers (Duncan, 1995; Prahalad & Krishnan, 2002; Sambamurthy *et al.*, 2003). Information systems must be flexible to satisfy user requirements, particularly in changing environments. Sufficient IS flexibility could extend the life cycle of information systems and expand the effectiveness of IT investment (Cha-Jan Chang & King, 2005; Chang & King, 2005; Gebauer & Schober, 2006; Moitra & Ganesh, 2005).

Truex et al. (1999) found users can never be satisfied in emergent organizations, because their needs are always changing. The user-to-systems relationship, which often experiences continuing conflict, requires application systems flexibility. This viewpoint holds that IS projects should not only focus on design and development activities, but also value the adaptation activities in both implementation and post-implementation stages (Markus *et al.*, 2003; Ross *et al.*, 2003; Truex et al., 1999). As emphasized in prior studies, this calls for considering IS flexibility through the overall life cycle in addition to planning and crafting an infrastructure of IT (Byrd & Turner, 2000; Lewis & Byrd, 2003). Despite a wealth of research on IS flexibility and its impacts on organizations and business processes (Gebauer & Schober, 2006; Moitra & Ganesh, 2005; Sambamurthy et al., 2003), decisions regarding IS flexibility, especially considering the entire IS life cycles, have rarely been included into the analysis. As a result, flexibility guidelines for managing IS have not been developed.

In addition, the benefits of IS flexibility are difficult to measure physically or objectively; particularly as they are perceived by both IS staff and system users. IS flexibility to accommodate changes in the supported business processes depends on the various ways staff members combine application functions with business activities (Askenas & Westelius, 2003; Moitra & Ganesh, 2005). Thus, this study uses an interpretive flexibility perspective that differs with most prior studies which consider IS flexibility as being built into IT artifacts through IS design and development activities (Byrd *et al.*, 2004; Byrd & Turner, 2000; Lewis & Byrd, 2003). In addition, this study asserts that the cognitive factors of staff members would influence the decisions and adaptation activities associated with IS flexibility.

Flexibility comes at the price of complexity and the additional investment required (Gebauer & Schober, 2006; Stigler, 1939). The decisions regarding IS flexibility are filled with the tradeoffs that need to find a balance between *IS rigidity* and *IS complexity* (Gebauer & Schober, 2006; Silver, 1991). IS implementation always involves the risk of failure from rigidity, changing requirements, or too much complexity to maintain. Therefore, we apply the concept of *perceived risk* from the consumer behavior literature to analyze the perceived requirement for IS flexibility. This perception is related to decisions for lowering or limiting the risk of failures on future IS usage. The perceived risk approach, based on the interpretive flexibility perspective, could be an original and important direction for analyzing IS flexibility. This leads to the following research questions:

1. What kinds of factors interact to change IS flexibility in each stage of IS adoption, implementation, and post-implementation?
2. How do these factors for IS flexibility differ between IS staff and users in each stage of IS adoption, implementation, and post-implementation?

THEORETICAL BACKGROUND

First, it is necessary to clarify the content of IS flexibility (for use and for change) and IS adaptation activities (including technology systems and task adaptation) since these are the primary means to alter IS flexibility in actual usage. Subsequently, the related concepts that form the foundation for the theoretical model: perceived risk and interpretive flexibility are reviewed.

Information System Flexibility

There are two types of IS flexibility: (1) *IS flexibility for use* is the range of possibilities provided by an information system until a major change is required, and (2) *Flexibility to change or* the potential adaptability for further changes of a given information systems (Gebauer & Schober, 2006; Knoll & Jarvenpaa, 1994). Mostly, scholars focus the issue of *flexibility to use* on the functions of the information system that can be determined by designers. All features should not be embedded in the IT products in advance. IT resources allow uses that are not yet envisioned by the developers of the resource (Knoll & Jarvenpaa, 1994).

In addition to the decision regarding the level of *IS flexibility to use (*as the result of the combined choices with functionality, data base and interface), another consideration is IS flexibility. This involves the choices influencing the effort required to change an information system after its initial implementation. *Flexibility to change* usually plummets as the system life cycle progresses from implementation to maintenance. That is why Duncan (1995) issued the concept of flexible IT infrastructure and identified basic components of IT infrastructures. However, Prahalad and Krishnan (2002) found that the quality of IT infrastructures, especially the flexibility of application systems, has lagged behind needs and became impediments. Many companies are still constrained by legacy infrastructure, including incompatible databases and applications, poor data quality, and restricted scalability on vender's software modules.

IS Adaptation Activities

Although *flexibility to use* and *flexibility to change* are properties of IS architecture and applications, are shaped in design stage, their actual impacts are also influenced by following technology adaptation activities in both implementation and post-implementation stages (Tyre & Orlikowski, 1994). These adaptations are major ways to increase user satisfaction and IS flexibility after the adoption stage of IS.

Technology adaptation is referred to as the adjustments and changes following the installation of a new technology in a given setting (Tyre & Orlikowski, 1994). Technology adaptation as IS adaptation activities is further grouped into two kinds of IS adaptation activities -- *system adaptation* and *task adaptation* (Hong & Kim, 2002). Even with the popularity of packaged software, IS implementation often requires organizations adapt the application systems and/or processes to fit operations embedded in the software of the adopted information systems. This software modification or adaptation increases the feature-function fit between systems and the adopting organizations. Such *system adaptation* is categorized into customization, extension, and modification (Brehm *et al.*, 2001). Another kind of adaptation that considers organizational change and the functions of package software is *task adaptation*. Task adaptation includes *process adaptation* and *operation adaptation*. Users change or adjust their processes to fit those embedded in the adopted application systems. Both *system adaptation* and *task adaptation* have become the main activities to prevent IS failure, improve the organizational fit of IS usage, and maintain IS flexibility.

However, most decisions for IS adaptation activities focus only on user satisfactory and organizational fit in short term, flexibility to use an information system. Each adaptation activity influences the flexibility range of IS today as well as in the future. This viewpoint is often ignored by most stakeholders and leads to the complexity of IS. It is important to clarify the cognitive factors of the staff members that influence the two types of IS flexibility via IS adaptation activities.

Interpretive Flexibility

The critical decision factors influencing adaptation approaches are primarily focused on *perceived fit,* which is popularly applied in technology acceptance model (TAM) in IS research (Amoako-Gyampah & Salam, 2004). In addition the proposed model includes cognitive factors based on the interpretive flexibility perspective: *perceived flexibility requirement* and *perceived IS control*.

From the technical point of view, information systems are considered as 'engineered artifacts' expected to do exactly what they are designed for (Orlikowski, 1992). Likewise, organizations are regarded as information processing systems, exchanging and handling information based on certain rules (Katzenstein & Lerch, 2000). According to this perspective, the organizations are assumed to have clear requirements and regular usages for IS.

In contrast, researchers argue, while information systems do have objective and touchable artifacts, they also have a subjective construct. Orlikowski argued 'technology is not an external object but a product of ongoing action, design and appropriation' (1992, p. 400). Included within this perspective of technology is *interpretive flexibility*, which refers to 'the degree to which users of a technology are engaged in its construction (physically or socially) during development' (Orlikowski, 1992:406). The same technology is likely to have different meanings and effects for different users (Pozzebon & Pinsonneault, 2005; Rose & Scheepers, 2001), particularly in the case of configurable software packages that are not developed in-house (Pozzebon & Pinsonneault, 2005). A configurable IS (i.e. Enterprise Planning Systems), designed with many individuals setting parameters to reflect the requirement of different organizational features, and is complex and challenging. People will have varying interpretations about a configurable IS based on their differing levels of knowledge, skill and experience with the systems.

In summary, the implementation and adaptation of an application systems could be analyzed as a cognitive process and the embedded IS flexibility is affected by the interpretive flexibility perspective of users and specifies. Although, the concept of interpretive flexibility has been considered in many studies, the detailed constructs and the conceptual definitions of interpretive IS flexibility have not been addressed.

RESEARCH MODEL

Figure 1 shows the proposed theoretical model, which posits that the embedded IS flexibility interacts with cognitive factors from staff members as well as from IS adaptation activities in their effects on interpretive IS flexibility. Unlike prior studies considering IS flexibility as embedded in IT artifacts, our proposed model focuses on the cognitive factors of staff members and their influence the adoption decisions for information technology. The model also includes the interaction of the cognitive factors with IS adaptation activities as they affect IS flexibility in the implementation and post-implementation stages. The underlying theories in our model are interpretive flexibility, the technology acceptance model and perceived risk theory. The main constructs of cognitive factors in the model are developed below.

Perceived Fit

The theoretical foundation of this study is that individuals' perceptions about using IT are posited to influence adoption behaviors (Moore & Benbasat, 1991). The technology acceptance model (TAM) is one of the most popular theories in IS dealing with behavioral intentions and usage of IT (Amoako-Gyampah & Salam, 2004). TAM proposes that *perceived usefulness* and *perceived ease of use* are most relevant in explaining the behavioral intention to use IS (Davis, 1989). Davis defined *perceived usefulness* as 'the degree to which a person believes that using a particular system would enhance his or her job performance' and defined *perceived ease of use* as 'the degree to which a person believes that using a particular system would be free of effort.'

In this study, we applied these two constructs to explain the factors influencing IS flexibility. However, the short-term view of perceived fit on IS usage will lead to the nearsightedness of focusing only on *IS flexibility to use*. Therefore, in addition to the perceived fit perspective based on TAM, we still include additional cognitive

Figure 1. A theoretical model of information system flexibility with interpretive flexibility perspective

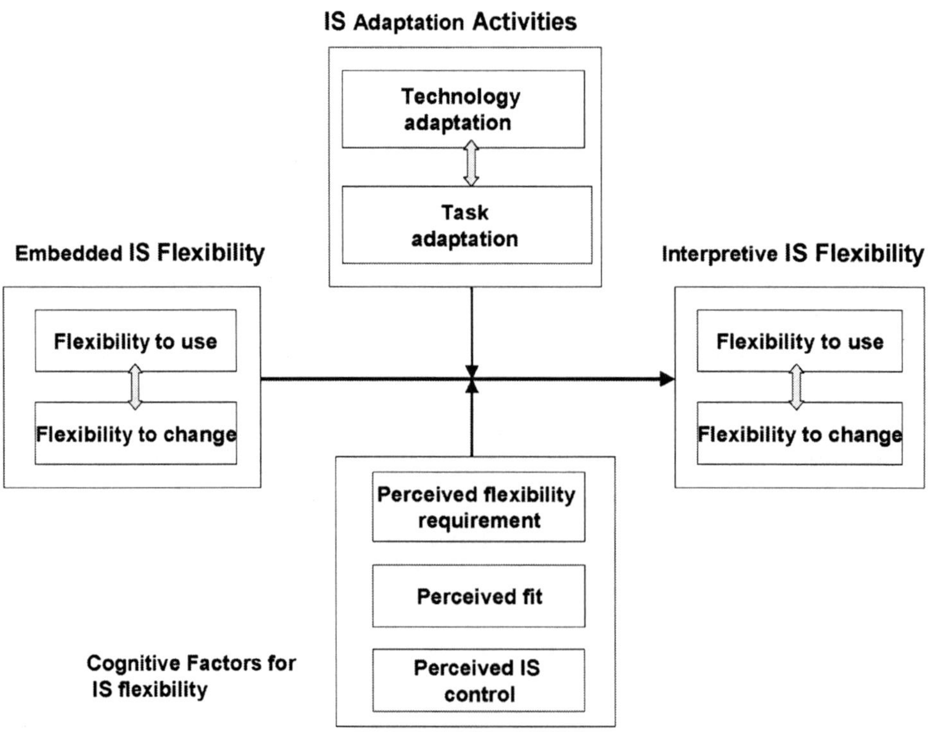

factors that explain when or how staff members recognize the impact of adaptation activities on *IS flexibility to change*. We define this construct as *perceived flexibility requirement,* which is similar TAM and founded on the concept of perceived risk.

Perceived Flexibility Requirement

The concept of *perceived risk* most often used by consumer researchers who define risk in terms of the consumer's perceptions of the *uncertainty* and the adverse consequences of buying a product (or service) (Dowling & Staelin, 1994). Just as the properties of products and services can lower perceived risk, the flexibility of an information system avoids usage situations with uncertain consequences that would cause staff members to feel 'uncomfortable' or 'anxious'. In addition, IS differs from general consumer products. The flexibility of information systems can be continuously changed by adaptation activities beyond the adoption stage. Thus, the perceived risk of staff members influences information systems purchase decisions but also influences their adaptation activities in implementation and post-implementation stages.

Consequently, we define the *perceived flexibility requirement* for IS as 'the perceived risk of staff members regarding the inflexibility of IS to use or to change with their involvement throughout the IS life cycle'. The perceived risk and involvement of staff members for IS implementation and usage will alter the level of perceived requirement for IS flexibility. And, the perceived flexibility requirement is one of major factors affecting the adoption decisions and the decisions for IS adaptation activities in both implementation and post-implementation stages. Although the flexibility of information systems can be altered somewhat after the adoption stage, it is not unlimited.

Perceived IS Control

Information systems not only support the tasks but also control how the work is performed (Askenas & Westelius, 2003). People's perception of how the system attempts to influence their work is termed *perceived IS control.* Thus IS control, to a large degree, is subjective. Because the more knowledgeable IS people are crafting the information systems, the easier it is to gain a sense of control (Askenas & Westelius, 2003; Besson & Browe, 2001).

In addition, perceived IS control varies among staff members based on their familiarity with IS functionality. At today's maturity stage of the IT industry with standardization of IT products and the popularity of commercial software packages, one important problem associated with perceived IS control is negotiations concerned with balancing the global development of information infrastructure and the various local contexts they are to operate across (Rolland & Monteiro, 2002). System adaptation strategy is not recommended due to integrity degradation as well as making future upgrade more difficult. But, forces of globalization on IS have led to a new control crisis—the system adaptation. These adaptation activities for local context often slow future maintenance due to the complexity of application systems.

In brief, IS unfamiliarity, IS rigidity caused by global standardization, and IS maintenance complexity form the main sources of perceived IS control for both IS staff and users. Perceived IS control has become another factor restraining IS flexibility in each life-cycle stage.

Table 1 provides the main constructs, mapped directly onto our research model in Figure 1. Table 1 also lists the key factors and their conceptual definitions for each construct, which are described in previous research and/or are modified by the researchers.

Table 1. Conceptual definitions of the constructs in the research model

Constructs	Dimensions	Conceptual definitions	Previous studies
IS flexibility for use	*System functionality*	The different features a system provides the users.	(Soh *et al.*, 2000)
	Scope of underlying database	The scope of the database support for deploying reports and analyses for decision making.	(Soh et al., 2000)
	User interface	The different features and methods an information system provides to users for interaction.	(Soh et al., 2000)
	Processing capacity	The capacity provided by an information system before major performance losses are experienced.	(Gebauer & Schober, 2006)
IS flexibility for change	*Integration*	The integration of data and functionality provided by open system architecture with compatibility of application across platforms.	(Byrd & Turner, 2000; Duncan, 1995)
	Modularity	Modularity as provided by the use of reusable software modules, vendor-independent database connectivity, and object-oriented development tools.	(Byrd & Turner, 2000; Duncan, 1995)
	Technology skills	The variety of skills and attitudes of the IS staff.	(Byrd et al., 2004; Byrd & Turner, 2000; Duncan, 1995)

continued on following page

Table 1. continued

Constructs	Dimensions	Conceptual definitions	Previous studies
System adaptation	*Enterprise application integration (EAI)*	A middle technology aimed at integrating individual applications into a seamless whole, enabling business processes and data to communicate with one another, across applications, without system customization.	(Hong & Kim, 2002; Soh et al., 2000; Sutherland & Heuvel, 2002)
	System customization	The adaptation activities utilizing configuration, extension and modification to fill the gap between IS functionality and organizational requirements.	(Brehm et al., 2001; Hong & Kim, 2002; Soh et al., 2000)
Task adaptation	*Process adaptation*	The implementing organization adapts its processes to fit those embedded in the adopted information systems	(Hong & Kim, 2002; Soh et al., 2000)
	Operation adaptation	The adaptation activities of users themselves within the operations and output styles of the adopted information systems.	(Soh et al., 2000)
Perceived flexibility requirement	*Involvement*	The personal relevance of IS flexibility based on inherent needs, values and interests.	(Laroche *et al.*, 2003; Zaichkowsky, 1985)
	Perceived risk	The staff members' perceptions of the *uncertainty* and adverse consequences of adopting and using an information system.	(Cox & Rich, 1964; Laroche *et al.*, 2003; Zaichkowsky, 1985)
Perceived fit	*Perceived usefulness*	The degree to which an individual believes that using a particular system would enhance their job performance.	(Davis, 1989)
	Perceived easy to use	The degree to which an individual believes using a particular system would be easy.	(Davis, 1989)
Perceived IS control	*Perceived IS control for users*	The user's perception of how the system is trying to influence their work	(Askenas & Westelius, 2003)
	Complexity on maintenance	The complexity and the constraints of maintenance perceived by IS staff about an adopted information system.	(Braa & Hedberg, 2002; Rolland & Monteiro, 2002)

PROPOSITION DEVELOPMENT

In this section, constructs introduced above to analyze the relationships with IS flexibility and IS adaptation activities are presented. These relationships are analyzed based on the key stages for IS usage: adoption, implementation and post- implementation. Differences on attitudes and behavior of IS staff and users is also provided.

IS Adoption Stage

The perceived risk theory predicts consumers engage in risk-reducing activities (i.e., information-search) (Dowling and Staelin, 1994). For IS adoption decisions, this can be achieved by collecting new information about the technology being applied, the available system functions, or the system's flexibility.

Building flexible IT infrastructure and adaptable IS are the most important issues for IS staff and users today. However, the IS flexibility emphasized by IS staff is different than the flexibility emphasized by users. Normally, users focus on *flexibility for use* because *perceived usefulness* and *perceived ease of use* are the main information system criteria that are evaluated. User satisfaction is changing; user needs may unfold rapidly in directions that are not well understood by the users themselves (Truex et al., 1999). The IS requirements of user evolve as organizations or environments change. This calls for the requirement of *IS flexibility to change*. If staff members interpret short life spans as an IS failure, staff members might develop an *IS flexibility to change* perspective for long-term ease of maintenance rather than a goal of short-term usage.

Who should be responsible for stressing IS flexibility? The perceived risk theory suggests the consumer's involvement with purchase decisions influence their perception of risk (Dowling & Staelin, 1994; Laroche et al., 2003; Zaichkowsky, 1985). The responsibility for successful IS projects usually rests with the IS staff (Reddy & Reddy, 2002). IS staff are involved with IT projects from beginning to the end. Usually, IS effectiveness is considered as a key performance indicator for IS staff. In contrast, the actual user contact with information systems begins after the new system goes on-line, which is close to the end of IS project. Thus, the involvement of users in the adoption and implementation stages is far behind IS staff. As a result, users hold lower perceived risk on IS flexibility than do the IS staff. These arguments yield the first and second research proposition:

Proposition 1: *In the IS adoption stage, if staff members involved in IS decision-making have a higher perceived risk, they will stress higher perceived flexibility requirements, giving more attention to the flexibility properties of the information systems under evaluation.*

Proposition 2: *In the IS adoption stage, IS staffs are more deeply involved with IS adoption decisions and IS projects compared with users causing IS staff to have higher perceived risks with IS implementation and usage.*

IS Implementation Stage

The fit between IS and organizations is positively related to IS implementation success and the fit will improve with high levels of system adaptations (Hong & Kim, 2002). System adaptations can reduce the gap between IS and organization. Thus, when staff members perceive IS fit is low the in implementation stage, they tend to apply a system adaptation strategy to increase the functional fit of IS with user requirements. This result in lower resistance reduced training needs, and less task adaptation (Bingi *et al.*, 1999).

System adaptation activities can increase the flexibility of IS, however, the activities may harm IS by limiting future software upgrades, increasing system complexity, and lowering system maintainability (Brehm et al., 2001). Implementation of packaged software requires the organization to adapt its processes to fit the operations embedded in the new IS. In the IS implementation stage, in particular, staff members often lack adequate knowledge about the adopted application software. They often perceive more control from the unfamiliar software than it warrants. This perceived IS control by IS staff influences them or other users to avoid applying a system adaptation strategy and to replace it with a task adaptation strategy. Collectively these findings suggest the following:

Proposition 3: *In the IS implementation stage, the lower perceived IS fit will result in the application of a system adaptation strategy, by IS staff members, to increase IS flexibility.*

Proposition 4: *In the IS implementation stage, the higher perceived IS control will mean IS staff members apply the task adaptation strategy to maintain IS flexibility for change.*

IS Post-Implementation Stage

Users with a better understanding of a system use its functions more efficiently to support their diverse daily operations (Laroche et al., 2003). Usually, the mostly widely used method to improve IS knowledge is via user training. However, user training emphasizes system operations rather than understanding the entire application systems or knowledge on how to applying the system in different situations. Thus, the understanding of a system for users largely develops after the actual usage of IS via the accumulation of experience and situation learning, or the learning and experience curve.

Proposition 5: *With the accumulation of experience and learning in the post-implementation IS stage, users will increase their IS knowledge. They will experience higher perceived usefulness and higher perceived ease of use. The user's interpretive IS flexibility will also increase.*

When an application system is on-line for daily usage, it is not the termination of IS adaptation activities. The post-implementation stage is critical to receiving value from information systems (Markus et al., 2003; Ross et al., 2003). This stage still involves opportunities for process redesign. Thus organizations have on-going requirements to add functionality to the information systems. As the business and its environment changes more frequently, the operations or the processes needed by users might change repeatedly. This lowers the perceived fit of IS, resulting in a requirement for more perceived IS flexibility.

Proposition 6: *When the business or environment changes more frequently, the perceived fit of staff members will decrease and the perceived IS flexibility will increase. The IS adaptation activities will increase to improve the flexibility of the information systems.*

Many new information systems that replace prior legacy systems now have become another kind of 'legacy system' after a period of usage number (Markus et al., 2003; Prahalad and Krishnan, 2002). This phenomenon results not only from technology and innovation but also from organizational changes. Especially, when organizations adopt the system adaptation strategy for process innovation, the complexity and rigidity of IS will rapidly increase and result in higher perceived IS control by staff members.

Proposition 7: *After long-term adoption of a system adaptation strategy, the complexity and rigidity of IS will increase and cause the higher perceived IS control for staff. The interpretive IS flexibility to change will decrease.*

CONCLUSION

This study provides a model of IS flexibility covering the stages of IS life cycles. This model considers the cognitive factors from both IS staff and users as important for leveraging IS flexibility with adaptation activities. A review of constructs based on interpretive flexibility perspective in the literature supports these cognitive factors. The results lead to the hypotheses about the relationships among these factors, IS flexibility, and adaptation activities. The theoretical basis of the proposed our research model is interpretive flexibility, which was identified in Orlikowski's (1992) structural model of technology.

Technology is a dynamic result of the interaction process between people and organizations. IS adaptation is the process by which staff members try to maximize an application's perceived fit, thus enhancing their satisfaction with IS. But, perceived fit for the users of the same application system is not stable because many organizations face ever-changing environments. Therefore, a dynamic and continuous view of the perceived IS fit is more appropriate for IS effectiveness today.

The proposed model combines two lines of reasoning to extend the current thinking of perceived fit on IS. The first line of reasoning is that the perceived IS flexibility requirement based on perceived risk theory, which considers IS flexibility requirement as a function of various kinds of risks on future IS usage. The other line of reasoning is that perceived IS control originates from limited opportunities offered by the application system. Along with other cognitive factors, perceived IS control also considers an individual's differentiated experience and subjective knowledge. Consequently, the perceived IS flexibility requirement and perceived IS control could be regarded as two different forces anchoring the balancing process between IS complexity and IS rigidity. After adding these two concepts, the model for interpretive IS flexibility is is more complete and more exhaustive than those identified or proposed prior studies.

In summary, this work contributes to the literature in three important ways. First, it extends prior IS flexibility research by highlighting the importance of cognitive factors between the embedded IS flexibility of application systems and IS adaptation activities. These cognitive factors have many effects on both IS flexibility for use and IS flexibility for change. In addition, the research model was designed to develop the propositions considering the temporal dimensions of IS implementation and usage. It points to the importance of managing the different levels of cognitive factors of IS staff and users, and proposes how these cognitive factors will change in each IS life-cycle stage. Finally, the model proposes a macro structure for comprehending and analyzing interpretive IS flexibility through the IS life cycle. The model can serve as the basis of developing strategies for reducing the dysfunctional behaviors associated with IS staff and users.

Therefore, future empirical study should use the model and its propositions to examine and statistically validate these relationships. The theoretical model is subject to systematic examination based on empirical data. A survey methodology is suggested as appropriate to test the research model. A measurement instrument must first be developed and validated for the research constructs. Primary data should then be collected from a cross-section of a variety of industries. It is also advisable to analyze the data gathered from different cultures, given the important role of cognitive factors. Results of cross-cultural empirical testing increases the generalizability of the theoretical model proposed in this research. The implications of these findings also could be better evaluated in future research through interpretive case studies.

REFERENCES

Amoako-Gyampah, K. K., & Salam, A. F. (2004). An extension of the technology acceptance model in an ERP implementation environment. *Information & Management, 41*(6), 731–745. doi:10.1016/j.im.2003.08.010

Askenas, L., & Westelius, A. (2003). Five roles of an information system: A social constructionist approach to analyzing the use of ERP systems. *Informing Science, 4*(3), 105–113.

Besson, P., & Browe, F. (2001). ERP project dynamics and enacted dialogue: Perceived understanding, perceived leeway and the nature of task-related conflicts. *The Data Base for Advances in Information Systems, 32*(4), 47–66.

Bingi, P., Sharma, M. K., & Godla, J. K. (1999). Critical issues affecting an ERP implementation. *Information Systems Management, 16*(3), 7–14. doi:10.1201/1078/43197.16.3.19990601/31310.2

Braa, J., & Hedberg, C. (2002). The struggle for district-based health information systems in South Africa. *The Information Society, 18*(2), 113–127. doi:10.1080/01972240290075048

Brehm, L., Heinzl, A., & Markus, M. L. (2001). *Tailoring ERP systems: A spectrum of choices and their implications.* Paper presented at the Proceedings of the 34th Hawaii International Conference on System Sciences.

Byrd, T. A., Lewis, B. R., & Turner, D. E. (2004). The impact of IT personal skills on IS infrastructure and competitive IS. *Information Resources Management Journal, 17*(2), 38–62. doi:10.4018/irmj.2004040103

Byrd, T. A., & Turner, D. E. (2000). Measuring the flexibility of information technology infrastructure: Exploratory analysis of a construct. *Journal of Management Information Systems, 17*(1), 167–208.

Cha-Jan Chang, J., & King, W. R. (2005). Measuring the performance of information systems: A functional scorecard. *Journal of Management Information Systems, 22*(1), 85–115.

Chang, C. J., & King, W. R. (2005). Measuring the performance of information systems: A functional scorecard. *Journal of Management Information Systems, 22*(1), 85–115.

Cox, D. F., & Rich, S. U. (1964). Perceived risk and consumer decision-making - the case of the telephone shopping. *JMR, Journal of Marketing Research, 1*(4), 32–39. doi:10.2307/3150375

Davis, F. D. (1989). Perceived usefulness, perceived ease of use, and user acceptance of information technology. *Management Information Systems Quarterly*, *13*(3), 318–340. doi:10.2307/249008

Dowling, G. R., & Staelin, R. (1994). A model of perceived risk and intended risk-handling activity. *The Journal of Consumer Research*, *21*(1), 119–135. doi:10.1086/209386

Duncan, N. B. (1995). Capturing flexibility of information technology infrastructure: A study of resource. *Journal of Management Information Systems*, *12*(2), 37–57.

Gebauer, J., & Schober, F. (2006). Information system flexibility and the cost efficiency of business processes. *Journal of the Association for Information Systems*, *7*(3), 122–146.

Hong, C.-S., & Kim, Y.-G. (2002). The critical success factors for ERP implementation: An organizational fit perspective. *Information & Management*, *40*(1), 25–40. doi:10.1016/S0378-7206(01)00134-3

Katzenstein, G., & Lerch, F. J. (2000). Beneath the surface of organization processes: A social representation, framework for business process redesign. *ACM Transactions on Information Systems*, *18*(4), 383–422. doi:10.1145/358108.358111

Knoll, K., & Jarvenpaa, S. L. (1994). *Information technology alignment or "fit" in highly turbulent environment: The concept of flexibility: SIGCPR Computer Personnel*. ACM.

Laroche, M., Bergeron, J., & Goutaland, C. (2003). How intangibility affects perceived risk: The moderating role of knowledge and involvement. *Journal of Services Marketing*, *17*(2), 122–140. doi:10.1108/08876040310467907

Lewis, B. R., & Byrd, T. A. (2003). Development of a measure for the information technology infrastructure construct. *European Journal of Information Systems*, *12*(2), 94–108. doi:10.1057/palgrave.ejis.3000449

Markus, M. L., Axline, S., Petrie, D., & Tanis, C. (2003). Learning from experiences with ERP: Problems encountered and success achieved. In Shanks, G., Seddon, P. B., & Willcocks, L. P. (Eds.), *Second-wave enterprise resource planning systems* (pp. 23–55). Cambridge: Cambridge University Press.

Moitra, D., & Ganesh, J. (2005). Web services and flexible business processes: Towards the adaptive enterprise. *Information & Management*, *42*(7), 921–933. doi:10.1016/j.im.2004.10.003

Moore, G. C., & Benbasat, I. (1991). Development of an instrument to measure the perceptions of adopting an information technology innovation. *Information Systems Research, 2*(3), 192–222. doi:10.1287/isre.2.3.192

Orlikowski, R. J. (1992). The duality of technology: Rethinking the concepts of technology in organizations. *Organization Science, 3*(3), 398–427. doi:10.1287/orsc.3.3.398

Pozzebon, M., and Pinsonneault, A. (2005). Challenges in conducting empirical work using structuration theory: Learning from IT research. *Organization Studies (Sage Publications Inc.), 26*(9), 1353-1376.

Prahalad, C. K., & Krishnan, M. S. (2002). The dynamic synchronization of strategy and information technology. *MIT Sloan Management Review, 43*(4), 24–33.

Reddy, S. B., & Reddy, R. (2002). Competitive agility and the challenge of legacy information systems. *Industrial Management & Data Systems, 102*(1), 5–16. doi:10.1108/02635570210414613

Rolland, K. H., & Monteiro, E. (2002). Balancing the local and the global in infrastructural information systems. *The Information Society, 18*(2), 87–100. doi:10.1080/01972240290075020

Rose, J., & Scheepers, R. (2001). *Structuration theory and information systems development; frameworks for practice.* Paper presented at the Proceedings of the 9th European Conference on Information Systems, Bled, Slovenia.

Ross, J. W., Vitale, M. R., & Willcocks, L. P. (2003). The continuing ERP revolution: Sustainable lessons, new modes of delivery. In Shanks, G., Seddon, P. B., & Willcocks, L. P. (Eds.), *Second-wave enterprise resource planning systems* (pp. 102–132). Cambridge: Cambridge University Press.

Sambamurthy, V., Bharadwaj, A., & Grover, V. (2003). Shaping agility through digital options: Reconceptualizing the role of information technology in contemporary firms. *Management Information Systems Quarterly, 27*(2), 237–263.

Silver, M. S. (1991). *Systems that support decision makers: Description and analysis.* Chichester: Wiley & Sons.

Soh, C., Kien, S. S., & Tay-Yap, J. (2000). Cultural fits and misfits: Is ERP a universal solution? *Communications of the ACM, 43*(4), 47–51. doi:10.1145/332051.332070

Stigler, G. (1939). Production and distribution in the short run. *The Journal of Political Economy, 47*(3), 305–327. doi:10.1086/255387

Sutherland, J., & Heuvel, W.-J. d. (2002). Enterprise application integration and complex adaptive systems. *Communications of the ACM, 45*(10), 59–64. doi:10.1145/570907.570932

Truex, D. P., Baskerville, R., & Kelin, H. (1999). Growing systems in emergent organizations. *Communications of the ACM, 42*(8), 117–123. doi:10.1145/310930.310984

Tyre, M. J., & Orlikowski, J. (1994). Windows of opportunity: Temporal patterns of technological adaptation in organizations. *Organization Science*, *5*(1), 98–119. doi:10.1287/orsc.5.1.98

Zaichkowsky, J. L. (1985). Measuring the involvement construct. *The Journal of Consumer Research, 12*(3), 341–352. doi:10.1086/208520

This work was previously published in International Journal of Enterprise Information Systems, Volume 5, Issue 1, edited by Madjid Tavana, pp. 32-43, copyright 2009 by IGI Publishing (an imprint of IGI Global).

Chapter 2
Contrasting Approaches to Preparedness:
A Reflection on Two Case Studies

Lorraine Warren
University of Southampton, UK

Ted Fuller
Lincoln University, UK

ABSTRACT

This chapter reflects on ongoing research in SMEs in the manufacturing and service sectors. It contrasts different approaches to the issue of preparedness from an organisational and social perspective, in two cases where new enterprise-wide business processes were implemented and integrated in different settings. In both cases, the emergence of new systems presented a huge challenge to companies hard-pressed to marshal the resources to mount effective change and implementation projects on this scale. The cases presented enable a comparison of different strategies used, one firm responding to organic growth, and the other to rapid industry-driven change. The chapter focuses not on the implementations per se, but instead on the issue of preparedness for change. The chapter concludes by drawing out general lessons concerning how to support and maintain organisational preparedness for enterprise wide change in different industry settings.

DOI: 10.4018/978-1-60960-529-2.ch002

INTRODUCTION

A few years ago, I worked with a small manufacturing company in the UK horticultural industry that was experiencing the need for improved communication and control across the enterprise as growth took place (Warren, 2002, 2003, ab). Parts of the business responsible for different product lines wanted to talk to each other, more efficient financial management systems were essential to meet increased orders, and further, there was a need to develop more internet-oriented customer management and marketing systems. This situation resulted in a two-year project with the local university under the (then) Teaching Company Scheme (which has now evolved into the Knowledge Transfer Partnership programme) which employed a graduate under university supervision to analyse and redesign the company's management and information systems in an enterprise-wide endeavour. During the scheme, through an extensive consultancy, development and training programme, we introduced Beer's Viable System Model (VSM) (Beer, 1981, 1985) as a learning vehicle to support the development of a conceptual design for integration that at the time, in itself, met the company's needs. Later on, this turned out to be a stepping stone on the road to a technological implementation of the design. The project was deemed successful, with the organisational learning that took place through using a simplified version of the VSM during the analysis and design phase being seen as essential to success. Through a variety of participative fora, staff across the enterprise developed insight into the need for change and made input into how the new systems would work. Over the period of the project, a sense of 'preparedness' for change emerged among all sections of the workforce.

Based on this experience, presented in the first case below, I went on to develop successfully this *modus operandi* for developing new business systems (in terms of preparedness for implementation) with other small companies, both service and manufacturing, public and private sector (Ragsdell and Warren, 1999; Warren, 2003c). It was only when I encountered a different kind of company that seemed to be operating and growing in a new way, that I realised I was seeing a different kind of preparedness. At this point, my research took a new direction. Thus, the second case I present examines a 'rapid response' to industry change from a service company in the airline industry. In this case, competitive advantage (and indeed survival) is linked to the rapid embedding of new systems in short time frames as new business models emerge across a whole industry. This chapter therefore examines, in reflective mode, the two projects that proved to be landmarks in my understanding of how small organisations organise for enterprise-wide change.

BACKGROUND

The first cluster of SMEs I worked with, although they were quite different in location and purpose, all had one thing in common: they were all relatively localised firms, experiencing fairly linear growth patterns, in relatively predictable sectors, that were yes, subject to change and competition, but by and large, the basic business models held true for quite long periods of time. What they seemed to be experiencing was growth in line with classical stage model theory, and as predicted by Greiner (1972), at a certain point, they were coming up against a 'crisis of control'. Classical 'stage models' of growth for small firms, whilst they differ in their detail, identify a series of phases through which growing businesses progress, each presenting different managerial challenges. Stage models suggest that an appropriate response from the owner-manager (OM) is required if the firm is to grow effectively, or indeed to survive (Greiner 1972; Churchill & Lewis 1983; Scott & Bruce 1987).

Although stage models have been criticised widely for their owner-centric, deterministic, linear perspective, it is notable that they all predict that problems may arise as existing management and information systems become unable to meet the needs of expanding firms, either in terms of coping with increased throughput, or providing the flexibility to meet the opportunities and challenges in the business environment. Greiner's model, for example, points to a phase of delegation, where OMs appoint others to deal with functional aspects of the business organisation that they once dealt with themselves. This can be followed by a 'crisis of control', if the result of delegation is poor communication between different parts of the organisation. It is suggested by the model that a phase of co-ordination should then follow, where management and information systems are reviewed and developed to improve communication and effect better reporting and monitoring procedures. Notwithstanding the critique of stage models, this does seem to reflect the experience of many small firms in conditions of organic growth. At this point, many OMs consider technological integration across the enterprise (Waring & Wainwright, 2000), the point where I was called in to oversee the project at the firm at the heart of the first case, APCO.

The situation at the second company, FD, was quite different from the above, where the enterprise-wide change appears manageable through quite rational management planning processes (albeit with a strong interpretive dimension as we shall see below). FD was established by two founders in 1984 to provide brokerage services in the air travel industry. This industry has certainly presented far more volatile conditions over the last twenty years than those experienced by the firms identified above. Airline service companies have had to survive an environment completely transformed by successive rounds of deregulation, the reshaping of the travel industry through new patterns of consumer behaviour, and the impact of new technology at every level of operation. The airline industry is distinctive in that it is international and truly global, yet it has a degree of uniformity imposed by safety and security considerations. It is also highly regulated in terms of who can participate and how – through what systems, both technological and regulatory bodies. FD has little power or influence over supra-national events that have the potential to threaten the survival of the firm unless decisive managerial action is taken, typically over relatively short timescales, and at the level of the enterprise. For example, the effects of terrorist action on the demand for travel, the continued opening of trading regulations, direct internet bookings and air-crashes are all features of the landscape outside the control of the firm. FD is remarkable in that it has survived for 24 years, having employed up to 100 people prior 9/11, in an industry which has been through huge political, economic, social and technical change on a global scale. Growth had occurred through what the OM described as 'enforced agility', where disruptive industry events had led to the rapid-fire development of new business models that operated as distinctive and separate business units within the firm. Nonetheless, there was still a need for the underlying system architecture of the firm to have a degree of interoperability that still allowed for the anticipation of speedily implemented change. The ongoing research carried at FD is being undertaken not to instigate phases of planned integration, but instead to gain better understanding of how such 'anticipatory systems management' contributes to the agility and sustainability of firms operating in volatile environments.

In the next section, the two case studies are presented, followed by a reflective conclusion that draws out contrasts concerning the idea of 'preparedness' for system-wide process change. In the first case, we see that preparedness is something that needs to be worked at and developed as step change approaches. In the second we see that preparedness is quite different, it is a 'way of being' in anticipation of constant and unpredictable change. These differences have consequences for the nature of enterprise design.

Case Studies and Reflection

1. APCO: Developing Preparedness

APCO are a small family company with a £2M turnover, producing and supplying a range of building and garden products to civil engineering contractors, large home improvement/garden centre companies, and directly to the end consumer. Starting out 70 years ago as a concrete products manufacturing company supplying to the building industry, the company had undergone a typical diversification of its customer and product base, into four departments, organised around the key product ranges: flood defence products, aggregates, concrete slabs and decorative garden products, all acting to some extent as separate production units, but drawing on the same operative and support staff pool. That 'mix' was seen as important in coping with seasonal and market fluctuations across the different sectors addressed. The firm was controlled by the Managing Director (OM) with the aid of his father, ex-OM, semi-retired and operating as Chairman. Alongside a four-person management team and a small administrative staff, 22 full-time production operatives were employed by the company, some in a supervisory capacity. Over time, the company had adopted a rather tall (though not inflexible) hierarchical structure, built around 5 levels of operations and management that were not functioning well in terms of information flows and needed a complete redesign, even to support current levels of activity. Further, the company was seeking to expand, while achieving economies of scale through automation of certain sections of the manufacturing operation. This brought further challenges to the management and information systems of the company, as in the need to develop and integrate new inventory control systems and new marketing systems to cope with increased orders and recognise the growing importance of the internet.

It was clear that the time had come to initiate a project to support the planned expansion and deal with an accumulated problem set at root and branch level (Waring & Wainwright, 2000). However, previous change initiatives had had mixed results, not due to a lack of top level support, but a lack of enthusiasm from middle managers as they became side-tracked by pressing production issues. This loss of enthusiasm had soon spread to the shop floor, where momentum rapidly dissolved. This past history of failed initiatives, and also a real fear of redundancy as rumours of the automation project circulated added up not only a lack of preparedness for systems integration, but resistance to change altogether.

This lack of enthusiasm did not come as a surprise. At the time of the project, a literature concerning success factors for enterprise systems integration had begun to emerge (Holland et al., 1999; Chen, 2001; Al-Mudimigh et al., 2001; Nah et al., 2001; Waring & Wainwright, 2000), which highlighted a range of organisational issues in addition to technically dominated concerns. This was in some part a backlash against the enthusiasm of software companies to sell 'off the shelf' integration packages to companies in the 90s, whether they were suitable or not. There was a consensus that the pre-implementation phase was crucial to the success of the eventual endeavour, with the need to:

- Establish the need for the project in line with the strategic objectives of the business
- Understand, simplify and perhaps re-engineer key business processes
- Establish appropriate change management procedures.

Yet achieving the above is not straightforward and raises complex issues, with a number of authors highlighting cases where poor conceptualisation and a lack of meaningful engagement of system users in the early stages had compromised success overall (Waring & Wainwright, 2000; Markus & Tanis, 2000; Van Stijn & Wensley, 2001). These general organisational complexities can take on a particular character in the small firm environment. (Fuller & Lewis, 2003), drawing on a 2-year qualitative study of 38 small firms, note the powerful influence of OMs in 'managing meaning' around technological projects (supporting stakeholder relationships in the supply chain in this study). This influence may be particularly powerful where no dedicated IS/IT professionals are employed, commonly the case in small firms.

Not surprisingly then, in light of the prevailing zeitgeist at the time, we took an interpretive approach to the pre-project phase which encouraged user ownership of solutions and prioritised learning about the organisational situation over a technologically-driven push towards a predetermined and poorly conceptualised notion of integration (or Fuller & Lewis, 2003's 'orderliness'). We also sought throughout to maintain an ethical stance towards the workforce, by trying to follow the tenets of Critical Systems Thinking (Jackson, 1991, 2000) a journey chronicled in (Warren, 2003a). This consisted of full workplace meetings, one-to-one meetings, and the formation of project workgroups, to address issues of data modelling, systems integration, organisational design and user engagement. Of course, this path, which lasted for the full two years of the project, is never smooth and there was some evidence in the early stages of our involvement that the academic input into project design was not welcome in all quarters, with comments such as:

What do those boffins know about a concrete company? Nothing! They're just here to put us out of a job!

You want to put us out of work and you don't have the guts to do it yourself, and you've brought that lot in, and their bits of paper, to do it for you.

If you want to sack me, just do it, I can't be bothered with all this.

I appreciate what you're trying to do, but me gathering all these facts and figures will just put me out of a job. That pretty picture [VSM schema] you're waving around is just a map to the [social welfare office] as far as I'm concerned.

Why do we need boffins from the university to tell you what's wrong, I've been telling you for years!

Yet in spite of this early suspicion and many wobbles along the way, the project was a success: automation of production took place, and notwithstanding an investment in plant of £200K, there was a corresponding increase in profit, without loss of any staff. This expansion is supported by effective management and information systems, which have addressed a range of immediate operational and tactical communication problems, in addition to supporting broader strategic objectives concerning better marketing and better relationships with customers and suppliers. At the time, this was a *conceptual* integration, to build an enterprise-wide system architecture, not a software implementation. Better business process and communication systems could be managed with existing software, and it was seen as more important to get people working effectively in new working patterns in a new organisational design. Of course, over time, as networking and the internet have become increasingly important, new hardware and software have been purchased, but the initial design held fast for many years, a testament to the rigorous values of the project.

One of the key elements in this success was the use of Beer's VSM (1981, 1985) to support the design of the new integrated management systems; this part of the journey is chronicled in (Warren, 2003b). In very simplified terms, Beer sees any organisation as being made up of five systems connected through communication and control channels, in contrast to traditional organisation charts:

System 5: Policy (policy formulation)
System 4: Development (intelligence gathering and reporting)
System 3: Control (day to day running of the organization)
System 2: Coordination (of System 1)
System 1: Implementation (directly concerned with the task of the organization)

Derived from cybernetic principles as a means of 'engineering' organisations with hard-wired communication channels, later applications of the VSM have drawn on more socially oriented thinking; Espejo et al. (1996) characterise the model as a hermeneutic enabler of organisational learning where systems of communication and control can be developed in interactive settings.

Of course the VSM in its 'raw' form is intimidating to new users. Yet without developing shared understanding of the principles of the model by a significant number of the project management team, the analysis and design phases would have been compromised. By building up from general discussions of accessible ideas such as strategic, tactical and operational information, varying depths of understanding concerning the VSM were shared. Many members of the workforce were happy with the general concept of a five-layer information architecture model and began to use the vocabulary of the five layers of the VSM directly in their contributions to design meetings, and further, to different extents, in implementation discussions with colleagues from across the whole workplace. It was clear that the model was being used in the hermeneutic sense (Espejo et al., 1996), not as a 'recipe' or 'cookbook' formula to produce a predetermined 'hardwired' structure. The vocabulary of the model led to explication, clarification and definition of existing procedures, which in many areas were rather vague and ad hoc. It could be argued that a Community of Practice (CoP) had grown up around the VSM, where learning took place and innovative ways of managing information were developed 'on the ground' using a new shared vocabulary. Like Lave and Wenger (1991, p. 56), masters (academic and associate), young masters (OM and team) and apprentices (those who were drawn into the project team from the periphery) could be identified at different times in the project. The 'meaning' of the VSM application was therefore ambiguous, dynamic and reflexively mediated by negotiation in practice. In conclusion, what has taken place here is that knowledge transfer could be equated with the establishment of a CoP around the VSM within the project context. Through the CoP, a spirit of preparedness for change came about.

2. FD: Gaining Insight into Preparedness

Like APCO, FD had diversified into different business areas over the years. However, unlike APCO, which had experienced largely linear growth, for FD, the pattern of expansion had been far more discontinuous, driven by both opportunities and shocks in the airline industry. In 1984, the business started with three people brokering between airlines and holiday tour operators. By 1992, four separate business units were operating, in various areas of brokerage. However, in 1993, deregulation removed the need for this type of brokerage role and FD downsized to two business divisions concentrating instead on niche brokerage activity between small airlines and large airports in the UK. Over the next few years, FD expanded again, and in 2001, pre 9/11, the company boasted over 100 employees, a brokerage division, a ticketing call centre and a branded charter service with two 737 aircraft. Post 9/11, the charter service was in liquidation and the call centre survived only at the 11th hour. Up to 2007, the business has continued in a highly dynamic and competitive environment, with around one hundred staff providing general sales agency (GSA, a development of the niche brokerage activity) and an overspill ticketing call centre.

During its existence, FD has had to innovate to remain 'fit' within the business environment, by repeatedly restructuring and rapidly establishing new corporate ventures in response to industry change. Each venture has remained under the FD umbrella: all the employees work in the same building and there is flexibility across operations as the workforce respond to different demand at different times. Yet while there is an overarching veneer of systems integration for basic functions such as payroll and marketing, the underlying architectures of the different divisions remain largely distinct, and dependent on dedicated industry systems. Unlike APCO then, there is no desire for consolidation and co-ordination to support expansion, rather the need is for a fast and flexible response that enables new divisions to be bolted on to the FD structure – and at the same time, such structures can be very quickly jettisoned if they become unprofitable.

Both authors have worked with FD for many years, researching into the sustainability of small entrepreneurial businesses in such volatile settings. Our latest study focussed on the emergence of yet another new business model in FD, this time for a 'long-tail' web-based internet onward-flight regional airline booking system, A-A.com, which is intended to cater for a niche market not covered by the large travel companies such as expedia or ebookers. Unlike the APCO case, the development of this potential new business up until almost the implementation point, was driven almost entirely from the top, by two members of the senior management team, P (the Managing Director) and J (the Technical Director and owner of a large shareholding in the firm). The full account of this journey is summarised in Warren et al, (2008).

The pre-launch phase of the development of A-A.com commenced in 2004. The idea was first articulated by P and J during a meeting in a Moscow hotel foyer, while waiting for a client who was late for an appointment. This conversation was part of ongoing discussions regarding the 'fitness' of FD, updating the GSA business' web presence and looking for higher growth opportunities to supplement the overspill call centre, which was being challenged by competition from India. Initially, A-A.com was expected to grow out of, and supplement the newly web-focussed GSA division. J then began to work on the feasibility of the idea with his commitment really crystallising when he attended a Travel Distribution Summit in Philadelphia in May 2005, where he developed a new *"sense of urgency"* about *"missing this bandwagon"*. Early in 2006, J began to seriously discuss online booking with system providers. Meanwhile, the GSA system continued its full migration to the web.

At this point, the idea underwent a major shift in its trajectory. Because both P and J were becoming increasingly convinced over time of the likelihood of A-A.com becoming highly profitable, a strategic decision was taken to fully exploit the idea by moving out of the model based on the GSA business (a relatively small airline base) to a GDS (dedicated travel industry Geographical Distribution System) system. Effectively this made FD a travel agency, for which IATA (International Air Transport Agency) approval would be required. This approval was achieved in July 2006. Going down this route brought with it the capability to fulfil bookings for hundreds of other airlines in IATA, not just the GSA base. The first booking was on 29 September through GSA, prior the launch of A-A.com as a separate entity in January 2007. Since then, A-A.com has operated as a separate arm within FD, with ongoing effort (through the appointment of new staff) being directed into the building of technological infrastructure, web presence, markets, and increasing the participating airline base. The underpinning architecture of the GSA and the GDS are linked, but A-A.com has a separate character.

During our research period with FD, our studies have shown that unlike APCO, senior figures in FD spend their time in constant state of preparedness for organisational change, a form of 'anticipatory systems management', where temporary, ephemeral, unstable organisational structures appear and develop ontological status over time. Some go on to 'become' part of the firm and others are discarded either before, or soon after, implementation. Elsewhere, we have used and developed understandings of emergence rooted in complexity theory to explore this situation in more detail (Fuller et al., 2007 a,b). In FD, preparedness manifests as repeating patterns of behaviour. (Fuller et al., 2004, 2006) and (Fuller et al., 2007 a,b) have characterised these 4 inter-related behaviour patterns, as 'processes of emergence', patterns that lead to the emergence of novelty in entrepreneurial settings: new services, new products, new careers, or in this case, new business models. These processes of emergence, set out in Table 1, have been characterised as the 'EROS' model – Experiments, Reflexivity, Organising, Sensitivity.

The processes in Table 1 should be seen as interconnected, not separate, and we argue that it is the multi-dimensional concentration on these patterns of behaviour that is at the heart of entrepreneurial competence through effective strategising over time to produce a *sustainable* business. The four EROS processes interact to produce new emergent structures over time. Each process inter-relates with the other through multi-layers of cognition, language, performance and relationships with others, albeit strongly influenced by the entrepreneur. For FD's directors, preparedness is a state of mind, a way of being, not a sit-down session at 2pm on a Tuesday afternoon. In brief:

Table 1. EROS processes of emergence

Process	Behaviour
Experimenting	Diverse exploratory behaviours that might (or might not) become part of the firm over time; new things tried out in often very informal ways, small scale; often developed through exploration of social interactions; shared experiential learning across project teams and stakeholders; 'what works'
Reflexivity	Continuous reflection on the identity of the firm and the self-identity of its owner(s) through the discourses within the business and with stakeholders; vision setting through narratives of self and firm; 'who we are'
Organising	Organising around a dominant logic (or project); patterns established through negotiated practice; pattern-making and pattern-breaking; 'what needs to be done now'
Sensitivity	Interpretation of shifts in industry landscape; detection of difference; weak signals; triggers and thresholds for change; 'what we might do'

Experiments

At FD, new things were constantly being tried out, often in very informal ways. There is a sense in which social interactions were used to search for and examine possibilities for new activities which might be formalised as experimental projects if judged to hold promise. If these worked, they were built upon. If they didn't work they were changed or dropped. The projects or reorganising of activities were relatively small scale and were talked about in terms of seeing what would work. Experiments could be as tenuous as conversations, mental models, thought experiments, or interactions with casual contacts, or, they could involve more significant discussions with suppliers or new partners. The character of the firm is to repeatedly experiment with new initiatives and projects, sometimes in the most tenuous of informal ways. A-A.com is a typical example of FD's tradition of doing things in this way. It began with the casual conversation in Moscow, which P remembers as significant, but J has a much more vague recall of the genesis of the idea. This was the start of a new discourse that might – or might not – persist over time. In this case, it did. Over time, the experiment, in the form of new identities, new products, new services and new stakeholders acquired precedence over the old order through the sensing of a changing business environment. This growing sense of project identity was something that P fostered, an example of this being the production of an internal newsletter, the Altimeter, that focussed on the project alone, not FD in its entirety. A key element of this experimental behaviour is that major resources are not committed till quite late on in the project, when there is a need for rapid embedding of systems. During the 2 years from conception to implementation (around the same period of time as the APCO project), the vision of A-A.com changed significantly on at least two occasions, prior to the rapid implementation stage at the end.

Reflexive Construction of Identity

The significance of identity for self, the firm and the industry, in which were constituted motivations, roles, daily practice and behavioural imperatives, was paramount in FD, particularly for P. Reflexivity describes the process by which the individual constantly assesses the relationship between 'knowledge' and the "ways of doing knowledge" (Calás & Smircich 1992). Reflexivity links the cognitive domain of the individual to their experienced environment which for the entrepreneur, includes the everyday practices of doing business with others. P, as shaper and decision maker influences the emergent structures of the firm and the context (Fuller & Lewis, 2003). A continuous reflection on the identity of the firm and the self-identity of its owner(s) through the discourses within the business and with stakeholders was central to the direction and identity of the firm, as well as the entrepreneur. For Stacey (2003), strategy is the evolving patterns of an organisation's identity. Thus, an inability to reshape organisational identity puts the future at risk for the firm. This does not mean that the FD was in a state of drift. Two constant themes in FD's history have been P's overwhelming self of 'being something' in the airline industry, and the sense of the company having a unique selling point developed from very specialist expertise in the industry. For A-A.com to work for P and FD, it had to have the distinctive qualities as a niche provider linking to the lesser known reaches of the airline industry. This is strongly bound in the ongoing intertwined life narrative of P and FD, the desire to be independent and the deep desire to be embedded in the specialist regions (geographically and conceptually) of the airline industry. It is also strongly bound in the relationship with J who realises the vision through continuous grasp of an industry that has seen enormous systems development and change since the first joined the firm. P trusts J to enable anticipation and response to change that has enabled the gradual development of a unique core competence around industry knowledge over time. Thus A-A.com becomes a realistic possibility, triggered by a sense of industry change yet rooted in the existing identity of the firm.

Organising Domains

An organising domain is a space where activities are organised around a dominant logic. Lichtenstein links activity domains, which "guide organizational activity and also prescribe limits to the system's capacity to get the work done" with "organizing domains," which in his studies of successful young businesses emerged rapidly in a self-organizing process, e.g. "*Once agreement for a new mission had been reached, a new set of organizing domains rapidly emerged to implement that goal*" (Lichtenstein, 2000). In volatile or high velocity landscapes in particular, the speed at which new regularised practices can be put into place contributes to the sustainability of the enterprise. The tension between innovative (pattern breaking) practices and recurrent practices (maintaining patterns) requires managerial judgement, and for A-A.com, occurs quite late on in the project. Yet the business cannot just 'act' overnight. A-A.com is shaped – both constrained and enabled by the regulatory requirement and the technical infrastructure, i.e. IATA registration and the GDS; these require anticipatory management and system building, a partial commitment of resource, even though at this stage, there is still a sense that the project may not necessarily come to fruition. The most significant resources are only committed at a very late stage, once the first order has been realised through the GSA system.

Sensitivity to Conditions

The evidence from FD suggests that the management were highly aware of changes in the external environment and also of the potential cash-flow and profitability produced by the business model. The main issue for this business seemed to be mainly one of when to enact new patterns, and more particularly when to break existing ones. The key trigger points for A-A.com were firstly, J's trip to the Philadelphia Conference when he realised with a sense of urgency that if FD did not act soon they would be beaten to the market by someone else. The second trigger point was the decision to move out of the GSA-driven model for A-A.com and purchase the GDS/IATA registration and (with reference to the point made earlier) adopt a slightly extended identity for the firm, in terms of the travel agency.

Taken in totality, these four areas of process provide an entrepreneurial mechanism that has proved significant in the sustainability of FD over a prolonged period of time demonstrating the ability to perform and survive in an industry which is increasingly dominated by dedicated travel industry systems that are deeply intertwined with advanced web analytics. This industry context is fast-moving and an excellent example of the need to strategise and anticipate on a contingent and agile basis. The conception and development of alternative-airlines.com is deeply embedded in this intricate context and decisions taken impact across the whole business; it is not a simple standalone project that can be picked up or put down on an *ad hoc* basis. There is evidence that the EROS processes are at the heart of FD entrepreneurial culture. Yet EROS is not simply a cultural model, a vague cultural soup which allows good things to somehow happen. It is based on the language and understandings of complexity theory and in part therefore explains how certain essential sets of activities result in the emergence of new systems, though the outcomes are not predetermined.

CONCLUSION

Unlike the APCO project, which was a step change redesign to provide an enterprise-wide platform for the future, A-A.com is another example in FD's long history of a business unit which is nurtured separately in isolation then rapidly embedded in the FD structure on a just-in-time basis, when it is sensed that the industry pressure to do so is becoming critical, if a competitive edge is to be obtained. Resources of money, people and time are only committed at the last moment and shifts in the trajectory of systems projects are to be expected. It cannot be said that the FD exemplified Pathfinding (Turner & Crawford, 1994) competences in its everyday approach to business. It did not routinely or explicitly undertake formal foresight activities, such as scenario planning, it was not able to assess the "total impact of any particular change" that strategic awareness assumes (Gibb & Scott, 1985). Nor was there evidence of the "highly visible vision of the future" that Hamel and Prahalad (1994) associate with Strategic Intent. Instead, the firm exists in a constant state of preparedness that results in the partial construction of new systems against the potential existence of developing projects that may or may not be realised. This means that full enterprise-wide integration to effect communication and control, which was an important need for APCO, is less significant for FD, where integration is not an issue in itself. It may be necessary for two underlying system architectures to be connected (as in the GSA and A-A.com projects), but it may not: in which case, separate development is the order of the day, as any given project may need to be jettisoned at a later stage.

This mindset, developed to cope with the exigencies of a volatile industry environment, is in complete contrast to the situation at APCO, where the need is to establish a robust platform that integrates and supports the needs of the company over the coming years in what is expected to be a relatively stable environment. Reflecting the stability of the past, in a firm that has existed in a rural environment for over 60 years, there is a need to develop a sense of preparedness in the workforce from the bottom-up. This took considerable time, effort and sensitivity, in context carefully informed by the principles of participative intervention.

In summary, the issue of preparedness is one that is often taken for granted in the literature. At one time, the concern was limited to technical matters related to data collection and user/system requirements. In the early 00s, the emphasis shifted to the social concerns of the pre-project phase. What these contrasting case studies show is that for some companies, the whole notion of systems integration is a moveable feast at best and may even be undesirable in certain types of industry/firm, where more flexible or readily disposable arrangements might be needed. The recent world financial crisis certainly tells us how volatile the business environment can be. We will be carrying out further research into the normative implications of our work.

REFERENCES

Al-Mudimigh, A., Zairi, M., & Al-Mashari, M. (2001). ERP software implementation: an integrative framework. *European Journal of Information Systems, 10*(4), 216–226. doi:10.1057/palgrave.ejis.3000406

Beer, S. (1981). *The Brain of the Firm*. Chichester: Wiley.

Beer, S. (1985). *Diagnosing the System for Organizations*. Chichester: Wiley.

Calás, M., & Smircich, L. (1992). Rewriting gender into organizational theorizing: Directions from feminist perspectives. In Reed, M., & Hughes, M. (Eds.), *Rethinking organization: New directions in organizational theory and analysis* (pp. 227–253). London: Sage.

Chen, I. J. (2001). Planning for ERP systems: analysis and future trends. *Business Process Management Journal*, *7*(5), 374–386. doi:10.1108/14637150110406768

Churchill, N., & Lewis, V. (1983, May/June). The five stages of small business growth. *Harvard Business Review*, 30–50.

Espejo, R., Schuhmann, W., Schwaninger, M., & Bilello, U. (1996). *Organisational Transformation and Learning*. Chichester: Wiley.

Fuller, T., & Fewster, R. (2006). *The emergence of Tesco.com: A study of Corporate Entrepreneurship*. Paper presented at the Babson-Kauffman Entrepreneurship Research Conferemce, Kelley Business School, Indiana

Fuller, T., & Lewis, F. (2003). Relationships mean everything. *British Journal of Management*, *13*, 317–336. doi:10.1111/1467-8551.00249

Fuller, T., Moran, P., & Argyle, P. (2004). Entrepreneurial foresight; a case in reflexivity, experiments, sensitivity and reorganisation. In Tsoukas, H., & Shepherd, J. (Eds.), *Managing the Future:Foresight in the Knowledge Economy* (pp. 171–178). Oxford: Blackwell.

Fuller, T., Warren, L., & Argyle, P. (2007a). Sustaining Entrepreneurial Business; a complexity perspective on processes that produce emergent practice. *The International Entrepreneurship and Management Journal*, *4*(1), 1–17. doi:10.1007/s11365-007-0047-y

Fuller, T., Warren, L., & Welter, F. (2007b, November). *Towards an emergence perspective on entrepreneurship.* Paper presented at RENT XXI, Research in Entrepreneurship and Small Business, Cardiff (pp. 22-23).

Gibb, A. A., & Scott, M. G. (1985). Strategic Awareness, Personal Commitment and the Process of Planning in the Small Business. *Journal of Management Studies*, *22*(6), 597–625. doi:10.1111/j.1467-6486.1985.tb00014.x

Greiner, L. E. (1972, July/August). Evolution and Revolution as Organisations Grow. *Harvard Business Review*, 37–46.

Hamel, G., & Prahalad, C. K. (1994). *Competing for the future*. Boston: Harvard Business School Press.

Holland, C. P., Light, B., & Gibson, N. (1999, June 23-25). A critical success factors model for emterprise resource planning implementation. In *Proceedings of the Seventh European Conference on Information Systems*, Copenhagen (pp. 288-301).

Jackson, M. C. (1991). *Systems Methodology for the Management Sciences*. New York: Plenum.

Jackson, M. C. (2000). *Systems Approaches to Management*. New York: Kluwer.

Lave, J., & Wenger, E. (1991). *Situated Learning: Legitimate Peripheral Participation*. New York: Cambridge University Press.

Lichtenstein, B. M. B. (2000). Self-organized transitions: A pattern amid the chaos of transformative change. *The Academy of Management Executive*, *14*(4), 128–141. doi:10.5465/AME.2000.3979821

Markus, M. L., & Tanis, C. (2000). The enterprise systems experience – from adoption to success. In Zmud, R. W. (Ed.), *Framing the Domains of IT Research: Glimpsing the Future through the Past* (pp. 73–207). Cincinnatti, Ohio: Pinnaflex Educational Resources Inc.

Nah, F. F. H., Lau, J. L. S., & Kuang, J. (2001). Critical factors for successful implementation of enterprise systems. *Business Process Management Journal*, *7*(3), 285–296. doi:10.1108/14637150110392782

Ragsdell, G., & warren, L. (1999). Learning from Beer: Using the Viable System Model for Organisational Design. *OR Insight*, *12*(4), 16-23.

Scott, M., & Bruce, R. (1987). Five Stages of Growth in Small Business. *Long Range Planning*, *20*(3), 45–52. doi:10.1016/0024-6301(87)90071-9

Stacey, R. D. (2003). *Strategic Management and Organisational Dynamics, the Challenge of Complexity*. London: FT Prentice Hall.

Trunick, P. A. (1999). ERP: promise or pipe dream. *Transportation and Distribution*, *40*(1), 23–26.

Turner, D., & Crawford, M. (1994). Managing Current and Future Competitive Performance: The Role of Competence. In Hamel, G., & Heene, A. (Eds.), *Competence Based Competition*. Chichester: Wiley.

Van Stijn, E., & Wensley, A. (2001). Organisational memory and the completeness of process modelling in ERP systems. *Business Process Management Journal*, *7*(3), 181–194. doi:10.1108/14637150110392647

Waring, T., & Wainwright, D. (2000). Interpreting integration with respect to information systems in organizations – image, theory and reality. *Journal of Information Technology, 15*, 131–148. doi:10.1080/026839600344320

Warren, L. (2002). Towards Critical Practice in a Teaching Company Scheme. *OR Insight, 15*(4), 11–19. doi:10.1057/ori.2002.16

Warren, L. (2003a). Towards Critical Practice in SMEs. *Systemic Practice and Action Research, 16*(3), 197–212. doi:10.1023/A:1023859805741

Warren, L. (2003b). The crisis of control: a progressive approach towards information systems integration for small companies. *Information Systems and E-business Management, 1*(4), 353–371.

Warren, L. (2003c). Supporting Knowledge Management through he Viable System Model. *Systemist, 25*, 156–165.

Warren, L., Fuller, T., Argyle, P., & Welter, F. (2008, September). *A complexity perspective on entrepreneurship: a new methodology for research in high velocity environments.* Paper presented at the British Academy of Management conference, Harrogate, UK.

This work was previously published in International Journal of Enterprise Information Systems, Volume 5, Issue 3, edited by Madjid Tavana, pp. 60-71, copyright 2009 by IGI Publishing (an imprint of IGI Global).

Chapter 3
A Complex Adaptive Systems-Based Enterprise Knowledge Sharing Model

Cynthia T. Small
The MITRE Corporation, USA

Andrew P. Sage
George Mason University, USA

ABSTRACT

This paper describes a complex adaptive systems (CAS)-based enterprise knowledge-sharing (KnS) model. The CAS-based enterprise KnS model consists of a CAS-based KnS framework and a multi-agent simulation model. Enterprise knowledge sharing is modeled as the emergent behavior of knowledge workers interacting with the KnS environment and other knowledge workers. The CAS-based enterprise KnS model is developed to aid knowledge management (KM) leadership and other KnS researchers in gaining an enhanced understanding of KnS behavior and its influences. A premise of this research is that a better understanding of KnS influences can result in enhanced decision-making of KnS interventions that can result in improvements in KnS behavior.

CAS-BASED MODELING OF ENTERPRISE KNOWLEDGE SHARING

The enterprise KnS model developed here models enterprise knowledge sharing from a complex adaptive systems perspective. Hypothetical concepts that are fundamental to the development of this CAS-based model and to this research include:

DOI: 10.4018/978-1-60960-529-2.ch003

1. Knowledge sharing is a human behavior performed by knowledge workers;
2. Knowledge workers are diverse and heterogeneous;
3. Knowledge workers may choose to share knowledge; and
4. The KnS decision is influenced by other knowledge workers and the KnS environment.

Enterprise knowledge sharing is the result of the decisions made by knowledge workers, individually and as members of teams, regarding knowledge sharing. As depicted in Figure 1, there are two major decisions (rectangles) that a knowledge worker makes: "Share Knowledge?" and "Type of Knowledge to Share?" This research models the KnS decisions as being influenced by the attributes of the individual knowledge worker, the KnS behavior of other knowledge workers, and the state of the KnS environment. Previous KnS studies and research identify factors that influence KnS behavior. However, few address the heterogeneity of knowledge workers and how the attributes of the individual knowledge worker, and knowledge worker teams, impact KnS behavior. The emergent enterprise KnS behavior, noted by the diamond shape in Figure 1, is the result of the interactions of the knowledge worker with the KnS environment and other knowledge workers. Relevant aspects of enterprise KnS behavior and the associated KnS influences are discussed in the sections that follow.

Enterprise KnS behavior takes on many forms. It can be a conversation around a water fountain, e-mail sent to a co-worker or a group forum, a presentation to a small group, an enterprise "best-practice" forum, or documents published to a corporate repository. Murray (2003) categorizes KnS activities into technology-assisted communication (videoconferencing, databanks/intranet, e-mail, and teleconferencing), meetings (face-to-face interaction, seminars and conferences, social events, and retreats), and training and development (mentoring, instructional lectures, video tapes, and simulation games). This research combines the two types of knowledge (tacit and explicit) and the ontological dimension (individual, group, and organization) of knowledge creation presented by Nonaka and Takeuchi (1995) to derive the types of KnS behavior for the model. The KnS behaviors investigated and incorporated in the enterprise KnS model are as follows:

1. **Individual tacit:** This behavior includes sharing tacit knowledge with an individual or individuals, such as face-to-face interactions in informal or formal meetings.
2. **Individual explicit:** This behavior includes sharing explicit knowledge with an individual or individuals, such as through sending e-mail or hard copy material to select individual(s).

Figure 1. Enterprise KnS influence diagram

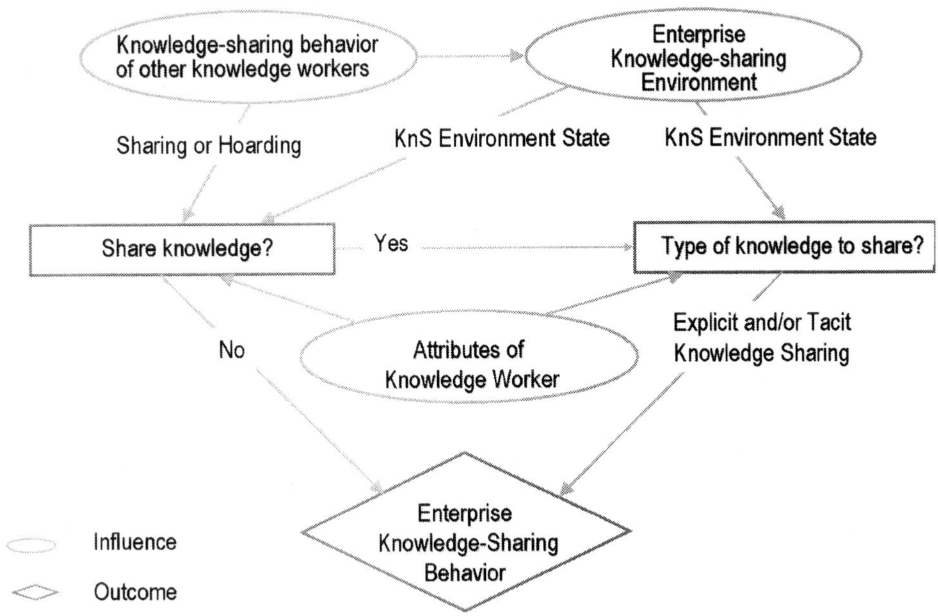

3. **Group tacit:** This behavior includes sharing tacit knowledge with a group, such as face-to-face interactions with a community of interest, community of practice (CoP), or organizational unit.
4. **Group explicit:** This behavior includes sharing explicit knowledge with a group, such as posting or contributing to a community of interest, CoP, or organizational unit repository, Web site, or mailing list server.
5. **Enterprise tacit:** This behavior includes sharing tacit knowledge in an enterprise-wide forum, such as presenting at a technical exchange meeting or other forum that is open to the entire enterprise.
6. **Enterprise explicit:** This behavior includes sharing explicit knowledge in a manner that makes it available to anyone in the enterprise, such as publishing in a corporate-wide repository or enterprise-wide intranet.

While we investigate KnS behavior as being comprised of six different types, both tacit and explicit knowledge are often shared in a given situation. For example, in an enterprise KnS forum, tacit knowledge, such as unrehearsed oral presentations and responses to questions, and explicit knowledge, such as hard copy presentations, are generally both shared.

We investigate three major KnS influences on the associated sharing of knowledge:

1. The enterprise KnS environment,
2. KnS behavior of other knowledge workers, and
3. Attributes of the knowledge workers.

The KnS literature, such as reviewed in Small and Sage (2006), identifies many factors that influence KnS behavior. A discussion of each of the major influences is provided in the sections that follow.

The enterprise KnS environment is closely aligned to the Japanese concept of "ba" which translates into English as "place." Nonaka and Konno (1998) adapted this Japanese concept for their knowledge creation theory. "Ba," as described by Nonaka and Konno (1998), is the shared space for emerging relationships that can be physical, virtual, mental, or any combination of these. It is the place where knowledge is created, shared, and exploited. The "ba" is comprised of the knowledge resources and the people who own and create the knowledge. The KnS environment or "ba" is comprised of many factors that influence KnS behavior. There are at least six important influence factors in the KnS environment modeled and investigated here. A brief description of each of these factors is appropriate here:

1. **KnS technology:** KnS technologies are those technologies that allow knowledge workers to share tacit or explicit knowledge. Technologies and tools reported (APQC, 2000) as critical to knowledge sharing at best practice firms included: e-mail, intranets, document sharing systems, collaboration tools, and video conferences. Chu (2003) included e-mail, Internet, intranet, databases, and teleconferences in his listing of these. With the advent of Web 2.0, wikis, blogs, and social networking applications are being used to enable enterprise knowledge sharing (APQC, 2008)
2. **Leadership:** Leaders and managers in an organization impact KnS behavior by directing behavior, rewarding or recognizing behavior, and by setting KnS behavior examples. Many studies indicate that organizations with appropriate KnS leadership behavior have more instances of appropriate KnS behavior than others.
3. **KnS culture:** Culture is an organization's values, norms, and unwritten rules. Most existing KM models and KnS investigations include culture as a critical enabler or influence on KnS behavior. Additionally, cultural issues are regularly cited as one of the concerns held by those implementing KM initiatives.
4. **Human networks:** This factor includes processes, technology, and resources that help to connect knowledge workers or support knowledge networks. Support for human networks, which includes informal and formal forums, is widely practiced among best practice organizations. They are often referred to as communities of practice or community of interests. Organizations can

enable these networks with knowledge stewards, online collaboration tools, and tools to facilitate easy publishing.

5. **Rewards and recognition:** This factor includes the approaches organizations use to encourage or reinforce the discipline of knowledge sharing. Approaches include rewards, recognition, alignment with performance assessment and promotion, and conducting visible KnS events. When establishing rewards, organizations must consider the generic type of behavior they are trying to stimulate. Many organizations have instituted reward and award programs for knowledge sharing and/or have integrated incentives for knowledge sharing with performance appraisals and promotions.
6. **Alignment with strategy:**This refers to the alignment of knowledge sharing with business strategy. Best practice organizations do not share knowledge for the sake of knowledge. Rather, knowledge sharing is deemed critical to achieving business goals and is linked to the business strategy (APQC, 1999). The alignment of knowledge sharing to business strategy can be either explicit or implicit. When organizations have explicit alignment, language regarding knowledge sharing can be found in documents such as strategic business plans, vision or mission statements, or performance measures. Organizations with implicit alignment are evidenced by knowledge sharing embedded in business practices. Fifty percent of the best-practice firms that participated in the APQC benchmarking study (APQC, 1999) on knowledge sharing were explicitly aligned, while the other half were implicitly aligned. Findings of two APQC benchmarking studies found that organizations where knowledge workers understood how knowledge sharing supported the business strategy had stronger KnS behavior.

The behavior of other knowledge workers within an organization affects the KnS decisions of a specific knowledge worker in many ways. Ford (2003) describes sharing knowledge as a risky behavior because the individual does not know how the shared knowledge will be used by the party who obtains it. Trust in, and some knowledge of, what the recipient of the shared knowledge will do with the shared knowledge are critical to knowledge sharing. From an enterprise perspective, knowledge workers must trust the organization not to cast them aside after the knowledge is harvested. From a peer interrelationship perspective, a knowledge worker must trust that the knowledge recipient will make ethical use of the shared knowledge (Bukowitz & Williams, 1999). If a knowledge worker shares and the knowledge recipient misuses the shared knowledge, from the perspectives of the intended purposes for sharing, then the knowledge worker may be reluctant to share knowledge in the future.

The KnS influence of individual knowledge workers attributes is very important because knowledge sharing is a human behavior in which the knowledge worker chooses to share. The decision to share is influenced by interactions. Leonard and Straus (1997), for example, assert that individuals have preferred habits of thought that influence how they make decisions and interact with others. Knowledge workers have many diverse attributes, some of which are fixed and others of which are variable. Some of the individual attributes or human factors identified in the KM and KnS literature include employees' means, ability, and motivation (Ives et al., 2000); job characteristics including workload and content (Chu, 2002); feelings of being valued and commitment to the project (Ipe, 2003); and conditions of respect, justice perception, and relationships with superiors (Liao et al., 2004).

Here, we model enterprise knowledge sharing as emergent behavior that is the result of decisions made by knowledge workers. The decisions, "Share Knowledge?" and "Type of Knowledge to Share?" depicted in Figure 1 are based on dynamic interactions and are influenced by factors in the KnS environment, KnS behaviors of other knowledge workers, and the individual attributes and perspectives of the knowledge worker. The CAS-based enterprise KnS model integrates the knowledge worker, KnS decisions, and the KnS influences into a CAS-based framework, which consists of two major components:

1. CAS-based enterprise KnS framework
2. Enterprise KnS simulation model (e-KnSMOD).

A detailed discussion of each of the components is provided in the sections that follow.

CAS-BASED KNS FRAMEWORK

The CAS-based KnS framework is the most critical element of our CAS-based KnS model and distinguishes it from other KM models, such as those described in Small and Sage (2006). The CAS-based KnS framework describes enterprise knowledge sharing from a complex adaptive systems perspective. The properties of a CAS, as described by Holland (1995), are aggregation, diversity, internal models, and non-linearity. Axelrod and Cohen (1999) identify variation, interaction, and selection as the hallmark of complex adaptive systems. Other important concepts of complex adaptive systems include the agent, strategy, population, type, and artifacts. For simplicity, the following constructs of a complex adaptive system have been addressed at the highest level of the enterprise KnS framework: agent, agent attributes, interactions, artifacts, and rules.

The CAS-based KnS framework, illustrated in Figure 2, is comprised of the following elements: knowledge worker(s); KnS environment (comprised of KnS influences/enablers and barriers); KnS behaviors; KnS rules; and attributes of the knowledge worker. The KnS behavior results from the interactions of the knowledge workers with each other and the KnS environment. The decision to share is influenced by individual attributes, KnS behavior of other knowledge workers, and the KnS environment. A mapping of the KnS influence diagram in Figure 1 to the CAS concepts used in the CAS-based framework of Figure 2 is as follows:

- **KnS Influence Diagram Elements**
    - Knowledge workers
    - KnS Environment
    - KnS Decisions
    - Enterprise knowledge sharing
    - Knowledge worker attributes
- **CAS-Based KnS Framework Elements**
    - KnS Agents
    - KnS Environment (artifacts)
    - KnS Rules

Figure 2. Major elements of the CAS-based KnS framework

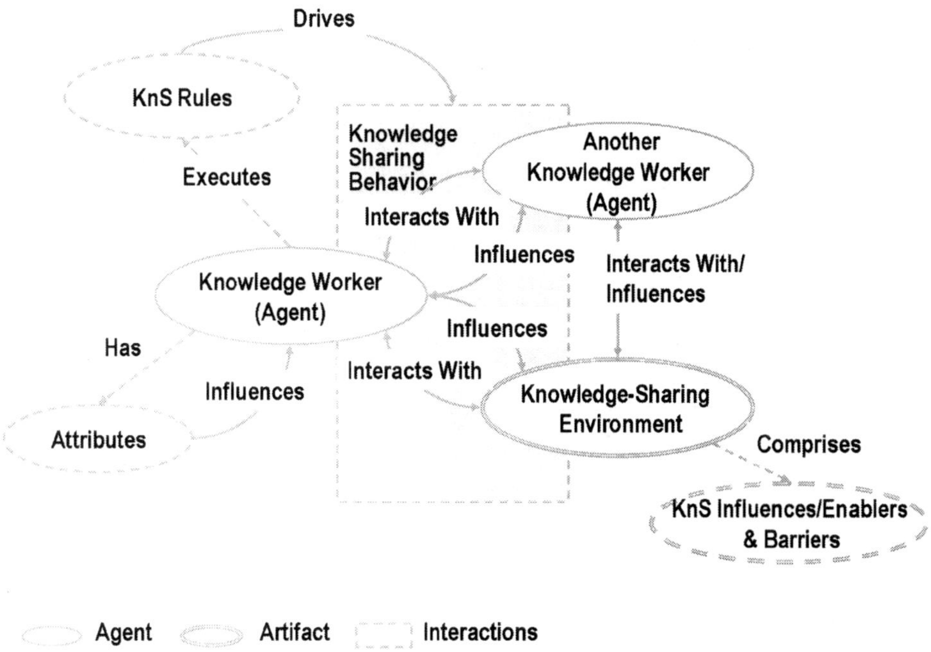

- KnS Behaviors (interactions)
- KnS Agent attributes

The knowledge worker is the KnS agent within the CAS-based model. Critical to this concept is the diversity and heterogeneity of this KnS agent. The knowledge worker within an enterprise is diverse in many ways: personality, gender, role, and job level. Figure 3 associates this segment of the KnS framework with the attributes of the knowledge worker. The KnS decisions (execution of rules) of a KnS agent depend on the agent's attributes and are influenced by the agents' interactions with other knowledge workers and the KnS environment.

The attributes of the knowledge worker investigated here include: personality, gender, level of knowledge acquired, years of affiliation, role, career goals, job level, internal organizational affiliation, external organizational affiliation, and job characteristics. These attributes are described as follows:

1. **Personality:** Such as introvert, extrovert, or a combination.
2. **Gender:** Male or female.
3. **Level of knowledge acquired:** The level of knowledge acquired over time (related to competency) by the knowledge worker.
4. **Years of affiliation:** The number of years a knowledge worker has been affiliated with the enterprise (i.e., number of years at the company).

Figure 3. Investigated attributes of knowledge worker

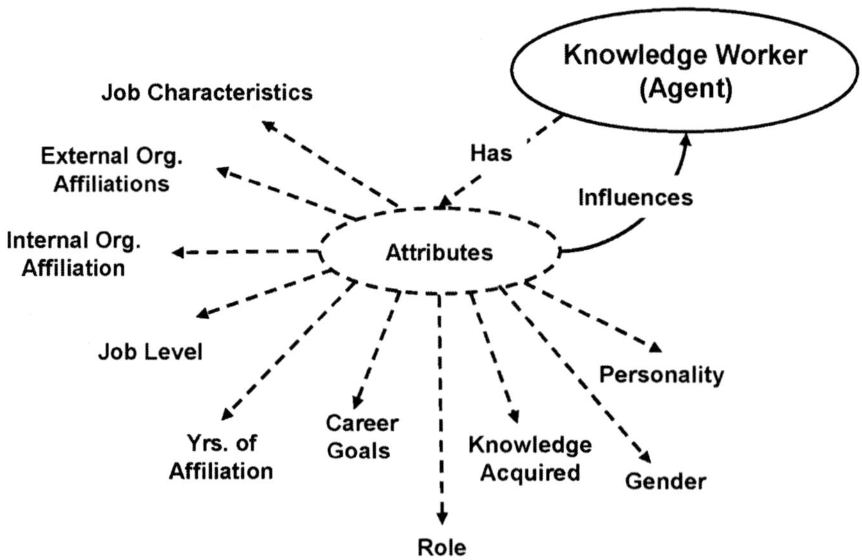

5. **Role:** The role (s) the knowledge worker has within the enterprise, organization, or project. Examples include manager, technical leader, or technical contributor.
6. **Career goals:** The job or career-related goals possessed by the knowledge worker. Goals investigated as part of this research include: career growth (promotion), knowledge growth opportunities, satisfying customers, satisfying management, recognition, and reward.
7. **Job level:** The job level that is assigned by the company to a given knowledge worker, ranging from entry/junior level people to executive management.
8. **Internal organizational affiliation:** An enterprise usually consists of many organizations. This is the internal organization to which the knowledge worker is assigned.
9. **External organizational affiliations:** The number of external professional organizations with which the knowledge worker is affiliated.
10. **Job characteristics:** This includes number of tasks supported, workload, pace, and content of work.

KnS rules drive the decisions the knowledge worker makes. A knowledge worker has two fundamental KnS decisions: "Share Knowledge?" and "Type of Knowledge to Share?" The KnS rules are the same for all KnS agents. They are parameterized based on the attributes of the agents, behavior or other knowledge workers, and the state of the KnS environment.

An enterprise KnS environment consists of many factors that influence or enable KnS behavior. A KnS artifact is an entity in the enterprise (not a person) with which the knowledge worker interacts that either influences or enables their KnS behavior. An enterprise has many KnS artifacts, including information technology, performance and reward systems, knowledge repositories, and information help desk. The KnS influences or enablers examined here and illustrated in Figure 4 include: KnS linked to corporate strategy, alignment of rewards and recognition, KnS embedded with work processes, KnS aligned with core values, enabling of human networks, and KnS technology (availability and ease of use). The artifacts that exist in an environment can have different enabling characteristics. A five-state characterization instrument was developed to characterize the KnS environment.

A knowledge worker (KW) gains or acquires knowledge by interacting with the environment and other knowledge workers. Knowledge sharing results in and from a KW interacting with another KW and/or with the KnS environment. Enterprise knowledge sharing is the result of knowledge workers interacting with other knowledge workers and the enterprise KnS environment. Included in the CAS-based framework are the following KnS behaviors: individual tacit, group tacit, enterprise tacit, individual explicit, group explicit, and enterprise explicit.

Figure 4. KnS influences/enablers investigated

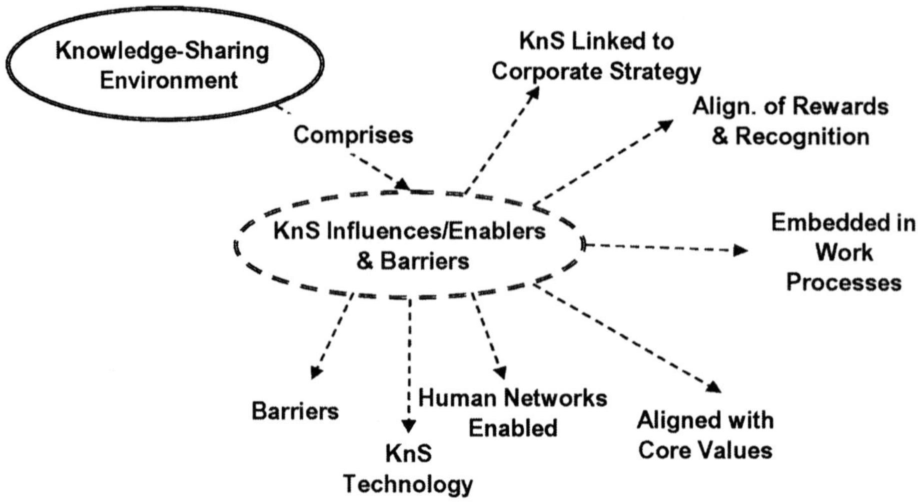

MULTI-AGENT ENTERPRISE KNS SIMULATION MODEL (E-KNSMOD)

The Enterprise KnS Model (e-KnSMOD) simulates enterprise knowledge sharing as the emergent behavior of knowledge workers, represented as agents, interacting with the KnS environment and other knowledge workers. The design of the e-KnSMOD is based on the CAS-based KnS framework described here. All of the constructs of the framework (KnS agent, agent attributes, KnS behavior, KnS environment, and rules) are implemented in the simulation model. For simplicity, the simulation model implements a subset of the attributes (level of knowledge, role, career goals, job level, and internal organizational affiliation) of the knowledge worker included in the CAS-based framework. The purpose of the model is to examine the effects of the KnS enterprise environment and behavior of other knowledge workers on the KnS behavior of a heterogeneous population of knowledge workers. Epstein and Axtell (1996) refer to agent-based models of social processes as artificial societies. The design and implementation of this model leverages the agent-based computer modeling of the artificial society known as The Sugarscape Model (Epstein & Axtell, 1996) and the Sugarscape source code developed by Nelson and Minar (1997) using Swarm (Minar et al., 1996; Johnson & Lancaster, 2000; Swarm Development Group, 2004).

The e-KnSMOD model simulates a population of knowledge workers that work in an artificial enterprise. As with Sugarscape (Epstein & Axtell, 1996), the e-KnSMOD leverages the research results that have been obtained using cellular automata (CA) for agent-based modeling. KnS agents represent the knowledge workers, and the CA represents the artificial enterprise, KnS-scape. The KnS agents interact with each other and their environment as they move around the enterprise gaining valuable knowledge (a goal of many knowledge workers). Agents acquire knowledge by engaging in a knowledge creation opportunity or by receiving knowledge shared by other knowledge workers. In order to satisfy their goals, they must continue to generate new knowledge. As conceptually depicted in Figure 5, the e-KnSMOD consists of three major elements:

1. KnS agents ("knowledge workers")
2. The artificial enterprise or KnS-scape
3. Interactions (driven by rules).

Each of these elements, as implemented in the e-KnSMOD, is described in the following subsections.

KnS Agent

A KnS agent represents a knowledge worker in the artificial enterprise. The KnS agents are heterogeneous. This implementation of e-KnSMOD models the fol-

Figure 5. Major elements of the e-KnSMOD

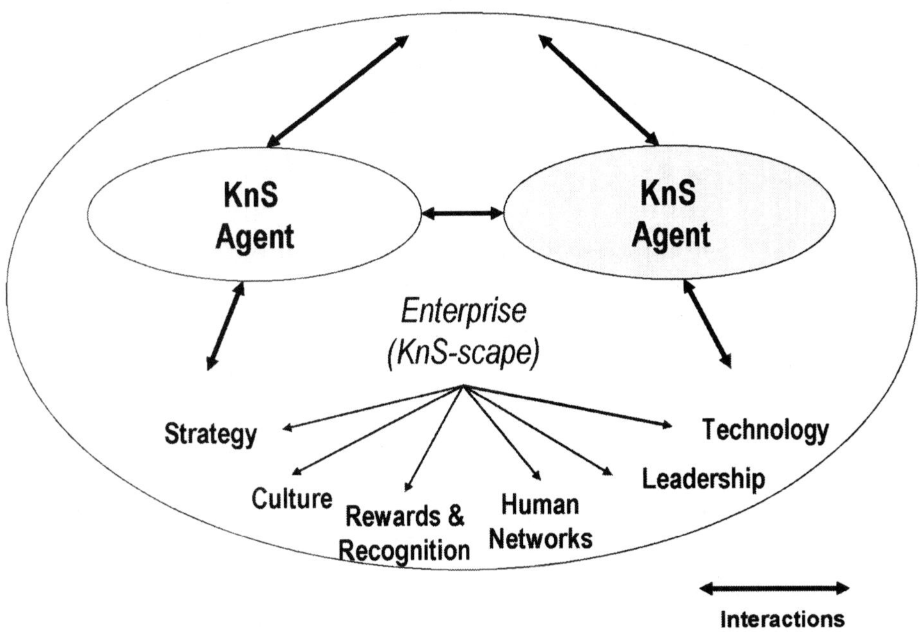

lowing subset of attributes included in the CAS-based KnS framework: level of knowledge acquired, role, job level, and organization affiliation. Each KnS Agent is characterized by a set of fixed and variable states that vary among the agents. The fixed states include:

1. Level of knowledge acquired (competency)
2. Job level (vision is based on job level) in organization (e.g., Jr. Analyst, Sr. Analyst, Principal, Director)
3. Role in organization (manager, non-manager)
4. Organizational affiliation.

Each agent has the following variable states:

- New knowledge gained
- Location on the KnS-scape
- KnS indicator (indicates if the agent shared in the previous run cycle).

The KnS agent comes to the KnS-scape with a specified competency. Upon entry, the agent is assigned a vision and organizational affiliation. The job level is then based on vision. The KnS agent moves (changes location) around the enterprise in order to participate in knowledge-creation opportunities that allow the KnS agents to gain knowledge. The agent's vision restricts what knowledge creation events the agent can see. The agent decides to share or hoard the knowledge gained. If the agent decides to share, it can participate in one or more KnS behaviors: individual tacit, individual explicit, group tacit, group explicit, enterprise tacit, and enterprise explicit. The shared knowledge indicator is set when the agent shares knowledge.

KnS-Scape: The Artificial "Ba"

The KnS-scape, which represents the "Ba," is represented by a two-dimensional (50 x 50) coordinate grid. The grid is built using the Swarm tool set. The grid has multiple views. Each point (x, y) on the grid has a knowledge-creation opportunity, an organization identifier, and a KnS environment state. The information needed by the model to create these views is read from data files, which can be specified at run time. A KnS agent is randomly placed on the KnS-scape. The organizational unit associated with the agent's initial location on the KnS-scape determines an agent's organizational affiliation. When a KnS agent engages in a knowledge-creation opportunity, it acquires the knowledge associated with the opportunity. An organization view of the KnS-scape would indicate that there are four different organizations within the enterprise. The KnS agents are colored by the organizational affiliation of their initial location on the KnS-scape.

Knowledge-Creation Opportunity

Each location on the KnS-scape, represented by an (x, y) coordinate, has a knowledge-creation event or opportunity. KnS agents interacting with their environment and with other KnS agents create knowledge. One of the ways a KnS agent interacts with the environment is by moving to a location and then acquiring the knowledge associated with a knowledge-creation event. When an agent acquires the knowledge at a given location, the knowledge is depleted (value = 0) until another knowledge creation event occurs. The value of the knowledge creation event is increased on each cycle of the simulation until the maximum value for that location is achieved. The amount of increase on each cycle is controlled by the "alpha" parameter, described later.

KnS Environment State

Each location on the KnS-scape has a KnS environment state. The states are as follows:

1. **Barrier:** KnS environment has a negative impact on KnS behavior.
2. **Neutral:** KnS environment has no or minimum impact on KnS behavior.
3. **Enabled:** KnS environment enables KnS behavior.
4. **Encouraged:** KnS environment encourages KnS behavior.
5. **Aligned:** KnS environment positively influences KnS behavior.

KnS Organization View

Each location on the KnS-scape, represented by an (x, y) coordinate, has an organizational identifier. When an agent enters the KnS-scape, it is given the organizational identifier of the location where it is placed. The organizational identifier is used in group KnS behaviors.

Interactions: Acquiring and Sharing Knowledge

The KnS agent interacts with the KnS-scape and with other KnS agents. As previously described, each KnS agent comes to the KnS-scape with a vision that allows it to see knowledge-creation opportunities. During each simulation cycle, an agent looks out over the KnS-scape and determines the location of the best knowledge-creation opportunity. It then moves there and acquires the knowledge. If the KnS agent acquires enough knowledge to share, the KnS agent then chooses to share or not to share. The KnS agent can participate in six types of KnS behaviors: individual tacit, individual explicit, group tacit, group explicit, enterprise tacit and enterprise explicit. The impact of each of these KnS interactions is briefly described as follows:

1. Tacit individual: Results in the "current knowledge" attribute of the recipient KnS agent being increased. The physical vicinity of KnS agents restricts this interaction.
2. Tacit group: Results in the "knowledge acquired" attribute of the recipient KnS agents being increased. The "current knowledge" attribute restricts this interaction.
3. Tacit enterprise: Results in the "current knowledge" attribute of all KnS agents being increased. The "organizational affiliation" attribute restricts this interaction.
4. Explicit individual: Results in the "current knowledge" attribute of the recipient KnS agent being increased.
5. Explicit group: Results in an increase of knowledge in the organizational or group repository.
6. Explicit enterprise: Results in an increase of knowledge in the enterprise repository.

The most important aspect of "ba" is interaction. Important to this research is that knowledge is created by the individual knowledge worker as a result of interactions with other knowledge workers and with the environment.

Rules for the KnS-Scape

Eptein and Axtell (1996) describe three types of rules: agent-environment rule, environment-environment rule, and agent-agent rule. There are three types of similar rules in the KnS-scape model:

1. Agent movement rule;
2. Generation of new knowledge creation events rule;
3. KnS rule.

A brief description of each rule is provided here:

- **Agent movement rule:** The KnS agent uses the movement rule to move around the KnS-scape. The movement rule processes local information about the KnS-scape and returns rank ordering of the state according to some criteria. The rules and functions used by the agents are the same for all agents. The values of the parameters change based on the attributes of the agent and the state of the environment. A summary of the movement rule is as follows:

1. Look out as far as vision (an agent attribute) permits and identify the unoccupied site(s) that best satisfies the knowledge acquisition goal.
2. If goals can be satisfied by multiple sites, select the closest site.
3. Move to the site.
4. Collect the knowledge associated with the knowledge-creation opportunity of the new position.

- **Generation of New Knowledge Creation Events:** A knowledge creation event has a knowledge value. After the knowledge is collected from the site on the KnS-scape, the value goes to zero (it no longer exists). The frequency of new events is driven by the "alpha" parameter. At the end of each cycle, each location on the KnS-scape is incremented by the "alpha" value until it reaches its maximum value.
- **KnS Rule:** After an agent completes the move to the new location and acquires the knowledge there, the KnS rule is executed. The decision to share and the type of knowledge to share is dependent on the KnS behavior of other agents, the KnS environment state, and the "level of knowledge acquired" attribute.
- **E-KnSMOD—Simulation of Enterprise Knowledge Sharing:** Enterprise knowledge sharing is simulated by the e-KnSMOD. Enterprise knowledge sharing is measured by the number of KnS agents participating in one of the six KnS behaviors, the percent of KnS agents that share, the frequency that KnS agents share, and the number of items deposited into the group or enterprise repositories.

Initializing the e-KnSMOD environment properly is important here. E-KnSMOD, built using the Swarm tool set, has two basic components: the Observer Swarm, and the Model Swarm. Swarms are objects that implement memory allocation and event scheduling. Upon execution of the e-KnSMOD, two probes and a program control panel are displayed. The observer (ObserverSwarm) and model (ModelSwarm) probes consist of default parameters that are modifiable by the user. After the parameters for the Observer Swarm and Model Swarm are processed, the e-KnSMOD environment is established by creating the Observer and Model objects and building the Scheduler. The Observer objects consist of the windows used to display the KnS-scape and KnS agents and other graphs specified by the user. The Model objects consist of the KnS-scape and the KnS agents. These steps are described next:

1. **Creation of the KnS-scape:** The KnS-scape, a 50 x 50 lattice, represents the KnS enterprise environment. Each location (x,y) on the KnS-scape has a knowledge creation opportunity, an organization identifier, and a KnS environment state. The KnS_event, organization, and KnS_environment datafiles (specified in the ModelSwarm probe) are used to build the characteristics of each (x,y) location, respectively. The knowledge creation events, which have a value of 1 through 5, are observable by the user of the KnS model from the KnS-scape window. The value of a knowledge creation (KC) event is distinguishable by color as represented in the KnS-scape window illustrated in Figure 6.
2. **Creation of the KnS Agents:** After the KnS-scape is created, the KnS agents are created and randomly placed on the KnS-scape. The "KnSnumAgents" parameter is used to determine how many KnS agents are created. The model creates a heterogeneous population of KnS agents. Some of the attributes are randomly generated, and others are based on where the agent is placed on the KnS-scape. The agents organizational affiliation is determined by the organization associated with the (x, y) coordinate at which the agent is placed. The initial value of current knowledge is based on the vision, which is randomly generated.
3. **Creation of the Scheduler:** The Observer Swarm and the Model Swarm create a schedule for activities to be performed during each cycle of the model. The Model Swarm schedules the actions to be performed by the KnS agents and the actions to be performed on the KnS-scape. The actions include:
    1. KnS Agent: Move and acquire knowledge.
    2. KnS Agent: Execute KnS behavior rule.
    3. KnS-scape: Update KnS-scape (Knowledge Creation Event View).
    4. KnS Repositories: Update group and enterprise repositories.
    5. Display: Update KnS-scape display window.
    6. Display: Update knowledge distribution graph.
    7. Display: Update KnS attributes over time.
    8. Summary File: Update KnS summary (metrics) file.
4. **Model Output:** The e-KnSMOD has three primary output windows that are updated after each cycle. The windows include: KnS Agent Attributes Over Time, Agent Knowledge Distribution, and the KnS-scape. Additionally, the model maintains a KnS summary data file that captures the KnS metrics of the KnS agents. This data file is used for additional data analysis outside the e-KnSMOD environment. The following KnS metrics are captured by the model: the number of KnS agents that shared, the number of agents that shared by organization, the average amount of knowledge acquired, the number of items contributed to a group repository, and the number of items contributed to an enterprise repository.

The e-KnSMOD is designed to allow the user to explore possible improvements in enterprise knowledge sharing by observing the impact of KnS influences. The influences identified in the enterprise sharing influence diagram, shown in Figure 1, are: KnS environment, KnS behavior of other knowledge workers, and attributes of the knowledge workers. Figure 7 shows the results of a 10-cycle run using the default "alpha" value (alpha = 1), which causes a depleted KC event to increase one unit per cycle until it reaches its maximum capacity. Examination of the KnS Agent Attributes Over Time window shows that an average number of KnS agents sharing during each cycle is approximately 50, with a steady increase of knowledge acquired. By changing the "alpha" parameter to zero (0), for example, the user can examine what the impact of the KC event not reoccurring has on KnS behavior. Here, the results of a 10-cycle run show that the number of KnS agents sharing began to drop until no sharing occurred. The resulting KnS-scape window shows that there are no KC events.

Sensitivity analysis may be performed on e-KnSMOD by executing the model of several varying conditions in order to determine if small changes to the parameters resulted in unexpected results. Analysis may be performed on the parameters that are used in either the KnS rule or the environment rules. A summary of the findings are:

1. **Number of agents:** the model was tested with the number of agents ranging from 100 to 500 with varying conditions. In most cases, the percent of agents sharing increases slightly (< 1.5%) as one increases the number of agents in increments of 50. The number of agents was more sensitive in the range of 100-300 than in the range of 200-500.

Figure 6. Knowledge creation (KC) events on the KnS-scape

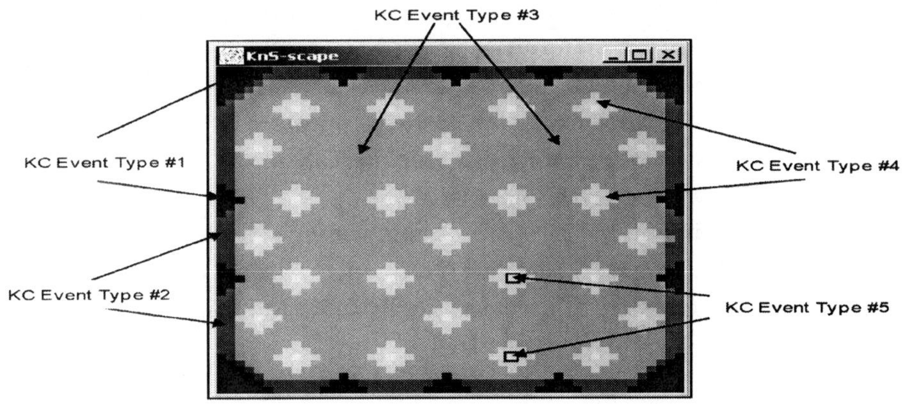

Figure 7. Example run: Recurring rate for KC events = 1

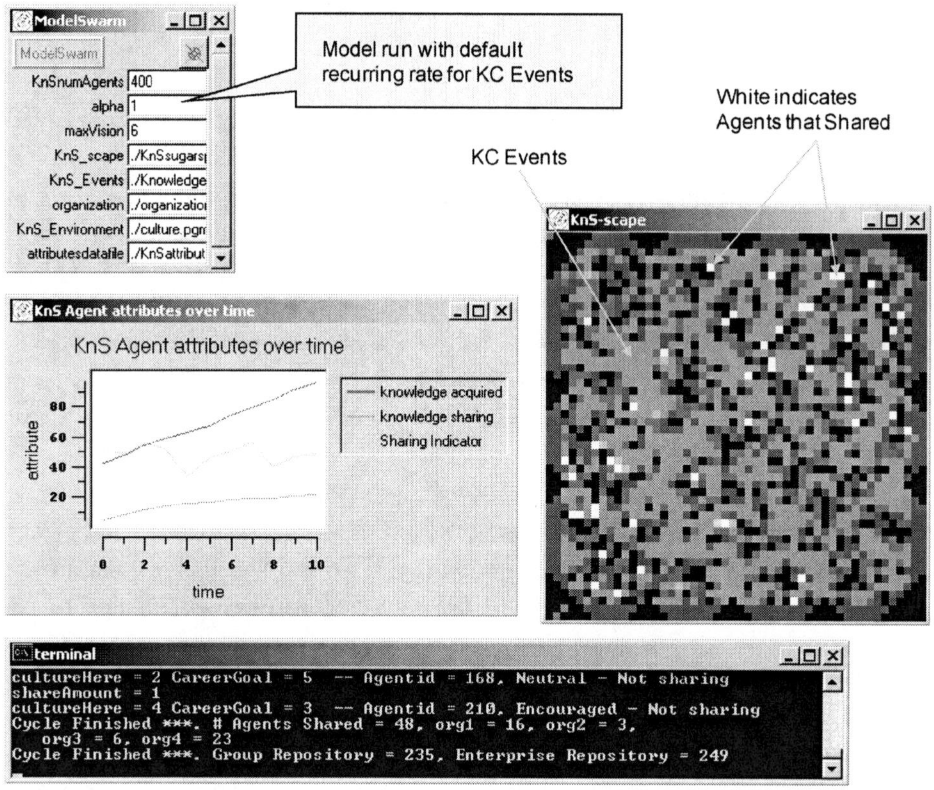

2. **Behavior influence:** the model was tested by setting this parameter to 0 and 1. In all the tests conducted the percent of agents sharing decreased in the range of 1.7 to 4.0 percent when the parameter was changed from 0 to 1.
3. **Max vision:** The maximum vision was tested with the values 7, 14 and 28. In most cases, as the vision increased (7 to 14 to 28) the resulting knowledge sharing increased ~ 1%. However, the percent was higher when the knowledge creation events with high value (part of the KnS_scape) were further apart.
4. **KnS_scape:**– the percent of agents sharing is impacted most by this parameter. The KnS agents acquire knowledge from the KnS_scape and if the agent does not have knowledge, it does not share.
5. **KnS_environment:** the percent of agents sharing is impacted greatly by this parameter. A difference of one state (i.e., barrier to neutral or neutral to enable) can change the percent of agent sharing from 5% to 14%.

Much more detailed discussions of the construction of this simulation model are presented in Small (2006).

As described in this article, the e-KnSMOD, is a simple multi-agent simulation based on simple environment and KnS rules. The environment is represented by three 2-dimentional (50 by 50) lattices: one for the knowledge creation events, one for the organization affiliation, and one for the state of the KnS environment. Many complex relationships among the KWs and the KnS environment are not included in the implementation of e-KnSMOD. The objective of the model is not to predict enterprise KnS behavior, but to be used with the other CAS-based tools to enhance the understanding of enterprise knowledge sharing.

One major use of this KnS model is to improve enterprise knowledge sharing. The CAS-based enterprise KnS model can assist enterprise KM leadership, managers, practitioners, and others involved in KM implementation to characterize the current KnS environment, identify influences of KnS behavior, and better understand the impact of KnS interventions. This model can be applied to enterprises that are about to embark on KnS initiatives, as well as those that have a rich KnS portfolio.

The CAS-based characterization instruments allow a practitioner to characterize enterprise KnS from the perspective of the KW and from that of KM Leadership. Both instruments characterize the frequency of KnS behaviors, the extent of influence of KnS influences and barriers, and the state of the KnS environment. The data gathered using these instruments provide the information needed to characterize and model an enterprise from a CAS perspective.

The KW Profiling Questionnaire is a critical element here. The purpose of the KW Profiling Questionnaire is to determine, from an individual knowledge worker perspective, the answers to four questions:

1. What are your attributes?
2. What is your KnS behavior?
3. What influences your KnS behavior?
4. What is the state of the KnS environment?

The answers to these questions allow a KM practitioner to investigate the extent of KnS influences on the heterogeneous knowledge worker populations. Addressing the attributes of the knowledge worker is a critical aspect of this CAS-based methodology.

The focus of the KM Leadership Characterization Questionnaire is to determine, from the perspective of KM leadership and implementers, the answers to the following four questions:

- Part I: What is the understanding of the KM Leadership Team regarding the KnS needs (mission perspective) and KnS behavior within the organization?
- Part II: What are the KnS influences and the extent of the influences within your enterprise?
- Part III: What is the state of the KnS enablers/influences within your enterprise?
- Part IV: What is the KnS Strategy for Improvement?

Part I and Part IV of the KM leadership characterization instrument relates to the KnS improvement strategy. Part I addresses the importance of KnS to support mission needs, and whether KnS is occurring at the right level (individual, group, enterprise) and frequency. Part IV addresses the KnS strategy, which includes areas of improvement and the priority for achievement. The relationships of these questions to the CAS-based KnS framework are depicted in Figure 8.

The CAS-based KnS improvement methodology can be used by either an enterprise about to embark on KnS improvement activities for the first time (Initial Stage) or an enterprise that has a KnS strategy and robust KnS portfolio (Learning Stage). The tools described here can be used to identify and prioritize KnS improvement courses of action. The CAS-based methodology consists of five primary steps:

1. Step 1: Determine KnS Needs in Context of Mission Effectiveness. During this step, the KM practitioner determines the importance of KnS to the organization and assesses whether KnS is occurring at the appropriate frequency to support mission needs. Part I of the KM Leadership Characterization Questionnaire is used to gather this information.
2. Step 2: Characterize Current State of KnS. During this step, the KW profiling instrument is used to characterize KnS in the organization from a CAS perspective. The frequency of KnS behavior, KnS influences, and the state of the KnS environment are characterized from the individual knowledge worker perspective.
3. Step 3: Establish KnS Target State. During this step, Part III of the KM Leadership Characterization Questionnaire is used to capture the target state of the KnS environment, identify factors in the KnS environment that need improvement, and to establish priority of their implementation.
4. Step 4: Perform CAS-based Analysis. During this step, population analysis is performed based on KW attributes of interest to the organization. A gap analysis is performed on areas targeted for improvement against the extent of influence of the KnS factors identified by the KWs.
5. Step 5: Develop KnS Improvement Strategy. During this step, the results of the CAS-based analysis are used to develop or align the KnS strategy. The

Figure 8. KM leadership characterization and the CAS-based KnS framework

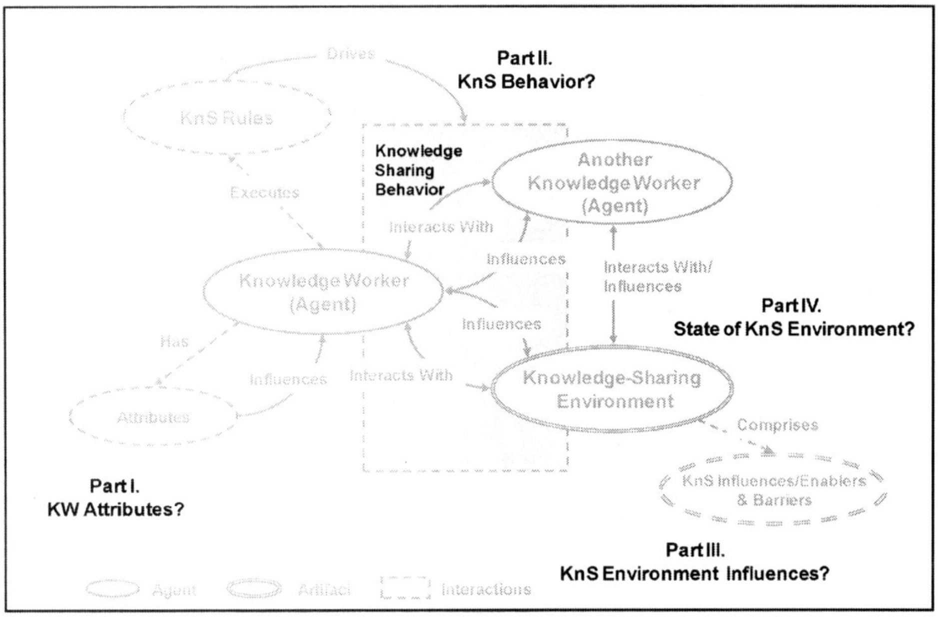

current state of the KnS environment (KW perspective), the target state of KnS environment (KM leadership), and the extent of KnS influence (KW perspective) are used to identify areas of improvement and their priority. The CAS-based simulation model can be used to model the planned improvements to gain insight into the possible impacts on KnS behavior.

The steps of the CAS-based KnS methodology should be integrated into the organizational improvement framework. We describe the CAS-based KnS improvement methodology in the context of the IDEAL^{SM} (SEI, 1996) model, an improvement process originally designed for software process improvement. The IDEAL^{SM} model consists of five phases:

1. Initiating: This phase lays the groundwork for a successful KnS improvement effort. It includes setting the context and sponsorship, and establishing the improvement infrastructure (organizations). Step 1 is conducted during this phase.
2. Diagnosing: Assessing the current state of KnS in the enterprise and determining where the organization is relative to the target state. Step 2, 3, and 4 are conducted during this phase.

3. Establishing: Developing strategies and plans for achieving the KnS target state. Step 5 is conducted during this phase.
4. Acting: Executing the plan to improve KnS.
5. Learning: Learning from the KnS experience and feedback from mission stakeholders, KM leadership, and knowledge workers.

As shown in Figure 9, Step 1 occurs during the Initiating phase. Step 2, 3, and 4 occur during the Diagnosing phase, and Step 5 concurs during the Establishing phase.

SUMMARY

A CAS-based enterprise KnS model is described in this article. The model was evaluated for validity and effectiveness in two case studies. The premise of our research was that modeling enterprise knowledge sharing from a complex adaptive systems (CAS) perspective can provide KM leadership and practitioners with an enhanced understanding of KnS behavior within their organization. This research found that the CAS-based enterprise KnS model and methodology provides KM leadership with an enhanced understanding of KnS behavior and the KnS influences. In the two case studies conducted in operational environments, members of the KM

Figure 9. CAS-based methodology: An IDEAL[SM] perspective

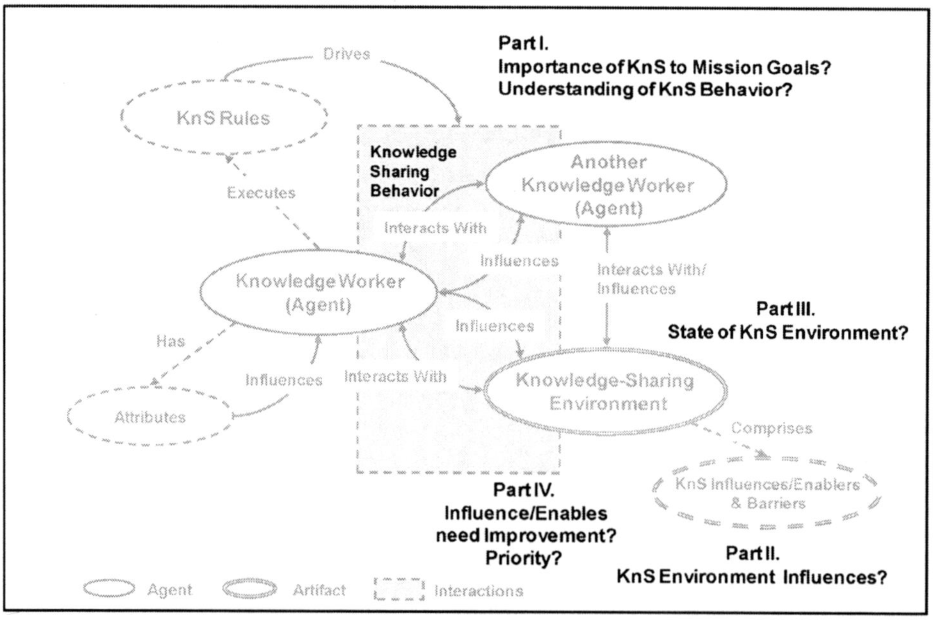

leadership teams indicated that they had gained a better understanding because of the CAS-based modeling approach. Enhanced understanding of the following was indicated: KnS behavior in their organization; KnS influences in their organization; and the extent of the KnS influences within their organization. KM leadership also indicated that because of the CAS-based modeling, they would either change the target KnS state of the KnS environment or the priority for achieving that state.

The CAS-based enterprise KnS model developed as part of this research was found to be valid. The CAS-based enterprise KnS model was exercised in two case studies. The results of the case studies (Small, 2006) provided support for the validity of the assumptions on which the CAS-based enterprise KnS model was developed. The claims associated with the validity of the CAS-based enterprise KnS model are as follows:

1. Claim 1 (C1): The KnS behavior of other KWs is a significant influence on KnS behavior.
2. Claim 2 (C2): The KnS environment factors are a significant influence on KnS behavior.
3. Claim 3 (C3): The attributes of the KW are related to the frequency of KnS behavior (how often a KW engages in a KnS behavior).
4. Claim 4 (C4): Enterprise KnS behavior can be characterized using a multi-agent CAS model, with a few basic rules that drive agent behavior.

REFERENCES

American Productivity & Quality Center (APQC). (1999). *Creating a knowledge-sharing culture*. Consortium Benchmarking Study -- Best-Practice Report.

American Productivity & Quality Center (APQC). (2000). *Successfully implementing knowledge management*. Consortium Benchmarking Study -- Final Report, 2000.

Anderson, P. (1999). Complexity theory and organization science. *Organization Science*, *10*(3), 216–232. doi:10.1287/orsc.10.3.216

Axelrod, R. (1997). *The complexity of cooperation: Agent-based models of competition and collaboration*. New Jersey: Princeton University Press.

Axelrod, R., & Cohen, M. (1999). *Harnessing complexity: Organizational implications of a scientific frontier*. New York: The Free Press.

Bukowitz, W., & Williams, R. (1999). *The knowledge management fieldbook*. London: Financial Times Prentice Hall.

Epstein, M., & Axtell, R. (1996). *Growing artificial societies: Social science from the bottom up*. Washington, D.C.: The Brookings Institution.

Ford, D. (2003). Trust and knowledge management: The seeds of success. In *Handbook on Knowledge Management 1: Knowledge Matters* (pp. 553–575). Heidelberg: Springer-Verlag.

HBSP. (1998). *Harvard Business review on knowledge management*. Cambridge, MA: Harvard Business School Press.

Holland, J. (1995). *Hidden order: How adaptation builds complexity*. MA: Perseus Books Reading.

Holsapple, C. W. (Ed.). (2003). *Handbook on knowledge management 1: Knowledge matters*. Heidelberg: Springer-Verlag.

Holsapple, C. W. (Ed.). (2003). *Handbook on knowledge management 2: Knowledge directions*. Heidelberg: Springer-Verlag.

Ipe, M. (2003). *The praxis of knowledge sharing in organizations: A case study*. Doctoral dissertation. University Microfilms.

Ives, W., Torrey, B., & Gordon, C. (2000). Knowledge sharing is human behavior. In *Knowledge management: Classic and contemporary works* (pp. 99-129).

Johnson, P., & Lancaster, A. (2000). *Swarm users guide*. Swarm Development Group.

Leonard, D., & Straus, S. (1998). Putting your company's whole brain to work. In *Harvard Business Review on Knowledge Management* (pp. 109–136). Boston: Harvard Business School Press.

Liao, S., Chang, J., Shih-chieh, C., & Chia-mei, K. (2004). Employee relationship and knowledge sharing: A case study of a Taiwanese finance and securities firm. *Knowledge Management Research & Practice*, *2*, 24–34. doi:10.1057/palgrave.kmrp.8500016

Minar, N., Burkhar, R., Langton, C., & Askemnazi, M. (1996). *The Swarm Simulation System: A toolkit for building multi-agent simulations*. Retrieved from http://alumni.media.mit.edu/~nelson/research/ swarm/.

Murray, S. (2003). *A quantitative examination to determine if knowledge sharing activities, given the appropriate richness lead to knowledge transfer, and if implementation factors influence the use of these knowledge sharing activities*. Doctoral dissertation. University Microfilms.

Nonaka, I., & Konno, N. (1998). The concept of Ba: Building a foundation for knowledge creation. [Special Issue on Knowledge and the Firm]. *California Management Review*, *40*(3), 40–54.

Nonaka, I., & Takeuchi, H. (1995). *The knowledge-creating company: How Japanese companies create the dynamics of innovation*. New York: Oxford University Press.

O'Dell, C. (2008). *Web 2.0 and knowledge management.* American Productivity & Quality Center (APQC). Retrieved from http://www.apqc.org.

Small, C. (2006). *An enterprise knowledge-sharing model: A complex adaptive systems perspective on improvement in knowledge sharing*. Doctoral dissertation, George Mason University. University Microfilms.

Small, C., & Sage, A. (2006). Knowledge management and knowledge sharing: A review. *Information, Knowledge, and Systems Management*, *5*(3), 153–169.

Software Engineering Institute (SEI). (1996). *IDEAL*[SM]*: A user's guide for software process improvement (Handbook CMU/SEI-96-HB-001)*. Pittsburgh, PA: Software Engineering Institute, Carnegie Mellon University.

Swarm Development Group. (2004). *Chris Langton, Glen Ropella*. Retrieved from http://wiki.swarm.org/.

This work was previously published in International Journal of Information Technologies and the Systems Approach, Volume 1, Issue 2, edited by Frank Stowell and Manuel Mora, pp. 38-56, copyright 2008 by IGI Publishing (an imprint of IGI Global).

Chapter 4
Conflicts, Compromises, and Political Decisions:
Methodological Challenges of Enterprise-Wide E-Business Architecture Creation

Kari Smolander
Lappeenranta University of Technology, Finland

Matti Rossi
Helsinki School of Economics, Finland

ABSTRACT

This article describes the architecture development process in an international ICT company, which is building a comprehensive e-business system for its customers. The implementation includes the integration of data and legacy systems from independent business units and the construction of a uniform Web-based customer interface. We followed the early process of architecture analysis and definition over a year. The research focuses on the creation of e-business architecture and observes that instead of guided by a prescribed method, the architecture emerges through somewhat non-deliberate actions obliged by the situation and its constraints, conflicts, compromises, and political decisions. The interview-based qualitative data is analyzed using grounded theory and a coherent story explaining the situation and its forces is extracted. Conclusions are drawn from the observations and possibilities and weaknesses of the support that UML and RUP provide for the process are pointed out.

DOI: 10.4018/978-1-60960-529-2.ch004

INTRODUCTION

Robust technical architecture is considered one of the key issues when building successful e-business systems. The design of technical architecture is usually seen as a set of trade-offs between available resources (such as available personnel and money) and operational requirements related to technical architecture, such as scalability, capacity, response times, security, and availability. The software architecture research provides design tools for technical architecture design, including, for instance, architecture description languages (Dashofy, Van der Hoek, & Taylor, 2005; Medvidovic & Taylor, 2000), common architectural patterns and styles (Monroe, Kompanek, Melton, & Garlan, 1997), architectural trade-off methods (Kazman, Klein, & Clements, 2000), architectural frameworks (Leist & Zellner, 2006), and technologies for e-business implementation (Bichler, Segev, & Zhao, 1998). In an ideal world, the work of an architect would be to find the explicit requirements for architecture, and select the best possible design tools and technologies to implement the architecture. Furthermore, the architecture development team would make rational trade-offs concerning the requirements, and produce the best realistic solution for the architecture with the selected design tools and implementation technologies.

However, the literature contains many examples of cases where technical rationality has not been sufficient for the success in IS projects (e.g. Sauer, Southon, & Dampney, 1997). Architecture researchers have found that the work of an architect and the usage of architecture are bound by more diverse organizational issues and limitations that the classical technical software architecture research ignores. These include for example the diverse role of an architect in an organization observed by Grinter (1999) and varying uses and meanings of architecture in practice (Smolander & Päivärinta, 2002a). The main message of these studies is that an architect has a social, and even political, role in an organization and that different stakeholders relate different meanings to architecture to fulfill their informational requirements in the development process. This phenomenon has remarkable similarities to information systems development in general. As pointed out by Klein & Hirscheim, the implicit assumption of rationality of the development processes hides the legitimating of the goals and differing political agendas of various stakeholders (Hirschheim & Klein, 1989).

To understand the issues involved in architecture development, we observed a project that was developing e-business architecture in an international ICT company. We interviewed various stakeholders to gain a deep insight into the process. The company already had several e-commerce systems in individual business units, but it needed a more uniform customer interface for its various systems. The e-business project included the integration of data and legacy systems from these units and the construction of a uniform Web-based customer interface hiding the differences of the business units. Our goal was to find ways for supporting architecture development by means of methods and description languages, such as UML. We were aware of efforts of supporting architecture design with UML (e.g., Conallen, 1999; Garlan & Kompanek, 2000; Hofmeister, Nord, & Soni, 1999b; Object Management Group, 1999, 2006), but these efforts were mostly targeted to technical software design and we did not know how well these would support a large socio-technical or organizational project, such as enterprise or e-business architecture development. Therefore we decided to observe a real world project and concentrate on the requirements that e-business architecture development in its complex organizational context state on description languages and development methods. Next, we decided to compare the observed requirements to the support that UML and RUP offer, because they, together, form the current methodological basis for many systems development organizations. UML is the de-facto standard language in software and systems development and RUP (Jacobson, Booch, & Rumbaugh, 1999) is a widely known process model that claims to improve development process maturity (Kuntzmann & Kruchten, 2003). We believed that this kind of knowledge would benefit both practitioners in process improvement and developers of UML extensions.

Another interest was to find out what factors influenced the creation of e-business architecture: was it designed purposefully by software architects through rational decisions and trade-offs, or did it emerge through somewhat non-deliberate actions obliged by the situation and its constraints, conflicts, compromises, and political decisions? This is a very important issue, as unlike software architecture, e-business architecture is very tightly coupled with the business models of the company and thus the architecture has a far more direct impact on business than for example low-level system architecture. Furthermore, if the business models are not supported by the e-business architecture, then the business strategy will not work (Ross, Weill, & Robertson, 2006).

We used open interviews of various actors in the projects to gather the necessary information about the project. We analyzed the qualitative data from the interviews using grounded theory (Glaser & Strauss, 1967) as the research method and concluded the analysis by categorizing the issues that had emerged using the taxonomy of Lyytinen (1987). Thus, we classified the issues as belonging into technical, language and organizational context. From this classification of issues, we extracted requirements for development methods when developing integrated e-business solutions and compared these requirements to the support that the combination of UML and RUP provides.

We observed that most of the problems encountered had very little to do with descriptions of the architecture per se. Rather what was problematic were the issues that architecture development exposed about the underlying organization. This is an important finding, as most of the research into architecture has been about effective description languages and design processes and there is a void of research about the organizational consequences of architecture development.

The article is organized as follows: we start by explaining in more detail what is meant by architecture in this article (section 2). In section 3, we describe the research process and method used. section 4 describes the situation the company is facing and the motives for the change and implementation of the e-business system. In section 5, we describe the situation and the context of the development project aiming at e-business implementation and the consequences of the situation for the progress of the development project. From the observed issues faced by the development project we draw conclusions and extract the requirements for development methods in e-business architecture development and compare the requirements to support that the combination of UML and RUP provides (section 6). We point out areas where current research is not supporting the needs of the practice of general and particularly e-business architecture development.

ARCHITECTURE IN SYSTEMS DEVELOPMENT

In this study, we describe a process where comprehensive e-business architecture is being created. In addition to e-commerce systems serving external customer transactions, e-business includes both the integration of and streamlining of internal information systems to serve the new digitally enabled business processes (Kalakota & Robinson, 2001) and the unified customer interface (Ross et al., 2006). For the sake of simplicity, we understand e-business here to cover both the transactions and processes within a firm and the integrated external e-commerce systems as in (Kalakota & Robinson, 2001). This enables us to interpret the process in the studied organization as the process of building an integrated e-business architecture. Ross et al. (2006) stress the architecture as the necessary foundation for execution of comprehensive, across the functions operating, e-business.

Conventionally, architecture is understood as a high-level logical abstraction of the system defining the main components of the system and their relationships. The term architecture is also used both in the context of an individual system and in the context of systems integration. The software architecture typically concentrates on the architecture of a single software system, whereas the terms information systems (IS) architecture and enterprise architecture (Kim & Everest, 1994; Ross et al., 2006; Sowa & Zachman, 1992) refer to the overall architecture of all information systems in an organization.

In practice, however, the borderline between a single system and a set of systems is difficult to determine. Practically no system today is isolated from other systems, and the relationship of a system to its environment may be architecturally more important than the inner structure of the system, especially when developing e-business systems. Usually, systems rely on a common technical infrastructure, (including networks, processing services, operation services, etc.) which is common for all the systems in an organization. Organizationally, architecture design is a co-operative effort involving many roles in the development environment. These roles include the role of an architect who is specifically associated with the task of architecture design. An architect needs contribution and commitment from many individuals, teams, and parts of organization to succeed in the effort (Grinter, 1999).

By architecture development, we mean a process where early design decisions are realized into an architecture defining that defines system's composition from various viewpoints. Architecture also contains the blueprints for system's implementation from conceptual and physical components. This process forms a set of documents which different stakeholders can use to relate their concerns to the issues made concrete by the architecture and discuss their needs in the terms defined by the common architecture. They can also make decisions concerning system development strategies and policies using architecture as a common reference. This conception sees architecture not only as a technical artifact but also as a boundary object (Star & Griesemer, 1989) having strong organizational connotations.

The conventional role of architecture is to serve as an enabler for further design and implementation (Hofmeister, Nord, & Soni, 1999a; Shaw & Garlan, 1996). Obviously, sound and well-designed technical architecture makes the detailed design and implementation of a system easier and less risky than it would be without such architecture. Architecture defines, for example, the modules or components which the system is composed of, and therefore it focuses and constrains the solution space of individual designers that develop individual components. This technical view of architecture has produced also studies related to UML. In the end of last decade, possibilities and weaknesses of UML as an architecture description language, and its complexity (Siau & Cao, 2001; Siau, Erickson, & Lee, 2005) were widely evaluated and enhancements were proposed (Conallen, 1999; D'Souza & Wills, 1998; Egyed & Medvidovic, 1999; Garlan & Kompanek, 2000; Hofmeister et al., 1999b; Medvidovic, Egyed, & Rosenblum, 1999; Rumpe, Schoenmakers, Radermacher, & Schürr, 1999). The recent developments in this area include the SysML extension of UML (Object Management Group, 2006). Different profiles and enhancements to UML have been proposed to tackle its limitations in electronic commerce (Dori, 2001).

RESEARCH PROCESS

The studied organization is a globally operating ICT company having thousands of employees worldwide. Its customers include both consumers and businesses for which the organization provides various products and services. Software is one of the key assets in the organization's service production and product development. Historically, the organization has had several independent business units targeted at diverging business sectors. In addition, the information management of the organization has been distributed to these business units and the functions of enterprise level information management have included mainly the provision of network infrastructure, enterprise level accounting, and basic office tools. Most of the information systems in use have been implemented and operated by the business units that have been quite independent in their decisions concerning strategies for information management. However, recent developments in markets and technology have led the organization to set its strategies to a more integrative direction. For this reason, the organization has set an objective to provide an integrated e-business solution to both its consumer and business customers. This will include both implementation of a uniform Web-based customer interface and sufficient integration between the distributed operative back-end information systems, such as customer management and billing systems.

The research process followed the grounded theory method (Glaser & Strauss, 1967), which is a research method developed originally for social sciences by Glaser and Strauss in the 1960s and later developed and re-interpreted by the original authors (e.g., Glaser, 1978; Strauss & Corbin, 1990) and others (e.g., Locke, 2001; Martin & Turner, 1986). Grounded theory promotes inductive theory creation from the data. The objective is not to validate or test theories but to create one. The analysis process of the grounded theory is explicitly defined and consists of several coding phases. The coding starts from *open coding* in which any incident, slice, or element of the data may be given a conceptual label for the identification of commonalities. These commonalities are called *categories* and they are described in terms of their properties (Fernández, Lehmann, & Underwood, 2002). The coding continues with *axial coding* (Strauss & Corbin, 1990) or theoretical coding (Glaser, 1978), where relationships between the categories are resolved. The coding ends at *selective coding* (Strauss & Corbin, 1990) where the resulting theory is "densified" (Glaser, 1978) or a core category selected (Strauss & Corbin, 1990) and theory about that is described. The data collection is based on the notion of *theoretical sampling*, which means adjusting the data collection process according to the requirements of the emerging theory. The sources of data may be adjusted during the process and the data collection can be stopped whenever a state of *theoretical saturation* is achieved, meaning a situation where no additional data would further develop the categories and their properties.

In the study, we interviewed 19 participants of the ongoing e-business system architecture design project during 2002, first in January and February and then later in November and December. The interviewees included six system architects, five enterprise system managers, three project managers, two software development managers, one project leader, one system analyst, and one marketing manager. Table 1 describes their relationship to the e-business development project. The interviews lasted from 45 to 120 minutes and they were completely transcribed as text.

The interview themes of this study were adjusted during the data collection to reflect better the developing theoretical understanding of the researchers and the specific knowledge of the interviewees. The emphasis of the interviews changed according to the interviewee and the special knowledge in his or her possession. Because the data collection proceeded partly in parallel with the analysis, the emerging theory also caused changes in the emphasis of the interview themes. In grounded theory this kind of adaptation is called *theoretical sensitivity*, and for theory-building research this is considered legitimate because "investigators are trying to understand each case individually and in as much depth as feasible" (Eisenhardt, 1989, p. 539). Eisenhardt calls the process where the emergence of a new line of thinking causes the altering of data collection *controlled opportunism* "in which researchers take advantage of the uniqueness of a specific case and the emergence of new themes to improve resultant theory" (Eisenhardt, 1989, p. 539).

The analysis in this study started with the open coding phase. In the beginning, we did not have any explicit *a priori* constructs for the analysis. Our task was to search mentions from the interviews that could be interpreted as meaningful related to the research question, "What are the conditions and constraints for creating and designing architecture in a large information systems development project?" The identified mentions related to this question were categorized using the software tool

Table 1. Interviewed persons and their roles

Role	Tasks	Interviews
System architect	Deals with technological solutions and architectural structures in the e-business development project	6
Enterprise system manager	Is responsible for a portfolio of systems and technologies that are used in a particular organization. Acts as a customer in the internal e-business development project or participates it as an expert.	5
Project manager	Manages resources and is responsible for the execution of a sub-project of the e-business development project	3
Software development manager	Is responsible for a permanent software development organization	2
Project leader	Manages the e-business development super-project and supervises its set of sub-projects.	1
System analyst	Participates the requirements gathering and analysis phases as an intermediate between customers and technical experts.	1
Marketing manager	Is responsible for the public image and services of the electronic channel. Requirements setter and a customer to the development project.	1

ATLAS.ti. During the open coding phase, altogether 187 emergent categories were found, and the categories were assigned to emerging scheme of super categories or category families, including for instance changes, conflicts, consequences, experiences, problems, purposes, and solutions occurring during the e-business architecture design and implementation process.

The axial coding started in parallel with the open coding and causal relationships between categories were recorded with Atlas.ti's semantic network capability. Figure 1 shows an example of such a network diagram. In the figure, the boxes represent categories, the arrows between them interpreted causalities, and the lines associations between categories. The number of categories and the number of identified relationships between the categories added up to 187 categories and 200 relationships, which created a problem of how to report such a multitude of categories and relationships. The solution was sought through abstracting out those categories that were rarely occurring in the data and interpreted as not so relevant regarding the research question. In addition, more attention was paid to those categories that occurred frequently in the data.

Inductively, we produced an explaining story to the events and forces under which the e-business development project had to work. The organization is facing market changes and changing the organization according to the changing markets. The objectives for the e-business development emerge from these changes and because the change is continuous and it brings all the time new requirements for the e-business system, the objectives are quite fluctuating. In addition, the history and legacy structures of the organization cause conflicts and problems in the development when combined with the need for change. These fluctuating objectives and emerging conflicts and problems brought certain consequences to the e-business architecture development in the organization. The formation and description of this explaining story can be considered as selective coding (Strauss & Corbin, 1990) and its details in the studied organization are explained in the next three sections.

The study has required extensive interpretation and exploration in the studied organization and therefore the main instruments of the research has been the researchers and their ability to interpret events and people's actions correctly. Robson (2002) lists three threats to validity in this kind of research, reactivity (the interference of the researcher's presence), researcher bias, and respondent bias, and strategies that reduce these threats. We have used these strategies in the following way:

- **Prolonged involvement:** Although this study lasted for one year, the research project altogether lasted for more than two years in the same organization and consisted of several phases and data collection rounds.
- **Triangulation:** The study has used data and observer triangulation as presented by Denzin (1978). To reduce the bias caused by researchers, we used

Figure 1. An example of a semantic network from axial coding

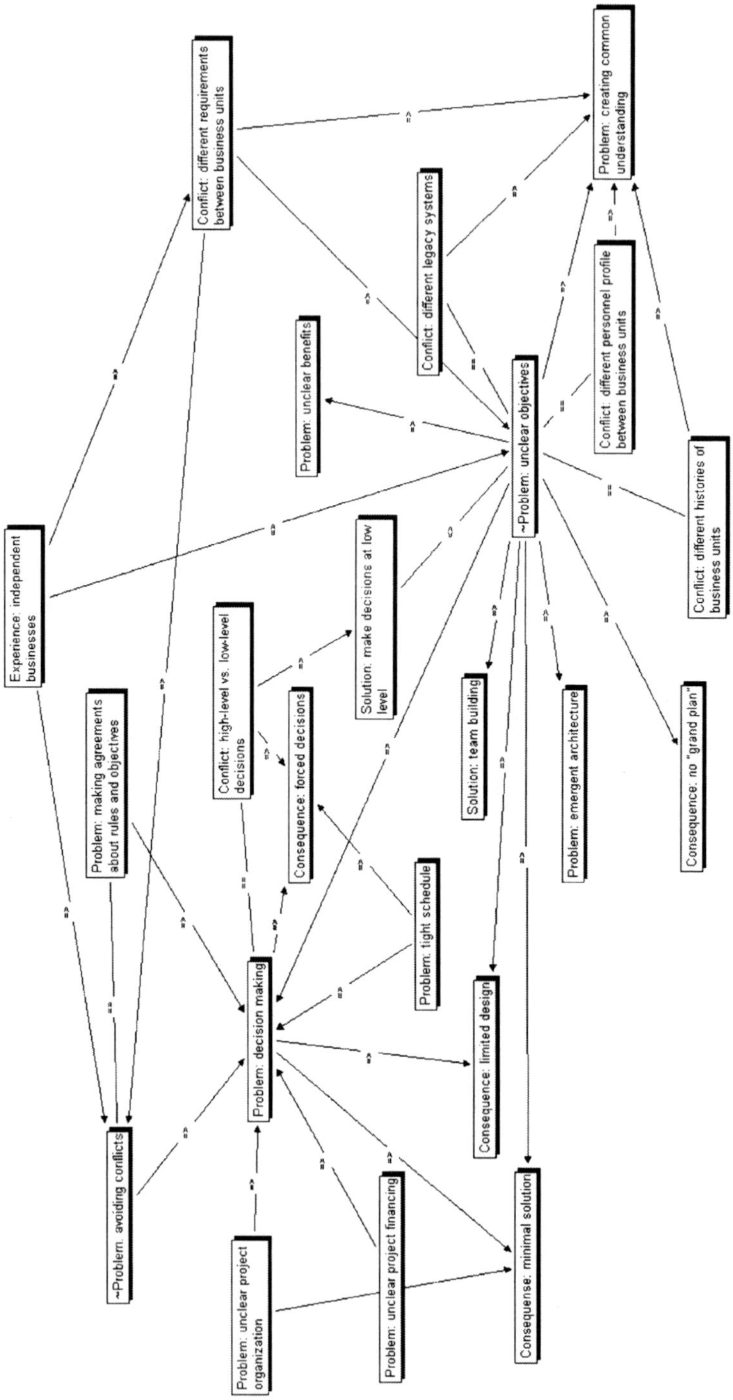

observer triangulation, because the data collection was done by two researchers. The bias caused by data was minimized using *data triangulation*, where different sources of data were used. Interviews were the primary data collection method, but we also received many kinds of project and company documents and architecture descriptions.

- **Peer debriefing and support:** The research has included regular meetings and discussions with involved research participants from several research institutions. In addition, preliminary results of research phases have been presented and discussed in conferences and workshops (Smolander, 2003; Smolander, Hoikka, Isokallio et al., 2002; Smolander & Päivärinta, 2002a, 2002b; Smolander, Rossi, & Purao, 2002, 2005).
- **Member checking:** The interpretation of the data has been confirmed by presenting the results to company participants in the research project.
- **Audit trail:** All interviews have been recorded and transcribed. The notes and memos of the study have been preserved and data coding and analysis results are available through the analysis tool used, ATLAS.ti.

CHANGES AND THEIR EFFECTS IN THE DEVELOPMENT CONTEXT

Starting Point: Changing Markets, Changing Organization

During the time of the data collection, there was a considerable change going on in the ICT market and the organization under study had undergone a deep change. A few years ago, the strategies emphasized growth and utilization of the possibilities in the stock market. This enforced independent business units inside the organization since the growth was easier to handle through independency. Each of the business units built independent e-commerce solutions and customer extranets, which resulted to a fragmentary set of e-commerce solutions to customers with own Internet sites, sales and billing systems, and Web-based customer support.

When the beliefs in the possibilities of ICT sector's continuing growth diminished, the organization had to change its strategies from growth to profitability and from stock market to customer orientation. With independent business units, there was no authority in the organization, which would see a customer as a whole. Instead, each business unit kept track of the customers only in the context of its independent business. To produce a unified customer interface a profound change to the way of building information systems and an integrated e-business solution was needed. This change would also require changes in business practices and organization. The organization should operate in a more integrated fashion and the barriers between independent units should be lowered.

The organization began to see technical e-business architecture as an enabler of change. The IS organizations in independent business units were obliged to cooperate and enforce commitment to the integration of information systems. This also emphasized the role of central information management, which had been in a minor role this far. Now, its roles would include the enforcement of information systems integration and enabling the unification of the sales channels and customer management for the planned e-business solution. At this point, the organization decided to establish a working group of systems architects from various parts of the organization. In the following section, we shall describe the context and the forces under which this group of architects were developing and designing the unified e-business architecture.

Conflicts, Problems and Varying Purposes

The context for e-business architecture development included many issues, which the working group for technical architecture development had to face and be aware of. These included the market changes as described above, historical organizational inertia, fluctuating requirements and objectives, and conflicts and problems emerging from the market changes, inertia, and unclear objectives.

Historical Inertia

The organization's history with independent businesses and their diverging functions and objectives had both psychological and technical consequences causing slow progress and conflicts in the integrated e-business development. Each of the business units had legacy systems with incompatible information structures, technical architectures, and operating principles. It was not possible in practice to replace these systems with a uniform solution at once.

The historical inertia had effects also on the organization responsible for information management and information systems. Because of the independence, the organization had no clear central information management that could take responsibility of the e-business architecture development. Many of the conflicts and problems described later arose from this situation.

The Observed Objectives for the E-Business System

The fluctuating objectives, meanings, and requirements for the e-business architecture created another source of conflicts and problems. In a large organization with a high degree of independency, the conceptions among different business units and individuals about the purposes of an e-business solution vary considerably. Among the interviewees, we identified a large set of different purposes for the e-business system, which were then classified in five distinct classes:

- Creation of a unified electronic customer interface.
- Reduction of costs.
- Integration of information systems.
- Gaining business advantage.
- Implementing an organization change.

This list of observed purposes for the e-business system looks quite comprehensive and ambitious. Different interviewees emphasized the purposes differently and many saw that the only realistic objective was to implement a single sign-on procedure with a minimal level of customer information integration. The list anyhow shows the complicated and conflicting nature of objectives for the e-business system when it is developed for a large enterprise.

Emerging Conflicts and Problems

Changes in markets and organization, the history of the organization, and the complicated objectives for the e-business system put the architecture development group in a difficult situation. The group and its members were obliged to respond by some means and these responses shaped mitigated the role of deliberate design in the development process. In open coding, we identified in total 48 categories of conflicts and problems. This list was further combined to seven main categories, as follows:

- Varying requirements and unclear objectives
- Problems in the cooperation between technical and business people
- Conflict avoidance and problems in decision-making
- Problematic role of the central information management and its missing working practices
- Difficulties in creating common understanding about the architecture
- Difficulties in determining the level of integration
- Problems of implementing the integration

As described earlier, the purposes of the system were manifold and complicated and the requirements varied according to the business needs in the business units. The architects held this ambiguity of objectives and requirements as the biggest obstacle in the development. Those in the managerial level recognized the problem as well, but explained it as unavoidable in the situation and expected that the first prototypes of the system will bring more clarity to the objectives. This resembles the chicken-egg problem: architects must know well the objectives to design the architecture, but the objectives are further clarified only after the first version of the architecture is built.

There were several mentions about the problems in the cooperation between technical and business people. Architects expected the business managers to explicate clear requirements and objectives for the system and its architecture. However, they considered the task impossible, because they thought that the business managers do not possess enough understanding about the possibilities of current technology. They felt that this leads to unrealistic objectives, which were manifested especially when considering the possibilities of legacy systems integration: people with business background had far more optimistic views than architects.

Conflict avoidance and problems in decision-making slowed the progress. Again, because of the history of independency, a central authority that could take care of the architectural decisions for the integrated e-business solution was missing. Because nobody took a full responsibility of the situation, this led to avoidance of conflicts and enforced the tendency towards compromises. A frequently occurring phrase among the architects included the term "lowest common denominator," which was usually noting to the compromised solution with a single sign-on procedure and a minimal level of customer information integration.

The role of the central information management was unclear and it was lacking the routine of large development efforts. The independency of businesses and the minor role of central information management had implications on the working practices. The architectural and development practices of the business units contained considerable differences implying that also common working practices needed to be established for the development process of the e-business system.

Even the understanding of the designed architecture and related technical solutions were difficult to communicate across the organization. Since the business units have had their own histories and produced their own legacy systems and information architectures, the interpretations on the situation and objectives diverged. This, combined with changing organization, unclear objectives, and missing common working practices, created difficulties in understanding and transferring architectural knowledge between the participants from different business units.

It was also difficult to determine the level of integration between the systems. The ownership of the information becomes an issue even in the most modest single sign-on e-business solution serving the whole organization. The question becomes, "who owns the customer information?" and relates to determining the integration level to the currently independent back-end legacy systems. The more ambitious integration, the more out-of-control the customer information (and possibly other information too) shifts from the business units.

In addition to determining the integration level, the actual implementation of integration proved to be problematic. Since the diverging legacy systems could not be replaced, they all had to be interfaced. Of the seven conflicts and problems occurring when creating e-business architecture, only the problem of implementing the integration was mainly a technical problem. The others were more related to the change in organization and practices that happen when developing an e-business system in a large organization with independent businesses. In the following, we shall look closer on what consequences these conflicts and problems cause for the architecture design and development process.

CONSEQUENCES: LIMITED DESIGNS AND MINIMAL SOLUTIONS

In the beginning of the project a unified architecture was seen as a panacea for solving the problems of systems integration, streamlining the organization and unifying the customer interface. However, during the project it became clear that the aforementioned conflicts and problems would have some unfavorable consequences. While it was of paramount importance for the company to be able to streamline its systems and develop a more coherent architecture enabling the creation of an e-business system, the realities of legacy systems and the organization led to situation where it was best to seek satisfying, even minimal, solutions instead of optimal ones.

In the early phases of the project architecture was seen as general blueprints or roadmaps, largely drawn from scratch. Soon, however, the technical experts realized that evolutionary prototyping was the only possibility for progress in the architecture development. Because the schedule was tight, the objectives and requirements unclear and changing, and because the business units were rather independent, it was hard to achieve common understanding and commitment. With prototyping, it would be possible to clarify objectives and commit stakeholders by showing them visible results and benefits. This could be seen as "extreme" architecture design (Merisalo-Rantanen, Tuunanen, & Rossi, 2005). This could however lead to new problems. The technically oriented architects were specially worried that, combined with the quarter-based reporting system in the organization, evolutionary prototyping can easily produce quick-and-dirty and ad hoc solutions. We could classify the interviewees to those with positive attitudes towards prototyping and to those with negative or doubtful attitudes. In general, the project management believed positively that "somehow" the prototypes would transform to the final e-business solution, whereas technical architects presented more doubts and wanted to have explicit requirements and objective statements before committing to certain architectural solutions.

Prototyping and minimal solutions formed a vicious circle that made the development of robust and clear architectures nearly impossible by severely limiting the options available for the architecture developers. Existing legacy systems, the evolutionary approach, varying requirements, unclear objectives, difficulties in creating common understanding, and problems in decision making created a complex situation where textbook methods, description languages, and rational architecture design, as it is conceived in the literature, had no possibilities for immediate success. The degrees of freedom of design became limited. The system and its architecture could not be designed rationally as a whole, but rather one needed to accept the conditions and limitations caused by the factors above and to keep the day to day operations running while the new systems are continuously created through evolution.

The situation had also organizational consequences. We found clear hints of low-level networking and formation of shadow organizations as the result of unclear project organization and problems of decision-making and objective setting. As the organization and responsibilities change, new and perhaps inexperienced persons come into crucial official positions related to the e-business development. At the same time, the experienced architects and other key persons continued to stay in contact with each other. This unofficial shadow organization balanced the mismatch in skills and experience that might otherwise seriously impede the development.

The final consequence from all the above is, that in fact the e-business architecture becomes emergent: it is created gradually through compromises, constraints, and conflicts (c.f., Ciborra, 2000; Hanseth, Monteiro, & Hatling, 1996). The exact objectives and responsibilities will be resolved as the architecture emerges through evolutionary prototyping. Compared to the conventional view on software architecture design (Hofmeister et al., 1999a), most of the claimed benefits of rigorous architecture development seem to be lost. There is no "grand plan" since the work is proceeding in a day-to-day basis and the well defined responses and interfaces between systems do not necessarily emerge in a rationally planned way, but rather most duplicate functions are kept and there is agreement only on a few items that become the "architecture."

DERIVED REQUIREMENTS FOR E-BUSINESS SYSTEMS DEVELOPMENT METHODOLOGY

From the previous observations and explanations, we can derive a set of requirements that an e-business systems development methodology should meet. The grounded theory process resulted in an explanation model (Figure 2), from which a set of methodological requirements can be extracted. Changing markets and organization, historical inertia, and unclear objectives for the development produced a complex combination of conflicts and problems that brought various difficult consequences to the e-business development process. We analyzed the complex socio-technical situation and its consequences and reasoned the set of most pertinent methodological requirements. This was done by identifying and coding the methodological requirements in the interview transcripts and further combining them in 13 requirements as described below.

According to Lyytinen et al. a design methodology should conform to a set of key requirements (Lyytinen, Smolander, & Tahvanainen, 1989). It must embed several conceptual structures and description languages, and support several levels of abstraction at which the development process takes place. It should also cover the whole spectrum of activities in information systems development (ISD), include a prescribed model of activities to be carried out during the development process, include a model of the organizational form of the development (a set of human roles), and try to reuse existing descriptions and implementations. Tools for drawing, manipulating, and managing the descriptions should also support the methodology, in a balanced manner.

We can further elaborate this conception of ISD methodology by distinguishing between three separate contexts in ISD, namely the technical, language, and organization contexts (Lyytinen, 1987). The technical context is concerned with the technical components of the system (like hardware and software), language context forms the environment for linguistic communication, and the organization context provides the environment for systematic human interactions, including decision-making and operative control. An ISD methodology includes assumptions, models, languages, and tools related to these three contexts. In the following, we shall extract from the case the general requirements for e-business development methodology and classify them according to these contexts. The objective of this classification is to illustrate the nature and requirements of e-business architecture development

Figure 2. Deriving the methodology requirements

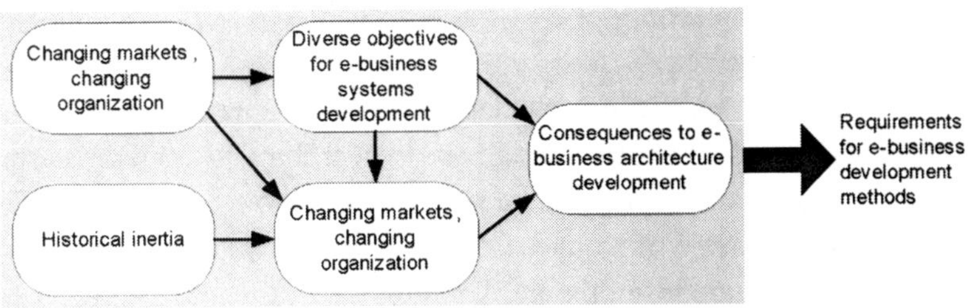

in large organizations with several business areas and to highlight the areas with a weak methodical support.

Lyytinen commented already in 1987 that most development methodologies have too limited scope and they tend to concentrate on technological issues late in the development lifecycle (Lyytinen, 1987). This limited scope omits most of the institutional and governance issues which seemed to be central for most stakeholders according to this study on architectural practice. One could argue that the organizational context is particularly relevant for e-business area, as most proponents of e-business emphasize the changes it brings about to work processes and organizations (Kalakota & Robinson, 2001).

The research into e-business architecture development is in a relatively immature stage. Previous literature has largely assumed that it solves technical issues for known problems (Taylor, McWilliam, Forsyth, & Wade, 2002). However, from the previous passages it has become obvious that methods for forming the problem statement and reaching a mutual agreement on what the architecture is in the end of the day are crucial. In this section, we take this as a starting point and observe the issues that rose in the described case starting from the inner, technical context and ending to the general organizational issues. This corresponds to Lyytinen's idea that the contexts are hierarchically ordered, because languages are presented by material carriers of technology context and language is needed for organized social action (Lyytinen, 1987). We identify e-architecture approaches in these areas and show how they propose solutions to the issues raised in our study.

In the following, we shall present the methodological requirements for each context. We also refer to the rows in Table 1 with the notation R1-R13.

Requirements from the Technology Context

Observed Requirements

The technical requirements of e-business development methods do not differ much from those of methods for traditional transaction-based information systems. E-business system development includes methodical requirements concerning e.g. distribution, error recovery, and networking, but those requirements can be met without a special "e-business support." A standard way to describe such technical solutions is of course required /R1/.

Integrated e-business architecture necessitates the integration of information systems in the organization and the rationalization of technology and development processes. Existing legacy systems will be integrated to the e-business functionality. This requires the selection of an integrative technology and the construction of development processes supporting the implementation of the integration. Because the integration is the basis and characteristic to e-business development, the development methodology should have specialized and usable techniques for describing information systems integration /R2/.

The key issue in the development of e-business systems is the keeping of the day-to-day operations running and at the same time implementing the integration between existing legacy systems and the new e-business functionality. This means that the nature of development is in many cases more analogous to a maintenance project than to a green-field development project. Current systems development methodologies and models of thought are mostly aimed at designing new systems instead of changing existing ones. This problem has been recognized before the advent of e-business, but it becomes more critical in the e-business development. From this we can derive a requirement that the development methodology for e-business systems should support evolutionary approaches to architectures and systems /R3/.

Existing Solutions

Most research on e-business systems development in general, and e-business architecture in particular, concentrates on this view. Much of the support that UML and RUP or their derivatives provide seems to concentrate on this area. Component aware methodologies, such as the Catalysis extension to UML, seem suitable for e-business. In addition, there are UML 2.0 extensions, such as SysML (Object Management Group, 2006), that provide better support for technical architecture design. Bischler and Segev (Bichler et al., 1998) investigate the possibilities of component oriented approach for e-business. They take a technical viewpoint, and provide a useful listing of enabling technologies for e-business. An applicable standard in this area is the SysML extension to UML (Object Management Group, 2006). A work by Rossi & Schwabe (Rossi & Schwabe, 2000) uses patterns and frameworks as building blocks for e-business systems. This kind of approach could be particularly useful for a relatively well-specified domain, such as trade processes, which are assumed to be generic in nature. Baskerville & Pries-Heje see a relatively fixed architecture as a common ground, on top of which e-business systems can be built (Baskerville & Pries-Heje, 2001).

As mentioned earlier, in the e-business domain there are several layers of components available. The InterNCA architecture in (Lyytinen, Rose, & Welke, 1998) describes some of these and outlines needs for new breed of development methodologies, which would take into the account the particular problems of e-business systems development. Greunz & Stanoevska-Slabeva present an extension of UML, which can be used to realize systems on top of "media platform" architecture (Greunz & Stanoevska-Slabeva, 2002).

Requirements from the Language Context

The language context provides a means and an environment for linguistic communication which encompasses the use, nature, content, context and form of signs (Lyytinen, 1987). The methodology requirements coming from the language context deal with the ability of stakeholders to communicate successfully during the e-business architecture development process.

Observed Requirements

The chicken-egg problem between objectives and architecture becomes problematic in e-business development. To design a robust technical architecture, one must have clear objectives, and to select realistic objectives, one must understand the possibilities of the technical architecture. To overcome this problem, it is necessary to have a close cooperation between technical architects and those responsible of the business. This, however, induces a language problem. These groups often do not have a common language. To overcome the language problem, we need architecture description languages that business managers understand /R4/ and business descriptions that are explicit enough for technical people /R5/.

The problems of objectives and integration culminate on architecture design because the designs and prototypes related to technical architecture become the first concrete artifacts in the development showing implications of decisions to businesses and to the information management. Before architecture design, the plans and designs have been on the "PowerPoint presentation" level, showing ambiguous and general roadmaps and noble objectives. The more concrete the architecture becomes, the more various stakeholders become aware of the consequences, conflicts, and problems they will be facing. This leads to two distinct requirements for the development methodology: the methodology should take the development to a very concrete level (both politically and technically) very soon after the project initiation /R6/ and the architecture designs and descriptions (and their implications) should be approachable and intelligible by the various stakeholders participating the process /R7/.

Existing Solutions

As a description language, UML and its extensions offer a fairly strong support for engineering in the language context. Yet, there are very few articles describing these issues of having a common language in e-business area, but one could expect that methodologies used in other domains for participative processes and joint application development could be applied here (August, 1991). In this context, architecture serves as a language between the participants in the development process, enabling communication and making the consequences of the implementation concrete to the participants. Using architecture as an enabler of communication between a diverse set of participants (including various levels of management and technical experts) requires informal and expressive approaches, which are practically non-existent in the field of software architecture research. This kind of conception of "architecture as language" can be associated with approaches that include rich and informal description techniques, like "rich pictures" in (Wood-Harper, 1985), the wall-charting technique (Saaren-Seppälä, 1988), and genre-based approaches (Päivärinta, Halttunen, & Tyrväinen, 2001).

Requirements from the Organization Context

Observed Requirements

These problems formed the largest bulk in our study. They included issues such as organizational inertia as well as environmental limitations, characteristics of a given business environment, codes of conduct in business, and regulatory and societal factors. These factors form together the 'ballpark' for an organization to act in relationship with its providers and customers.

The first organizational requirement comes from the overall conclusion of the case. The transition from heterogeneous e-commerce to integrated e-business is not only technically challenging. It is more a profound change to the organization. In fact, the primary challenge is in the change of the organization, not in the implementation of the technology. Therefore, e-business systems development methodology should support also the description of organizational change /R8/.

In this change of organization and implementation of technology, the role of central information management or some kind of central authority in the organization is crucial. The central authority should take care of the multitude of conflicts occurring when aiming at integration and coordinate the creation of objectives for the system. An e-business development methodology should enable the creation of a common vision /R9/, which can then be enforced by the central authority.

Evolution with modest but growing objectives may be the only way to develop integrated e-business systems. To foster commitment, some immediate benefits should be shown with the prototypes for each stakeholder. However, at the same time, the path to robust architecture should also be secured and enough time and resources must be given to technical architects. This very difficult and complex trade-off must be made in every e-business project /R10/.

The implementation of e-business integration deals not only with technical issues but also with difficult political ones. An organization shifting to integrated e-business must resolve issues concerning the internal ownership of information related for instance to customers, sales, contracts, and products. The ownership and responsibilities related to information must be decided and described during the development process. The development methodology should include descriptions for organizational responsibilities and ownership of information /R11/.

Identifying and agreeing about objectives became the most difficult problem in this case. Thus, to become valuable in practice, e-business development methodology should support not only the formation and recording of objectives but also measuring of success related to objectives /R12/.

The requirements directed to an e-business development organization are quite conflicting. On the other hand, the development requires a strong authority that can control the process through conflicts, and on the other hand, the formation of unofficial and shadow organization (peer-level networking) should be fostered to allow creative solutions and frictionless cooperation between businesses /R13/. This requirement is, however, not a new one when developing organizations.

Existing Solutions

From a more managerial and decision oriented view one could look at business- and strategy development methods, which aim at creation of a common understanding and vision of business strategy. This view sees building of architecture as a common vision building effort rather than a system building effort. It could also be argued that e-business architecture building is quite similar to organizational change processes, especially the introduction of enterprise wide information systems, such as ERP. Koontz has argued for this by presenting e-business architecture development model, which is very generic (Koontz, 2000).

Organizational issues are largely neglected by the traditional systems development methodologies, but form important context and frame for the implementation of the e-business systems and architectures. The work on organizational change and observation of the power-play could be fruitful if applied to early stages of architecture development. However, they do merely observe the issues than provide solutions. Checkland's SSM methodology is one of the few general-purpose methodologies that identifies and models the "essence" of the organizational idea of the system and then proceeds to actual development of the system (Checkland & Scholes, 1990). It is clear from the observations in this case study that the explicit identification and framing of the problem to be solved, and then resolving the actual goals of the architecture forms the basis for architecture development.

Most studies thus far seem to assume that the development of e-architecture and infrastructure can be guided by the deliberate actions and decisions of management. However, as can be seen here the technological changes often evolve from designers' and users' experience with such technologies and are often unpredictable (Ciborra, 2000).The problem of loosing the original target while developing partial solutions and prototypes (e.g., see R10) could be helped by explicitly recognizing emergent and opportunistic possibilities created on the process.

Summary of Issues

The list above shows that most solutions and research this far, has concentrated on the technical level. Unfortunately, most of the problems seem to be non-technical in nature, they are rather more of the linguistic or organizational. E-business cuts across functional borders in organization and is built on a complex infrastructure of ERP and legacy systems and it shares many of the challenges and opportunities of these organizational technologies.

Table 2 summarizes these derived requirements for e-business development methodology. The requirements and their rationale are described in the text above. The 'Type' column places the requirement to the appropriate context or contexts (T: technology, L: language, O: organizational). The last column in the table ("Support in RUP employing UML") analyzes how unified modeling language (Object Management Group, 2005) and the Unified Process (Rational Software Corporation, 2001) support the e-business specific characteristics of the development process. This is important, because UML and RUP together form the current methodological basis for many software organizations. The column shows that the support is generally poor. The e-business specific requirements are not met by UML and RUP —only the standard technical issues are well covered. This conclusion calls for method development supporting better these e-business specific requirements.

In the technical context we noted that e-business development would benefit from method enhancements in IS integration and evolutionary development. However, the language and especially the organization context appeared to have more importance in the development. In the language context, there was an urgent need for more understandable and concrete architecture descriptions that could be used among many groups involved in the process, including technical and non-technical people. The organization context appeared as the most important target for research and practical methodical improvements. In that context, we could identify a multitude of issues requiring improvements, including better understanding and usable methods for the design and implementation of organization change, organizational vision, organizational ownership of information, and organizational responsibilities.

Figure 3 shows concisely our findings. When creating e-business or enterprise architecture, the major problems to be solved are organizational. This does not align with the support that UML and RUP provides, because they mostly concentrate on solving the problems in the language and technical contexts. It is the task of future

Table 2. Summary of the requirements for e-business development methodology

	Requirement	Type	Rationale	Support in RUP employing UML
R1	Technical issues (like distribution, error recovery, and networking) must be described in a standard way.	T	These issues will occur as in all modern systems development	Good; this is what UML and RUP are for
R2	Specialized techniques for describing the information systems integration	T	IS integration is characteristic to e-business development	Poor; no specialized technique for the description of integration in standard UML. Some UML 2.0 extensions are however available.
R3	The development methodology should support evolutionary approaches to architectures and systems.	L/T	The change and maintenance of existing systems forms a major part of the e-business systems development	Moderate; UML and RUP are mainly targeted at the development of new systems
R4	Architectural description languages that business managers understand	L	To enable realistic objective selection, business managers must have some understanding on architecture	Poor; the descriptions necessitate too much technical skills and knowledge
R5	Business descriptions that are explicit enough for technical people	L	To understand the objectives, technical people must have understanding on business	Moderate; no description techniques showing overall aggregate view
R6	The methodology should take the development to a very concrete level (both politically and technically) soon after the project initiation	T/L/O	The more architecture becomes concrete, the more stakeholders become aware of the consequences, conflicts, and problems	Good (technically), none (politically)
R7	The architecture designs and descriptions (and their implications) should be approachable and intelligible by the various stakeholders participating the process	L/O	To enable wide understanding to the consequences of architectural selections (cf. R4).	Moderate; no relevant description technique besides Use Case diagrams
R8	Support for the description of organizational change	O	e-business involves deep changes to organization	Poor; some thoughts of "organization engineering" in RUP's Business Architecture
R9	Support for the description of a common vision	O	Resolve conflicts, build objectives	Poor; no common language for all stakeholders
R10	Both prototyping and careful architecture design needed	T	Gain commitment and resolve objectives through prototyping, aim at robust architecture	Moderate; iterative basis in RUP, but its implementation is difficult in practice
R11	Methodology should contain descriptions for organizational responsibilities and ownership of information	L/O	The ownership of information becomes an issue when aiming at e-business integration	Poor; only general thoughts
R12	e-business development methodology should support the formation and recording of objectives and measuring of success related to objectives	L/O	Identifying and agreeing about objectives is one of the most difficult issues in e-business development	Poor; the objectives are mostly supposed to be given to the development project
R13	The development process should support organizationally both effective control structures and flexibility	O	Strong authority is needed to handle the conflicts and unofficial structures for creative solutions	Poor; development organization "design" in a general level

research to provide improvements to this, but, as can be seen from Table 2, it might need quite radical extensions or changes to UML and RUP to be able to support effectively the formation of e-business architecture.

CONCLUSION

We have described a process where a large ICT company is building architecture for a comprehensive e-business system. From the case, we extracted 13 requirements for methodology supporting integrated e-business systems development and classified the requirements to technology, language, and organization contexts. We also compared the requirements to the support that UML and RUP offers and concluded that the e-business specific requirements are not met in UML and RUP. Successful e-business development requires alternative approaches that support better organization change, communication between stakeholders, systems integration, objective formation, and evolutionary development.

In our study, architecture manifested itself as a catalyst that makes business and organizational conflicts and problems concrete. When making decisions about architecture, the systems architects had to take into account the organizational situation in the company. At the same time the architecture starts shaping and changing the organization, thus forming a double mangle (e.g., Jones, 1998). The architects also realized that technical rationality is not enough for success in this kind of a situation. To succeed in e-business architecture development, one has to be aware of the political and organizational forces that are driving the development and its objectives. E-business architecture development can therefore be characterized as a process of seeking boundaries, finding sufficient consensus, and identifying commonalities across organizational borders. Most previous literature on architectural methods has neglected this and sought to develop description languages for describing the actual architectures for systems with clear problem statements, whereas we claim that it

Figure 3. Support and requirements

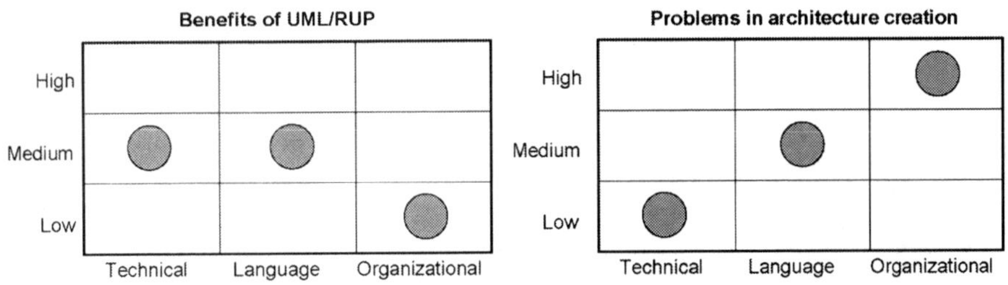

would be more important to seek tools that aid in building common understanding about the system and its architecture and tools for processing the emerging conflicts. Thus, we maintain that the field of architecture for e-business would benefit from tools that help to identify and process the emerging conflicts than tools that aid in developing a technically "perfect" and optimized solution. These tools could be used in early phases of development to augment UML and RUP based tools. Examples of such tools are group support systems and different participation facilitation systems. Thus we do not call for replacing UML, but rather adding tools that can be used to communicate with non-technical people about the architecture.

ACKNOWLEDGMENT

We would like to thank the anonymous reviewers of this paper for their valuable instructions and especially the reviewer that gave us the simple idea of Figure 3.

REFERENCES

August, J. H. (1991). *Joint application design: The group session approach to system design*. Englewood Cliffs, NJ: Yourdon Press.

Baskerville, R., & Pries-Heje, J. (2001, July 27-29). *Racing the e-bomb: How the internet is redefining information systems development methodology.* Proceedings of the IFIP TC8/WG8.2 Working Conference on Realigning Research and Practice in Information Systems Development: The Social and Organizational Perspectice (pp. 49-68). Boise, Idaho.

Bichler, M., Segev, A., & Zhao, J. L. (1998). Component-based e-commerce: Assesment of current practices and future directions. *SIGMOD Record, 27*(4), 7–14. doi:10.1145/306101.306102

Checkland, P. B., & Scholes, J. (1990). *Soft system methodology in action*. Chichester: John Wiley and Sons.

Ciborra, C. (2000). Drifting: From control to drift. In Braa, K., Sorensen, C., & Dahlbom, B. (Eds.), *Planet internet*. Lund: Studentlitteratur.

Conallen, J. (1999). Modeling web application architectures with UML. *Communications of the ACM, 42*(10), 63–70. doi:10.1145/317665.317677

D'Souza, D. F., & Wills, A. C. (1998). *Objects, components, and frameworks with UML: The catalysis approach*. Addison-Wesley.

Dashofy, E. M., Van der Hoek, A., & Taylor, R. N. (2005). A comprehensive approach for the development of modular software architecture description languages. *ACM Transactions on Software Engineering and Methodology*, *14*(2), 199–245. doi:10.1145/1061254.1061258

Denzin, N. K. (1978). *The research act: A theoretical introduction to sociological methods*. McGraw-Hill.

Dori, D. (2001). Object-process methodology applied to modeling credit card transactions. *Journal of Database Management*, *12*(1), 4. doi:10.4018/jdm.2001010101

Egyed, A., & Medvidovic, N. (1999, Oct). *Extending Architectural Representation in UML with View Integration.* Proceedings of the 2nd International Conference on the Unified Modelling Language (UML), (pp. 2-16). Fort Collins, CO.

Eisenhardt, K. M. (1989). Building theories from case study research. *Academy of Management Review*, *14*(4), 532–550.

Fernández, W. D., Lehmann, H., & Underwood, A. (2002, June 6-8). Rigour and relevance in studies of IS innovation: A grounded theory methodology approach. [ECIS]. *Proceedings of the European Conference on Information Systems*, *2002*, 110–119.

Garlan, D., & Kompanek, A. J. (2000). *Reconciling the needs of architectural description with object-modeling notations.* Proceedings of the Third International Conference on the Unified Modeling Language - UML 2000, (pp. 498-512). York, UK.

Glaser, B. (1978). *Theoretical sensitivity: Advances in the methodology of grounded theory*. Mill Valley: Sociology Press.

Glaser, B., & Strauss, A. L. (1967). *The discovery of grounded theory: Strategies for qualitative research. Chigago*. Aldine.

Greunz, M., & Stanoevska-Slabeva, K. (2002). *Modeling business media platforms.* 35th Annual Hawaii International Conference on System Sciences, Maui, HI.

Grinter, R. E. (1999). Systems architecture: Product designing and social engineering. *ACM SIGSOFT Software Engineering Notes*, *24*(2), 11–18. doi:10.1145/295666.295668

Hanseth, O., Monteiro, E., & Hatling, M. (1996). Developing information infrastructure: The tension between standardization and flexibility. *Science, Technology & Human Values*, *21*(4), 407–426. doi:10.1177/016224399602100402

Hirschheim, R., & Klein, H. K. (1989). Four paradigms of information systems development. *Communications of the ACM, 32*(10), 1199–1216. doi:10.1145/67933.67937

Hofmeister, C., Nord, R., & Soni, D. (1999a). *Applied software architecture*. Reading, MA: Addison-Wesley.

Hofmeister, C., Nord, R., & Soni, D. (1999b). *Describing software architecture with UML*. Proceedings of the First Working IFIP Conference on Software Architecture (WICSA1), (pp. 145-160). San Antonio, TX.

Jacobson, I., Booch, G., & Rumbaugh, J. (1999). *The unified software development process*. New York: Addison-Wesley.

Jones, M. (1998). *Information Systems and the Double Mangle: Steering a Course Between the Scylla of Embedded Structure and the Charybdis of Strong Symmetry*. IFIP WG8.2/8.6 Joint Working Conference, Helsinki, Finland.

Kalakota, R., & Robinson, M. (2001). *e-Business 2.0: Roadmap for Success*: Addison-Wesley.

Kazman, R., Klein, M., & Clements, P. (2000). *ATAM: Method for Architecture Evaluation* (Technical report No. CMU/SEI-2000-TR-004): Software Engineering Institute.

Kim, Y.-G., & Everest, G. C. (1994). Building an IS architecture: Collective wisdom from the field. *Information & Management, 26*(1), 1–11. doi:10.1016/0378-7206(94)90002-7

Koontz, C. (2000). Develop a solid e-commerce architecture. *e-Business Advisor*(January).

Kuntzmann, A., & Kruchten, P. (2003). The rational unified process—an enabler for higher process maturity. Retrieved April 19, 2007 from http://www-128.ibm.com/developerworks/rational/library/content/03July/0000/0579/Rational_CMM_WhitePaper.pdf.

Leist, S., & Zellner, G. (2006, April 23-27). *Evaluation of current architecture frameworks*. SAC'06, (pp. 1546-1553). Dijon, France.

Locke, K. (2001). *Grounded theory in management research*. SAGE Publications.

Lyytinen, K. (1987). A taxonomic perspective of information dystems fevelopment: Theoretical constructs and recommendations. In Boland, R. J. Jr, & Hirschheim, R. A. (Eds.), *Critical issues in information systems research* (pp. 3–41). John Wiley & Sons.

Lyytinen, K., Rose, G., & Welke, R. (1998). The brave new world of development in the internetwork computing architecture (InterNCA): Or how distributed computing platforms will change systems development. *Information Systems Journal, 8*(3), 241–253. doi:10.1046/j.1365-2575.1998.00037.x

Lyytinen, K., Smolander, K., & Tahvanainen, V.-P. (1989). *Modelling CASE environments in systems development.* Proceedings of CASE'89 the First Nordic Conference on Advanced Systems Engineering, Stockholm.

Martin, P. Y., & Turner, B. A. (1986). Grounded theory and organizational research. *The Journal of Applied Behavioral Science, 22*(2), 141–157. doi:10.1177/002188638602200207

Medvidovic, N., Egyed, A., & Rosenblum, D. S. (1999). *Round-trip software engineering using UML: From architecture to design and back.* Proceedings of the 2nd Workshop on Object-Oriented Reengineering (WOOR), Toulouse, France, Sept. 1999, 1-8.

Medvidovic, N., & Taylor, R. N. (2000). A classification and comparison framework for software architecture description languages. *IEEE Transactions on Software Engineering, 26*(1), 70–93. doi:10.1109/32.825767

Merisalo-Rantanen, H., Tuunanen, T., & Rossi, M. (2005). Is extreme programming just old wine in new bottles: A comparison of two cases. *Journal of Database Management, 16*(4), 41. doi:10.4018/jdm.2005100103

Monroe, R. T., Kompanek, A., Melton, R., & Garlan, D. (1997). Architectural styles, design patterns, and objects. *IEEE Software, 14*(1), 43–52. doi:10.1109/52.566427

Object Management Group. (1999). *UML Profile for Enterprise Distributed Object Computing: Request for Proposals (ad/99-03-10).* OMG.

Object Management Group. (2005). *Unified modeling language: Superstructure version 2.0* (No. formal/05-07-04).

Object Management Group. (2006). *OMG SysML Specification (ptc/06-05-04).*

Päivärinta, T., Halttunen, V., & Tyrväinen, P. (2001). A genre-based method for information system planning. In Rossi, M., & Siau, K. (Eds.), *Information modeling in the new millennium* (pp. 70–93). Hershey, PA: Idea Group. doi:10.4018/9781878289773.ch005

Rational Software Corporation. (2001). Rational Unified Process [Online documentation, Version 2001A.04.00].

Robson, C. (2002). *Real world research* (2nd ed.). Blackwell Publishing.

Ross, J. W., Weill, P., & Robertson, D. C. (2006). *Enterprise architecture as strategy: Creating a foundation for business execution*. Harvard Business School Press.

Rossi, G., & Schwabe, D. (2000). Object-oriented web applications modeling. In Rossi, M., & Siau, K. (Eds.), *Information modelling in the next millennium*. Hershey: IDEA Group Publishing.

Rumpe, B., Schoenmakers, M., Radermacher, A., & Schürr, A. (1999). *UML + ROOM as a Standard ADL*. Fifth IEEE International Conference on Engineering of Complex Computer Systems, (pp. 43-53).

Saaren-Seppälä, K. (1988). *Wall chart technique: The use of wall charts for effective planning*. Helsinki: Kari Saaren-Seppälä Ky.

Sauer, C., Southon, G., & Dampney, C. N. G. (1997). *Fit, failure, and the house of horrors: Toward a configurational theory of IS project failure*. Proceedings of the eighteenth international conference on Information systems, (pp. 349-366). Atlanta, Georgia.

Shaw, M., & Garlan, D. (1996). *Software architecture: Perspectives on an emerging discipline*. Prentice Hall.

Siau, K., & Cao, Q. (2001). Unified modeling language (UML)—a complexity analysis. *Journal of Database Management, 12*(1), 26–34. doi:10.4018/jdm.2001010103

Siau, K., Erickson, J., & Lee, L. Y. (2005). Theoretical vs. practical complexity: The case of UML. *Journal of Database Management, 16*(3), 40–57. doi:10.4018/jdm.2005070103

Smolander, K. (2003, January 6-9,). *The birth of an e-business system architecture: Conflicts, compromises, and gaps in methods*. Hawaii International Conference on System Sciences (HICSS'36), Hilton Waikoloa Village, Big Island, Hawaii.

Smolander, K., Hoikka, K., Isokallio, J., Kataikko, M., & Mäkelä, T. (2002, April, 8-11). *What is included in software architecture? A case study in three software organizations*. Proceedings of 9th annual IEEE International Conference and Workshop on the Engineering of Computer-Based Systems (pp. 131-138). (ECBS) 2002, Lund, Sweden.

Smolander, K., & Päivärinta, T. (2002a, May 27 - 31). *Describing and communicating software architecture in practice: Observations on stakeholders and rationale*. Proceedings of CAiSE'02 - The Fourteenth International Conference on Advanced Information Systems Engineering, (pp. 117-133).Toronto, Canada.

Smolander, K., & Päivärinta, T. (2002b, Aug 25-30). *Practical rationale for describing software architecture: Beyond programming-in-the-large.* Software Architecture: System Design, Development and Maintenance - IFIP 17th World Computer Congress - TC2 Stream / 3rd Working IEEE/IFIP Conference on Software Architecture (WICSA3), (pp. 113-126). Montréal, Québec, Canada.

Smolander, K., Rossi, M., & Purao, S. (2002, December 18). *Software architecture: Metaphors across contexts.* AIS Theory Development Workshop, Barcelona.

Smolander, K., Rossi, M., & Purao, S. (2005, May 26-28). *Going beyond the blueprint: Unraveling the complex reality of software architectures.* 13th European Conference on Information Systems: Information Systems in a Rapidly Changing Economy, Regensburg, Germany.

Sowa, J. F., & Zachman, J. A. (1992). Extending and formalizing the framework for information systems architecture. *IBM Systems Journal, 31*(3), 590–616. doi:10.1147/sj.313.0590

Star, S. L., & Griesemer, J. R. (1989). Institutional cology, "translations" and boundary objects: Amateurs and professionals in berkeley's museum of vertebrate zoology, 1907-39. *Social Studies of Science, 19,* 387–420. doi:10.1177/030631289019003001

Strauss, A. L., & Corbin, J. (1990). *Basics of qualitative research: Grounded theory procedures and applications.* Newbury Park, CA: Sage Publications.

Taylor, M. J., McWilliam, J., Forsyth, H., & Wade, S. (2002). Methodologies and website development: A survey of practice. *Information and Software Technology, 44*(6), 381–391. doi:10.1016/S0950-5849(02)00024-1

Wood-Harper, T. (1985). Research methods in information systems: Using action research. In Mumford, E., Hirschheim, R. A., Fitzgerald, G., & Wood-Harper, T. (Eds.), *Research methods in information systems.* New York: North-Holland Publishers.

This work was previously published in International Journal of Database Management, Volume 19, Issue 1, edited by Keng Siau, pp. 19-40, copyright 2008 by IGI Publishing (an imprint of IGI Global).

Section 2
Managing Intervention

Chapter 5
Information System Conversion Strategies:
A Unified View

Efrem G. Mallach
University of Massachusetts Dartmouth, USA

ABSTRACT

Information system conversion has been with us since users of punched-card tabulating systems first moved to vacuum-tube computers. However, it has generally been seen as an afterthought: once the "interesting" development stages of analysis, design and so on are done, it will just happen. This article attempts to view the process holistically, from both the technical and human viewpoints, reflecting the fact that information systems have both technical and human components. It shows how ignoring one side or the other can lead to problems, which can be avoided if all aspects are considered together. It proposes a systematic approach to considering these issues and points out benefits to both researchers and practitioners from using it.

INTRODUCTION

Conversion from one information system (IS) to another is common in all organizations, regardless of type, size or location. On the information technology (IT) side, conversion can involve hardware, operating system (OS), database management system (DBMS) and the database it supports, and/or application portfolio. On the human side, procedures must be changed and people must be, if not changed, at least moved (in the sense of change theory (e.g., Schein 1990), not geographically) and retrained.

DOI: 10.4018/978-1-60960-529-2.ch005

Effective management of conversion is vital to the long-term success of any IS. Choosing a conversion strategy from one information technology environment to a new one is not easy. A conversion effort may affect any of the four IT components to varying degrees, as well as the human and procedural components of the IS as a whole.

The existing literature focuses on either the technical or human side of conversion, the latter often under the broader label "implementation." This leads to a narrow view of the issues, treating IT and the human components of an IS in isolation from each other, and can lead to local optimization at the expense of global optimization.

The aim of this article is to provide an overall framework of information system conversion, including all aspects of the information system. It also updates the literature to provide a 2008 view of conversion, both to provide guidance to professionals faced with a new conversion situation and to serve as a basis for future research in this area.

A Note on Terminology

Some writers use *conversion* to refer only to the technological (IT) aspects, calling either the human side or the entire process "implementation." Here "conversion" will refer to the entire process. We will use more specific terminology (such as "IT conversion") for its subsets when necessary to avoid confusion.

SYSTEM COMPONENTS AND CONVERSION FRAMEWORK

An information system consists of five components: hardware, software, data, procedures and people (originally Kroenke 1981; more accessibly today in, e.g., Kroenke 2009). Figure 1, adapted from that source, shows the relationships.

All five IT components must be considered in any conversion. Conversion of any element may impact elements to either side. For example, database conversion will affect usage procedures (to its right); a new application may require hardware changes (to its left).

Figure 1. Five components of an information system

Hardware	Software	Data	Procedures	People

IT CONVERSION METHODS

The literature, including standard textbooks such as (Baltzan & Phillips 2008) and (Stair & Reynolds 2008), generally recognizes four conversion methods:

- **Direct cutover**[1]**:** an entire organization stops using the old system at one time and begins using the new one immediately thereafter. (This may be after a natural activity break such as overnight.) The organization ends one day using the old system, begins the next day with the new. This is the riskiest method: Lee (2004) discusses how the Nevada Department of Motor Vehicles gave itself problems by using it. Other methods reduce this risk.
- **Pilot conversion:** Part of an organization uses the new system while the rest of it continues to use the old. This localizes problems to the pilot group so support resources can focus on it. However, there can be interface issues where organizational units share data.
- **Phased (modular) conversion:** Part of the new system is introduced while the rest of the old one remains in use. This localizes problems to the new module so support resources can focus on it. However, there can be interface issues where modules share data.
- **Parallel conversion:** The new system is introduced while the old one is still in use. Both systems process all activity and the results are compared. Once there is confidence that the new one operates properly, the old one is shut down. Because parallel conversion isn't as useful today as some people believe (and many authors suggest), it is discussed separately below.

As Palvia *et al.* (1991) point out, risk reduction methods are orthogonal and can thus be used in any combination. Figure 2, adapted from that source to make the terminology consistent with the present article, shows the concept. The three axes refer to three ways in which indirect conversion methods reduce risk: by reducing the organizational scope of the conversion, the technological scope of the conversion, and/or the time pressure of the conversion. The four combination methods are pilot-phased, pilot-parallel, phased-parallel and pilot-phased-parallel. They are shown at the four vertices of the cube in the figure that do not lie along at least one of the axes.

As an example of pilot-phased conversion, the University of Massachusetts converted to integrated enterprise-wide software in the early 2000s in a modular fashion. Major modules were introduced via pilot groups: its Lowell campus, for example, was first to use it for student registration. After that campus had used it for a semester, the others adopted it. Other modules were introduced on different schedules, with various pilot campuses.

Figure 2. Combinations of technical approaches to system conversion

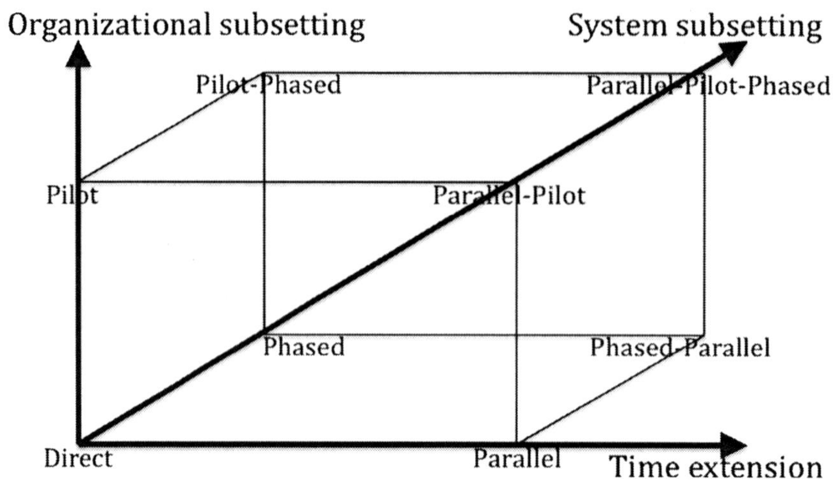

Yusuf *et al.* (2004) give another example of this combination in the Rolls-Royce manufacturing firm's adoption of ERP, where the overall project was divided into phases with pilot conversion then used in most. They chose the "number 4 shop" facility for their ERP pilot because it produced a small number of parts and had low volumes of material flows. They then used separate pilot projects for purchasing and other subsystems.

Issues with Parallel Conversion

Parallel conversion has been a staple of textbooks for decades. Most (Rainer and Turban 2009 is an exception) do not recognize that it is no longer appropriate in the 21st century. It is important to correct this misconception.

Parallel conversion is no longer widely applicable for two reasons (Mallach 2006):

1. When both old and new systems are online, as is nearly always the case today, it is impractical to have users (especially customers) enter transactions twice.
2. Timing differences can lead to different outputs even when each system is internally consistent. Consider a bank whose old system processed checks overnight, but whose new one processes them as they arrive. A $100 check on an account with a balance of $150 arrives at 9 am. Its holder tries to withdraw $100 at noon. The old system would have dispensed the cash and later bounced the check at night. The new one pays the check but then refuses the cash withdrawal. Each is correct, but their outputs differ.

As a result, parallel conversion is only practical today in a few situations:

1. Advisory (decision support/business intelligence) systems, discussed below.
2. The few remaining conversions from older manual systems, also discussed below.
3. Systems with critical financial or legal implications, where assurance of identical outputs is mandatory. These are hardly ever customer-facing. Input timing differences cannot be allowed to affect their results.

Parallel conversion is not the same as keeping an older system around as insurance! With falling storage costs, there may be little reason to remove older software (license arrangements permitting) even if the possibility of ever needing it is remote. If the old and new systems are not both used to process the same work, it is not parallel conversion.

CHOOSING A CONVERSION METHOD

There is no "best" conversion strategy. This section gives considerations in choosing an approach. They must be taken as a group, along with other factors that are specific to an organization or system and which can therefore not be covered here.

Impact of Conversion Type on Conversion Strategy

System conversions tend to fall into three main categories, as follows:

1. **Manual to automated:** This is no longer common, as manual systems that are candidates for computerization grow increasingly rare, but still happens in small organizations or with specialized functions.

Manual systems are typically easy to partition because the use of physical records limits data sharing. For example, in converting from paper to electronic voting, it is easy to use different methods in different polling places. This lends itself to the pilot approach.

Parallel conversion can also work here, if duplicate outputs going down the line in the organization or to customers don't create problems. (A restaurant kitchen shouldn't receive the same orders on both slips of paper and overhead monitors.) Presumably the computerized system involves less work than the manual one, so the incremental work of processing each transaction twice may be acceptable. This can help alleviate employee concerns about the accuracy of a newly computerized way of doing business.

2. **Like systems:** An example of this would be CRM to CRM, perhaps moving from hosting the application on a firm's own servers and clients to software-as-a-service or vice versa.

This type of conversion does not argue for any particular conversion approach. The best one to use depends on other factors.

3. **Unlike systems:** This might involve, for example, moving from functional "silo" systems to ERP. A major issue here is data conversion: it is virtually certain that the set of older systems plus the new one use, together, a variety of different files and databases.

In this situation the older system is typically partitioned while the new one is more integrated. This lends itself to phased conversion. Each part of the older system can be converted individually to the corresponding module of the new one.

Impact of System Type on Conversion Strategy

Whether a system is automated or advisory affects conversion strategy.

The issue here is whether or not a system updates an organizational database. Those that update a database automate some organizational function. Advisory systems (data warehouses, decision support, business intelligence, information retrieval, data mining, etc.) do not update one, though decisions made with their support may at some later time lead to database updates.

Advisory systems offer more conversion flexibility than automated systems. Parallel use to build confidence (though not precisely parallel conversion as defined above) is practical, as two advisory systems need not produce identical outputs; the new one need only produce output that is at least as useful as the old one's. Furthermore, since usage of advisory systems tends to be more sporadic than that of automated systems, and the volume of data entered into them manually tends to be small, the disadvantage of requiring people to enter input twice is less of a concern.

Information retrieval systems, which do not modify their database, are a form of advisory systems. (A data warehouse can be viewed as an information retrieval system whose purpose is to provide advisory information.)

Advisory systems can also use a pilot approach. The pilot group can be self-selected: early adopters can try the new system while the rest of the organization continues to use the old one, and can easily revert to the older system if the new one doesn't meet their needs. If decision-making consistency in an area is important, which would argue for use of a single advisory system, a pilot group can convert as a unit without impacting others.

Phased conversion is less applicable to pure advisory systems, though in a system that has some advisory functions, it may be possible to split those out as part of a phased approach to the overall conversion process.

Impact of Organization Size on Conversion Strategy

Organization size is correlated with other factors. Smaller organizations are more likely to convert from a manual system, less likely to convert to an unlike system, than larger enterprises. They are also less likely to use advisory systems than are large ones, since the benefit of such a system is proportional to the size of the organization using it but its cost goes up more slowly. It is important not to confuse the size factor with other factors with which it is correlated.

Large organizations typically have more organizational units than smaller ones. Data may pertain only to one geographic location or line of business. This facilitates the creation of self-contained pilot groups. In small organizations it may be more difficult to find these, though not always impossible: the author is aware of a three-CPA accounting firm whose owner used a new package himself for one tax season, the other two accountants moving to it the year after.

Small organizations have less data in total than larger ones, making it practical to recover from a bad conversion and reducing the value of risk-mitigating strategies. This can make direct cutover practical.

Smaller organizations also have, obviously, fewer people. As a result, people in different areas are more likely to know each other personally and to have developed informal relationships. This gives managers in different work areas a level of personal credibility that their opposite numbers in large organizations would not have, and allows such firms to relax some of the "MIS managers should do this; user managers should do that" guidelines given below.

HUMAN FACTORS IN CONVERSION

As noted earlier, most of the limited literature on conversion focuses on its technical aspects. This is understandable, since IS literature is written largely by IS professionals for other IS professionals, and IS professionals tend to focus on the technical side, but is still unfortunate.

Human factors have not been completely ignored. Meyers *et al.* (1999) and Kuruppuarachchi *et al.* (2002), among others, have examined the human factors that influence implementation success. However, authors who have examined human factors in conversion have ignored technological considerations, just as those who have studied technical issues have ignored the human side. In addition to the above two references, examples of this tendency include Kuipers 1995, Reisman and Dear 1998, and Shin and Edington 2007. All three of this group ignore the technology side of conversion strategy, though Reisman and Dear, for one, devote a great deal of space to other technology issues. Conversion involves all five information system components. Managers ignore either side at their peril.

For example, a study of ERP implementation in China (Yusuf *et al.* 2006) found that state-owned enterprises (SOEs) had more difficulty implementing ERP systems than non-SOEs. Most factors (hardware, software, nature of previous systems, etc.) were similar in both groups. Organizational culture was not. Had the technical managers who led SOE conversions been aware of the human factors that led to difficulties in their environment, they could have dealt with them proactively and thus been more successful.

System conversion is, after all, not just *technical* change. It is also *organizational* change. Organizational change has been studied since well before information technology entered the picture. One seminal work was (Lewin 1947). It led to the popular "unfreeze-move-refreeze" model of change management elaborated by Schein (1990) and others, known today as the Lewin/Schein model. Other models have up to eight steps (e.g., Kotter 1990) or more. The ADKAR method (Hiatt 2006) sets five requirements for successful change:

- **Awareness** of why change is needed
- **Desire** to support and participate in the change
- **Knowledge** of how to change
- **Ability** to implement new skills and behaviors
- **Reinforcement** to sustain the change

The second and fifth stages must be driven by user-side management. No amount of exhortation by MIS experts can create, for example, a desire for change. Only users' peers and managers have the requisite credibility. Knowledge and ability can come from MIS trainers. Awareness of the need for change can come from either side, though the support of users' managers can help technical reasons carry weight. If change is to succeed, user and technical managers must coordinate their activities to cover all five building blocks.

As an example of doing this right, an Australian water utility used the following methods, some of which overlap, to ensure conversion success (Mandal & Gunasekaran 2003):

- Formulate and use a network to collect user requirements and feedback at each stage.
- Prepare to handle unexpected crises and deviations from plans.
- Provide strong leadership with concern for the welfare of people and a resource commitment.
- Provide a professionally stimulating work environment.
- Obtain top management support for the project and an adequately resourced launch.
- Promote consultation, with user participation and approval throughout the project.
- Communicate proactively, tailoring communications to each organizational unit, to establish realistic expectations about the technology's capabilities.
- Promote collaborative system development between users and developers.
- Use multi-functional project teams to bring complementary capabilities together during the life of the project.
- Familiarize staff with the new technology, train users involved with the system.
- Use intra-project teams, and intra- and inter-industry networking, for technology transfer.
- Provide stakeholders with a detailed plan of the implementation process, explain how it achieves business objectives, and keep them informed about its progress.
- Propose ways to restructure personnel and systems in light of the new technology.

Multi-functional project teams, the fifth bullet from the end, helped ensure that both technical and human factors were considered. While this utility's managers undoubtedly also had to choose pilot groups and decide which modules to convert first, those technical issues probably weren't the hard ones!

"Conversion Myopia"

Theodore Levitt's seminal paper "Marketing Myopia" (Levitt 1960) showed how organizations often misunderstand their strengths, focusing instead on what they think they do, and thus miss opportunities that they could have taken advantage of. The classic example is railroads, which could have become successful airlines had they recognized the value of understanding passenger handling, baggage handling, ticketing and so on rather than seeing their business as rolling large boxes along steel rails.

This error, seeing value in specifics of what one does rather than in underlying strengths, is common among people who go through an information system conversion. Employees see their value to their employer as based on their knowing the existing system at the keystroke and submenu level. Since any new hire will know a new system as well as they do in this regard, they feel that their value to the company will drop—as does their sense of security.

This is, of course, not the case. The value is not in knowing which submenu allows one to change a customer discount percentage, but in understanding when to change it. Unfortunately, few people see the true business value of their day-to-day work.

"Conversion myopia" can disable a department or more. In extreme cases it can lead to slow-downs and even sabotage. Managers in charge of a conversion must prevent this by discussing with employees what it is that they truly contribute to the organization. This is in part a training issue, but has more to do with raising their collective consciousness about what aspects of their competence are most important to the business.

RELATIONSHIP BETWEEN TECHNICAL AND HUMAN CONSIDERATIONS

A successful conversion must take into account both technical and human factors. While historically a given researcher or manager has focused on one or the other, it is better to see them as parts of an integrated process. The approach to the technical IT conversion and the human side have implications for each other. For example:

- If direct cutover is used, procedures may be needed to maintain an audit trail of some or all work in case it is necessary to revert to the previous system and re-enter it. (This may be a good idea in any case, but the lower risk associated with other conversion strategies may make it less of a requirement.)

If such procedures require extra work on the part of system users, their purpose, their likely duration and the way those who will work overtime (if any) were selected must be explained. If practical, some indication of management appreciation beyond overtime pay is appropriate.

- If pilot conversion is used, it is important not to create status distinctions on the basis of being, or not being, first to use the new system. MIS managers are most likely not sensitive to how users read unintended messages in such choices.

Example: In converting a network of distribution centers, it is natural to convert the closest one to headquarters first, as it is most convenient to IT support staff in case of problems. If this is not explained, staff at other centers may think "They always get the good stuff first; we're second-class citizens." Few MIS managers will anticipate this user reaction, recognize it when it happens, or understand the reasons for it if it is pointed out.

- If parallel conversion is used, the need for extra work should be explained even if overtime is compensated

As with the extra work that may be required for in direct cutover, its purpose, its likely duration and the way those who will work overtime were selected must be explained. If practical, some indication of appreciation beyond overtime pay is appropriate here as well.

Change management, as conducted by user managers, must suit the technical IT conversion process. Therefore, user managers must in turn understand the reasons that led to the technical choices. This can only happen through interaction with the IT personnel who made those choices.

In the other direction, the technical approach must be organizationally (or operationally) as well as technically and economically feasible. No matter how desirable a pilot approach may be on technical grounds, for example, it won't work if the organizational division of labor does not lend itself to the creation of a pilot group.

It follows that, as a minimum, the manager responsible for each side must be aware of the other and be in close touch with the person responsible for it.

THE OVERALL FRAMEWORK

We can conclude:

- Conversion must be approached from the technical, human, and occasionally economic sides. This is analogous to the requirement, familiar to every systems analyst, that a feasibility study address these aspects.
- A particular type of manager—technical or user—must be responsible for each aspect of the process. Some technical parts cannot be managed from the user side. Some user issues cannot be addressed effectively by technical managers.
- Those responsible for the two aspects of the process must coordinate their work.

Accordingly, we recommend this sequence of planning activities:

1. The organization is studied to see which technical approaches are organizationally feasible. This comes first because the purpose of any information system is to facilitate the work of the organization, not vice versa. It is far more difficult to change how an organization works, especially the informal processes rooted deep in its culture, than to do almost anything on the technical side.

This stage must be led by a user-side manager or a user-focused systems analyst, in close consultation with MIS experts who can explain what the different technical strategies imply (for example, for database conversion).

2. If more than one technical approach is feasible, cost, time and risk estimates for all feasible approaches are made so that one can be chosen. This may involve a one-minute meeting ("We can do direct or pilot, direct is too risky, does everyone agree? OK, then, that settles it.") or an in-depth study.
3. A project plan is drawn up showing both the human and technical aspects of the conversion with their interrelationships and dependencies. These interrelationships and dependencies are fundamental, since only through them is it possible to adjust one side of the process if the other goes awry and thus manage the conversion as a whole.

For example, it is probably obvious that a delay in conversion should lead to a revised training schedule. However, training is not the only way in which system conversion affects people. All aspects of change management should be put on hold. This may require notifying managers who are not otherwise directly involved with either training or the IT conversion itself.

4. The conversion itself is carried out. Organizational culture permitting, and assuming suitable candidates exist, this process should be co-managed by two people: one for its technical aspects, one for its human side.

The benefits of using this framework are:

For practitioners: Implementation failures based on the use of a conversion approach which is inappropriate for technical reasons, human reasons or both, are less likely. In other words, the probability of a successful system—since a system whose implementation fails has failed just as surely as a system that fails in any other way—are increased.

In addition, the framework forces cooperation between technical and user-side managers. In environments where this would not happen otherwise, which are unfortunately not rare, this removes another potential cause of implementation failure.

For researchers: Research questions can be couched in terms of a specific aspect of the issue and/or a specific step of the process. Researchers will also be less likely to lose sight of other issues that may affect the specific topic they are studying, which their personal perspectives might otherwise cause them to overlook.

Someone embarking on a research career can now also see conversion as a unified area with considerable potential. In the past, when it was fragmented and the fragments put willy-nilly with other topics, this would have been at best difficult.

For MIS textbook authors: It is as important to be current in this area of practice as it is to have up-to-date processor speeds in that table. It can be argued that the typical businessperson is more likely to need to know how to manage a conversion effectively than what the CPU state of the art was in 2009 (or whenever he or she was a student). Their discussions of parallel conversion as a viable approach to transaction processing systems in the 21st century stand out as in need of change. More specific suggestions are made in (Mallach 2006).

CONCLUSION

No organizational information system can be put in place without conversion. No matter how well a system was developed in a technical sense, failure at this stage renders all that went before useless.

Conversion has both technical and human aspects. Therefore, some of its tasks must be done by those who are competent in the technical area, while others must be done by those who understand and are respected by the people who will use the system. In all but the smallest organizations these are unlikely to be the same managers. It is therefore necessary for managers in both areas to work together to arrive at a joint plan that considers both types of needs. Following the above sequence can make this possible.

REFERENCES

Baltzan, A., & Phillips, P. (2008). *Business driven information systems*. Boston, Mass.: McGraw-Hill.

Hiatt, J. (2006). *ADKAR: A model for change in business, government and our community*. Loveland, Colo.: Prosci.

Kotter, J. (1990). *Force for change: How leadership differs from management*. New York: Free Press (Div. of Simon & Schuster).

Kroenke, D. (1981). *Business computer systems*. Santa Cruz, Calif.: Mitchell Publishing.

Kroenke, D. (2009). *Using MIS* (2nd ed.). New York: Prentice-Hall.

Kuipers, W. (1995). Surviving a system conversion. *Catalog Age*, *12*(3), 67.

Kuruppuarachchi, P., Mandal, P., & Smith, R. (2002). IT project implementation strategies for effective changes: A critical review. *Logistics Information Management*, *15*(2), 126. doi:10.1108/09576050210414006

Lee, O. (2004, March). A case study of Nevada DMV system. *Journal of the Academy of Business and Economics, 3*.

Levitt, T. (1960). Marketing myopia. *Harvard Business Review*, *82*(7–8), 138.

Lewin, K. (1947). Frontiers in group dynamics, Part II-B: Feedback problems of social diagnosis and action. *Human Relations*, *1*, 147.

Mallach, E. (2006). System conversion: Teaching versus reality. *International Journal of Information and Communication Technology Education*, *2*(2), 17. doi:10.4018/jicte.2006040102

Mandal, P., & Gunasekaran, A. (2003). Issues in implementing ERP: A case study. *European Journal of Operational Research*, *146*, 274. doi:10.1016/S0377-2217(02)00549-0

Meyers, P., Sivakumar, K., & Nakata, C. (1999). Implementation of industrial process innovations: Factors, effects, and marketing. *Journal of Product Innovation Management*, *16*, 295. doi:10.1016/S0737-6782(98)00044-7

Palvia, S., Mallach, E., & Palvia, P. (1991). Strategies for converting from one IT environment to another. *Journal of Systems Management*, *42*(10), 23.

Rainer, R. K., & Turban, E. (2009). *Introduction to information systems: Supporting and transforming business* (2nd ed.). Hoboken, N.J.: John Wiley & Sons.

Reisman, S., & Dear, R. G. (1998). Managing platform conversion in educational institutions. *International Journal of Educational Management, 12*(5), 225. doi:10.1108/09513549810225934

Schein, E. (1990). Organizational culture. *The American Psychologist, 2,* 109. doi:10.1037/0003-066X.45.2.109

Shin, N., & Edington, B. H. (2007). An integrative framework for contextual factors affecting information technology implementation. *Journal of Information Technology Theory and Application, 8*(4), 21.

Stair, R., & Reynolds, G. (2008). *Principles of information systems,* Boston, Mass.: Cengage (then Thomson Course Technology).

Yusuf, Y., Gunasekaran, A., & Abthorpe, M. (2004). Enterprise information systems project implementation: A case study of ERP in Rolls-Royce. *International Journal of Production Economics, 87,* 251. doi:10.1016/j.ijpe.2003.10.004

Yusuf, Y., Gunasekaran, A., & Wu, C. (2006). Implementation of enterprise resource planning in China. *Technovation, 26*(12), 1324. doi:10.1016/j.technovation.2005.12.003

ENDNOTE

1 Sometimes called *plunge* conversion, for the sake of alliteration and/or to mimic the well-known "four Ps" of the marketing field.

This work was previously published in International Journal of Enterprise Information Systems, Volume 5, Issue 1, edited by Madjid Tavana, pp. 44-54, copyright 2009 by IGI Publishing (an imprint of IGI Global)

Chapter 6
Information Technology Interventions for Growth and Competitiveness in Micro-Enterprises

Sajda Qureshil
University of Nebraska at Omaha, USA

Mehruz Kamal
University of Nebraska at Omaha, USA

Peter Wolcott
University of Nebraska at Omaha, USA

ABSTRACT

The use of Information and Communication Technologies (ICTs) by Small and Medium Sized Enterprises (SMEs) have the potential to enable these businesses to grow through access to new markets and administrative efficiencies. However, the growth of the smallest of these SMEs which are micro-enterprises is hindered by their inability to adopt ICTs. This paper investigates how micro-enterprises can adopt ICTs to grow and achieve competitiveness. It investigates a set of seven micro-enterprises through an interpretive field study in which action research was used to diagnose and treat the micro-enterprises. This was done using interventions through a process called "Information Technology (IT) Therapy". This process involved providing individualized IT solutions to pressing problems and opportunities. The increase in competitiveness of these micro-enterprises was assessed using the Focus Dominance Model and their growth through a modified model of micro-enterprise growth. This research contributes to assisting micro-enterprises achieve sustained growth and competitive advantage.

DOI: 10.4018/978-1-60960-529-2.ch006

INTRODUCTION

There is evidence to suggest that use of Information and Communications Technology (ICT) can play an important role on the growth of small businesses (Matthews 2007, Sullivan 1985, Qiang et al 2006, Raymond et al 2005). In this sense, IT can be employed to bring about increased competitiveness if it enables businesses to create new jobs, increase productivity and sales through access to new markets and administrative efficiencies (Qureshi 2005, Matthews 2007). These outcomes can be achieved through measurable improvements in the lives of people living with limited resources to sustain themselves. Duncombe and Heeks (2003) suggest that there is a role for the ICT intermediary in providing the needed information on markets, customers and suppliers. In their study of 1000 small business enterprises in the US, Riemenschneider et al (2003) found that businesses were prepared to overcome obstacles to IT adoption to achieve web presence. This is because pressures to keep with the competition and promote services to customers are greater than the obstacles to setting up websites. There is a sense that small and medium enterprises hold the promise of growing incrementally on existing capabilities, and providing a seedbed for the emergence of dynamic and efficient larger national firms (Levy 2001, Mathews 2007, Servon and Doshna 2000).

It also appears that the promise of eBusiness adoption by micro-enterprises can potentially provide these businesses with the ability to access new markets and reduce costs through administrative efficiencies (Brown and Lockett 2004, Pateli and Giaglis 2004). However, the use of ICT by Small and medium Sized Enterprises (SMEs) remains a challenge in both developed as well as developing countries (Schreiner and Woller 2003, Sanders 2002, Lichtenstein and Lyons 2001, Hyman and Dearden 1998, Honig 1998, Piscitello and Sgobbi 2004). In particular the opportunities opened up by the internet are limited in SMEs especially due to the challenges faced by globalization (Piscitello and Sgobbi 2004). Small and medium sized businesses are seen to be organizations that employ less than 500 people and typically have problems adopting IT due to competitive pressures and underestimation of time taken to implement IT (Riemenschneider et al 2003). A form of small business being investigated in this article is the micro-enterprise. Micro-enterprises are tiny businesses with fewer than 10 employees - often just one. The micro-enterprises studied in this article are part of a Micro-enterprise development program. Such programs make loans and or provide classes to poor people to help them start or strengthen their businesses (Schreiner and Woller 2003).

The challenges faced by micro-enterprises make it even more difficult for them to adopt ICTs for competitiveness. In particular, Piscitello and Sgobbi (2004) suggest that the key barrier to the adoption of ICTs is not size but the learning processes followed by the firms and access to networks of similar internet enabled business services. While a great deal has been written about the challenges faced by micro-enterprise adoption of ICTs, little has been done to provide business models that enable micro-enterprises to use ICTs competitively. According to Grosh and Somolekae (1996), barriers to growth of micro-enterprises are access to capital, educational level of the entrepreneur, legal barriers and start-up financing. In their study of information systems for rural micro-enterprise in Botswana, Duncombe and Heeks (2003) suggest that the role of ICT in enabling information and knowledge is important for both social and economic development. They found that there was a reliance on localized, informal social networks for their information for rural micro-enterprise. Information from these networks was of poor quality and not readily available; it appeared to fail the poorest and most disadvantaged entrepreneurs. In this sense, ICTs can represent an unaffordable addition to costs and the benefits of using them are not always apparent (Duncombe and Heeks 2003, Matthews 2007, Southwood 2004).

This article investigates how micro-enterprises can adopt ICTs to grow and achieve competitiveness. The question investigated in this article is: How can micro-enterprises adopt ICTs to achieve competitiveness? In order to answer this question, this article investigates a set of seven micro-enterprises in the underserved communities of Omaha, Nebraska. The micro-enterprises had received hardware and software through a grant from the eBay Foundation administered by a micro-enterprise development program called the New Community Development Corporation. Through a series of action research steps carried out by the researchers, the ICT challenges faced by the micro-enterprises were diagnosed and treated with interventions through a process of "Information Technology (IT) Therapy" (Wolcott et al, 2007; Qureshi et al, 2008). This process involved providing individualized IT solutions to pressing problems and opportunities and the development of a longer-term IT project plan, customized for each of the businesses. In addition to the IT therapy process, the researchers were able to analyze the potential use of the awarded technology to help achieve operational efficiency and competitive advantage. This was done by mapping each of the micro-enterprises' current IT use combined with increase in IT awareness (on the part of the micro-entrepreneur) and transferred IT skills (to the micro-entrepreneur) – both as a result of the IT therapy process - to a theoretical model.

THEORETICAL BACKGROUND

Small Businesses and Information Technology

Past studies have shown that the use of ICT can play an important role on the growth of small businesses (Matthews 2007, Sullivan 1985, Qiang et al 2006, Raymond et al 2005). Cragg and King (1993) have shown that there is a gradual increase in the number of small firms that either adopt various new technologies or take steps to upgrade what they currently possess. The studies suggest that IT can be employed to bring about increased competitiveness if it enables businesses to create new jobs, increase productivity and sales through access to new markets and administrative efficiencies (Qureshi 2005, Matthews 2007). Small and medium sized businesses that have adopted and used ICTs have seen positive outcomes related to operational efficiencies, increased revenues, and are able to better position themselves within their market niche. Qiang et al. (2006) observed that businesses that utilized e-mail to communicate with their customers experienced sales growth 3.4 per cent greater than those which did not. Similar outcomes were also observed for productivity and reinvestment. Both these components were found to be greater for more intensive users of IT (Qiang et al., 2006). Other research in this area also highlights the positive impact of IT use within small businesses. A 4% increase in sales as well as 5% increase in export performance was obtained when e-business techniques were adopted by SMEs in the manufacturing sector in Canada (Raymond *et al.,* 2005). Specifically, Raymond et al. (2005) mention that by using technologies such as websites, email and telephones to communicate with customers, SMEs can provide better customer service as well as expand their customer base to help reach out to both local as well as international consumers for their products. In another study Southwood (2004) found that ICT investments by SMEs in South Africa resulted in profitability gains from cost savings rather than from increase in sales.

In addition, studies have established that Information Systems play a significant role in small firms (Harrison et al. 1997, Igbaria et al. 1997). In particular, Street and Meister (2004) conducted a study that showed that improved internal transparency is a key component for small business development. The study concluded that Information Systems play a major role in enhancing communication and that the need for an appropriate IS occurs at a very early stage, even before many of the other structural or organizational changes are required. There also exist a number of studies that take the focus away from the direct impacts of IT in small businesses and instead look into various other angles of IT adoption and use in such types of businesses: Raymond (1988) studied the effect of computer training on attitudes and usage behavior; Montazemi (1988) investigated the relationship between computing issues and satisfaction of end-users; DeLone (1988) examined the link between CEO involvement and computer use effectiveness. While developing upon current research, this article focuses on the adoption of ICTs by micro-enterprises to achieve competitiveness.

Although current literature supporting adoption of technology by small businesses exists, in practice, this is not the scenario – particularly in the case of micro enterprises. In a study of a set of micro enterprises in North Omaha, many entrepreneurs who had received state-of-the-art technology to assist them with their businesses had not even opened the packaging within which these technologies were contained six months after they had received them (Wolcott *et al.* 2007)! In another study by Qiang *et al* (2006), among the *micro firms*, only 27 percent use e-mail and 22 percent use Web sites to interact with clients and suppliers. The study suggests that if computer use affects firm productivity and ICT expands networking within sectors and industries, the micro firms may not be benefiting from these externalities – benefits from ICTs. In addition, Bharati and Chaudhury (2006) surveyed micro, small and medium manufacturing firms within the Boston metropolitan area and found that most of the micro firms were using simple technologies such as basic e-mail, and simple software packages as compared to more complex technologies that were being used by the medium sized firms. Their survey results showed that the micro firms were not aware of most technologies that could be used for improving their business performance.

Challenges Facing Small Businesses

In order for micro-enterprises to benefit from ICTs and reach a level where they may be competitive, they need to overcome some of the barriers that are holding them back. Relevant literature in this area has identified a number of different challenges facing these small businesses.

- *Affordability* (Mansell & When, 1998; Hazan, 2002): This is a major issue with small businesses as they operate on very restricted budgets and do not have sufficient capital to invest towards state-of-the-art technologies.
- *Awareness about IT* (Owen & Darkwa, 1999): Most micro-entrepreneurs do not possess any technical skills and are oblivious to the capabilities that ICT has to offer. As a result, their ignorance on the power of IT may inhibit small businesses from growing and flourishing.
- *Infrastructure* (Baark & Heeks, 1998; Latchem & Walker, 2001; O'Farrell, Norrish, & Scott, 1999; Barton & Bear, 1999): A core requirements for any form of ICT implementation is to have a basic infrastructure in place that will support the new form of technology that is being introduced into that environment. Lack of such infrastructure will be a major barrier to the adoption and use of ICT.
- *Private/Government sectors* (Lefebvre and Lefebvre, 1996): These two agencies in any community play an important role in either facilitating or inhibiting the development of IT infrastructures to promote increased ICT adoption and use.

- *Management's capacity* (Lefebvre and Lefebvre, 1996): Management's capacity to incorporate IT into small business environments are also a crucial aspect in successful IT adoption and use; and lack of such capacity could become a major hindrance.

In other studies by Duncombe & Heeks (2002) as well as Moyi (2003), obstacles faced by rural micro-enterprises were highlighted. The challenges related to issues of remote locations, lack of education and literacy on the part of the business owner, poor business skills, poverty and lack of affordability, and lack of transportation.

Information Technology and Competitiveness

Despite these limitations, the competitive advantages of using ICT by the micro-enterprises outweigh the challenges. The relationship between IT and competitive advantage was first researched by McFarlan and McKenney (1983) who came up with a grid to place organizations based on the strategic impact of existing IT applications and the strategic impact of current IT applications development within the firm. The grid was helpful to the extent that management could utilize it to consider the right alternatives to pursue for improved competitiveness. Information technology can add economic value to an organization through 1) the reduction in the costs incurred by the organization, and 2) by differentiating the organization's products or services (Bakos and Treacy, 1986; McFarlan, 1984; Wiseman, 1988). Taking this notion that IT can add value to a firm, Porter and Millar (1985) moves the discussion further by analyzing how advances in information technology have changed the way organizations conduct business and how it may serve to provide a competitive advantage. They explain three core ways in which IT may impact competitiveness: 1. by changing the industry structure, 2. by supporting cost and differentiation strategies, and 3. by creating opportunities to generate new businesses from within existing businesses. Ives and Learmonth (1984) narrow down the focus of a firm to emphasize customer relationships, and they show how information system technology can enhance relationships with the company's customers. They outline a 13-step customer resource lifecycle highlighting potential uses of IT at the various stages to enable competitive advantage for the firm providing the product or service to the customer (Ives and Learmonth,1984).

Sethi and King (1994) have attempted to measure the extent to which IT applications may provide competitive advantage. They referred to the construct measuring this notion as "CAPITA" (competitive advantage provided by an information technology application) and operationalized it through five main dimensions–efficiency (degree to which an IT application enables a company to produce lower priced products than competing products), functionality (degree to which an IT application provides users with the functionality they desire), threat (impact of the IT application on the bargaining power of customers and suppliers), preemptiveness (early and successful penetration of the IT application into the market), and synergy (the degree to which the IT application is tightly integrated with the business goals, and strategies of the organization). In summarizing the early notions of how IT may impact an organization's competitive advantage, see four distinct strategies emerge: 1) Low-cost leadership – using information systems and technology to produce products and services at a lower price than competitors while enhancing quality and level of service; 2) Product differentiation – using information systems and technology to differentiate products, and enable new services and products; 3) Focus on market niche – using information systems and technology to enable a focused strategy on a single market niche; and 4) Customer and supplier intimacy – using information systems to develop strong ties and loyalty with customers and suppliers.

Due to rapid changes in markets, customer expectations, as well as technologies and most importantly globalization, has made competitive advantages short lived. Along those lines, Mata, Fuerst, and Barney (1995) talk about how IT may provide not only competitive advantage but also *sustained* competitive advantage using a resource-based analysis. They emphasize that the "create-capture-keep" paradigm (Clemons and Kimbrough, 1986; Clemons and Row, 1987, 1991b; Feeny and Ives, 1990) whereby customers make certain investments (switching costs) specific to a particular supplier of IT, enabling those suppliers of IT to achieve competitive advantage does not truly hold when it comes to the sustainability of the competitive advantage. Instead, Mata et al (1995) takes the resource-based view of the firm (Clemons, 1991; Barney, 1991; Conner, 1991). In the resource-based view of the firm, resources and capabilities may provide a unique set of competencies that may serve to address either cost reduction or product differentiation strategies to eventually create value for the organization. This is summarized in Figure 1.

Using the resource-based perspective, Mata et al (1995) put forward two major notions to explain sustained competitive advantage. The first concept is that of resource heterogeneity which states that competing firms may vary in their resources and capabilities. The second concept is that of resource immobility which says that the differences in resources and capabilities between competing firms may be long lasting. Their argument is that if a firm's IT resources are distributed heterogeneously among competing firms and if the firms without the resources find it more costly to develop, acquire and implement the same strategy as the firms that already have the resources, then those resources can serve to be a source of sustained competitive advantage. Mata et al (1995) develop a framework using the concepts of resource heterogeneity and resource immobility to depict how these two notions relate to competitive advantage. They then apply this model to four characteristics of IT – access to capital (McFarlan, 1984), proprietary technology, technical IT

Figure 1. Resource-based view of the firm

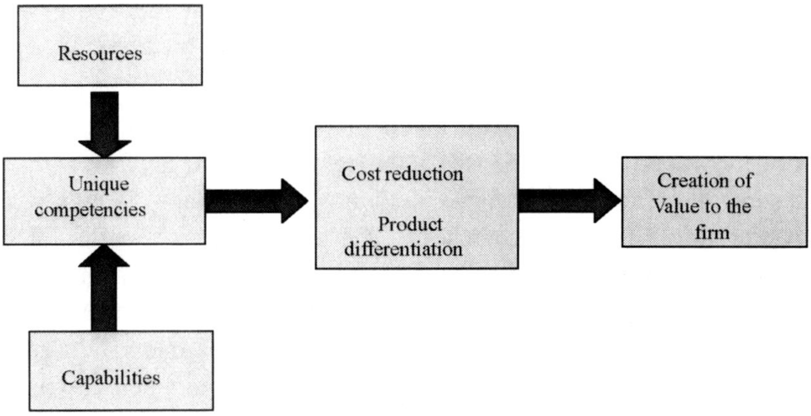

skills (Copeland and McKenney, 1988), and managerial IT skills (Capon and Glazer, 1987) – that prior literature has suggested to be sources of sustained competitive advantage. Their findings imply that organizing and managing IT within a firm, or in other words, managerial IT skills are the only source of sustained IT competitive advantage and that less focus should be made on the information technology itself.

In order to be able to achieve competitive advantage through its adoption of ICTs, what should a micro-enterprise facing multiple challenges do? Prior research has shown that there are two distinct routes by which small businesses incorporate ICTs. One route is to enhance day-to-day operational support and transaction processing activities (Blili and Raymond, 1993; Foong, 1999; Levy and Powell, 1998; Poon and Swatman, 1999). These studies have shown that small businesses adopt and use simple ICTs without any form of planned strategy to integrate other aspects of the business. And so any form of IT-based competitive advantage is accidental rather than planned (Hashmi and Cuddy, 1990). The second route that is typically taken is to use ICTs to improve interaction and relationships with customers. SMEs, and in particular micro-enterprises are strongly influenced by customer needs. Porter (1980) states, that in many small businesses, customer power is very high. It has been seen that a majority of SMEs depend on a small number of customers who purchase large amounts of goods and services. These major customers are then in a position to influence the price of goods and services that are being produced by the small businesses (Reid and Jacobsen, 1988). Close relationships among SMEs and their customers enable these businesses to respond quickly to customers' changed requirements. Lefebvre and Lefebvre (1993) have shown that there is a link between the innovative efforts of an SME and its competitive position.

Levy et al. (2001) formulated an analytical framework (focus-dominance model), that incorporates both forms of strategic focus - the issue of cost reduction versus value added and the second one being customer dominance i.e. few versus many customers - that emerged from prior research described above. The model examines the potential for SMEs to realize value from IS capabilities. The framework shows where SMEs would fit in terms of the trend they show in IT investments and market strategies. The model is shown in Figure 2. The framework may be viewed as providing four different approaches to ICT adoption as a result of integrating the two dimensions of strategic focus. The *efficiency* quadrant may comprise SMEs that exploit simple systems such as word processing and trivial accounting processes (Naylor and Williams, 1994). The *co-ordination* quadrant is composed of those SMEs that have a need to increase market share and their customer base. The *collaboration* segment then attracts SMEs that attempt to incorporate emerging technologies to manage relationships with the businesses' major customers. And finally the *innovation* quadrant comprises of those SMEs that actively seek to adopt new information and communication technologies to help achieve competitive advantage. In a follow-up study, Levy *et al.* (2002) investigated 43 SMEs to observe their positions in the focus-dominance model. The results revealed that most of the 43 SMEs make only one move, from *efficiency* to *co-ordination*, or from *efficiency* to *collaboration*. SMEs taking either one these routes tend to avoid losing control and so opt to stay within their current markets. It was also seen that only 17 of the 43 SMEs wanted to move to the *innovation* quadrant possibly due to an environment scan whereby they become aware of "best practices" and strategies that would assist them to manage business growth.

This focus-dominance model was chosen to investigate how micro-enterprises can adopt ICTs to achieve competitiveness. This model is seen to be a valuable means for the analysis of each of the micro-enterprises in the study because it enables us to: 1) Identify the strategic position of each micro-enterprise at the time the study was conducted; 2) Predict the strategic position the micro-enterprise will be in a few years based on the context-specific business goals of each micro-enterprise; 3) Identify the information systems that will support the micro-enterprise in its current strategic position and 4) Map what information systems will be needed to support the micro-enterprise in its projected strategic position.

Moreover, the four quadrants of the focus-dominance model is an outcome of the true conditions encountered by SMEs highlighted through prior research. The unique contribution of the research taken up by the authors of this article is to apply this model to the context of micro-enterprises (as noted earlier, these are the smallest form of businesses) – which has not yet been studied in the realm of this or any other theoretical model. The results will show that micro-enterprises do indeed fall into distinct categories and we provide support for our results by using

Figure 2. The focus-dominance model (Source: Levy et al., 2001)

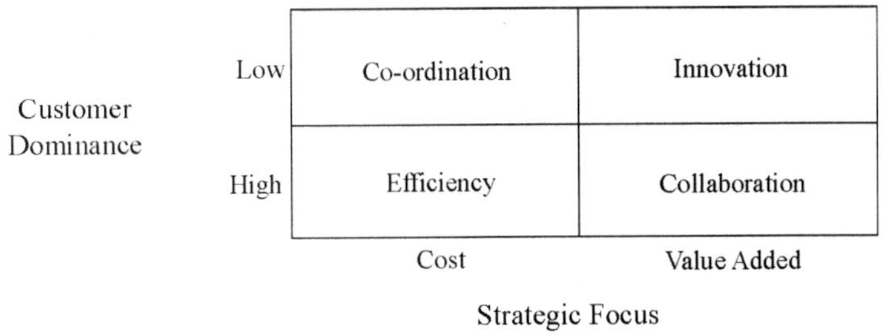

the established notion of resource-based view of the firm to illustrate competitive advantage (Clemons, 1991; Barney, 1991; Conner, 1991; Mata et al., 1995). Our analysis reveals that through the micro-enterprises' current IT resources – combined with capabilities provided through the IT therapy process, produce unique competencies to position these small businesses to be competitive.

METHODOLOGY

In order to investigate how the micro-enterprises can use ICTs to increase their competitiveness, an interpretive field study was carried out. According to Klein and Myers (1999), Information Systems research can be classified as interpretive if it is assumed that our knowledge of reality is gained only through social constructions. Interpretive methods in IS are aimed at producing an understanding of the context of the information system and the process by which the information system influences and is influenced by the context (Walsham 1993). This research follows an interpretive field study approach in which seven case studies are carried out. These case studies are carried out using Klein and Myers (1999) principles of the hermeneutic circle, contextualization, interaction between researchers and subjects, abstraction and generalization, dialogical reasoning, the principle of multiple interpretations, and the principle of suspicion. Within each case study, the data was collected and analyzed in iterative cycles of action research. Action research involves the application of tools and methods from the social and behavioral sciences to practical problems with the intention both of improving the practice and of contributing to theory and knowledge in the area studied. Action researchers participate directly or intervene in a situation or phenomenon in order to apply a theory and evaluate the value and usefulness of that theory (Checkland, 1981, 1991; Galliers, 1991). This conforms to Klein and Myers (1999) third principle which requires that there is critical reflection on how the data are socially constructed through interaction between researchers and participants. Action research is a change oriented research methodology that seeks to introduce changes with positive social values, the key focus being on a problem and its solution (Elden and Chisholm 1993). Action research is typically carried out as part of an attempt to solve problems by allowing the researcher to become a participant in the action, the process of change itself becoming the subject of research (Checkland 1981).

Research Setting

This study investigated seven micro-enterprises undergoing change through the adoption of ICTs for competitiveness. Each business has been given an arbitrary name for the purpose of this study and to maintain confidentiality of the businesses. All of the businesses are located in Omaha, Nebraska. Following are brief descriptions of each of the micro-enterprises studied:

1. LD specializes in high quality soups and sandwiches. During the period of this study LD moved its deli from its original location to a better one that could serve local businesses and students.
2. FD specializes in the design of elegant, conservative women's clothing. The owner has aspirations of being a player in the global fashion market.
3. CZ is a franchise that pairs individuals of all ages who need tutoring in any subject with tutors who can provide the service.
4. HH offers a structured residence with treatment and support services to individuals who are transitioning from a treatment program back to society.
5. HE offers massage therapy services. The owner is seeking to diversify into the retail sale of a variety of natural health products.
6. EP is a modeling agency that provides models who reflect the diversity of "normal" (non-glamorous) Americans.
7. HC This on-line business sells wedding cake toppers that reflect the ethnic diversity of customers.

The micro-enterprise owners were all recipients of small technology grants from eBay Foundation's Techquity Grant Program. The Techquity Grant Program offers small grants, typically around $2000, to be used for purchasing hardware, software, and training that would promote the development of micro-enterprises. The grant program was locally administered by the New Community Development Corporation (NCDC), a non-profit that provides affordable housing and business development services in the greater Omaha area. The anticipated benefit to the micro-enterprises would be more effective utilization of technology, improved thinking about technology and the role of information, and, in general, economic and human development.

Research Design

The design of the research involved seven case studies in which action research was carried out to diagnose the problem in each case, intervene to solve the problem, collect data through interviews and observations of the effects of the interventions and analyze the results in preparation for the next cycle. Action research used in this way was an iterative cycle in which the researcher begins with a *plan* of how to carry out the activity, then *act* to intervene to solve the immediate problem, *observe* the results of the intervention and *reflect* on the impact and next steps (Zuber-Skerrit, 1991, Avison et al. 1999). Carried out as part of an academic service-learning course – *Information Technology for Development* (IT4D), the action research was supplemented by the *absorbing* of knowledge through classroom lectures and discussion. The participative learning process took place in the form of group discussions in which problems were discussed and solutions arrived at collectively.

In this study, the plan was to assist the micro-enterprises through partnership with New Community Development Corporation (NCDC). The cycle continued to action or intervention, to solve the problem or manage the change process; this is where the researcher collected the data. On location at the micro-businesses, the ITD innovators worked with business owners to understand the business and existing technology, implement technology-based projects, and train business owners as appropriate. This process was referred to as "IT therapy" in which assistance was given to the micro-business owner to solve their immediate IT needs.

These steps were carried out within each case study using Klein and Myers (1999) principles. These principles guide our assessment of the action research steps taken to understand the current situation and map it on to Levy et al's (2001) focus-dominance model. Then diagnose the problem, carry out the IT therapy interventions, collect the data and map the future state of each micro-enterprise using Levy et al (2001)'s model. This iterative data collection and analysis process was designed to enable each micro-enterprise's ability to adopt ICTs to achieve competitiveness to be investigated. This is illustrated in Table1.

The design of this field study conforms to the principles that guide the evaluation of interpretive field studies model by Klein and Myers (1999). The *Principle of the Hermeneutic Circle* states that an understanding of a complex whole is obtained from preconceptions regarding the meanings of its parts and their interrelationships. Applying this principle to the current study, the *parts* are the researchers' and the micro-entrepreneurs initial understandings and the *whole* are the shared meanings (e.g. increased awareness and acceptance of the utility that the awarded technology can help the micro-entrepreneurs in their business) that arise from the close interactions between them. The multiple interventions in the IT therapy process is supported by the view that in a number of iterations of the hermeneutic circle, a com-

Table 1. Data collection steps

Action Research	Case 1: LD	Case 2: FD	Case 3: CZ	Case 4: HH	Case 5: HE	Case 6: EP	Case 7: HC
Plan	Researchers' and the micro-entrepreneurs share initial understandings in Hermeneutic dialogue. Contextualization of the social and historical background of the micro-enterprise and diagnosis of the problem to arrive at the current state of the micro-enterprise on the focus-dominance model.						
Act	IT Therapy interventions through interactions between the researchers and participants to solve the problem. Principle of abstraction and generalization adhered to through the use of two theoretical models to frame and interpret findings from this study.						
Observe	Collection of data through interviews and observations. The principle of multiple interpretations was achieved through class discussions when the ITD innovators implementing the IT interventions discussed the results in class and the second form of interpretation came from the subjects, or in other words, the micro-entrepreneurs						
Reflect	Analysis of the data and interpretation to reveal future state on the focus-dominance model.. Principle of dialogical reasoning used to analyze how context-sensitive assistance (IT therapy) may enable micro-entrepreneur to overcome some of the technical and social barriers that they face.						

plex whole of shared meanings emerges. *The Principle of Contextualization*: is addressed by treating the micro-entrepreneurs as active actors (e.g. learning new IT skills, gaining trust over technology, working together with the ITD innovators to develop technology plans, etc.) and through the action research steps that were used to collect data for this research, they served as producers of history. *The Principle of Interaction between the Researcher and the Subjects was* addressed by the close and continuous interaction of the researchers with the microentrepreneurs as described in the action research steps utilized for the data collection phase of the study (Klein and Myers, 1999).

In developing the theoretical contributions of this research, *the Principle of Abstraction and Generalization* guided our use of the focus-dominance model (Levy et al., 2001) which was used to provide a systematic means for understanding the historical, current as well as the future predicted IS-based positions of each of the micro-enterprises. The resource-based view of the firm helped us tie in the concept of IT therapy as a *capability* that when integrated with IT resources within each of the micro-enterprises may help bring about competitiveness. *The Principle of Dialogical Reasoning* formed the basis of the context-sensitive assistance (IT therapy) may assist small businesses to overcome some of the technical and social barriers that they face (Klein and Myers, 1999).

Data on each case being studied was gathered through observation while implementing the IT therapy. The reflection entailed interpretation of the data, and consequences of action that then fed into the planning stage to modify the methodology or model that then determine what action would be taken in the next cycle. On their own time, the ITD innovators maintained a reflective journal, worked on assigned class exercises and readings, and prepared a technology plan for the micro-businesses. Using the techniques provided to them, the ITD innovators implemented the IT interventions by interacting closely with the micro-entrepreneurs. In this way they interacted as *IT for Development (ITD) innovators* as they implemented the IT and training interventions that enabled the technology to be adopted in innovative ways. The IT4D class sessions served as a sounding board for issues and proposed solutions, offered advice or relevant information, and offered constructive criticism of proposed courses of action to address any IS/ICT adoption/implementation issues specific to any of the micro-businesses. Further cycles of activities continued until a desired end-state is achieved (Zuber-Skerrit, 1991, Avison et al. (1999, p.96).

RESULTS

The current and the future trends in how each of the micro-enterprises use their IS have been mapped onto the focus-dominance model (Levy et al., 2001) after the researchers in the study had an opportunity to discuss and observe the manner in which these small businesses carry out their activities following the action research steps outlined in the methodology section. The IT therapy phase involved the ITD innovators working with business owners to understand the business and existing technology, implementing technology-based projects, and training business owners is also mentioned. This process of "IT therapy", or in other words, assistance given to the micro-business owner to solve their immediate IT needs, is important to the extent that it supports a major resource capability that is lacking and in much needed demand on the part of the micro-enterprises. The future IS trends for each of the businesses were based on the researchers' understanding of the micro-enterprise's future strategic growth plans and their IS requirements. The results were discussed with the business partners (the micro-enterprises) in the study. Following are the individual mappings for each of the micro-enterprises in the study.

- **LD:** LD specializes in high quality soups and sandwiches. During the period of this study LD moved its deli from its original location to a better one that could serve local businesses and students. (see Figure 3)
    - **Current state:** LD has high customer dominance because it is currently dependent on a specific client group. The owner of LD typically uses a PDA, Cell phone, email and a simple software package such as, QuickBookas for the business operations. The old register system is merely a calculator. It does not provide any data to the owner on trends, sandwich purchases, inventory usage, or payroll. Although, the owner is aware of the benefits of the technology the business currently pos-

sesses might bring, due to lack of skills and IT knowledge, the business is yet to exploit the technology for competitive advantage. LD's current state of affairs makes it position itself in the *efficiency* quadrant of the focus-dominance model since according to Levy et al. (2001), the main focus of IS use in the *efficiency* quadrant is for control of the business, primarily financial control. The information systems in this context are concerned with improving the efficiency of internal processes.

  - **IT therapy:** The ITD innovators helped the owner select a register system that will not only handle ideal usage issues (ideal usage is the total amount of use of a particular item that is an ingredient for various menu items) but also maintain payroll information – thus eliminating the problems of previously manually calculating payroll at the end of each pay period. The Internet café implementation is a work in progress. A wireless communication network through a local Internet Service provider was set up. For a small fee per month, LD will have enough bandwidth to operate 20-25 computers on the same network.
  - **Future state:** LD's biggest struggle is going to be integrating a logical inventory and database system into the business. The owner is really working hard to be innovative with the move to the new location. The owner knows what it will take for the business to be successful at this new location and part of that will be incorporating a better inventory system and a customer database. The new location will have free wireless access for customers. Eventually, the business web site will have a customer information database that will be used as an advertising and marketing tool for LD for improved customer service. Since LD is looking to grow and build its customer base, it will eventually have low customer dominance (many customers i.e. few customers will not be able to dominate the business) and moreover the owner's intention of integrating the heart of the business which is the inventory management system with the other aspects of the business makes it position itself distinctly within the *innovation* quadrant. Levy et al. (2001) state that in this quadrant, the IS are a tightly woven part of the business strategy.

- **CZ:** CZ is a franchise that pairs individuals of all ages who need tutoring in any subject with tutors who can provide the service. (see Figure 4)
  - **Current state:** The current state of CZ can be classified as residing in both the *coordination* as well as in the *collaboration* quadrants. CZ's presence in the coordination quadrant arises from the fact that CZ has to deal with a large number of students and tutors and so customer dominance is low. CZ already has its own coordination components such as

Figure 3. Focus-dominance model mapping for LD

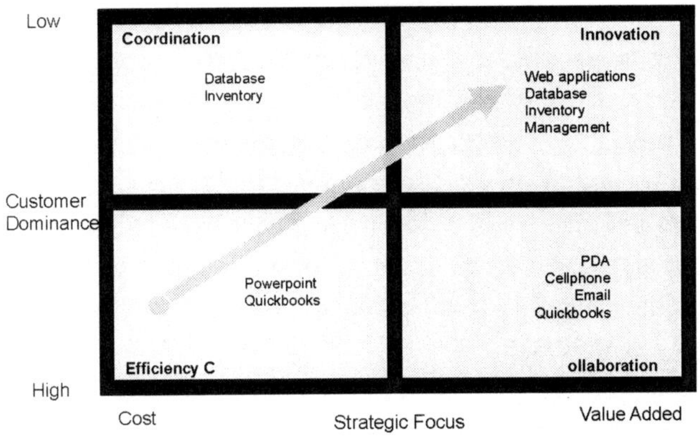

infrastructure, database, accounting system and marketing means from the franchiser to help it maintain its relationships with its customers (Levy et al., 2001). Additionally, CZ is viewed to reside in the collaboration quadrant since they have collaborative systems such as internal work processes using manual and automatic tools.

- **IT therapy:** The owners of CZ would like to have the process of matching tutors with students automated through online means. In addition they would like to have a software package that can take care of scheduling issues. In response to the needs of CZ, the following IT therapy interventions were carried out: creation of a decision-making framework to resolve whether it would make more sense to build the matching and scheduling system in-house versus purchasing an off-the-shelf application and customizing it to fit the needs of the micro-enterprise.

Figure 4. Focus-Dominance model mapping for CZ

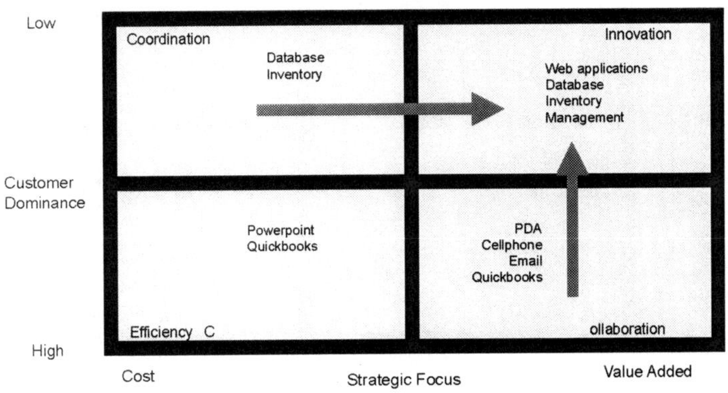

- **Future state:** CZ is heading to a possible *innovation* state from both the *coordination* and *collaboration* quadrants for its business. Once the owner invests money to develop their own application or purchase an existing off-the-shelf one, the business will generate exponential growth based on their current footing. Once they confirm their decision in investing capital on IT development, they will get more customers and tutors online. It will bring them financial freedom exponentially. The owner is clear as to what needs to be done to align the business strategy with the needed IS requirements to be a competitive force in the market (Levy et al., 2001).

- **HH:** HH offers a structured residence with treatment and support services to individuals who are transitioning from a treatment program back to society. (see Figure 5)
    - **Current state:** HH had an office management system which included a desktop and a laptop computer. Both computers were used for normal operations such as writing assessment reports, working on Power Point, internet research and e-mail communications. The desktop was the main repository for historical records including past guest records and financial information. The desktop was used for writing standard forms used in operations such as rules violation notices. The laptop was mainly used by the owner and is used in the same way as the desktop except in the case of the financial information. This redundancy in operations increased the ability for all employees to work on separate assignments

Figure 5. Focus-Dominance model mapping for HH

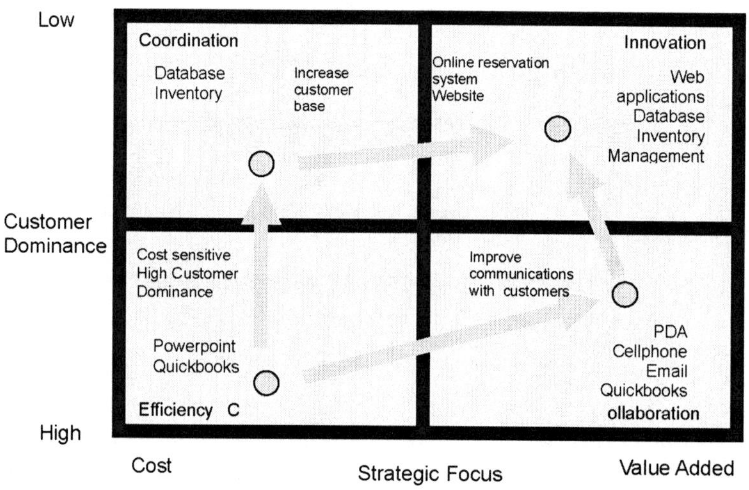

simultaneously. Some of the functions of the laptop system were that the owner is managing progress and evaluative data in an Excel spreadsheet and used offsite for presentations and guest evaluations. In addition HH had a guest computer lab consisting of one desktop computer located in a common area. The intent of this system was to give guests a resource for looking for jobs and staying in contact with family and friends. The computers could be used for resume writing and for enhancing computer skills as well computer based training. The computer lab accessed the internet from the same wireless connection as the management system. WiFi capability in the house made the guest computer systems expandable with relative ease and low cost. The state of HH was purely in the *efficiency* quadrant of the focus-dominance chart since the focus was on low-cost IS to maintain operational effectiveness (Levy et al., 2001).

- **IT therapy:** In responding to the immediate IT needs of HH, the following IT therapy interventions were carried out: Streamlined business practices including system maintenance and backup of standard procedures; financial data updated and used for making proposals to prospective lenders; business input, output and outcome data updated for display to potential donors and stake holders as well as referral services; data prepared for a database on resident statistics.
- **Future state:** HH is looking to take a phased incremental approach via *coordination* and *collaboration* to reach its desired spot in the *innovation* quadrant. The owners of HH realize that there is a need for better data management as well as improved communication with donors and guests and stakeholders. In attempting to move to the *coordination* and *collaboration* quadrants from their current state, HH is aware that the business will need to 1. Develop a website to get more exposure in the community and provide URL address to key stakeholders (increase customer base by reducing customer dominance and moving into the *coordination* quadrant); 2. Network with local education providers to allow guests to obtain needed training for the future (improve relationships with few customers i.e. local educational institutes through increased customer dominance by moving into the *collaboration* quadrant); 3. Work with local businesses to develop a community and a pool of potential job opportunities (improve relationships with few customers i.e. local businesses through increased customer dominance by moving into the *collaboration* quadrant); and 4. Present successful outcomes either in person through presentations or online through their website to stakeholders. In addition, the owners of HH want to go a step farther and

maintain a strategic focus to drive them into the *innovation* quadrant. They would like to have innovative web-based applications that will enable online reservation capability. The website should also offer capabilities to allow referral services to contact HH and eventually develop a treatment and payment plan online through a range of treatment options and payment types. Such an IS will tie in all of their business strategies to show relevant outcomes to stakeholders – thus moving them towards the *innovation* quadrant as a result of aligning IS with their overall business strategies (Levy et al., 2001).

- **HE:** HE offers massage therapy services. The owner is seeking to diversify into the retail sale of a variety of natural health products. (see Figure 6)
  - **Current state:** The owner has technology already available to her, but needs help utilizing it. There was an unopened PDA, a laptop, and a desktop. The owner would like to get things organized between the two computers and the PDA. The owner wanted help learning QuickBooks and possibly setting up a company website. She needed security on her laptop and Microsoft Office 2003 installed on both computers. This business lies in the *efficiency* quadrant as it is only beginning to set-up the technology for the business and the primary focus of the IS will be for controlling the business by improving the efficiency of internal processes (Levy et al., 2001)
  - **IT therapy:** The ITD Innovators provided the following IT therapy interventions: installing Microsoft Office 2003; setting up security on the

Figure 6. Focus-Dominance model mapping for HE

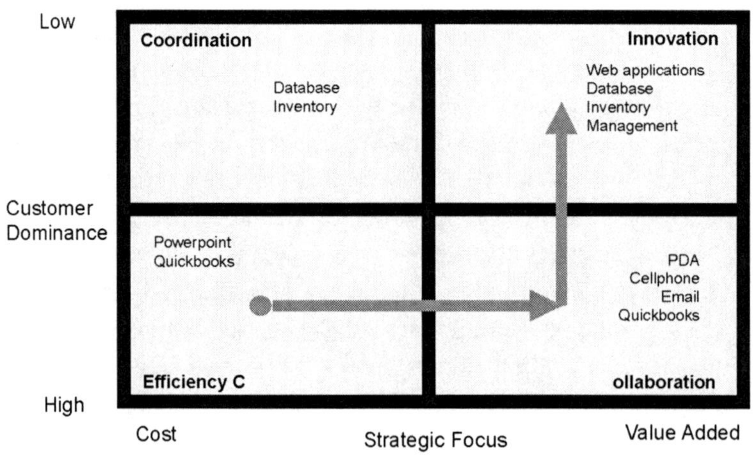

laptop computer; connecting the PDA to both the laptop and desktop; installing a CD-backup system; helping the owner learn how to organize her contact information in Microsoft Outlook.

- **Future state:** Since HE is only at the very early stages of incorporating technology into the business, the owner did not have a well thought out plan as to how the business would want to grow using the technology. The owner did express the intent to have a company website to eventually sell the company's products.

- **EP:** EP is a modeling agency that provides models who reflect the diversity of "normal" (non-glamorous) Americans. (see Figure 7)
  - **Current state:** EP has two dimension of the concept of customer. There are the models who sign up online that can be seen as customers and EP as the agency. The companies who require models for shoots are also customers of EP. EP has low customer dominance since it deals with a large number of models as well as agencies and so very few customers can dominate EP. EP's current state makes it reside in the *coordination* quadrant of the focus-dominance model since according to Levy et al. (2001), the primary use of IS in the *coordination* quadrant is to maintain customer relationships – which is a function of the larger customer base. Typically, information systems in this context hold basic customer data.
  - **IT therapy:** A major task for the ITD innovators in this case was training the business owner to help her understand the strategic importance

Figure 7. Focus-Dominance model mapping for EP

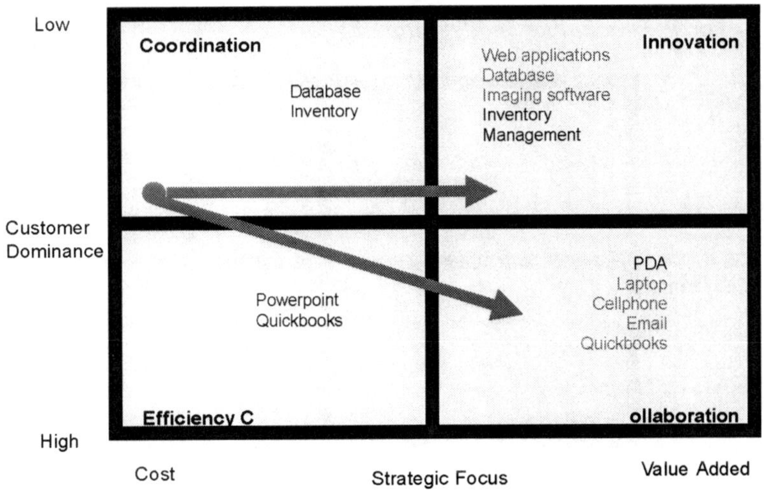

of technology in the business. Remote desktop was installed and demonstrated to show how greater mobility and convenience could be achieved through technology. Basic workstation maintenance such as ensuring critical patches and updates were current. The differences between critical and non-critical updates were explained. Desktop security and wireless security were explained to the users. Using QuickBooks to cut down on time spent on non-value added services was explained. Website ranking and place was also explained with possible solutions. It is important to mention here that an ITD innovators role was to increase the owner's comfort level with the technology.

- **Future state:** EP is heading towards both the *collaboration* as well as the *innovation* quadrants. It is heading to the *collaborative* quadrant since the owner has to maintain close contact with current clients as in photographers, ad agencies and also the listed models. Laptop and cell phone use allow the owner to have a mobile office when the owner travels, in addition to keeping in touch with clients that need models. This mode of operation is consistent with Levy et al.'s (2001) description whereby they state that businesses in the *collaboration* quadrant need to communicate and exchange information with major customers in a cost-efficient manner. In addition, EP is also heading to the *innovation* quadrant since the business model of EP relies on a web presence and is looking to be ahead of its competitors by enabling models to sign up online and get scheduled for photo shoots which will enable it to align its core business strategy with its online presence (Levy et al., 2001).

Figure 8. Focus-Dominance model mapping for HC

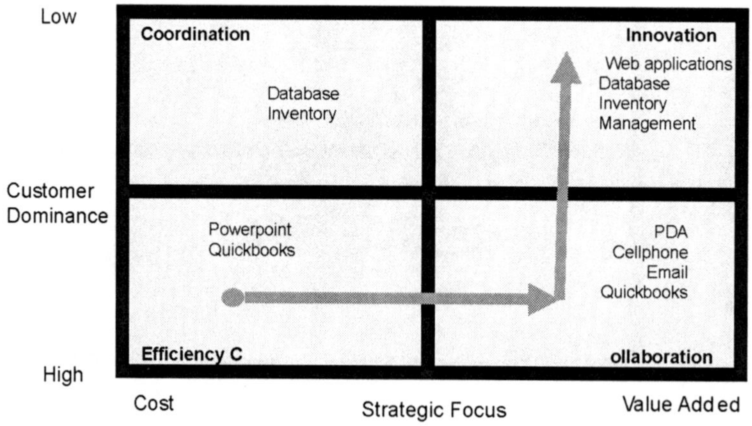

- **HC:** HC is an on-line business that sells wedding cake toppers that reflect the ethnic diversity of customers. (see Figure 8)
    - **Current state:** The business started in the *efficiency* quadrant. The customer dominance is currently quite high as the business has only had a few sales and relies on a small number of customers. Although HC is an online business, the owner has minimal interaction with the business website and uses minimal ICT for day-to-day business operations. In addition, HC's current state can be considered to reside in the *collaboration* quadrant since the owner of HC interacts with a small number of suppliers to obtain the cake toppers. And this trend is consistent with Levy et al.'s (2001) description since in this quadrant, the businesses need to communicate with major customers (in the case of HC, its major customers are its suppliers).
    - **IT therapy:** Some of the significant IT therapy interventions that were carried out for HC are as follows: *New website* – A completely new website was developed. The new website has a more organized and efficient layout comparable to other leading online competitors of similar products. *Training* - Training for the owner has come in the form of providing her with a manual to help add/delete products on the website so that customers will always have the new and updated product list. And most importantly, the owner will not have to depend on someone else to change the products for her – she will be able to perform the changes herself by following the steps outlined in the manual. A couple of hands-on sessions were done with the ITD innovator so that any confusion could be cleared. *Perceptions and attitude changes* - One of the owner's needs is to have the business website look more "crisp" and professional. On doing some preliminary research as to the look and feel of other comparable businesses, we had to suggest to the owner to change the colors and layout of her current site to help attract more customers. We had to persuade the owner to shift away from her inefficient current layout and existing bold colors (red and black) to a more "crisper" organized layout and softer colors to help attract more customers.
    - **Future state:** HC is primarily an internet business which entails web applications. The owner understands that in order to be competitive, the business will need to take a strategic focus to carrying out business online by selling its products through a professional looking website. The owner is looking to take the necessary steps to align HC's business strategy to its IS needs and the design and implementation of the newly developed website was the first step towards achieving that goal.

Figure 9. Focus-Dominance model mapping for FD

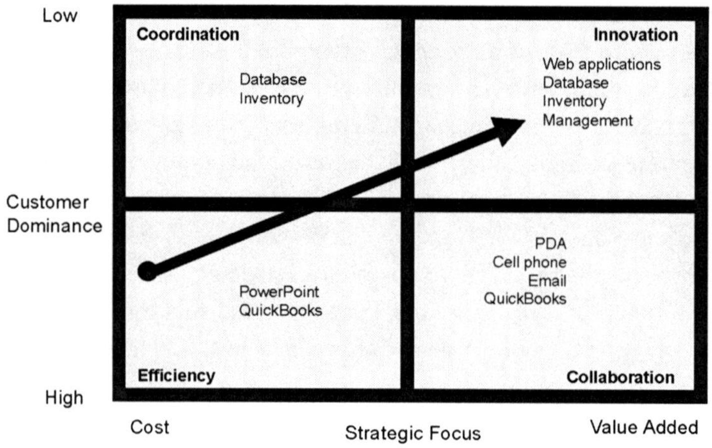

- **FD:** FD specializes in the design of elegant, conservative women's clothing. The owner has aspirations of being a player in the global fashion market. (see Figure 9)
    - **Current state:** FD has a laptop and an electronic cash register with some back-office software. FD currently resides in the *efficiency* quadrant since the owner has been using the technology available to the business for primarily basic day-to-day operational activities (Levy et al., 2001).
    - **IT therapy:** On meeting with the owner of FD and analyzing the technology needs of the business, The ITD innovators came up with the following list of items to be carried out to assist in the growth of the business: develop a website to promote its products, a developer to update and to do maintenance, and training and technical support for FD's staff to be able to update the website regularly; FD may benefit from online free technical assistance programs.
    - **Future state:** FD's main objective is to grow and attract new customers. The owner realizes that the only way to effectively achieve that goal is to have a web presence on the internet through a business website. The owner would like the following goals to be accomplished through the website: 1. To use it as a place to target new customers by advertising the owner's fashion designs; 2. To sell and promote the business on the web**;** 3. To advertise and provide information about FD. Achieving these three goals will enable it to align its core business strategy with its IS (Levy et. al, 2001).

ANALYSIS

The results from the analysis indicate that five out of the seven micro-enterprises in this study start off in the *efficiency* quadrant in the focus-dominance model. According to Levy et al. (2001), this implies that the focus of the IS was to help reduce costs and achieve simple administrative efficiencies. On initial meetings with the microentrepreneurs, the researchers found that the business owners had no clear business strategy and was not aware of how they could derive the maximum benefit from the IS or technology that they had been awarded through the e-bay Techquity grant. Through the action research steps described in the methodology section, the researchers were able to instill an awareness and understanding of how the microentrepreneurs needed to align the goals of their business and how the available technology could help them reach that end state. The IT therapy process used with each of the micro-enterprises helped to address some of the immediate IT needs of the business. The immediate visible and measurable outcomes were in the area of improved day-to-day business administrative activities mainly through automation of many of the tedious manual activities. This form of outcome seems to support the view coming out from the strategic IT literature which states that one of the core ways in which IT may add value to a firm is by reducing costs incurred by the organization (Bakos and Treacy, 1986; McFarlan, 1984; Wiseman, 1988).

It can be seen that in all the micro-enterprises in this study, the final strategic position that resulted lay in the *innovation* quadrant of the focus-dominance model. The path to the *innovation* quadrant was different for each of the micro-enterprises. Depending on their context, some showed a tendency for a direct shift from the *efficiency* quadrant to the *innovation* quadrant. Whereas, others tended to take routes via either the *coordination* quadrant, or the *collaboration* quadrant, or via both. This implies that all the micro-enterprise owners are looking to integrate their IS with their business strategies by taking into consideration both internal (improving operational efficiency) as well as external (improved relationships with suppliers and customers) aspects of the business (Levy et al., 2001). This form of alignment of IS with business strategy will enable the micro-enterprises to reach a state whereby they will have a strong platform to be competitive with other businesses in their market.

The resource-based view of the firm (Clemons, 1991; Barney, 1991; Conner, 1991; Mata et al., 1995) to explain competitive advantage provides support for not only the outcomes from this study, but also for the *process* by which IT therapy was used to assist the microeneterprises to have the potential to be competitive. In the resource-based view of the firm, resources and capabilities may provide a unique set of competencies that may serve to address either cost reduction or product differentiation strategies to eventually create value for the organization. Applying this perspective to the context of our study, the term *resources,* refers to the technology that was awarded to each of the micro-enterprises through the e-bay techquity grant program. The term, *capabilities,* refers to the context-sensitive technical assistance or the IT therapy that was provided by the ITD innovators in the case of each of the micro-enterprises.

Integrating the awarded IT (resources) with the IT therapy process (capabilities) produces certain context-sensitive competencies (for some of the micro-enterprises these were in the form of improved awareness of IT and for some others these were in the form of immediate solutions to technical problems that helped them clear the bottleneck that they were facing) for each of the micro-enterprises that as our results show, addressed cost reduction strategies through improved administrative efficiencies. Figure 3 shows a modified version of the resource-based view of the firm that incorporates the process of IT therapy. It shows how the integration of the IT therapy process with existing IT resources within the micro-enterprises creates added value to the firm – supporting and providing a means for competitiveness with other organizations. The effect of aligning the resources with the capabilities is illustrated in Figure 10.

This model illustrates how the IT therapy interventions bring about unique competencies that enable value to be created in the firm through cost reduction and administrative efficiencies. More specifically, the IT Therapy component of the work was focused on the entrepreneurs' strongly perceived issues and problems: LD's Internet connection was very unreliable; HH needed to provide better statistics to stakeholders; FD wanted to be able to show potential customers a PowerPoint show of her fashions; HE had customer information scattered in many different places; EP was frustrated by having to maintain duplicate accounting systems at work and at home; HC had ideas for enhancing her web site; CZ needed a more effective means of tracking tutors. In addition, the ITD innovators applied their

Figure 10. Model of micro-enterprise growth

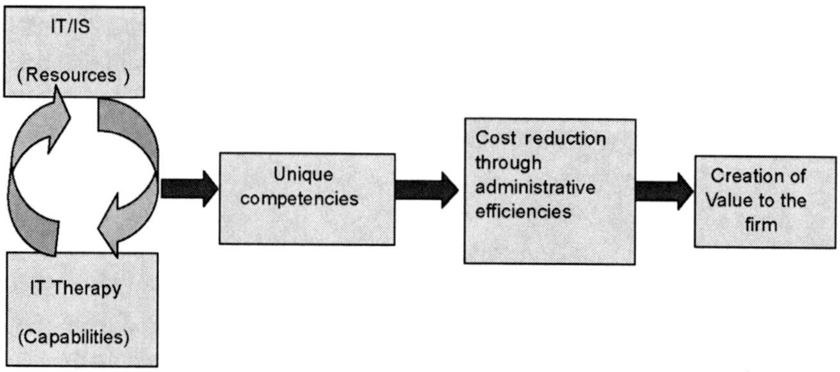

skills and experiences to identify solutions to problems the entrepreneurs may not have been aware of.

The resource based view of the firm suggests that sustaining the growth of these micro-enterprises would require sustaining the skills and experience developed through the IT therapy process. Competitive advantages that these micro-enterprises gain from the direction of their growth can be stimulated through additional interventions guided by the focus-dominance model. This research has also brought to light a unique set of skills and experiences that ITD innovators can bring to bear in helping micro-enterprises achieve sustained growth and competitive advantage.

CONCLUSION

This research suggests that while micro-enterprises have the potential to serve as the seedbed for economic development, they must overcome a number of challenges that obstruct their path. Very few micro-enterprise entrepreneurs possess the technical skills or information systems necessary to streamline their business operations and help them compete and expand into new markets. This is why they need interventions by ITD innovators who can give them the skills that enable the micro-entrepreneurs to diagnose business problems, design IT and training interventions and implement processes to support IT adoption. An innovative approach was developed by integrating context-sensitive technical assistance, or in other words, "IT therapy" with existing IT resources in micro-enterprises to show how these small businesses may become competitive. This research has investigated how through the process of context-sensitive IT assistance has the potential to enable micro-enterprises to achieve competitiveness. This research is based on an interpretive field study method of inquiry as outlined by Klein and Myers (1999) with data collection being carried out using action research steps (Zuber-Skerrit, 1991; Avison et al., 1999). This article used the Focus-Dominance model to investigate the adoption of ICT for competitive advantage by a set of seven micro-enterprises and the resource based view of the firm to develop a model of micro-enterprise growth. Further research needs to consider the effect of multiple interventions across a broader range of micro-enterprises over time through a longitudinal design.

REFERENCES

Avison, D. E., Lau, F., Myers, M., & Nielsen, P. A. (1999). Action Research. *Communications of the ACM, 42*(1), 94–97. doi:10.1145/291469.291479

Baark, E., & Heeks, R. (1998) "Evaluation of Donor-Funded Information Technology Transfer Projects in China: A Life-Cycle Approach". Retrieved Dec 12, 2007, from http://idpm.man.ac.uk/wp/di/di_wp01.htm.

Bakos, J.Y. and Treacy, M.E. "Information Technology and Corporate Strategy: A Research Perspective," *MIS Quarterly* (1 0:2), June 1986, pp. 107-1 19.

Barton, C., and Bear, M. (1999) "Information and Communications Technologies: Are they the Key to Viable Business Development Services for Micro and Small Enterprises? Report for USAID as part of the Microenterprise Best Practices Project. March". Retrieved December 12, 2007, from http://www.mip.org/PUBS/MBP/ict.htm.

Bharati, P., & Chaudhury, A. (2006). Current Status of Technology Adoption: Micro, Small and Medium Manufacturing Firms in Boston. *Communications of the ACM*, *49*(10), 88–93. doi:10.1145/1164394.1164400

Blili, S., & Raymond, L. (1993). Information technology: threats and opportunities for small and medium-sized enterprises. *International Journal of Information Management*, *13*, 439–448. doi:10.1016/0268-4012(93)90060-H

Brown, D. H., & Lockett, N. (2004). Potential of critical e-applications for engaging SMEs in e-business: a provider perspective. *European Journal of Information Systems*, *13*, 21–34. doi:10.1057/palgrave.ejis.3000480

Capon, N. and Glazer, R. "Marketing and Technology: A Strategic Coalignment," *Journal of Marketing* (51:3), July 1987, pp. 1-1 4.

Checkland, P. (1981). *Systems Thinking*. Systems Practice, New York: John Wiley & Sons.

Checkland, P. (1991) "From Framework through Experience to Learning: The Essential Nature of Action Research," in: Nissen, H.-E., Klein, H. and Hirschheim, R. (eds.) Information Systems Research: Contemporary Approaches and Emergent Traditions, North Holland: Elsevier Publishers, 397-403.

Clemons, E.K. "Corporate Strategies for Information Technology: A Resource-Based Approach," Computer (24:1 I), November 1991, pp. 23-32.

Clemons, E.K. and Row, M.C. "Sustaining IT Advantage: The Role of Structural Differences," *MIS Quarterly* (1 5:3), September 1991 a, pp. 275-292.

Clemons, E.K. and Row, M.K. "Information Technology at Rosenbluth Travel: Competitive Advantage in a Rapidly Growing Service Company," *Journal of Management Information Systems* (8:2), Fall 1991 b, pp. 53-79.

Conner, K.R. "A Historical Comparison of Resource-Based Theory and Five Schools of Thought Within Industrial Organization Economics: Do We Have a New Theory of the Firm?" *Journal of Management* (1 7:1), March 1991, pp. 121-1 54.

Copeland, D.G. and McKenney, J.L. "Airline Reservation Systems: Lessons from History," *MIS Quarterly* (12:3), September 1988, pp. 353-370.

Cragg, P. B., & King, M. (1993). Small-Firm Computing: Motivators and Inhibitors. *Management Information Systems Quarterly, 17*(1), 47–60. doi:10.2307/249509

DeLone, W. H. (1988). Determinants of Success for Computer Usage in Small Business. *Management Information Systems Quarterly, 12*(1), 51–61. doi:10.2307/248803

Duncombe, R., & Heeks, R. (2003). An information systems perspective on ethical trade and self-regulation. *Information Technology for Development, 10*(2), 123–139. doi:10.1002/itdj.1590100206

Feeny, D.F. and Ives, B. "In Search of Sustainability: Reaping Long-Term Advantage from Investments in Information Technology," *Journal of Management Information Systems* (7:1), Summer 1990, pp. 27-46.

Foong, S.-Y. (1999) Effect of end user personal and systems attributes on computer based information systems success in Malaysian SMEs. *Journal of Small Business Management*, July, **37**(3), 81–87.

Galliers, R. D. (1992) "Choosing Information Systems Research Approaches, in: Galliers, R.D. (Ed.) Information Systems Research: Issues, Methods and Practical Guidelines," Henley-on-Thames: Alfred Waller, 144-162.

Grosh, B., & Somolekae, G. (1996). Mighty oaks from little acorns: Can microenterprise serve as the seedbed of industrialization? *World Development, 24*(12), 1879–1890. doi:10.1016/S0305-750X(96)00082-4

Harrison, D. A., Mykytyn, P. P., Jr., and Riemenschneider, C. K. "Executive Decisions About Adoption of Information Technology in Small Business: Theory and Empirical Tests," *Information Systems Research* (8:2), 1997, pp. 171-195.

Hashmi, M. S., & Cuddy, J. (1990) Strategic initiatives for introducing CIM technologies in Irish SMEs. In *Computer Integrated Manufacturing – Proceedings of the Sixth CIM-Europe Annual Conference*, Faria, L. and Van Puymbroeck, W. (eds.) (Springer Verlag, Lisbon).

Hazan, M. (2002) "Virtual South: E-Commerce for unprivileged artisans" Retrieved Dec 12, 2007, from http://www.iicd.org/stories/.

Honig, B. "What determines success? Examining the human, financial, and social capital of Jamaican microentrepreneurs," *Journal of Business Venturing*, (13:5), 1998, pp.371-94.

Hyman, E.L. and Dearden, K. "Comprehensive impact assessment systems for NGO microenterprise development programs. *World Development*, (26:2), pp. 261-276.

Igbaria, M., Zinatelli, N., Cragg, P. B., and Cavaye, A. L. M. "Personal Computing Acceptance Factors in Small Firms: A Structural Equation Model," *MIS Quarterly* (21:3), 1997, pp. 279-305.

Ives, B., & Learmonth, G. P. (1984). The Information Systems as a Competitive weapon . *Communications of the ACM, 27*(12). doi:10.1145/2135.2137

Klein, H. K., & Myers, M. D. (1999, March). A Set of Principles for Conducting and Evaluating Interpretive Field Studies in Information Systems. *Management Information Systems Quarterly, 23*(1), 67–94. doi:10.2307/249410

Latchem. C. & Walker, D. (2001) "Telecentres: Case Studies and Key Issues", Vancouver: The Commonwealth of Learning.

Lefebvre, L., & Lefebvre, E. (1993). Competitive positioning and innovative efforts in SMEs. *Small Business Economics, 5*, 297–305. doi:10.1007/BF01516250

Lefebvre, L., & Lefebvre, L. A. (1996) "Information and Telecommunication Technologies: The Impact of their Adoption on Small and Medium-sized Enterprises." Retrieved Dec, 12, 2007, from http://web.idrc.ca/en/ev-9303-201-1-DO_TOPIC.html.

Levy, M., & Powell, P. (1998). SME flexibility and the role of information systems. *Journal of Small Business Economics, 11*, 183–196. doi:10.1023/A:1007912714741

Levy, M., P. Powell & P. Yetton. (2001) "SMEs: Aligning IS and the Strategic Context", *Journal of Information Technology*, forthcoming.

Levy, M., Powell, P., & Yetton, P. (2002). The Dynamics of SME Information Systems. *Small Business Economics, 19*, 341–354. doi:10.1023/A:1019654030019

Lichtenstein, G.A. and Lyons, T.S. "The entrepreneurial development system: Transforming business talent and community economies," *Economic Development Quarterly*, (15:1), 2001, pp.3-20.

Mansell, R., & Wehn, U. (1998). *Knowledge Societies: Information Technology for Sustainable Development*. Oxford: Oxford University Press.

Matthews, P., "ICT Assimilation and SME Expansion," *Journal of International Development*. (19), 2007, pp. 817–827.

McFarlan, F.W. "Information Technology Changes the Way You Compete," *Harvard Business Review* (62:3), May June 1984, pp. 98-1 03.

McFarlan, F. W., & McKenney, J. L. (1983). *Corporate Information Systems Management*. Homewood, Ill.: Richard D. Irwin.

Montazemi, A. R. (1988). Factors Affecting Information Satisfaction in the Context of the Small Business Environment. *Management Information Systems Quarterly, 12*(2), 239–256. doi:10.2307/248849

Moyi, E. D. (2003). Networks, information and small enterprises: New Technologies and the ambiguity of empowerment. *Information Technology for Development, 10*, 221–232. doi:10.1002/itdj.1590100402

Naylor, J., & Williams, J. (1994). Successful Use of IT in SMEs. *European Journal of IS, 3*(1), 48–56.

O'Farrell, C., Norrish, P., & Scott, A. (1999) "Information and Communication Technologies (ICTs) for Sustainable Livelihoods." Burton Hall: Intermediate Technology Development Group.

Owen, W., & Darkwa, O. (1999). Role of Multipurpose Community Telecentres in Accelerating National Development in Ghana. *First Monday, Vol, 5*(1), 1–23.

Pateli, A. G., & Giaglis, G. M. (2004). A research framework for analyzing eBusiness models. *European Journal of Information Systems, 13*, 302–314. doi:10.1057/palgrave.ejis.3000513

Piscitello, L., & Sgobbi, F. (2004, June). Globalisation, E-Business and SMEs: Evidence from the Italian District of Prato. *Small Business Economics, 22*(5), 333. doi:10.1023/B:SBEJ.0000022208.34741.55

Poon, S., & Swatman, P. (1999). An exploratory study of small business Internet commerce issues. *Information & Management, 35*, 9–18. doi:10.1016/S0378-7206(98)00079-2

Porter, M. E. (1980). *Competitive Strategy: Techniques for Analyzing Industries and Competitors*. New York, NY: Free Press.

Porter, M.E. and Millar, V.E. "How Information Gives You Competitive Advantage," *Harvard Business Review* (63:4), July-August 1985, pp. 149-1 60.

Qiang, C. Z., Clarke, G. R., & Halewood, N. (2006). The Role of ICT. In World Bank (Ed.), *Doing Business Information and Communications for Development—Global Trends and Policies*. Washington, DC: World Bank.

Qureshi, S. "How does Information technology effect Development? Integrating Theory and Practice into a Process Model." *Proceedings of the eleventh Americas Conference on Information Systems*, Omaha, NE, 2005.

Qureshi, S., Kamal, M., & Wolcott, P. (2008). *Sustainability of Information Technology Therapy on Micro-enterprise Development*. HICSS.

Raymond, L. (1988). The Impact of Computer Training on the Attitudes and Usage Behaviour of Small Business Managers. *Journal of Small Business Management, 26*(3), 9–13.

Raymond, L., Bergeron, F., & Blili, S. (2005). The assimilation of E-business in manufacturing SMEs: determinants and effects on growth and internationalization. *Electronic Markets, 15*(2), 106–118. doi:10.1080/10196780500083761

Reid, G., & Jacobsen, C. (1988). *The Small Entrepreneurial Firm*. Aberdeen University Press.

Riemenschneider, C. Harrison, D. and P. Mykytyn. (2003) "Understanding IT Adoption Decisions in Small Business: Integrating Current Theories" Information and Management, Vol 40.

Sanders, C.K. "The impact of micro-enterprise assistance programs: A comparative study of program participants, non participants, and other low-wage workers," *Social Service Review*, (76:2), 2002, pp.321-40.

Schreiner, M., & Woller, G. "Micro-enterprise Development Programs in the United States and in the Developing World," *World Development* (31:9), 2003, pp 1567-1580.

Servon, L. J. and Doshna, J.P. "Microenterprise and the economic development toolkit: A small part of the big picture" *Journal of Developmental Entrepreneurship*. (5:3), 2000, pp. 183.

Sethi, V., & King, W. R. (1994, December). Development of Measures to Assess the Extent to Which an Information Technology Application Provides Competitive Advantage. *Management Science, 40*(12). doi:10.1287/mnsc.40.12.1601

Southwood, R. 2004. ICTs and Small Enterprise: A Motor of Economic Development in Africa, IICD Research Briefs, IICD, The Hague: IICD Research Briefs 9.

Street, C. T., & Meister, D. B. (2004). Small Business Growth and Internal Transparency: The Role of Information Systems. *Management Information Systems Quarterly, 28*(3), 473–506.

Sullivan, B. C. "Economics of Information Technology" *International Journal of Social Economics*. Bradford. (12:1), 1985, pp. 37.

Thong, J., Yap, C., & Rahman, K. (1996). Top management support, external expertise and information systems implementation in small businesses. *Information Systems Research, 7*(2), 248–267. doi:10.1287/isre.7.2.248

Wiseman, C. (1988). *Strategic Information Systems*. Homewood, IL: Irwin.

Wolcott, P., Qureshi, S., & Kamal, M. "An Information Technology Therapy Approach to Micro-enterprise Adoption of ICTs" *Americas Conference on Information Systems (AMCIS)* 2007

Yap, C. (1989). Computerization problems facing small and medium enterprises: the experience of Singapore, in: *Proceedings of the 20th Annual Meeting of the Midwest Decision Sciences Institute*, Miami University, Miami. *OH. Osteopathic Hospitals, 19-21*, 128–134.

Zuber-Skerrit, O. (1991). *Action Research for Change and Development*. Aldershot: Gower Publishing.

This work was previously published in International Journal of E-Business Research, Volume 5, Issue 1, edited by In Lee, pp. 117-140, copyright 2009 by IGI Publishing (an imprint of IGI Global)

Chapter 7
Small Firm Process Re-Engineering Success

Li-Jen Chang
London South Bank University, UK

Margi Levy
University of Warwick, UK

Philip Powell
University of London, UK & University of Groningen, The Netherlands

ABSTRACT

Small firms are undertaking business process re-engineering (BPR), but the factors contributing to success of these activities are not clearly understood. This research reviews the main contributing factors to BPR success using a framework that considers culture, structure, technology, and resource. Evidence from Taiwanese firms is used to explore issues contributing to, or impeding, successful process re-engineering in small firms. The analysis shows that BPR success is empowered by innovation, employee empowerment, top management commitment, and strategic direction and is dependent upon customer relations, Information Systems involvement, and financial resources.

1 INTRODUCTION

Many forces, including competition and globalization have led enterprises to re-structure to focus on managing change. Business process re-engineering (BPR) is an approach to business transformation that emphasizes customer-driven, process-oriented management practice, often enabled by IT. Raymond et al (1998) argue

DOI: 10.4018/978-1-60960-529-2.ch007

that the literature focuses on BPR in large firms. They pose the question as to whether BPR success factors are the same for small and medium-sized enterprises (SMEs) as for large enterprises. While the first phase of activity involving process re-engineering is long over, the moves towards enterprise systems forces firms to refine and align their processes in order to fit with the software (Hicks et al, 2010, Muscatello et al, 2003 Webb and Schlemmer 2006, Ashton and Stacey 2009, Ashima, 2010, Alexandre, 2006, Montoni, 2007, Galinac, 2009, Girish, 2007).

This research investigates BPR to identify the success and failure factors in small firms. The chapter briefly outlines the nature of BPR. It then adapts Chang and Powell's (1998) framework to explore BPR in SMEs by focusing on culture, technology, structure and resources. The research explores, using a case approach, the BPR response of eight Taiwanese firms. This leads to underststanding of the different success and failure factors for BPR in SMEs A revised model for successful BPR in SMEs is then presented and the implications for theory and practice are discussed.

2 NATURE OF BPR

BPR is 'radical redesign of business processes to achieve dramatic improvements on critical measures of performance' (Hammer 1990). BPR emphasizes horizontal integration across organizational boundaries - the analysis and design of work-flows and processes within and between organizations (Davenport 1993). The main elements are fundamental work process redesign, adding value to final customers, integration of cross-functional specialization, and exploitation of IT. The challenges of BPR initiatives are both technical and socio-cultural. It is technically problematic to develop radical process improvements. The socio-cultural challenge is in dealing with people's reactions to the likely serious organizational changes required (Reijers and Mansar 2005).

Past research suggests many factors are inherent in successful BPR. First, top management commitment is important to ensure the initiative is maintained and focused. Second, re-engineering focuses on providing customers with greater value (Cameron and Braiden 2004). Third, re-engineering places a major emphasis on employees and their role in resolving problems (Larsen and Myers 1999). Process improvement involves changes to jobs and the social structure to increase motivation, reduce stress and improve performance by empowerment (Wastell et al. 1994). Fourth, IT is an *enabler* in creating and maintaining flexible business networks (Tinnila 1995). Finally, a BPR strategy is key, incorporating critical inputs from both corporate and IT planning (Teng et al 1994,Talwar 1993). However, as BPR involves changing the firm's competences, it is more likely to be successful if it is emergent, benefiting from organizational learning (Craig and Yetton 1997).

2.1 BPR in SMES

There is limited research into process re-engineering in small firms but studies indicates that firms benefit if they respect the underlying principles of BPR (Muscatello et al., 2003). In particular, SMEs need to review their business processes around customer requirements by using IT more innovatively. Top management commitment and a methodological approach are essential (Ursic et al 2005). Involvement from employees is also beneficial (Raymond et al 1998). These principles are evident in Chang and Powell's (1998) SME BPR framework (Figure 1). This framework identifies four key criteria that affect SME BPR success: culture, structure, resources and technology.

Culture: BPR does not work without profound cultural change as it emphasizes leadership, teamwork, empowerment, entrepreneurship, and risk-taking (Tersine et al 1997, Ursic et al 2005). SMEs are often perceived as more innovative than larger firms (Carrier 1995) and employees are often given operational responsibility (Brady and Voss 1995). Decision-making in SMEs is often dominated by the CEO: this may aid or hinder re-engineering.

Structure: Small businesses tend to encourage team and cross-functional orientations (Kinni 1995). The lack of bureaucracy makes for efficient and informal internal communication networks to manage processes. SMEs are able to respond readily to changing customers' needs. Due to the lack of management layers, small

Figure 1. BPR Framework for SMEs (adapted from Chang and Powell 1998)

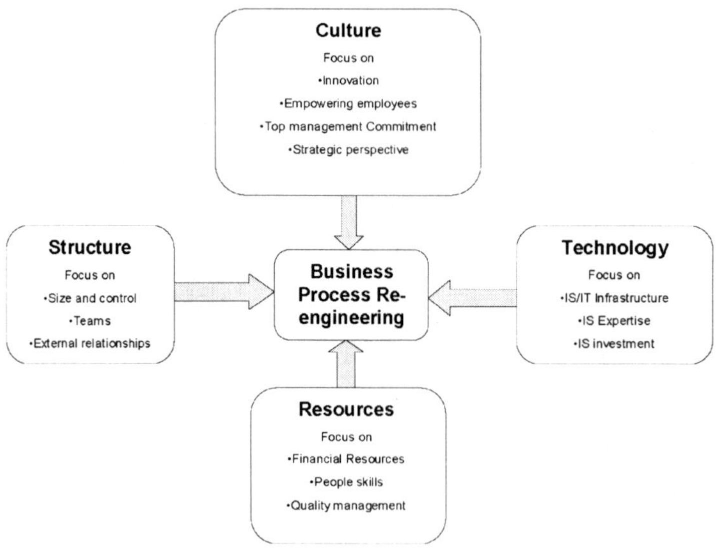

businesses are closer to their customers (Brady and Voss 1995). Thus, SMEs should be well positioned for re-engineering with their focus on process.

Resources: Two serious problems SMEs face when trying to implement quality management are the owner's lack of business experience and a lack of financial and human resources which may restrict growth (Haksaver 1996, Witherill and Kolak 1996). Thus, while survival is the first concern in SMEs, financial constraints may inhibit SMEs undertaking BPR.

Technology: IT infrastructure can be a significant enabler of, or barrier to, the practical options available to planning and changing processes for BPR (Grover et al 1993). Most re-engineering efforts are technology-driven, with the role of IT changing from producing data to integrating new technologies and assisting people as independent information gatherers (Ribbler 1996). However, SMEs are unlikely to employ IT staff, IS skills are limited and IS investment is often seen as a necessary evil.

This analysis leads to the research question: *what factors enable or inhibit BPR success in SMEs?*

3 RESEARCH APPROACH

There is little previous research available to investigate BPR success or failure factors. This research is therefore exploratory. Case studies are a powerful method for conducting exploratory research, as it is possible to pose reflective questions. Also, case research is effective when theory is relatively under-developed (Eisenhardt 1989). Particularly, when the research boundaries are unclear, there is a need to investigate the issue within a real life context, drawing on multiple views (Yin 1994). Multiple cases ensure that common patterns are identified rather than being generalized from what might be chance occurrences (Eisenhardt 1989).

3.1 Research Background

In Taiwan, SMEs constitute 95% of all enterprises (Lee and Chen 1992) Taiwanese SMEs are confronting dramatic environmental changes. Export-oriented SMEs are restricted to labour-intensive and mature-technology industries that constrain technology upgrading, enlarging operations and marketing (Wu and Chou 1992). Labour shortages and rising wages have led to SMEs losing competitiveness. Financial problems are a major obstacle. Macro-environmental transition has forced SMEs to investigate their internal operations and management. Hence, approaches such as BPR have become popular.

Eight cases are considered (Table 1). In order to mitigate contextual bias, the cases include four SMEs in manufacturing and four in services. Three firms are small and five are medium-sized. Data was gathered through semi-structured interviews with the CEO/management team from each SME. SMEs' perceived BPR satisfaction is a determinant for BPR success. Interview questions were developed based on the themes presented in the BPR framework (Figure 1). SMEs' perceived BPR satisfaction is a surrogate for BPR success or failure. For each sector, two 'successful' and two 'failure' cases are selected to compare success and failure factors.

Most of the SMEs are seeking to grow by business expansion. For example, Telecoms Supplier is enlarging its sales division to diversify into new markets with new products. Supersonic Machinery is developing technology to manufacture semiconductors. In contrast, Automatic Assembling and Freight Shipping tend to have steady orders and loyal clients. A feature of the SMEs is that their purpose in adopting BPR derives from a desire either to improve efficiency or to enhance capacities, rather than from a 'crisis situation' (Kinni, 1995) (Table 2).

4 CASE ANALYSIS

Case findings are organized around four criteria: structure, culture, resources, technology (Figure 1). The analysis investigates success/failure factors that influence BPR performance. Interview data are analysed to determine interviewee perspectives. Table 3 summarizes the findings discussed in detail.

Table 1. Characteristics of BPR case firms

Cases	Employees	BPR Outcome	Industry	Strategy	Market	Sub-contract
Automatic Assembling	10	Success	Manu	Market Segmentation	Steady	Yes
Supersonic Machinery	40	Success	Manu	Diversification	Growing	Yes
Geodetic Surveying	15	Success	Service	Expansion	Steady	No
Freight Shipping	150	Success	Service	Market penetration	Competitive	No
Shoes Trading	100	Failure	Manu	Market penetration	Growing	Yes
Telecoms Supplier	300	Failure	Manu	Expansion	Competitive	No
Financial Institution	200	Failure	Service	Market Development	Steady	No
Retail Grocer	200	Failure	Service	Product develop	Competitive	No

Table 2. Purpose of BPR in case firms

Purpose of BPR	Case Firms	Number
Process Improvement	All Firms	8
Cost Reduction	Telecoms Supplier, Retail Grocer, Shoe Trading	3
Customer Satisfaction	Supersonic Machinery, Automatic Assembling, Freight Shipping, Financial Institution	4
Quality	Geodetic Survey, Freight Shipping, Financial Institution	3

4.1 Culture

Owner-led SMEs with ambitious strategies that focus on product innovation and empowering employees are more likely to benefit from BPR than those with limited top management commitment, an autocratic management style with little top-down communication.

Innovation is primarily seen in rapid growth firms. In these firms product innovation takes precedence over process innovation. Since the case rapid growth firms, are technology-oriented, use of the latest IT tools and applications to support product innovation is common supporting Wind and West's (1991) observation that innovation is fostered in decentralised, integrated, informal organizations. The cases suggest that innovation is positively correlated with a team-based orientation. For example, Retail Grocer encouraged 'unconventional ideas' among project members when creating the firm's new image.

Empowering employees is recognized as critical for successful BPR (Janson 1993, Larsen and Myers 1999). Higher employee autonomy is more likely in decentralised SMEs, such as Automatic Assembling and Supersonic Machinery. These firms demonstrate that small businesses operate as an empowered team (Kinni, 1995) where knowledge workers are involved in decisions and product discussion.

Top management commitment, coupled with good top-down communication, is considered by all SMEs as the most critical factor in BPR success (Stevenson, 1993, McKeown and Philip, 2003), highlighting the need for direct CEO involvement. Automatic Assembling represents a 'top-down' approach to BPR. The owner-manager oversees several functions - personnel, finance and accounting. His enthusiastic involvement ensured the re-engineering project encountered few difficulties. Such direct involvement tends to occur in smaller firms where structures are less formal and communication lines shorter. In Geodetic Surveying the owner participated in building its network with clients that was instrumental in BPR success.

The only BPR initiative that was not CEO-led was Telecoms Suppliers, it derived from departmental managers. When the R&D director was asked about the owner's

Table 3. Success and failure factors for BPR

Criterion	Elements	Success factors	Failure factors
Culture	Innovation	• Product innovation [Supersonic Mach] • Innovative environment [Retail Grocer]	
	Empowering Employees	• High employee autonomy [Geodetic Surveying; Supersonic Machinery; Automatic Assembling]	• Autocratic management style [Financial Institution; Shoe Trading]
	Top Management Commitment	• Top-down approach [all cases expect Telecoms Supplier] • Direct involvement [Geodetic Surveying; Supersonic Machinery; Automatic Assembling] • Good top-down communication [Automatic Assembling]	• Lack of management support [Telecoms Suppliers] • Poor top-down communication [Retail Grocer; Financial Institution; Shoe Trading]
	Strategic Perspective	• Strategic thinking and customer focus [Geodetic Surveying; Supersonic Machinery]	• Lack of strategic vision [Financial Inst; Telecoms Supplier; Retail Grocer]
Structure	Process		• Formal hierarchy [Telecoms Sup]
	Teams	• Teamwork efficiency [Automatic Assembling; Geodetic Surveying]	
	External Relations	• Good relations with customers and suppliers [Supersonic Machinery] • Good relation with suppliers [Automatic Assembling] • Good relation with customers [Freight Shipping; Shoe Trading]	
Resources	Finance		• Lack of funds [Retail Grocer]
	People Skills	• Knowledge workers [Geodetic Surveying; Supersonic Machinery; Automatic Assembling]	• Lack of managerial skills [Telecoms Supplier; Retail Grocer; Financial Institution]
	Quality Management	• Integrating TQM and BPR within strategic context [Geodetic Surveying; Supersonic Machinery] • Organizational learning [Automatic Assembling]	• Lack of long-term business plans [Retail Grocer; Shoe Trading
Technology	IT/IS infrastructure	• Applying IT to core processes [Freight Shipping; Automatic Assembling] • Inter-organizational co-operation [Geodetic Surveying]	• Lack of IT tools [Shoe Trading]
	IS Expertise	• Skill Training [Geodetic Surveying]	• Lack of IT expertise [Financial Institution; Shoe Trading]
	IS Investment	• High IT spending [Geodetic Surveying]	• Lack of funds for IT investment [Retail Grocer]

attitude to BPR, he replied: *'We're thinking some good ideas, but the owner's just not interested'*. Limited top management support meant they could not find sufficient financial backup to launch process change.

A *strategic perspective* tends to be lacking in many SMEs. Re-engineering firms' core processes into strategic capabilities increases the chances of BPR success (Wastell et al 1994, Hale and Cragg 1996). Five case firms are re-engineering their core processes, which suggests some recognition of the need for strategic thinking. For example, Geodetic Surveying's firm-client interface is largely involved with customer services and product development. Automatic Assembling's integrated IS comprises three major processes: ordering, client/supplier database and manufacturing. Most of the unsuccessful cases demonstrate a lack of strategic vision. For example, Telecoms Supplier focused on distribution channel expansion and improving sales network efficiency rather than competition issues. Retail Grocer focused on business image, ignoring quality issues. They lost competitive advantage due to a focus on short-term pay-off and failure to implement continuous process change. Shoe Trading's BPR, which focused on process improvement was also limited. They put this down to their lack of competitive power due to their position as a sub-contractor.

Similarly, Financial Institution launched its Internet banking without considering client resistance about security concerns. The on-line banking system was created by external IT support without careful planning and management backup. The Investment Manager recalls: *'The initial idea was to reduce the workload of operators and to simplify the banking procedures. Clients only need to install the software provided and key in their usernames and passwords. We believed this was the trend of future banking. However, there aren't many people taking advantage of this facility. One reason is that customers are suspicious about this due to security concerns'*. A similar situation is seen at Telecoms Suppliers. The R&D director notes: *'We did not consider the feasibility of the on-line ordering system while creating our web site. Because of the nature of our products, customers are used to buying with sales staff's assistance'*.

4.2 Structure

The cases show that the structural factors that influence BPR success are teamworking and effective external relations. However, formal hierarchies inhibit success.

Team-based operations bring greater involvement and motivation (Sellers 1997). These are more likely in smaller businesses, e.g. Automatic Assembling and Geodetic Surveying due to their decentralised structure and shorter lines of communication. In SMEs, a major benefit from team-based operations is to bring greater involvement, increased motivation and communication, and enhanced job performance.

The owner of Geodetic Surveying believes: *'All our employees are professionals. They are talented and responsible. There's only about 15 of us and we work as a team. We respect each other and this is the best way to get things done. I never feel superior because I am the boss'.*

The importance of *External relations* is seen with customers and suppliers. Unusually for SMEs, which usually cluster near customers (Brady and Voss 1995), most of the case firms operate internationally. For example, Supersonic Machinery sells in SE Asia. Shoe Trading's clients are US and Australian. Thus, using IT as an enabler of re-engineering is likely to be beneficial. Cross-functional integration can be expanded to inter-organizational co-operation (Davidow and Malone, 1992). For example, the focus of Shoe Trading's BPR was improving communication with its 150 contracted manufacturers while building up relationships with foreign clients to secure regular orders.

Geodetic Surveying built an integrated IS with a customer interface to facilitate mutual information sharing, technical support and the latest information about surveying tools. Their clients, mainly civil-engineers, have similar IT infrastructure. Otherwise, costs for establishing such a network would be prohibitive. When asked how they use IT inter-organizationally, the owner replied: *'We are one of the few firms that use computers in geodetic surveying. It's different from traditional manual drawing and the quality is significantly improved. Recently we've built a network system linking to our clients' computers. This on-line network saves time and costs'.*

Automatic Assembling is subcontracted to several major clients while at the same time acting as a subcontractor for about 50 satellite manufacturers. Their re-engineering project is designed to reduce the complexity of business processes by integrating its ordering system, production line and supplier/clients databases. A senior technician describes their current relations with clients/customers/contractors: *'We have been trying to maintain a sound relationship with our clients and downstream satellite plants. And we're at an advantage of being located in an industrial park where we get support from other SMEs, such as sharing materials and facilities. With different market differentiation/segmentation, we have good relationship with other firms in the industry. There is no malicious competition'.*

The cases reinforce the view that strategic behaviour is the main reason for building relations. Geodetic Surveying's client-oriented interface and Automatic Assembling's integrated ordering system are related to their core processes.

The cases show that *size and control*, particularly in more formal and hierarchical structures may inhibit BPR. This occurs in larger firms, such as Telecoms Supplier, where the main purpose of BPR is to de-emphasize divisions of labour to streamline processes and reduce administrative costs. A reason for this is that processes in SMEs are often lean and owners may not accept the need to change, even within a BPR exercise.

4.3 Resources

Success factors in the cases include skilled staff, an emphasis on quality management, and recognition of the value of organizational learning. Failure factors are primarily limited financial resources, limited managerial skills and short term strategic planning.

Limited capital *financial resources* are a major constraint on SMEs' BPR efforts. Financial deficiency restricted Shoe Trading and Retail Grocer from advanced use of IT for functional integration and inter-organisational linkage. Retail Grocer's Planning Manager notes: *'The main reason for adopting BPR was to reduce administrative costs and increase internal efficiency. The owner is not good at financial planning. We had no idea about the return on investment. It's not easy to get the capital we need. So we haven't even gone half-way though our BPR project. Survival is more important'.*

The cases suggest that the amount SMEs spend on IT for BPR depends on the owner-manager's perceived benefits to individuals and the firm (Cragg and King, 1993). For example, the use of IT for BPR at Geodetic Surveying results from the owner's awareness of technological advances enabling better client service.

People skills are important in re-engineering success. This is seen in case firms that are technology-oriented and employ skilled staff (Geodetic Surveying, Supersonic Machinery and Automatic Assembling). However, limited people skills, particularly poor IT understanding, also restrict success. The Design Manager from Shoe Trading states: *'We built a web site on which the photos of our latest designs are exhibited. However, because of security concerns, on-line ordering has not been feasible. The designers are still drawing manually, which takes much longer, but they seem to be happy with what they are doing... Although we have installed 3D software that aids design, few people are able to use it'*

SMEs' managerial skills are often limited and may not provide support for radical process change. For example, Shoe Trading had difficulties in retaining its talented designers. The Design Manager describes this it: *'Since the owner started this re-engineering programme, we have felt terribly insecure about everything. You never know...when you'll be sacked. You suspect everybody is seeking new employment. The owner never told us...even though the business condition hasn't been that bad'.*

Quality management is seen by the case firms as important to demonstrate the provision of excellent service to customers. Quality management is only of value when it contributes to organizational learning. Automatic Assembling is an example of empowering and training employees to create ownership and develop the knowledge base. A senior technician stated: *'We care very much about the process by which new employees learn from the senior technicians. We can't afford lots of time for training. Thanks to IT, we are now able to standardize our products. This is the most efficient way to accumulate our experiences and knowledge. It saves time and simplifies the ordering process'.*

The lack of strategic direction in most case firms limits the benefits from quality initiatives. Retail Grocer had difficulty sustaining their initial benefits from re-engineering and failed to deliver 'core value' to their customers due largely to a lack of strategic vision and long-term business plans. Similarly, the absence of a BPR plan led to Shoe Trading being unable to deal with the consequences of radical process change. A major problem was its inability to retain the firm's main designers, since it could not provide sufficient support and establish a proper reward system to deal with workload.

4.4 Technology

In growing SMEs, IT is most likely to be applied to product development, usually coupled with R&D. Innovation in SMEs is significantly related to team-based operations and efficiency supported by a good IT infrastructure. Concomitant are sufficient IS skills in the firm. The role of IT in BPR is illustrated by the general manager from Supersonic Machinery: *'BPR to us is not merely process improvement. With our IT professionals, we are trying to broaden our business services, which is consistent with our current policy of differentiation. It allows us to redefine our business direction and customer target'.*

An effective *IS/IT infrastructure* plays an important supportive role as a tool in eliminating time and distance for process integration (Carr and Johansson, 1995). The Internet is extensively used for linking firms with customers, suppliers and others. The case firms use IT widely for process integration and product innovation. Applications, such as spreadsheets, databases, and document imaging for inter-organizational linkage are evident. IT

Automatic Assembling combined three major functions: ordering system, clients/supplier databases, and production lines. This was achieved by several IT tools such as spreadsheets and workflow software. These tools have increased speed and flexibility in customized production and improved customer satisfaction through efficient communication with customers and satellite manufacturers. A senior technician explains: *'All the contracted down-streamed plants and customers are detailed in a database and connected to the ordering system in which all the firm's products are standardised and numbered. This simplifies the ordering process and results in increased flexibility in catering for customers' needs'.*

However, a lack of IT tools, as in Financial Institution and Shoe Trading, inhibits functional integration. Similarly, the use of non-standardized IT platforms between Supersonic Machinery and its 200 contracted satellite firms demonstrates an obstacle to successful implementation.

IS Expertise is often limited in SMEs, with few in-house experts able to undertake new developments (Ferrell 1996). Financial Institution sought assistance from consultants due to a lack of IT skills, but relying too much on external IT vendors resulted in a loss of control.

IS investment is often constrained by limited finances, as in Retail Grocer. The cases reinforce that IT investment should be aligned with firms' strategic IT planning and business strategy. For example, investment in IT for Internet banking at Financial Institution was suggested by consultants rather than the firm, only to reveal that the time and costs could not be justified.

5 ISSUES FOR MANAGEMENT

SMEs need to examine whether they are culturally and structurally ready for re-engineering. Specifically, re-engineering requires a strong commitment from owner-managers since they play a decisive role in determining strategic direction. Employee motivation and empowerment is essential to effective internal communication and responsiveness to customers. Training is useful in enhancing managerial knowledge as well as inter-functional work skills. The IS function has to be repositioned to facilitate BPR by investing in IT tools and provide required end-user skills. Change issues, such as resistance and lack of required skills needs to be managed strategically at two levels: organizational and technological. This is to ensure that re-engineering efforts are implemented as planned and assessed by new performance standards and targets. Conducting pilots and measuring results regularly may significantly increase efficiency.

Despite much debate on whether IT is a necessity for BPR, this research shows the powerful potential of IT in re-engineering. The role of IT/IS has evolved from automating existing outdated processes to providing firms with an array of opportunities by shortening communication lines and eliminating space and time. This is achieved, in essence, by the innovative use of IT. Alignment of IT strategy and BPR strategy derived from a strategic vision is critical. This is to ensure that IT investment and any required end-user training can be evaluated by internal and external customers, or 'process outputs,' rather than by functional performance or cost savings. Given limited financial and human resources, the knowledge and experiences accumulated from the innovative use of IT and the efforts of R&D provide a valuable basis for continuous process improvement.

6 ISSUES FOR RESEARCH

Process re-engineering was introduced as requiring top management support, customer focus, IT, employee empowerment and strategic direction. The cases demonstrate that the main issues for success in BPR for SMEs are the strategic direction of the firm, top management commitment and external relations with customers.

The cases suggest that those SMEs with a positive attitude to risk are more likely to benefit from BPR. SMEs tend to engage in more incremental process change methods to cope with reality rather than adopting a radical approach as recommended by many BPR proponents (Johansson et al, 1993). However, strong commitment from top management is essential. In keeping with Tushman et al (1986), the cases indicate that direct involvement is strongly related to strategic control and project efficiency. Lack of owner support or an autocratic style, as in Financial Institution and Shoe Trading, can hinder re-engineering. However, size and control is possibly less relevant due to SMEs' inherent flexibility. In contrast, greater success is found where top management commitment extends to empowering employees to take greater responsibilities and adapt to new performance standards and requirements.

IS investment integrated with strategic direction is necessary for success. The cases indicate that IT has powerful capacities to eliminating time and distance to help firms to achieve functional integration and improve cross-company linkage. Supersonic Machinery and the Telecom Supplier, apply IT to both product innovation and improving client/supplier relations. Geodetic Surveying is expanding IT use to establish a firm-client interface for mutual support and information sharing, success is helped by their clients' similar IT infrastructure. For either functional linkage or inter-organizational co-operation, firms need to have sufficient IT investment and provide training for employees. Apart from the integrated system at the Automatic Assembling that combines ordering system, production, and client/supplier data-bases, the use of IT for 'process innovation' is relatively rare. IT provides essential support for SMEs' re-engineering. The other technology factors are less important. Financial resources are the main constraint or SMEs. The other resource issues are not as influential on BPR in SMEs. This leads to a revised model to consider BPR in SMEs (Figure 2).

7 CONCLUSION

The motivations and purposes for SMEs to re-engineer may be different from those for larger firms. In SMEs re-engineering is often a response to positive trends - they tend to re-engineer from a position of strength (Kinni 1995). First, small firms are short of the time and resources needed to re-engineer and it is unlikely that a small

Figure 2. Revised model for BPR in SMEs

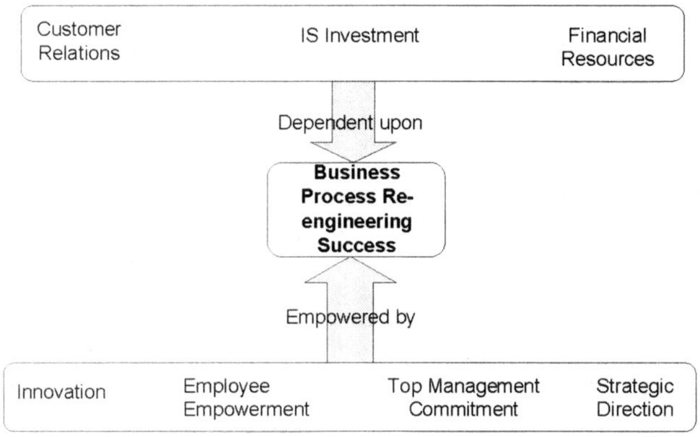

firm that is faltering can muster the required energy. Second, the by-products of success - rapidly increasing volume, straining processes, and increased profits are the impetus for small companies to re-engineer. They need to counter fast growth with processes improvement. Firms pursuing a growth strategy tend to re-engineer in order to enhance their external flexibility, relations with customers and suppliers, and internal efficiency, quality and production.

BPR initiatives are classified by two dimensions: scope and scale (Levene and Braganza 1996). *Scope* includes the number of functions integrated to form the process (Rockart and Short, 1989). *Scale* is the extent of change in terms of how radical the BPR project (Hagel 1993). Davenport and Short (1990) identify types of processes as inter-personal, inter-functional, and inter-organizational. Broadbent et al (1994) contrast approaches to process redesign as simplification and innovation. Based on the strategic nature and radical orientation, Childe et al (1994) depict a spectrum of process improvement activities, from personal/group improvement, quality improvement teams, process simplification, process re-engineering, business integration, to business re-engineering. While Craig and Yetton (1992) argue that process simplification offers firms the potential to capture some performance advantages and to minimize risk factors, higher levels of BPR, such as business integration, involve organizational and job redesign and new developments in IT. The higher levels of BPR are, in turn, viewed as more strategic and radical with the potential for substantial gains. Therefore, BPR projects in SMEs will involve lower scale and less scope, e.g. individual/group improvement and process simplification, as SMEs' policies are more conservative and owners try to avoid risks.

REFERENCES

Alexandre, S. (2006). A gradual approach for software process improvement in SMEs. *Proceeding of 32nd EUROMICRO Conference on Software, Engineering and Advanced Applications*, (pp. 328–335).

Ashima, H. (2010). Essence of software process reengineering in SME's: Towards process customization and automation. *Global Journal of Enterprise Information Systems*, *2*, 2.

Ashton, B., & Stacey, G. (2009). Technical intelligence in business: Understanding technology threats and opportunities. *International Journal of Technology Management*, *10*(1), 79–104.

Brady, A., & Voss, B. (1995). Small is as small does. *The Journal of Business Strategy*, *16*(2), 44–52. doi:10.1108/eb039690

Broadbent, M., Butler, C., & Hansell, A. (1994). A business and technology agenda for Information-Systems executives. *International Journal of Information Management*, *14*(6), 411–426. doi:10.1016/0268-4012(94)90016-7

Cameron, N., & Braiden, P. (2004). Using BPR for development of production efficiency in companies making engineered to order products. *International Journal of Production Economics*, *89*, 261–273. doi:10.1016/S0925-5273(02)00448-6

Carr, D., & Johansson, H. (1995). *Best practices in re-engineering*. New York, NY: McGraw Hill.

Carrier, C. (1995). Intrapreneurship in large firms and SMEs. *International Small Business Journal*, (April-June): 54–61.

Chang, L., & Powell, P. (1998). Toward a framework for business process reengineering in SMEs. *Information Systems Journal*, *8*(3), 199–216. doi:10.1046/j.1365-2575.1998.00035.x

Cragg, P., & King, M. (1993). Small-firm computing: Motivators and inhibitors. *Management Information Systems Quarterly*, (March): 47–60. doi:10.2307/249509

Craig, J., & Yetton, P. (1992). Business process redesign. *Australian Journal of Management*, *17*(2), 285–306. doi:10.1177/031289629301700207

Craig, J., & Yetton, P. (1997). The real event of re-engineering. In C. Sauer., P. Yetton, & Associates (Eds.), *Steps to the future*. San Francisco, CA: Jossey-Bass.

Davenport, T. H. (1993). Need radical innovation and continuous improvement? *Planning Review*, *21*(3), 6–12.

Davenport, T. H., & Short, J. E. (1990). The new industrial engineering. *Sloan Management Review*, *31*, 4–16.

Eisenhardt, K. (1989). Building theories from case research. *Academy of Management Review*, *14*, 532–550.

Ferrell, J. (1996). Help for the other SMEs. *Manufacturing Engineering*, *117*(2), 20.

Galinac, T. (2009). Empirical evaluation of selected best practices in implementation of software process improvement. *Information and Software Technology*, *51*(9), 1351–1364. doi:10.1016/j.infsof.2009.05.002

Girish, H. (2007). Software quality and IS project performance improvements from software development process maturity and IS implementation strategies. *Journal of Systems and Software*, *80*(4), 616–627. doi:10.1016/j.jss.2006.06.014

Grover, V., Jeong, S. R., Kettinger, W., & Teng, J. T. C. (1995). Implementation of business process re-engineering. *Journal of Management Information Systems*, *12*(1), 109–144.

Hagel, J. (1993). Keeping BPR on track. *The McKinsey Quarterly*, *1*, 59–72.

Hale, A., & Cragg, P. (1996). Business process re-engineering in the small firm. *INFOR*, *34*(1), 15–27.

Hammer, M. (1990). Re-engineering work: Don't automate, obliterate. *Harvard Business Review*, *68*(4), 104–122.

Hicks, B., Culley, S., McMahon, C., & Powell, P. (2010). Understanding Information Systems infrastructure in engineering SMEs. *Journal of Engineering and Technology Management*, *27*, 52–73. doi:10.1016/j.jengtecman.2010.03.004

Janson, R. (1993). Technology – Tomorrows determinate. *The Ohio Journal of Science*, *93*(4), 78–82.

Johansson, H. (1993). *BPR: Breakpoint strategies for market dominance*. Chichester, UK: Wiley.

Kinni, T. (1995). Process improvement part 2. *Industry Week*, *244*(4), 45–50.

Larsen, M., & Myers, M. (1999). When success turns into failure: A package-driven BPR project in the financial services industry. *The Journal of Strategic Information Systems*, *8*, 395–417. doi:10.1016/S0963-8687(00)00025-1

Lee, C., & Chen, S. (1992). *The overall environment and the development of Taiwan's SMEs*. Chung-Hua Institution for Economic Research.

Levene, R. J., & Braganza, A. (1996). Controlling the work scope in organisational transformation. *International Journal of Project Management, 14*(6), 331–339. doi:10.1016/0263-7863(96)00048-8

McKeown, I., & Philip, G. (2003). Business transformation, Information Technology and competitive strategies: Learning to fly. *International Journal of Information Management, 23*(1), 3–24. doi:10.1016/S0268-4012(02)00065-8

Montoni, M. (2007). *MPS model and TABA workstation: Implementing software process improvement initiatives in small settings*. 5th International Workshop on Software Quality, (pp. 57-63).

Muscatello, J., Small, H., & Chen, I. (2003). Implementing enterprise resource planning systems in small and midsize manufacturing firms. *International Journal of Operations & Production Management, 23*(8), 850–871. doi:10.1108/01443570310486329

Raymond, L., Bergeron, F., & Rivard, S. (1998). Determinants of BPR success in SMEs. *Journal of Small Business Management, 36*(1), 72–85.

Reijers, H., & Mansor, S. (2005). Best practices in business process redesign: An overview and qualitative evaluation of successful redesign heuristics. *Omega, 33*, 282–306. doi:10.1016/j.omega.2004.04.012

Ribbler, J. (1996). Delivering solutions for the knowledge economy. *On-line, 20*(5), 12-19.

Rockart, J., & Short, J. (1989). IT in the 1990s. *Sloan Management Review, 30*, 7–17.

SBS. (2003). Retrieved from www.sbs.gov.uk/statistics/smedefs.php

Sellers, G. (1997, September). Tools for managing your business process. CMA Magazine, 25-27.

Stevenson, R. (1993). Strategic business process engineering. In Spurr, K., Layzell, P., Jennison, L., & Richards, N. (Eds.), *Software assistance for business re-engineering*. Chichester, UK: Wiley.

Talwar, R. (1993). Business re-engineering. *Long Range Planning, 26*(6), 22–40. doi:10.1016/0024-6301(93)90204-S

Teng, J., Grover, V., & Fiedler, K. (1994). Re-designing business processes using IT. *Long Range Planning, 27*(1), 95–106. doi:10.1016/0024-6301(94)90010-8

Tersine, R., Harvey, M., & Buckley, M. (1997). Shifting organisational paradigms. *European Management Journal, 15*(1), 45–57. doi:10.1016/S0263-2373(96)00073-4

Ursic, D., Anteric, S., & Mulej, M. (2005). Business process re-engineering in practice - A medium-sized Slovenian company in difficulties. *Systemic Practice and Action Research, 18*(1), 89–117. doi:10.1007/s11213-005-2461-9

Wastell, D., White, P., & Kawalek, P. (1994). A methodology for BPR. *The Journal of Strategic Information Systems, 3*(1), 23–40. doi:10.1016/0963-8687(94)90004-3

Webb, B., & Schlemmer, F. (2006). Resilience as a source of competitive advantage for small IT companies. *Transfer and Diffusion of IT for Organizational Resilience: IFIP, 206*, 181–197. doi:10.1007/0-387-34410-1_12

Wind, J., & West, A. (1991). Reinventing the corporation. *Chief Executive*, 72-75.

Witherill, J. W., & Kolak, J. (1996). Is corporate re-engineering hurting your employees? *Professional Safety, 41*(5), 28–32.

Wu, H., & Chou, T. (1992). *Obstacles and reactions of Taiwan's SMEs*. Chung-Hua Institution for Economic Research.

Yin, R. (1994). *Case study research. Design and methods* (2nd ed.). Newbury Park, CA: Sage.

Section 3
Managing People

Chapter 8
Aligning Systems, Structures and People:
Managing Stakeholders in Enterprise Information Systems Projects

Albert Boonstra
University of Groningen, The Netherlands

ABSTRACT

This chapter focuses on how managers and sponsors of enterprise information system (EIS) projects can identify and manage stakeholders engaged in the project. This chapter argues that this activity should go beyond the traditional ideas about user participation and management involvement. Also suppliers, customers, government agencies, business partners, and the general public can have a clear interest in the ways that the system will be designed and implemented. This chapter proposes to apply identification, analysis, and intervention techniques from organization and management disciplines in the IS field to enhance the changes for the successfulness of enterprise information system implementations. Some of these techniques are combined in a coherent method that may help implementers of complex IS projects to identify and categorize stakeholders and to consider appropriate ways of involvement during the various stages of the project.

INTRODUCTION

Information system implementation projects traditionally affect a number of parties, including managers, developers, and users. The notion that managers and developers

DOI: 10.4018/978-1-60960-529-2.ch008

allow users to participate in system development has been a core topic of IS research and practice since the 1960s. Mumford is one of the main advocates of this notion, by arguing that "people at any level in a company, if given the opportunity and some help, can successfully play a major role in designing work systems" (Mumford, 2001, p. 56). Main reasons for participation are the assumed link between participation and system success in terms of system quality, user satisfaction, user acceptance, and system use (Markus & Mao, 2004). Mintzberg (1994) argues that people who have been consulted and have participated in the process will better understand the trade-offs between project benefits and disadvantages and have greater trust. Consequences of neglecting participants, on the other hand, may lead to system failure and resistance towards the system (Gonzalez & Dahanayake, 2007).

During recent decades, however, the traditional notion of users has been eroded by new trends in IS development, such as package installations, outsourcing, enterprise systems, and systems that cross organizational boundaries, and has changed the nature of IS practice. These trends indicate that modern information systems are increasingly complex since they affect a broader range of stakeholders both from within and from outside the organization. This wider group of stakeholders is also becoming an integral part of EIS implementation and is part of the 'sociology of technology.' Depending on the impact and scope of the system, these stakeholders may include suppliers and customers, business partners (such as banks), providers of IS/IT services, competitors, government agencies, and, in some cases, may well extend to the press and the general public. Information systems tend to increase the scope from smaller, internal, and functional areas to enterprise wide systems (such as ERP-systems) and systems that cross company boundaries and may well impact on personnel from different countries, with their own language and different value and legal systems.

This means that system development is increasingly an undertaking where many different people believe that they can affect or can be affected by the process or the outcome of the system. Many of these people will respond to system proposals according to their interests and their perception of the impact, the function and the objectives of the system (Rost, 2004). If project managers and others, responsible for the development and the implementation, are not prepared to take into account these wider requirements, they will be reactive rather than proactive. In such circumstances, as Boonstra (2006) elucidates, the progress will be shattering and shocked by all kinds of unexpected actions and responses from a variety of stakeholders during the various stages of the project.

To take into account such considerations and be proactive, a systematic stakeholder management is needed in the more complicated information system projects. Stakeholder management means that stakeholders around EIS (Enterprise Information System) projects are identified and analyzed so that appropriate actions are taken in ways that support the project (McElroy & Mills, 2003). To address this need for stakeholder management, the objective of this chapter is to propose a coherent set of techniques that can be used to identify and categorize stakeholders and stakeholder relations in EIS projects as well as to define appropriate actions towards stakeholders.

Of course methods exist for stakeholder identification and categorization. However, these methods are diverse in focus and nature and not specified to EIS development and implementation. Some exclusively focus on identification of stakeholders (Vos & Achterkamp, 2006), others on assessing their relative importance (Mitchell, Agle, & Wood, 1997) or on ways to involve them (Bryson, 2004). The contribution of this chapter is that it will specifically focus on stakeholders within complex enterprise IS projects and that it combines various theories and approaches into a practical and consistent method.

The chapter is structured as follows. It begins with some theoretical backgrounds of the stakeholder management approach. This section will briefly discuss literature on stakeholders and its most important findings. The next section discusses the seven activities of the method and combines these activities into a coherent method. The details of the proposed method will be illustrated by a case study. The discussion section examines the extent to which the method contributes to solving the stakeholder identification, categorization and intervention problem in IS contexts. Finally, the conclusion section will discuss the strengths and limitations of the method, by providing some suggestions for further work and by suggesting some guidance for practitioners.

BACKGROUND

Orlikowski (1992) proposes that the results of information systems depend on the interaction of both technology and people over an extended period. Information systems are both a product of human action and an influence of human action. People initiate, design, and use an IT system. Designers construct the system according priorities and expectations. Then, various stakeholders, such as users and managers, react in different ways, for example, by welcoming, rejecting, or adapting it. In doing so, they socially construct the technology in the sense that these reactions may become features of the system. This continuing interaction means that the results eventually obtained are different from those, which were originally expected. Orlikowski also suggests that stakeholders around the system can modify technologies during design, implementation, and use, since people and technology interact. Because of this, information systems are not primarily technical systems but social systems and their design, implementation, and use involve dynamic social and political processes in articulating interests, building alliances, and struggling over outcomes (Levine & Rossmoore, 1994). To understand how a system functions in a business, we must understand the nature of the relationship between various stakeholders and their interactions with the system. Stakeholder management should be based on such an understanding.

According to Mitchell et al. (1997), stakeholders can be defined in many different ways. Different kinds of entities can be stakeholders, such as persons, groups inside as well as outside an organization. Within this research, Freeman's classical definition is a useful starting point. He defines stakeholders as follows: "A stakeholder is any group or individual who can affect or is affected by the achievement of the organization's objectives" (Freeman, 1984, p. 46). In the case of an EIS project, this implies that any person or group who can affect or is affected by the EIS system is a stakeholder. Stakeholders' interests can be very diverse, since information systems affect many aspects of the business, including strategic position, cost-effectiveness, job satisfaction, security, customer satisfaction, and commercial success. This implies that many parties around an EIS project can be stakeholders.

McLoughlin (1999) adds an important perspective to the definition of Freeman by arguing that stakeholders are "those who share a particular set of understandings and meanings concerning the development of a given technology." He emphasizes the interpretive nature of stakeholders. Stakeholders are groups or individuals *who believe* that they can affect or are affected by an information system. This means that stakeholders are determined by perceptions and not by objective realities. This is in line with social constructivist (Pinch & Bijker, 1997) and interpretive (Walsham, 1993) views on reality and technology. Walsham argues that people act according to subjective interpretations of their world, "our knowledge of reality... is a social construction by human actors ... there is no objective reality which can be discovered by researchers and replicated by others" (1993, p.5). Stakeholders interpret the existing context and may act to change it to promote personal, local, or organizational objectives (Boddy, 2004). This implies that stakeholders are potential actors—people or groups with the power to respond to, negotiate with, and change the specifications and eventually impact the success of the system. Project managers and other promoters of new information systems have the responsibility to manage this process of stakeholder activity by creating a context for dealing with stakeholders in effective ways. The method as presented in this chapter is developed to facilitate the creation of this context.

STAKEHOLDER MANAGEMENT ACTIVITIES

Figure 1 briefly describes the method as presented in this chapter by seven activities that can be conducted to form the basis for sound stakeholder management. These activities are 1) identify stakeholders, 2) determine the phase of involvement, 3) determine their roles within the project, 4) determine objects of involvement and related interests, 5) assess the relative importance of stakeholders, 6) determine the degree of involvement, and 7) develop an action plan. Each activity will be explained in more detail in the following paragraphs.

The order of these activities will depend on the preference of the user of the method and the specific project characteristics. The order as presented in Figure 1 can be followed at the start, but often activities have to be reconsidered, given the results of subsequent activities. Mintzberg also argues that stakeholder management should be "... an ongoing and adaptive process ..." (1994, p. 74). Therefore, the activities of stakeholder management are often interactive and dynamic (see Figure 2). When time elapses, stakeholder managers may come to new insights, often caused by unexpected actions of stakeholders or because stakeholders influence each other, which may lead to redoing certain activities and to an adaptation of the action plan to manage stakeholders (Activity 7).

Figure 1. Stakeholder management activities

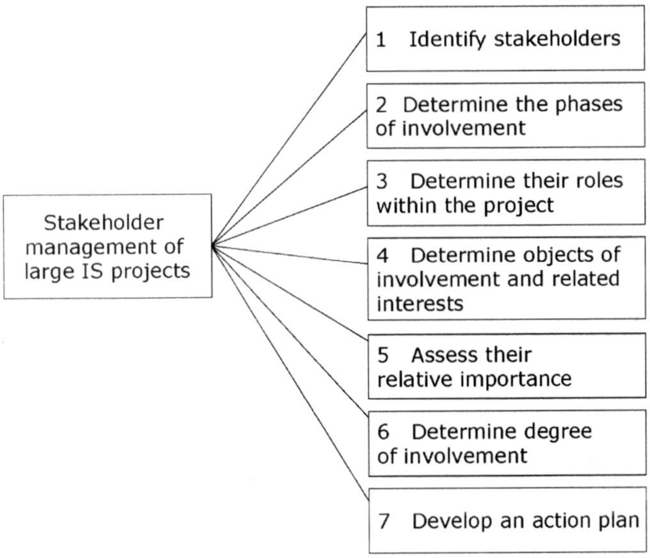

Identify Stakeholders

An important activity of deliberate stakeholder management is to identify relevant players. Identifying stakeholders comes in essence to the question "who are they?" For dealing with this question, stakeholder literature offers a variety of classification models (Mantzana, Themistocleous, Irani, & Morabito, 2007; Mitchell et al., 1997; Pouloudi & Whitley, 1997; Vos & Achterkamp, 2006; Wolfe & Putler, 2002).

Identifying stakeholders around IS means that a stakeholder mapper makes a subjective interpretation about who affects and who will be affected by a new information system. This means that groups or individuals have to be identified and that boundaries have to be drawn. There are various approaches to identify stakeholders, which can be regarded as complementary.

One is to use frameworks (Mantzana et al., 2007), often in the form of checklists relevant to the generic types of stakeholders, such as "customers, suppliers, competitors, users, managers, and developers" (Cummings & Doh, 2000). Such checklists can be adapted to make them more suitable for particular industries, for example, *doctors, patients, pharmacies, pharmaceutical companies*. They can then be used to determine which specific groups of stakeholders are important in relation to the information system. For example, *neurologists, patients with neurological diseases, pharmacy A, Merck*. This way of identifying stakeholders is quite generic but could serve as a useful starting point.

Figure 2. Enterprise information system stakeholder management as an interactive and dynamic activity

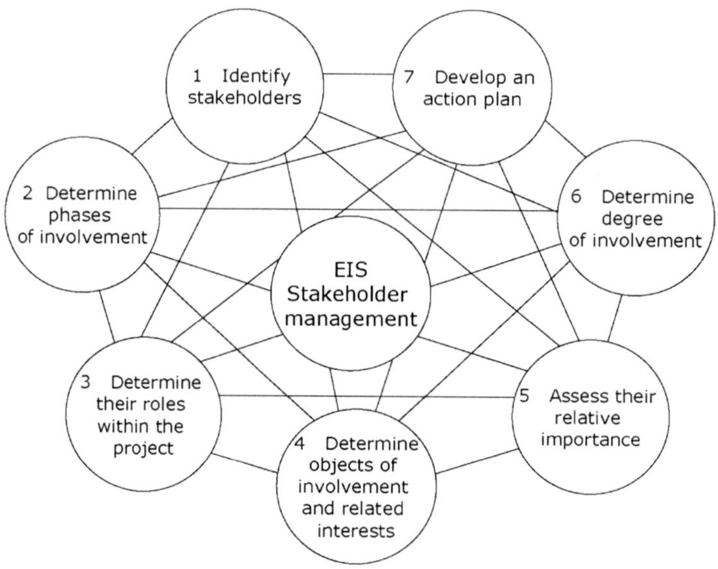

A second approach is posing questions concerning the information system and its nature. Relevant questions that may help to identify relevant groups and individuals in this context are (Cavaye, 1995; Pouloudi & Whitley, 1997):

- Who are the initiators of the system?
- Who are the sponsors of the system?
- Who have to adopt the system and make it work?
- Who are the intended users?
- Who will receive the output of the system?
- Who are the intended developers and operators of the system?
- Who will be impacted and affected by the system?
- Who will win or lose by using the system?

Answers to these questions may reveal stakeholders not yet identified by the first approach or make it possible to refine certain categories of stakeholders into relevant subgroups.

A third approach that complements the other ones is the network approach. In this context, stakeholders are actors in a network because they "perform activities and/or control resources within a certain field" (Håckanson, 1987, p. 14). This approach is very important in the diagnosis of complex information systems, because it focuses on the network of relations within and among organizations. Analyzing these dynamic networks of interactions and activities may help to identify stakeholders and their roles (Walsham, 1993). Network theory also emphasizes the dynamic, flexible, and contextual nature of complex information systems. This implies that it is not possible to draft one static stakeholder map. Stakeholders depend on a specific context that may change in time. In addition, stakeholders are related and may influence each other and therefore they cannot be viewed in isolation. Perceived interests and power of stakeholders are interactive and they may change over time (Pouloudi & Whitley, 1997).

Determine the Phases of Stakeholder Involvement

An information system follows a life cycle that begins when the system is conceived and ends when it is no longer available for use. Various authors have proposed phases that can be distinguished in this life cycle (e.g., Markus. Axline, & Petrie, 2000; Turner, 2006). A typical IS life cycle includes a concept stage, a development stage, an implementation stage, an operation and maintenance stage, and a termination stage. However, in practice, these processes can be quite different and more complicated (Boonstra, 2003). Some information system life cycles can take place in a strict sequential order, sometimes phases will overlap, run in parallel, or be repeated.

Attention for the life cycle in relation to stakeholders is important because it draws attention to the point that stakeholder activity and involvement may differ over different phases. This implies that stakeholder management is a dynamic process since new players may enter the field and others may leave or move to the periphery over time. In the proposed method, these dynamics are explicitly acknowledged. Others authors also stress the dynamic nature of stakeholder identification are Mitchell et al. (1997) and Mantzana et al. (2007). However, they have not made this essential dynamics an integral part of their methods.

During the conceptual phase, a reason for a certain stakeholder to propose the implementation of an information system may be that a system may strengthen its position in the organization or in the value chain, e.g. by providing more reliable information and transparency. Other stakeholders may interpret the availability of such information as a threat. During the development phase, a stakeholders' main concern is to shape the system to fit its interests. The implementation phase can be used by stakeholders to support implementation activities or to hinder these, depending on its specific interests. During the operational phase, the main concern is to align the system with the stakeholders' going concerns. Actions of stakeholders may also vary during the various stages, from dormant to very active and vice versa. For stakeholder managers, this may imply that it can be important to involve stakeholders actively in phases that they are dormant, to prevent for upright opposition during later stages.

Determine Stakeholders' Roles within the Project

Within complex EIS projects, different stakeholders will often have different roles. For an understanding of stakeholder attitudes and responses toward EIS initiatives, it is important to attach such roles explicitly to stakeholders. Roles and responsibilities that people have are a determining factor of attitudes and responses to initiatives and change ideas. Based on Turner (2006), Vos and Achterkamp (2006), and Mantzana et al. (2007), Table 1 lists the possible roles among the stakeholders in EIS projects.

Vos and Achterkamp (2006) also distinguish stakeholders in being directly involved or being represented. In relation to EIS projects, this is relevant since many stakeholders are often represented by others who formally may act on their behalf. In practice, stakeholders can play different roles at the same time and roles also may change in time or during subsequent phases. For example, a project manager of a large information system project can also be business manager who eventually has to work with the system.

Determine Objects of Possible Involvement and Related Interests

Stakeholders are generally interested in certain objects of the system. It is important to identify those objects as well as their interests. Objects can vary from the scope and objectives of the system to programming issues and from security to consequences for work and employment. Zachman (1999) provides a useful contribution for identifying relevant objects of involvement with his work on information system architectures. Based on this work, Table 2 identifies the objects and related issues.

In many EIS projects, decision makers, such as business managers, tend to focus mainly on the first three objects, whereas developers are more directed to objects 3–6. Users, on the other hand, tend to be interested in objects 2–4. For effective stakeholder management, it is important to identify objects that are relevant for each group of stakeholders to keep them interested.

When these objects are identified, it is important to determine the specific interests that are at stake in relation to these objects of the information system. Freeman (1984) uses the term "stake" interchangeably with "interest." Stakes or interests motivate stakeholders and are important determinants of stakeholders' priorities.

Stakeholders do often have different interests and different priorities among shared interests. Interests can also be conflicting (e.g., some stakeholders may be in favor of central decision making, while others may strive towards local autonomy). Besides, it may be possible that certain interests are not realistic, meaning that they cannot be realized by the system. Because of this, stakeholders tend to follow different agendas to achieve their goals.

Examples of interests of stakeholders in enterprise information systems (e.g., Doherty, King, & Al-Mushayt, 2003; Müller & Turner, 2007; Saarinen, 1996; Shenhar, Levy, & Dvir, 1997) are that the system:

Table 1. Stakeholders roles in EIS projects

Owner:	Who provides resources to develop or buy the system;
Project manager:	Who monitors the performance of the project and takes action if the project does not achieve the desired progress;
User:	Who will use the system by entering data or by retrieving information from it;
Developer:	Who designs, develops, or adapts the system; this includes consultants who contribute to the IS project;
Decision maker:	Who will be involved in decisions with regard to the scope and design of the system;
Passively involved:	Who will be affected by the consequences of the system but is not willing or able to play one of the above mentioned roles.

Table 2. Objects and related issues within EIS projects

	Objects	Related Issues
1.	Scope of the system	Goals and business advantages of the system
2.	Business model	Work flow model and business processes
3.	Functioning enterprise	Inputs and outputs of the system
4.	System model	Human interface architecture
5.	Technology model physics	Presentation architecture
6.	Component configuration	Security of the system, compatibility
7.	System Project	Project performance, time, money

- promotes the realization of strategic objectives of the company or the business unit (scope);
- delivers a positive return on investment of the system (scope);
- will strengthen business process performance (business model);
- provides good value and quality of information (functioning enterprise);
- is easy to use and user friendly (system model and presentation architecture);
- promotes work satisfaction (system model);
- promotes employment (functioning enterprise);
- has a good technical performance, maintainability and security (technology model physics);
- project will be completed in time and within budget (system project).

The objects in which stakeholders are interested imply criteria to which they will assess EIS projects. These criteria will often by highly related to the roles that these stakeholders may have (Fowler & Walsh, 1999; Wolfe & Putler, 2002). For example, top managers (a function) will often have roles as owner/decision maker. Given this function and these roles, they will be interested in the objects, scope and business model and will generally assess EIS projects against the criteria strategy, return on investment, business process performance, and project performance. Users of the system, on the other hand, will be focused on objects like business model and functioning enterprise and will be interested in issues like work satisfaction, employment, and user friendliness. If customers of the implementing organization are users (e.g., in case of a Web site for ordering goods or services), they may assess the system against criteria such as compatibility with their own systems, ease of use, and attractiveness of the system compared to those of alternative suppliers. These examples show that it is important to understand the roles that stakeholders play, the objects in which they have an interest, and the specific interests that they may have, as a consequence of those roles.

Assess Their Relative Importance

It is also useful to categorize stakeholders by their relative salience during the various stages of the project. Salience is the degree to which managers may give priority to stakeholder claims. For classifying stakeholders, Mitchell et al. (1997) developed the stakeholder salience model. Stakeholder salience theory (Mitchell et al., 1997) categorizes stakeholders against the possession of three relationship attributes: power, legitimacy, and urgency (see Figure 3).

A group has *power* to the extent it has access to coercive, utilitarian, or normative means for imposing its will in the relationship. *Legitimacy* is a social good and more over-arching than individual self-perception and is shared amongst groups, communities, or cultures. *Urgency* is based on time sensitivity and criticality. Combining these attributes generates eight types of stakeholder: dormant, discretionary, demanding, dominant, dependent, dangerous, definitive, and non-stakeholder (Mitchell et al., 1997). Stakeholder salience theory suggests that the amount of attention attributed to these categories should not be equal and that it can be used to give priority to competing claims of stakeholders.

Determine Degree of Involvement

Promoters of an EIS project should think about a successful project by considering the interests and relative importance of stakeholders to realize a balance of pluralist and sometimes contrasting perceived interests and power. Whether this negotiation is explicit or not, the stakeholders and their interests have to be managed to move forward and to achieve the objectives. Thus, once a decision has been made about involving a stakeholder on a certain object, the degree of involvement should be clarified. Many managers will let this depend on the salience of the stakeholder during a particular phase of the project and the interests, roles and expertise of that stakeholder. Degrees of engagement can vary (Bryson, 2004):

- *inform* (stakeholder is provided with information on the system without further real influence);
- *consult* (stakeholder and project members exchange information and opinions and there is real openness for advice);
- *involve* (stakeholder has a main influence on the development and implementation of one or more objects of the information system);
- *collaborate* (stakeholder becomes co-responsible for the development and implementation of one or more objects of the information system);
- *empower* (stakeholder is responsible for the development and implementation of one or more objects of the information system).

Figure 3. Stakeholder salience model (Mitchell et al., 1997)

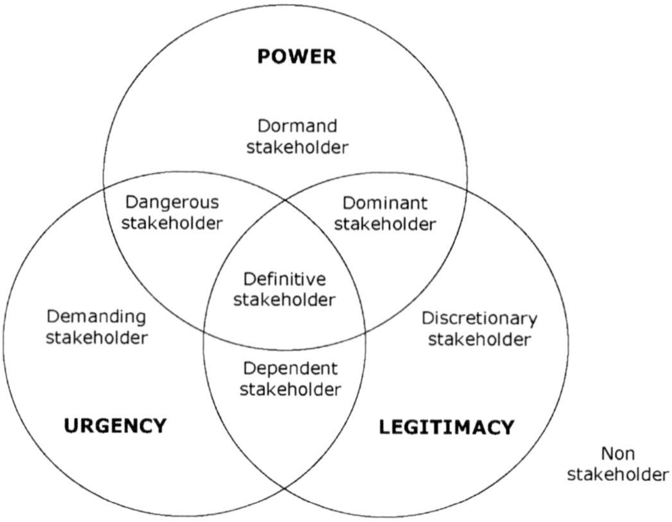

Develop an Action Plan

Based on the activities described above, promoters of the EIS can develop a stakeholder management action plan. Such a plan will normally consist of ideas, structures, and systems of communication and interaction with stakeholders (Cummings & Worley, 2005). It sets out what will be done to engage the various stakeholders of the project in ways that correspond with their roles, interests, and salience. Appropriate ways of communication with the range of stakeholders helps EIS project managers to become sensitive and to know the parties that are supportive and the ones that are indifferent, critical, or opposed to the development and implementation of a new enterprise information system. It also helps the project leader to become credible and to communicate with stakeholders in appropriate ways.

METHOD AND CASE STUDY

Based on these stakeholder management activities a generic form of the systematic stakeholder management approach can be developed (see Table 3). This table can be used to identify stakeholders (column1), to determine in what phases of the project they may play a role (column 2), to determine the roles they have within each phase (column 3), their interests and objects of involvement (column 4), their salience (column 5), and the possible degree of involvement throughout the various phases (column 6).

Based on such an analysis, a specific action plan has to be developed. Table 3 implies that some stakeholders can become participants during certain phases. Participants are subsets of stakeholders who are actually given the chance to participate in concept, development, implementation, or operation activities (Markus & Mao, 2004). Other stakeholders may only be informed or consulted. Some groups may be more able and willing to participate in certain stages than others. Project managers will tend to provide opportunities to participate to the more salient stakeholders (column 5). Involvement and participation activities (column 7) may differ throughout the various phases and can be more and less intensive. Examples of such activities are discussion meetings, requirements generation, testing, training sessions, information sessions, and brainstorming sessions. Various methods and techniques can be used to engage stakeholders, such as working via prototypes, Joint Application Development (JAD), brainstorming sessions, and forums.

The following case study shows how the method has been applied during the development of an electronic patient record in a regional health care system. The description does not intend to provide a complete stakeholder management approach; it only gives an impression of how the method can be used in practice

This electronic patient record was proposed by the management of a large hospital. The system was intended to enable hospital doctors, hospital departments, GPs, and pharmacies to share medical data. Within this concept, authorized users could access patient data from any location, and the system would conduct automated checks for drug and allergy interactions, record clinical notes and prescriptions, schedule appointments, and distribute laboratory data. The hospital's Information Systems (IS) department would manage the system; costs would be shared; and a representative council would provide control. Since the management of the hospital felt that this would be a complex project, not only from a technical viewpoint but also from a contextual perspective, they decided to explore in depth how this context is in terms of stakeholders by using the method as explained above.

Promoters of the system first identified the most relevant stakeholders by using a combination of methods that are described in the previous section. These promoters included a manager of the hospital responsible for information systems, the IS director, and an external consultant. For each stakeholder group, the other cells were also completed, in most cases per phase or per object. This led to a preliminary action plan (column 7 of Table 4 references specific action plans). (Table 4 only shows a part of the table to give an impression of the use of the method.)

Completion of this table led to extensive discussions about the identification of stakeholders (who are they), but also interests, power, roles, and ways to include their interests in the concept and development of the system. During the concept phase, two sessions of 2 hours were held to develop this table and make a first sketch of an action plan (consisting of references to ideas of stakeholder involvement, see

Table 3. Stakeholder management method

1	2	3	4		5	6	7
Stakeholder	**Involvement in phase**	**Roles**	**Objects of involvement & related interests**		**Relative importance**	**Degree of involvement**	**Specific action plan**
Pouloudi & Whitley (1997) Vos & Achterkamp (2006) Bryson (2004) Mantzana et al. (2007)	Markus et al. (2000)Turner (2006)	Turner (2006) Vos & Achterkamp (2006) Mantzana et al. (2007)	Zachman (1999) Shenhar et al. (1997) Saarinen (1996) Doherty et al. (2003) Müller & Turner (2007)		Mitchell et al. (1997)	Burke (1997) Bryson (2004)	Cummings & Worley (2005)
Name of individual, unit, or organization	*Phases:* Concept Development Implementation Operation Maintenance Termination	*Roles:* Owner Project manager User Developer Decision-maker Passively involved Direct involved or Representative	*Objects:* Scope of the system Business model Functioning enterprise System model Technology model physics Component configuration System project	*Interests:* Strategy Return on investment Business process performance Work satisfaction and employment User friendliness Technical performance and security Quality of information Project performance	*Salience is based on:* Legitimacy Urgency Power *Stakeholder can be:* Dormant Discretionary Demanding Dominant Dependent Dangerous Definitive or Non stakeholder	*Modes of Involvement:* Inform Consult Involve Collaborate Empower	

column 7 of Table 4). This plan was used by the project manager, who was appointed at a later stage.

During the use of the method, the project manager discovered that power and interests of some stakeholders were sometimes assessed in ways that proved to be inadequate. In other cases, certain stakeholders received too much attention from the project manager, which led to a degree of influence that did not match with their actual degree of salience. This led to adaptations of the plan throughout the project. During the activity "identification" promoters ignored the general public (and potential patients) and perceived them as "non stakeholders." For that reason, the general public did not have a place in the stakeholder management table and were ignored by the project manager. However, press coverage in a regional newspaper paid attention to the development of an electronic patient record. Based on those articles, a patient organization asked about the reasons for the system and about privacy issues. During an evaluation, project managers agreed that a more pro-active approach to the public by providing information brochures and advertisements would have prepared the public supported the project.

DISCUSSION

The method as described combines various theories and brings them together into a practical approach for managing stakeholder relationships that can be used by managers to consider stakeholders in a systematic manner. The method helps users to link stakeholder identification and analysis with influence and intervention. The method also goes beyond traditional ideas of user participation, since it suggests identifying all affected parties around a project. Using the method raises attention for developing strategies of managing stakeholder relationships: for example, engaging the participation of powerful supportive stakeholders and simultaneously attempting to deal with opponents through processes of negotiation, communication, and education.

It is important to recognize the dynamic nature of the stakeholder map, which means that the actual stakeholder approach has to be reviewed. This is because stakeholders depend on a specific context, which may change over time in ways that are difficult to predict in advance (Pouloudi & Whitley, 1997, p. 5). One reason for this dynamic nature of the stakeholder environment is that stakeholders are often inter-related, and the effects of these relationships are hard to predict. For that reason, it is not possible to design a complete stakeholder map if only the relations between stakeholders and the project are considered and the effects of the project on their mutual relationships are ignored.

In the illustrated case, one specific group of hospital doctors (dermatologists) was not cooperative in the attempt to develop one electronic patient file. They preferred to use their own system. When other specialists became aware of this resistance of the dermatologists, they also tended to become less cooperative. As a consequence, representatives of all specialties had to become involved in the development process, instead of one representative for all. That meant a major change in the stakeholder management process. This example shows how stakeholders can influence each other in unexpected ways, which may have an impact on the development process.

Another reason to review a stakeholder approach is changing circumstances. For example, when project costs or project duration become higher or lower than expected initially, attitudes of stakeholders may change. In the case of the electronic patient file, hospital directors became more critical towards the system once they

Table 4. Stakeholder management plan for electronic patient record system

1	2	3	4		5	6	7
Stakeholder	**Involvement in phase**	**Roles**	**Objects of involvement & related interests**		**Relative importance**	**Degree of involvement**	**Specific action plan**
Hospital directors	Concept	Owner / decision maker	Scope of the system Business model Functioning enterprise	Strategy Return on investment	Definitive	Empower	Ref 1
	Development	Decision maker	Business model Functioning enterprise	Business process performance Project performance	Dominant	Involve	Ref 2
	Implementation		Functioning enterprise	Project performance System use		Consult	Ref 3
	Operation	Passively involved	Functioning enterprise	Quality of information	Dormant	Inform	Ref 4
IS department of hospital	Concept	Passively involved	Business model	Technical feasibility	Demanding	Consult	Ref 5
	Development		System model Technology model physics Component configuration	Technical performance and security	Dependent		Ref 6
	Implementation	Decision maker	System model Technology model physics Component configuration		Definitive	Involve	Ref 7
	Operation	Owner	Functioning enterprise System model Technology model physics Component configuration			Empower	Ref 8
Project manager	Development & implementation	Project manager	System project	Project performance	Dependent	Collaborate	Ref 9
External consultancy	Development	Developer	Business model Functioning enterprise	Business process performance Project performance	Dependent	Collaborate	Ref 10
Hospital doctors	Concept	Decision maker	Scope of the system Business model Functioning enterprise	Quality of work Autonomy Financial consequences Quality of information	Definitive	Involve	Ref 11
	Development		Business model Functioning enterprise				Ref 12
	Implementation	User	Functioning enterprise				Ref 13
	Operation					Collaborate	Ref 14
General practitioners	Concept	Passively involved	Scope of the system Business model	Autonomy Financial consequences Quality of work and information	Discretionary	Inform	Ref 15
	Development						Ref 16
	Implementation	User				Involve	Ref 17

discovered the increasing costs of the development and the growing resistance from many other stakeholders. This led to a review of the relations around the system and to other stakeholder management approaches. The project leader had to "empower" directors again during the development process to make decisions about the further course of actions.

Despite the issues mentioned above it still may be useful to design a preliminary plan on how to deal with stakeholders at the start of an EIS project. Such a plan can be used to establish stable communication structures and to identify the issues to be dealt with as well as the status of the meetings, for instance informative, consulting, or for making decisions.

The method has been applied by more than 50 managers, responsible for IS projects, as well as by general managers who were a decision maker of such projects. During feedback sessions, these managers generally commented that the method helped them to consider the stakeholder environment and stimulated them to think in advance as well as during the project about stakeholders and appropriate actions. However, data analysis about their experiences is not yet sufficiently advanced to evaluate the effectiveness of the method.

FUTURE TRENDS

An agenda for further research can be directed at specifying how certain degrees of stakeholder involvement can lead to effective action plans (Activity 7). The approach as described in this chapter leaves this issue quite open. However, it is very relevant to include effective action plans into the method, which can be related to the various degrees of involvement throughout the various stages of the life cycle. Another interesting piece of future work is to address the question whether stakeholder analysis does help to produce desirable (or better) information systems. Finally, there is limited literature of how stakeholders around information systems are interrelated. Such research should provide suggestions about implications of inter-relatedness for action plans of stakeholder involvement.

CONCLUSION

Since information systems do increasingly affect interests of many parties, it is essential for management to focus on these parties by identifying them and by assessing their interests and their capabilities to influence the design, implementation and use of the proposed system. It is a common mistake to rush the implementation of a complex information system and to ignore the interests of various parties or to take them for granted. This may lead to system failure, troubled relations with parties or other undesirable effects. IS development in complex environments is often a situation where no one is fully in charge and many are involved, affected, or have certain responsibilities (Bryson, 2004). In such a diffuse situation, it is essential to think about policies and actions that promote effective development and implementation activities.

The main contribution of this chapter is that it suggests a practical method that helps managers to identify stakeholders as well as their interests and power and to develop possible actions to involve them or include their interests in the specifications of an information system. Taking deliberate steps to diagnose EIS initiatives and to involve relevant parties and divide benefits among stakeholders prior, during, and after implementation may prevent failure and disappointment. The method may help managers to be sensitive for their environment and to shift from a one dimensional, technological, and linear approach to system development to a multiple perspective assessment.

The method is flexible and acknowledges and addresses the time dimension of stakeholder management. Stakeholders may come and go during the process and interests and power positions may change during the design and implementation process. Because of this, the method should be used on a continuous basis to revise and monitor the positions and interests of stakeholders.

A limitation of the method is that it does not address the philosophies that project managers may have towards stakeholders. Some emphasize normative, moral, or ethical views on stakeholder management (Yuthas & Dillard, 1999; Gibson, 2000), while others hold a more instrumental view that emphasizes a contingent relationship (Donaldson & Preston, 1995). Independent of those views, managers can use the method as an integrated approach that combines theories on stakeholder management and is intended to help implementers and managers think systematically about how to deal with various social groups that affect or are affected by the system. It emphasizes instrumental, pragmatic, opportunistic, as well as normative, views on stakeholder management (Hirschheim & Klein, 1989).

REFERENCES

Achterkamp, M. C., & Vos, F. J. F. (2006). A framework for making sense of sustainable innovation through stakeholder involvement. *International Journal of Environmental Technology and Management*, *6*(6), 525–538. doi:10.1504/IJETM.2006.011895

Boddy, D. (2004). Responding to competing narratives: Lessons for project managers. *International Journal of Project Management*, *22*(3), 225–234. doi:10.1016/j.ijproman.2003.07.001

Boonstra, A. (2003). Structure and analysis of IS decision making processes. *European Journal of Information Systems, 12*(3), 195–209. doi:10.1057/palgrave.ejis.3000461

Boonstra, A. (2006). Interpreting an ERP implementation from a stakeholder perspective. *International Journal of Project Management, 24*(1), 38–52. doi:10.1016/j.ijproman.2005.06.003

Bryson, J. M. (2004). What to do when stakeholders matter. Stakeholder identification and analysis techniques. *Public Management Review, 6*(1), 21–53. doi:10.1080/14719030410001675722

Cavaye, A. L. M. (1995). User participation in system development revisited. *Information & Management, 28*(5), 311–326. doi:10.1016/0378-7206(94)00053-L

Cummings, J. L., & Doh, J. P. (2000). Identifying who matters: Mapping key players in multiple environments. *California Management Review, 42*(2), 83–105.

Cummings, T. G., & Worley, C. G. (2005). *Organization development and change*. Mason, OH: Thomson.

Doherty, N. F., King, M., & Al-Mushayt, O. (2003). The impact of inadequacies in the treatment of organisational issues on Information Systems development projects. *Information & Management, 41*(1), 49–62. doi:10.1016/S0378-7206(03)00026-0

Fowler, A., & Walsh, M. (1999). Conflicting perceptions of success in an information systems project. *International Journal of Project Management, 17*(1), 1–10. doi:10.1016/S0263-7863(97)00063-X

Freeman, R. E. (1984). *Strategic management, a stakeholder approach*. Boston, MA: Pitman.

Gibson, K. (2000). The moral basis of stakeholder theory. *Journal of Business Ethics, 26*(3), 245–257. doi:10.1023/A:1006110106408

Gonzalez, R., & Dahanayake, A. (2007). Responsibility in user participation in information system development. In Khosrow-Pour, M. (Ed.), *Managing worldwide operations and communications with Information Technology* (pp. 849–851). Hershey, PA: IGI Publications.

Håckanson, H. (1989). *Corporate technological behaviour: Co-operation and networks*. London, UK: Routledge.

Hirschheim, R., & Klein, K. (1989). Four paradigms of information system development. *Communications of the ACM, 32*(10), 1199–1217. doi:10.1145/67933.67937

Levine, H. G., & Rossmoore, D. (1994). Politics and the function of power in a case study of IT implementation. *Journal of Management Information Systems, 11*(3), 115–134.

Mantzana, V., Themistocleous, M., Irani, Z., & Morabito, V. (2007). Identifying healthcare actors involved in the adoption of Information Systems. *European Journal of Information Systems, 16*(1), 91–102. doi:10.1057/palgrave.ejis.3000660

Markus, M. L., Axline, S., & Petrie, D. (2000). Learning from adopters experiences with ERP: Problems encountered and success achieved. *Journal of Information Technology, 15*(4), 245–265. doi:10.1080/02683960010008944

Markus, M. L., & Mao, J. Y. (2004). Participation in development and implementation—Updating and old, tired concept for today's IS contexts. *Journal of the Association for Information Systems, 5*(11-12), 514–544.

McElroy, B., & Mills, C. (2003). Managing stakeholders. In Turner, R. J. (Ed.), *People in project management* (pp. 99–118). Aldershot, UK: Gower.

McLoughlin, I. (1999). *Creative technological change*. London, UK: Routledge. doi:10.4324/9780203019870

Mitchell, R. K., Agle, B. R., & Wood, D. J. (1997). Toward a theory of stakeholder identification and salience: Defining the principle of who and what really counts. *Academy of Management Review, 22*(4), 853–886.

Müller, R., & Turner, J. R. (2007). Matching the project managers' leadership style to project type. *International Journal of Project Management, 25*(1), 21–32. doi:10.1016/j.ijproman.2006.04.003

Mumford, E. (2001). Action research: Helping organizations to change. In Trauth, E. (Ed.), *Qualitative research in IS: Issues and trends* (pp. 46–77). Hershey, PA: Idea Group Publishing. doi:10.4018/9781930708068.ch003

Orlikowski, W. J. (1992). The duality of technology: Rethinking the concept of technology in organisations. *Organization Science, 3*(3), 398–427. doi:10.1287/orsc.3.3.398

Pinch, T. J., & Bijker, W. E. (1997). The social construction of facts and artifacts: Or how the sociology of science and the sociology of technology might benefit each other. In Bijker, W. E., Hughes, T. P., & Pinch, T. J. (Eds.), *The social construction of technological systems* (pp. 17–50). Cambridge, MA: MIT Press.

Pouloudi, A., & Whitley, E. A. (1997). Stakeholder identification in inter organisational systems: Gaining insights for drug use management systems. *European Journal of Information Systems*, *6*(1), 1–14. doi:10.1057/palgrave.ejis.3000252

Rost, J. (2004). Political reasons for failed software projects. *IEEE Software*, *21*(6), 104–107. doi:10.1109/MS.2004.48

Saarinen, T. (1996). An expanded instrument for evaluating information system success. *Information & Management*, *31*(2), 103–118. doi:10.1016/S0378-7206(96)01075-0

Shenhar, A. J., Levy, O., & Dvir, D. (1997). Mapping the dimensions of project success. *Project Management Journal*, *28*(2), 5–13.

Turner, J. R. (2006). Towards a theory of project management: The nature of the project. *International Journal of Project Management*, *24*(2), 1–3. doi:10.1016/j.ijproman.2005.11.008

Vos, F. J. J., & Achterkamp, M. C. (2006). Stakeholder identification in innovation projects: Going beyond classification. *European Journal of Innovation Management*, *9*(2), 161–178. doi:10.1108/14601060610663550

Walsham, G. (1993). *Interpreting Information Systems in organizations*. Chichester, UK: John Wiley & Sons.

Wolfe, R. A., & Putler, D. S. (2002). How tight are the ties that bind stakeholder groups? *Organization Science*, *13*(1), 64–80. doi:10.1287/orsc.13.1.64.544

Yuthas, K., & Dillard, J. F. (1999). Ethical development of advanced technology: A postmodern stakeholder perspective. *Journal of Business Ethics*, *19*(1), 35–49. doi:10.1023/A:1006145805087

Zachman, J. A. (1999). A framework for information systems architecture. *IBM Systems Journal*, *38*(2/3), 454–471. doi:10.1147/sj.382.0454

Chapter 9
People-Oriented Business Processes

Giorgio Bruno
Politecnico di Torino, Italy

ABSTRACT

Current notations and languages do not emphasize the participation of users in business processes and consider them essentially as service providers. Moreover, they follow a centralized approach as all the interactions originate from or end in a business process; direct interactions between users cannot be represented. What is missing from this approach is that human work is cooperative, and that cooperation takes place through structured interactions called conversations. However, the problem of effectively integrating conversations and business processes is still open, and this chapter proposes a notation called POBPN (People-Oriented Business Process Notation) and a perspective, referred to as conversation-oriented perspective, for its solution.

INTRODUCTION

In general, the notion of process denotes a standard way to achieve a given goal. It is a result coming from experience and investigation. It can be applied to the action of a single individual or to the actions of a community; the latter case is particular relevant when business systems are addressed and, in this context, processes are referred to as business processes.

DOI: 10.4018/978-1-60960-529-2.ch009

If the community involved belongs to the same organization, business processes are usually inspired to a centralized perspective: they present the viewpoint of a central authority having the power of distributing the work to the members of the organization. A business process is then a global model of work, i.e., a centralized description of the units of work (called tasks or activities) to be carried out by the various members subdivided in roles.

Tasks fall into two categories: human tasks (also called user tasks) are those performed by human participants playing suitable roles (associated with the tasks), while automated ones are implemented by services.

In the context of Process-Aware Information Systems or PAIS (Dumas, van der Aalst & ter Hofstede, 2005), tasks are meant to operate on the business entities residing in the underlying information system, and they are carried out by participants through graphical user interfaces.

From a technological point of view, tasks and process descriptions need different implementation tools: process descriptions are handled by process engines, while tasks are mapped into enterprise application software. The contact point is provided by todo lists, through which participants receive work from the process engine.

As the tasks are developed separately from the processes, current notations and languages, e.g. BPMN (OMG, 2008) and BPEL (OASIS, 2007), consider business processes essentially as orchestrators of work, which accomplish this function by means of interactions with external tasks; it makes little difference if the interaction is directed to a human task or to an automated procedure. This approach, referred to as orchestration-oriented perspective, makes the representation more homogeneous but at the expense of handling human activities as a special case of automated ones. If people are involved, they are considered as service providers. Moreover, each interaction that logically takes place between two users, say, A and B, such as A asking B for the approval of a certain request, is mediated by the process and therefore it results in two sequential actual interactions, the first between A and the process and the second between the process and B.

What is missing from the orchestration-oriented perspective is that, in most cases, human work is cooperative and therefore human activities are not performed in isolation but in structured frameworks referred to as conversations (Winograd & Flores, 1986). Conversations are the basis of the language/action perspective or LAP (Weigand, 2006), which was proposed for the design of information systems and business processes.

An example of conversation is the one governing the approval of a purchase requisition (PR). It takes place between two users, denoted as requester and approver: the former is the initiator and the latter is the follower of the conversation. The requester starts the conversation by sending a PR to the approver, who evaluates the PR and sends it back to the requester with three alternative outcomes, i.e. "accepted", "rejected" or "to be revised". In the first two cases, the conversation ends, in the third one the conversation continues and the requester may withdraw the PR or submit a revised version. In the latter case, the approver is expected to re-evaluate the revised version and to provide the final outcome ("accepted" or "rejected").

If user tasks are abstracted away, a conversation consists of a number of interactions organized in a control flow specifying their sequence. Interactions are defined in terms of three major attributes: name (embodying the interaction meaning, e.g. "request", "acceptance" or "rejection"), direction (i.e. initiator-follower or follower-initiator) and the business entity conveyed by the interaction (such as a PR). If the business entities are left unspecified, what remains is the flow that characterizes a particular kind of conversation. This flow, referred to as conversation protocol, is a template which can be specialized by providing the actual types of the business entities exchanged.

Several modeling approaches based on LAP have been proposed (a short survey is given in the next section); however they mainly focus on the nature of the underlying interactions and do not provide an adequate solution to the integration of conversations and business processes. This integration is a major purpose of this chapter, which proposes a notation called POBPN (People-Oriented Business Process Notation) and a perspective referred to as conversation-oriented perspective.

In POBPN the top-level representation of a business process clearly separates the contribution of the users involved (in terms of their roles) from that of the automatic activities. The roles participating in the process appear as building blocks and their refinement (in second-level models) is given as a combination of the conversations they are involved in. Such conversations are actualizations of standard conversation protocols obtained by providing the actual types of the business entities exchanged during the interactions. These types come from an information model that complements the process model: this way the behavioral aspects embodied in a business process are integrated with the informational aspects provided by the companion information model. The automatic activities are meant to support the conversations for which the process itself plays the initiator role or the follower one; in the top-level representation of a business process, they are represented by a specific building block, called System.

The RAD approach (Ould, 2005) is based on interacting roles as well, but these roles encompass tasks and control flow activities, while, in POBPN, roles are based on conversations.

This chapter is organized as follows. First, a discussion on the major limitations of the orchestration-oriented perspective is presented and then conversation protocols are introduced. Subsequent sections illustrate the proposed notation, POBPN, with the help of an example. Finally, the differences between the conversation-oriented perspective and the orchestration-oriented one are discussed.

BACKGROUND

Business processes can be addressed with different orchestration-oriented notations, such as BPMN (OMG, 2008) and UML activity diagrams (OMG, 2007); however they all have a number of features in common, as follows. They place great emphasis on the control flow of business processes, on the basis of research on workflow patterns (van der Aalst, ter Hofstede, Kiepuszewski & Barros, 2003); in contrast, they overlook the information flow (although information items can be included for documentation purposes) and tend to incorporate user tasks as execution steps in the process structures.

In particular, BPMN provides building blocks to represent the actual user tasks. Such building blocks can be placed in swim lanes associated with the roles needed; from an operational point of view, they enable the process to activate a user task, by sending it input information along with the indication of the actual performer(s) required, and then to wait for output information, which notifies the completion of the user task.

This approach, being an attempt at incorporating user tasks in the process structure, does not cope with all the situations taking place in practical applications. It only covers one interaction pattern between a process and a user task, i.e. the one in which the user task receives one input message (on its activation) and delivers one output message (on its completion); this pattern is referred to as (1, 1). There are three more task interaction patterns, as follows.

Pattern (1, *) indicates that the task sends a number of intermediate output messages before the completion one. These additional output messages signify that the task has produced information items requiring immediate attention. For example, task "reviewPapers" is started on the arrival of a folder of papers to be reviewed and allows the reviewer to release the reviews one by one.

Pattern (*, 1) indicates that the task may receive additional input messages, after its activation. For example, task "assignPapers" is activated with an initial group of papers and then it may receive additional papers, before its completion.

The fourth pattern (*, *) denotes both a flow of input messages and a flow of output ones. For example, task "evaluatePapers" receives a flow of reviews and provides a flow of papers evaluated, each of which will trigger an immediate notification to its author.

In order to overcome the above-mentioned limitations, the process, instead of incorporating the user tasks in its control flow, should emphasize the underlying interactions taking place with them.

The notion of interaction is important because it leads to a clear separation between processes and user tasks; however, interactions are part of larger structures encompassing all those exchanged between two parties for a common purpose. At this point, the notion of conversation comes into play.

Winograd and Flores (1986) introduced the term "conversation for action" to indicate the kind of conversation aimed at producing an effect on the real world through the cooperation of two parties. Taking advantage of the theory of speech acts (Austin, 1976), which studies how people act through language, they proposed a novel perspective, referred to as language/action perspective (LAP), for the design of information systems and business processes. Conversations may be carried out for different purposes: Winograd (1987-1988) mentions conversations for clarification, for possibilities and for orientation in addition to conversations for action.

Several modeling approaches based on LAP have been proposed, among which stand out Action Workflow, DEMO and BAT.

In the Action Workflow approach (Medina-Mora, Winograd, Flores R. & Flores F., 1992), a typical conversation takes place between a requester and a performer and is made up of four major phases, i.e. request, commitment, performance and evaluation, forming the so-called "workflow loop". The first two phases establish a commitment between the parties and the last two phases bring the parties to an agreement on the result. The actual workflow might be complicated because negotiations can be made in each phase.

In the DEMO approach (Dietz, 2006), workflow loops are subdivided in three phases, i.e. order, execution and result, and are encapsulated in transactions. Business processes are compositions of roles and transactions, where transactions connect two transactional roles. Transactional roles are compound entities including transactional tasks (i.e. the tasks being part of the transactions the role is involved in) and the control-flow logic handling their ordering. In the hierarchical structure provided by DEMO, tasks are compared to atoms, transactions to molecules and business processes to fibers (Dietz, 2003). Transactional roles might not have a one-to-one mapping to organizational roles, because the tasks included in a transactional role might be assigned to different organizational roles: this is needed to support delegation (i.e., the situation in which the actor who receives the order is not the one who delivers the result) but could make the model more difficult to understand.

BAT (Goldkuhl & Lind, 2004) draws upon the ideas of Action Workflow and DEMO and addresses business interactions in an inter-organizational framework. In particular, it analyzes the relationships between a supplier and a customer in a number of situations including single business transactions and frame contracting (with embedded transactions).

While the above-mentioned LAP approaches yield a deeper understanding of the nature of interactions, they do not provide an operational solution to the integration between business processes and user tasks through conversations. This integration is pursued by the conversation-oriented perspective illustrated in the next sections along with the related notation, POBPN.

CONVERSATION PROTOCOLS

This section illustrates the notion of conversation protocol and shows the notation adopted in POBPN, with the help of a number of examples to be reused in the next sections.

A conversation implies a flow of interactions between two parties, an interaction being the communication of one party's intention to the other party. Intentions can be categorized and identified by specific symbols, as illustrated later on in this section. Examples of intentions are making a request, accepting a request, and providing a reply. An interaction conveys the business entity that is the object of the intention. This business entity is referred to as the business content of the interaction.

Conversations can be categorized on the basis of their purpose: for example, there are conversations for approval and conversations for action. If the details of the business content are ignored, all the conversations with the same purpose turn out to have the same interaction flow, and the structure of this flow, called conversation protocol, is the major concern of this section.

A conversation protocol is an abstraction as it is defined independently of the types of the business entities exchanged by the parties; it is a template in which such types are given generic names. When a protocol is actualized, generic types will be replaced with actual types: as will be shown in the next section, an actualized protocol relies on an information model providing the definition of the types of the business entities involved.

State models are often used to define conversation protocols graphically (Winograd, 1987-1988). POBPN, instead, adopts UML sequence diagrams (OMG, 2007), because they focus on the essential elements, i.e., the interactions, while providing a simple hierarchical structuring mechanism based on fragments.

Four examples of protocols are shown in Figure 1.

As a general rule, the lifelines of the two actors involved in the conversation are not shown; however, the initiator is meant to be located on the left side of the diagram and the follower on the right side. The first interaction of a conversation is called initial interaction and the business entity that it conveys is referred to as initial business entity. Timing constraints are not considered so as to keep the examples reasonably simple.

The first protocol in Figure 1 addresses conversations for approval and is called "Approval conversation protocol" (ApprovalCP in short). These conversations start with a request, indicated by symbol "r"; the business content, i.e., the entity for which

Figure 1. Examples of conversation protocols

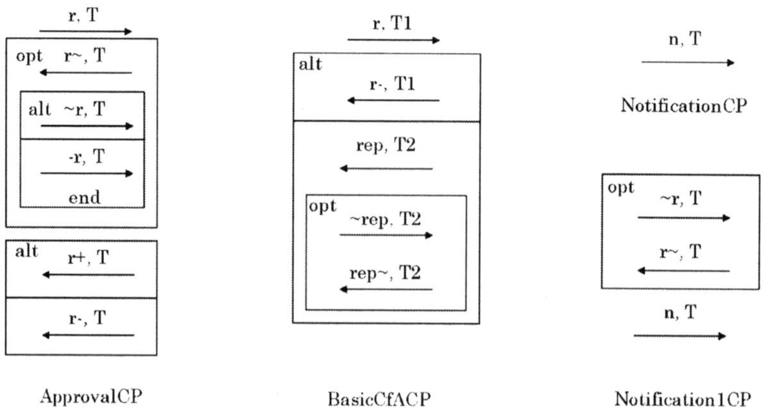

the approval is asked, is denoted by a generic type, such as "T". The follower can accept the request (r+), reject it (r-) or ask for some improvement (r~). In the first two cases, the conversation is ended; in the third one, the initiator can then withdraw the request (-r) thus ending the conversation or they can submit a revised version (~r) which will be followed by an acceptance (r+) or a rejection (r-). In the sequence diagram, the request for improvement is handled in an optional fragment (marked with "opt") following the initial interaction; the "end" appearing after interaction -r signifies that the conversation is ended. Alternative flows of interactions are placed in the partitions of alternative fragments (marked with "alt").

There is only one generic type involved, T, because the business entities exchanged during this kind of conversation are meant to be all of the same type.

Protocol BasicCfACP defines simple conversations for action. As in the first example, the conversation is started with a request (r) coming from the initiator. The follower may reject the request (r-) or may provide a reply. The interaction conveying the reply is indicated with a specific keyword, "rep". It is accompanied by a different business entity, denoted by generic type T2, because the purpose of a conversation for action is to make the follower deliver a new entity as the result of the action caused by the initiator's request. Upon receiving the reply, the initiator may then ask for a clarification (~rep) to be followed by a clarification (rep~) after which the conversation is ended. The sequence of interactions ~rep and rep~ is optional.

The protocol of conversations for action can become more complicated if counter-offers are included (Winograd, 1987-1988).

Protocol NotificationCP consists of one interaction (n), interpreted as a notification (i.e., a simple communication requiring no reply).

Protocol NotificationCP1 ends in a notification, which may be preceded by an optional sequence consisting of a request for clarification (~r) followed by a clarification (r~).

AN EXAMPLE OF PEOPLE-ORIENTED BUSINESS PROCESS

As mentioned in the introduction, the conversation-oriented perspective places great emphasis on the participation of users in business processes, and the notation proposed, POBPN, aims at providing an effective integration between conversations and business processes. In order to clarify the features of POBPN, an example concerning a business process handling purchase requisitions (PRs) is worked on in this section and in the following ones. The process is referred to as PRBP and its requirements are as follows.

PRs are submitted by users entitled to do so; such users play the Requester role with respect to process PRBP. When a PR is submitted, it may be automatically approved or it may be sent for evaluation to the appropriate supervisor. The first case occurs when the amount of the PR is less than the personal expenditure threshold associated with the requester; in this case, the PR is considered to be an "inexpensive" one. When the second case occurs, the (expensive) PR is directed to the requester's boss (who becomes the supervisor involved). The requester is informed of the result (acceptance or rejection). The supervisor may also ask for some improvement and the requester may provide a revised version of the PR or may withdraw it.

The PRs approved are sent to the purchasing department where they are handled by a number of equivalent buyers. Buyers are assumed to pick pending PRs from a common queue and to include them in purchase orders. In case a buyer has some doubts, they can ask the PR requester to make the necessary clarification; when a buyer has included the PR in a purchase order, they send a confirmation to the PR requester.

Sometimes supervisors may ask one or more reviewers to provide third-party reviews of PRs considered to be critical. How this is done can be subjected to different rules: in this case study, the conversation related to a single review is expected to conform to conversation protocol BasicCfACP shown in Figure 1. In addition, if a supervisor has started a review conversation for a certain PR, they must wait for its conclusion before starting a new review conversation for this PR or taking the final decision.

The analysis of the requirements above leads to the discovery that five roles are involved. Four of them are user roles: Requester, Supervisor, Reviewer and Buyer. The fifth role involved, the System role, is responsible for all the activities to be performed automatically (such as the approval of inexpensive PRs). These roles take part in several conversations, as follows. For the approval of a PR, its requester interacts with either his/her supervisor or the System; in order to get support for a critical PR, a supervisor may interact with a number of reviewers. When processing a PR, a buyer interacts with the PR requester (at least to notify him/her that the PR has been included in a purchase order). In addition, since approved PRs need to be processed by the purchasing department, notifications are sent by the System to the buyers.

The above-mentioned four conversations fit the patterns presented in the previous section, however it is necessary to indicate which business entities are involved. An information model is then needed, which defines the business entity types along with their most relevant attributes and relationships. This information model is the companion of the process model for two major reasons: firstly, the actualization of conversation protocols into actual conversation types is carried out by replacing the generic types used in the protocols with the actual types included in the information model. Secondly, in the process model there are a number of data-driven aspects, such as the selection of a conversation follower (to be illustrated later on in this section), and they can be adequately expressed only if an information model is provided.

The companion information model for process PRBP is shown in Figure 2 as a UML class model (OMG, 2007). Only the major items are considered, for the sake of simplicity.

Users are represented by classes marked with stereotype <<role>>. Such classes are not meant to be the actual ones, because the decision on how to represent users in the information system is postponed to the software development phase; they can be considered as interfaces to the actual classes.

Figure 2. The companion information model of process PRBP

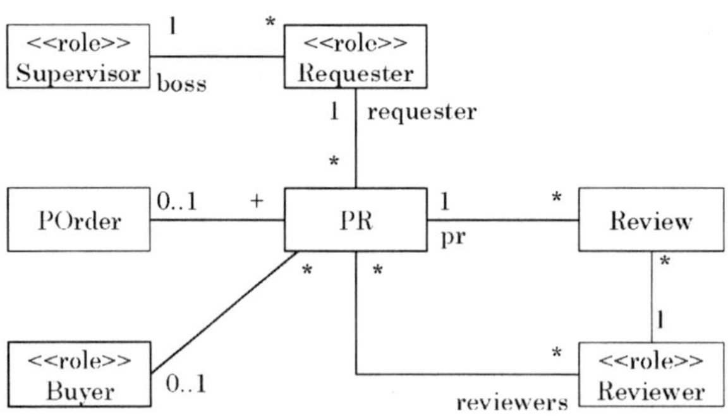

Attributes

PR: float amount. Requester: float threshold.

The relationship between role Requester and role Supervisor is a consequence of the requirement that an expensive PR has to be approved by the requester's boss, who acts as the supervisor for the PR. Associative attribute "boss" enables the navigation from a requester entity to the corresponding supervisor entity.

A PR is related to one requester entity (which can be reached through associative attribute requester) and possibly to one buyer entity (only in case the PR has been approved). A PR may also be linked to one purchase order (in case it has been approved), to a number of reviewers as well as to a number of reviews. A review is linked to the reviewer entity representing the reviewer who has provided it. Associative attribute "pr" denotes the PR associated with a given review. Relationships PR-Review and PR-Reviewer are both needed in that a reviewer could refuse to provide the review they have been asked for. Associative attribute "reviewers" indicates the list of Reviewer entities associated with a given PR. Purchase Orders are represented by class POrder.

Two relevant attributes are also shown in Figure 2, because they are mentioned in the requirements of PRPB: the amount attribute in PR entities and the threshold (for expenditure) attribute in Requester entities.

On the basis of the analysis made so far, the model of process PRBP can be worked out. Its top-level portion is presented in Figure 3 and consists of three parts: the process diagram, the section defining conversation types and the one (Links) showing how the followers of the conversations will be determined.

The approach adopted in POBPN is to represent participating roles as the top-level building blocks (referred to as role participations or simply participations) of

Figure 3. The top-level representation of process PRBP

Conversation types:

a: ApprovalCP (T = PR); b: NotificationCP (T = PR);

c: Notification1CP (T = PR); v: BasicCfACP (T1 = PR, T2 = Review);

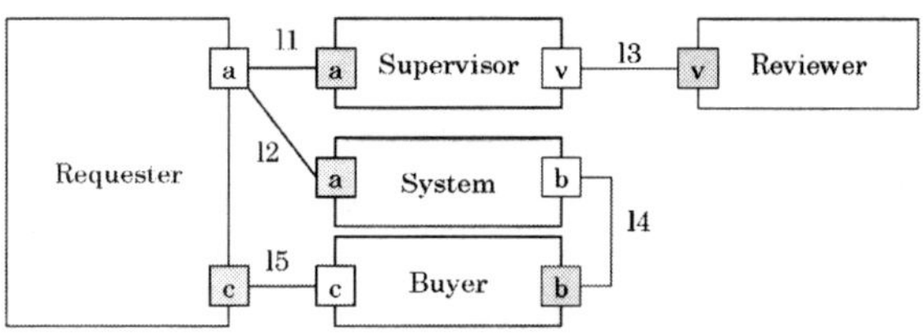

Links:

l1 (PR pr): [pr.amount > pr.requester.threshold] pr.requester.boss.

l2 (PR pr): [pr.amount <= pr.requester.threshold].

l3 (PR pr): pr.reviewers.last(). l5: (PR pr): pr.requester.

the process diagram and to show the conversations involved as ports, depicted as small squares on the participation icons. Each conversation gives rise to two ports, one in the initiator role (referred to as initiator port) and the other in the follower role (follower port). Such ports are given identical names but different colors; initiator ports are white, while follower ones are grey. Ports are connected through labeled links, whose details are shown in the Links section. The port names are names of conversation types.

Section "Conversation types" declares conversation type "a" to be based on conversation protocol ApprovalCP in which generic type T is replaced with entity type PR, while conversation types "b", "c", and "v" are actualizations of protocols NotificationCP, Notification1CP and BasicCfACP, respectively.

Section "Links" contains a number of link definitions, whose purpose is to show how the followers of the corresponding conversations are determined.

A link definition consists of four elements: name, formal parameter, guard (included between square brackets) and follower clause. The formal parameter refers to the initial business entity, i.e. the entity conveyed by the initial interaction. In all the definitions shown, the initial business entity is a purchase requisition (whose type is PR) and the formal parameter introduces the name, pr, used to refer to this entity, in the guard and in the follower clause of the link definitions.

A conversation of type "a" is initiated by a requester and may be followed by a supervisor or by the System. There are two links in competition, l1 and l2, because they have the initiator port in common: the choice is made on the basis of their guards.

The guard of l1, "pr.amount > pr.requester.threshold", consist of two terms, "pr. amount" and "pr.requester.threshold". The evaluation of the first term returns the amount of the current PR, and the evaluation of the second one gives the personal expenditure threshold of the PR requester: if the guard is true, the follower will be the requester's boss.

In most cases, the follower of a conversation is represented by a business entity related, through a certain path of associations, to the initial business entity: then, the follower clause consists of a navigational expression indicating how to reach the follower business entity from the initial one. Two associative attributes are involved in the follower clause of l1, i.e., requester and boss: in the information model shown in Figure 2, they determine a path from a PR to a Supervisor entity.

In the definition of link l2, the follower clause is missing, because the follower role is System: when the guard of l2 is true, the conversation is followed by automatic activities and no supervisor is involved.

The definition of link l4 is missing because both the guard and the follower clause are not needed. In general, when the follower clause is missing and the follower role is a user role, such as Buyer in link l4, the assignment of a particular follower will take place at run-time; it is up to the members of the role to decide which of them will follow a new conversation, as it happens with buyers who autonomously pick pending PRs from a common pool. In general, the selection of the performer is a critical issue and several patterns have been proposed (Russell, van der Aalst, ter Hofstede & Edmond, 2005).

The follower clause in link l3 specifies that the reviewer to be involved is the last added to the collection of reviewers associated with the PR that started the conversation. Before starting a conversation with a reviewer, a supervisor has to establish an association between the business entity representing the reviewer and the PR: this newly generated association determines the follower of the intended conversation. Link l5 indicates that the follower is the requester of the current PR.

It is now common opinion that business processes and information systems are two complementary aspects on which the operation of modern enterprises and organizations is based (Dumas, van der Aalst, & ter Hofstede, 2005). For this reason, recent research is aimed at leveraging their interrelations (Kumaran, Liu & Wu, 2008). In POPBN information models play a central role as shown by the above-mentioned follower rules.

Process diagrams are mainly architectural models, as they show the roles participating in the process and the conversations that may take place between them. Participation building blocks can be refined into second-level models, called participation models, and the next section is dedicated to their illustration.

PARTICIPATION MODELS

Participation models define the involvement of the users (identified by their roles) or the contribution of the System, in the business process being considered. Those related to users are called user participation models and fulfill two major aims: firstly, by looking at them, users get an insight into the overall sequence of interactions they will be involved in; secondly, they are the basis of the implementation of the actual user tasks.

The System participation model (there is at most one in a business process) is mainly meant to handle the automatic activities.

Both types of models are described in this section and the examples given refer to process PRBP: its user participation models are shown in Figure 4.

Basically, user participation models are combinations of conversations. For this reason, their structure is like the one of conversation protocols with interactions replaced by references to conversation types. Such references are placed in constructs similar to the "InteractionUse" items available in UML sequence diagrams (OMG, 2007); however, in POBPN they are called "ConversationUse" items, since their meaning is different. In these items, the conversation type name appears in a small rectangle at the upper left corner: the rectangle is white or grey depending on whether the current role is the initiator or the follower, respectively.

The Reviewer participation model is based only on conversation “v”, and reviewers are followers of such conversations.

The Buyer participation model is a simple sequence of conversations “b” and “c”; buyers are followers of conversations “b” and initiators of conversations “c”.

The Requester participation model is based on conversation “a”, which, if it ends successfully (i.e., if it ends in r+), is followed by conversation “c”. In the optional fragment, operator opt is followed by an informal expression describing when conversation “c” is carried out.

An important feature of user participation models is the ability of structuring conversations hierarchically, as shown in the Supervisor participation model. According to the PRBP requirements presented in the previous section, a supervisor, during conversation “a”, and precisely after receiving a new PR or a revised one, may carry out a number of sequential conversations “v”. What is needed is the possibility of including a number of conversations “v” into a conversation “a”. The original conversations are not modified, but they are combined so as to define the overall behavior of the role. POBPN supports the nesting of ConversationUse items, as follows. ConversationUse items are not black boxes, but they can include one or more extensions. An extension is a partition made up of two parts: the first part shows the interaction(s) preceding the extension (referred to as extension points), and the second part contains the conversations (represented by their ConversationUse items) to be carried out before resuming the enclosing conversation. If the enclosed conversations are subjected to constraints, they are placed in appropriate fragments. The Supervisor participation model extends conversation “a”: the extension points are interactions “r” or “~r” (referring to the receipt of a new PR or of a revised one,

Figure 4. The user participation models in process PRBP

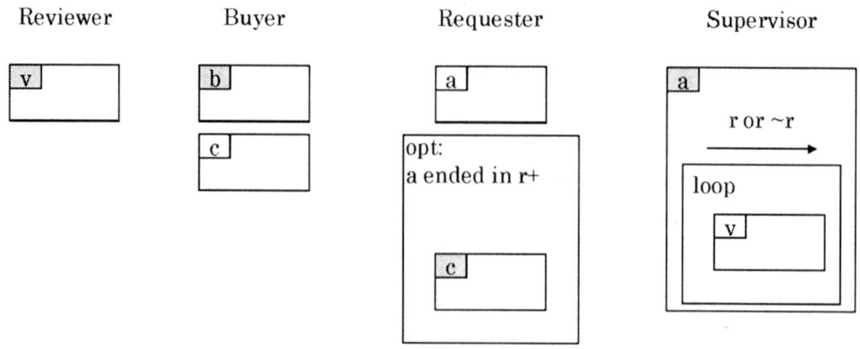

respectively), which are followed by a loop fragment including conversation "v". The loop operator introduces a sequence (possibly empty) of conversations "v".

The System participation model addresses those conversations for which the process itself plays the initiator role or the follower one. In PRBP there are two such conversations: the process is the follower of conversations "a" for inexpensive PRs and the initiator of conversations "b". The related interactions must be dealt with by means of automatic activities and, moreover, control-flow logic is needed to enforce ordering constraints between the activities.

The notation used in System participation models is different from the one adopted in user participation models and follows an orchestration-oriented perspective. The System participation model for the case study is shown in Figure 5.

The orchestration-oriented notation used in POBPN is an extension of colored Petri nets (Kristensen, Christensen & Jensen, 1998) and is called "interaction nets" to emphasize that its major purpose is to handle interactions, on which, as a matter of fact, orchestrations are based.

This chapter does not provide a formal definition of interaction nets; instead, it provides a number of examples, the first of which, shown in Figure 5, defines the System participation model in process PRBP.

Interaction nets are made up of places, transitions, arcs and interaction symbols.

Places are containers of tokens, which refer to business entities, such as PRs. They have a name and a label (the place type): the former is written in the circle representing the place and the latter outside the circle and close to it. The label is the name of the type of the business entities that are referred to by the tokens contained in the place. The business entity types are those defined in the companion information model of the process being considered; the one related to process PRBP is shown in Figure 2. This solution eliminates the need for complex data patterns (Russell, ter Hofstede, Edmond & van der Aalst, 2005) as all the data needed are associated with the tokens: as a matter of fact, the information flow is integrated with the control flow.

Places may have input arcs and output ones: the input arcs of a place come from its input transitions and the output ones are directed to its output transitions. Transi-

Figure 5. The system participation model in process PRBP

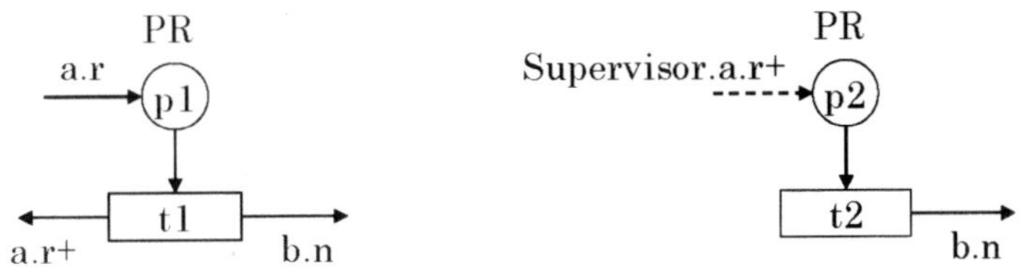

tions have input arcs and output ones, as well: the input arcs of a transition come from its input places and the output ones are directed to its output places.

Tokens are added to places by their input transitions and are removed by their output transitions; they can also be added by followed interactions as described later on in this section.

Transitions are the automatic activities performed by the process; they are token-driven as they are activated when the proper tokens are available in their input places. The basic rule is that a transition fires as soon as there is one token in each of its input places. When it fires, a transition takes the input tokens (i.e., it removes the activating tokens from the corresponding input places), performs an action (which can operate on the business entities referred to by the input tokens) and delivers the appropriate (output) tokens to its output places. When there is a correspondence between the types of the input places and those of the output places, tokens are moved from the input places to the output ones: this behavior is referred to as automatic propagation rule. In the other cases, the output tokens must be generated in the action.

The behavior of transitions can be complemented by a textual description that is made up of two sections, i.e., the precondition (introduced by keyword "p") and the action (introduced by keyword "a"). These sections may include operational code, but the examples shown only include informal descriptions, for the sake of simplicity. Preconditions serve two purposes: one is to make the firing of a transition depend on the contents of the business entities linked to its input tokens, and the other is to select the suitable input tokens from the input places. In the first case, preconditions act as guards and they are used with conflicting transitions in order to determine which of them has to be performed; in the second case, they provide a selection mechanism for the tokens to be acted on by transitions.

If a transition has no precondition, the basic rule is applied.

Interaction symbols are depicted as labeled arcs, which may be either input arcs of places or output arcs of transitions. They represent ordinary interactions or monitored ones.

Ordinary interactions are those in which the process is directly involved and may be divided into followed interactions and initiated ones. Their labels, such as "a.r", consist of the names of a conversation type and of an interaction belonging to that conversation type, separated by a dot. The conversation types correspond to the names of the ports that appear in the System building block in the process diagram.

Followed interactions are depicted as input arcs of places, because the effect of a followed interaction is to add a new token (referring to the business entity conveyed by the interaction) to its output place. Initiated interactions are depicted as output arcs of transitions: when a token flows along such an arc, the corresponding interaction is started and the follower is determined on the basis of the links defined in the top-level process model.

When an inexpensive PR is submitted by a requester, interaction "a.r" is performed and its effect is to add a token (referring to the PR) to place p1 whose type, PR, coincides with the type of the incoming business entity. Transition t1 is then triggered and its action consists in performing two interactions, "a.r+" and "b.n". On the basis of the automatic propagation rule, the business entity taken from place p1 is sent through output interactions "a.r+" and "b.n", without the need of writing any code in the action of t1. The recipient of interaction "a.r+" is the one that started conversation "a", while the recipient of interaction "b.n" is determined by link l4 shown in Figure 3, because this interaction is the initial one of a conversation "b".

Monitored interactions are those interactions the process has to be aware of so as to take appropriate actions, although it is not their follower. They are shown dashed and their labels include the initiator role before the conversation type name and the interaction name. One such interaction appears in the right part of Figure 5: its purpose is to enable the activation of conversation "b" when conversation "a" for an expensive PR ends successfully. Conversations "a" for expensive PRs are handled by supervisors, who are not supposed to decide what has to be done after the successful approvals of PRs. It is up to the process to trigger the subsequent processing of approved PRs and, therefore, it must be informed of the successful conclusion of a conversation "a" so as to start a conversation "b" with the buyers; these two conversations operate on the same PR.

Monitored interactions can only provide tokens to the process in that they are used to trigger complementary behavior.

FINE-GRAINED USER PARTICIPATION MODELS

The user participation models shown in Figure 4 are coarse-grained combinations in that conversations appear as building blocks that are combined sequentially or hierarchically.

It is not always possible to treat conversations as units, but it may be needed that the combination rules operate at the level of the single interactions. In such cases, POBPN proposes the use of interaction nets with the purpose of providing a fine-grained behavioral description of the users involved.

As an example, the Supervisor participation model is shown in Figure 6.

An incoming request (interaction a.r) is received in place p1 and then one of four transitions (t1, t4, t5 and t6) may take place. The ε-arc connecting place p1 and place p3 simply means that all the output transitions of p3 are also output transitions of p1; it is a means of simplifying the graphical representation.

Although interaction nets are used both in System participation models and in user participation ones, their meaning is different. In System participation models, transitions represent automatic activities performed by the process and, if there are conflicts between transitions, they are automatically solved by means of the pre-conditions associated with the transitions. As a consequence, conflicting transitions must have preconditions.

In user participation models, conflicting transitions need not have preconditions: the reason is that the selection of the transition to be carried out is in charge of the user. In other terms, such conflicting transitions allow a user choice. As a matter of fact, transitions t1, t4, t5 and t6 allow a supervisor to ask for some improvement of the request, to approve the request, to reject the request or to ask for a review, respectively.

If the requester cancels the request (interaction a.-r), the participation ends because transition t2 has no output. A reviewer may reject the request to review the purchase requisition (transition t7) or they may reply with a review (transition t8). In the first case, as transition t7 puts a token in place p3, the supervisor may then select t4, t5 or t6. In the second case, a token is put in place p5 and therefore the choice is about t4, t5, t6 or t9.

The model shown in Figure 6 has the same functionalities as the Supervisor model presented in Figure 4, which is more compact. However, the use of interaction nets

Figure 6. The Supervisor participation model in detail

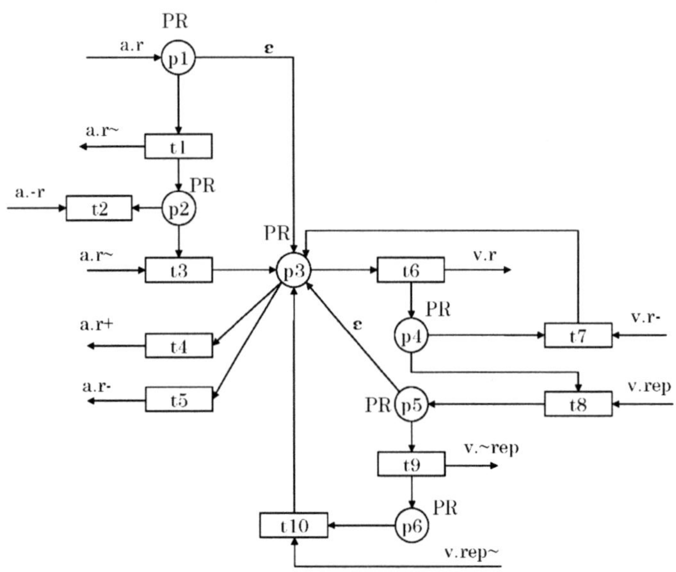

allows dependencies between interactions belonging to different conversations to be more easily expressed.

As an example, the behavior of supervisors is modified as follows. They may get only one review per PR and, moreover, they must notify the reviewer in case they accept the PR.

The revised model of the Supervisor participation is shown in Figure 7a, while the revised Reviewer protocol is shown in Figure 7b.

The reviewer protocol needs to be extended with an optional final notification (n) originated by the protocol initiator (i.e. the supervisor in the case study being considered).

The constraint that a supervisor may get only one review per PR is met by making transition t6 unreachable from place p5. Place p5 is not connected to place p3 as it is in Figure 6, but it is linked to a new place, p3', whose purpose is to enable the choice between transitions t4 and t5 (the acceptance or the rejection of the PR, respectively). If transition t4 is performed, two interactions are carried out, one (a.r+) signaling the acceptance to the requester and the other (v.n) informing the reviewer of the positive outcome of their work.

A user participation model, like the one presented in Figure 7, shows the expected behavior of a given role (i.e. of the users playing that role) in terms of: a) the interactions to handle, and b) the choices allowed. It is a road map from which the actual tasks can be developed and the interface between the user and the process can be worked out.

Figure 7. Revised Supervisor model (a) and revised Reviewer protocol (b)

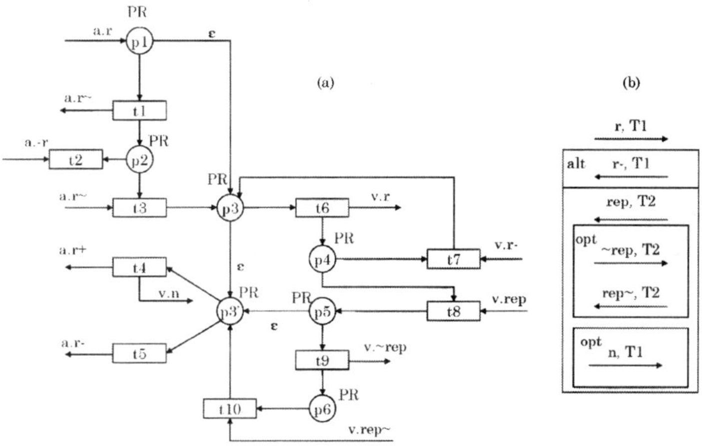

Transitions producing interactions (like t1, t4 and t6) correspond to tasks: t1 represents the task of requesting a PR to be improved, t4 and t5 represent the tasks of accepting or rejecting a PR, respectively.

The interface between users and processes is a todo list, through which users receive work from the processes they are participating in. Usually, a todo list includes a number of task entries: when a user clicks a task entry of their todo list, the main window of the task interface is shown and they can perform the specific work related to the task. In POBPN, user participations are driven by interactions and hence todo lists contain input interactions like a.r, a.-r or v.rep. When a user clicks an entry, two situations may occur: if the interaction is connected to only one transition, then the task related to the transition is directly activated; otherwise, if the interaction is connected to a place, then a list of possible tasks is shown, these tasks corresponding to the conflicting transitions coming out of that place. Interactions a.-r and a.r are examples of the two situations, respectively. When entry a.-r is clicked, only task t2 can be performed, while clicking entry a.r implies selecting t1, t4, t5 or t6.

The relevant presence of human decisions distinguishes knowledge-intensive processes from processes aimed at repetitive, standardized work (i.e. routines), and this calls for a more flexible control flow (Riss, Rickayzen, Maus & van der Aalst, 2005).

Several approaches have been proposed to improve flexibility in business processes (Nurcan, 2008). In the case-handling approach (van der Aalst, Weske & Grünbauer, 2005) a stronger integration between control-flow issues and data-flow ones is pursued, because a process is meant to take care of a certain business entity, referred to as the case of the process, and the process evolution is driven by the state of the case rather than by the completion of its activities (Künzle & Reichert, 2009).

BPMN (OMG, 2008) provides the notion of ad hoc sub-process, which is a group of tasks without a predefined control flow; the order of execution is decided by the users.

The BCPN approach (Lu, Sadiq & Governatori, 2009) supplements ad hoc sub-processes with a number of constraints (e.g. mandatory, prohibitive, inclusion and exclusion) that can be indicated graphically. First, an actual sequence of steps conforming to the constraints must be produced and then the execution can be started. This approach is like building a process model at run time. In the Declare approach (van der Aalst, Pesic & Schonenberg, 2009) there are ad hoc sub-processes with constraints like in BCPN, but there is no need to define a complete variant in advance: any task of the ad hoc sub-process can be performed as long as the mandatory constraints are not violated.

The major difference between POBPN and the above mentioned approaches is the presence of explicit decision points that are related to specific business entities, e.g. place p1 in Figure 7a.

COMPARISON OF NOTATIONS

The aim of this section is to provide a comparison between the notations used in the conversation-oriented perspective and in the orchestration-oriented one.

In the former approach, the emphasis is placed on the conversations between users and on how they are organized in participations: the explicit contribution of the process is restricted to the definition of the automatic activities, as shown in Figure 5 for process PRBP.

In the orchestration-oriented perspective, processes are thought of as explicit orchestrators of all the activities, both the automatic ones and the user tasks. Conversations are not a first-class notion of the approach and therefore the process has to make up for the lack of conversation-oriented constructs by directly handling the corresponding flow of interactions.

Conversation-oriented notations provide a higher-level representation than orchestration-oriented ones and the difference between them can easily be recognized on the basis of a simple scenario, as follows. The scenario refers to a particular occurrence of process PRBP involving four users: requester R, his/her supervisor S, reviewer V and buyer B. Requester R submits an expensive PR, which is sent to S for evaluation. S asks the support of V and then approves the PR. Buyer B receives the PR from the process and then notifies R of its inclusion in a purchase order.

On the basis of the scenario proposed, process PRBP shown in Figure 3 gives rise to a number of interactions that are graphically represented in the sequence diagram presented in Figure 8. The interaction flow develops as follows. When requester R submits an expensive PR, the process starts a conversation between R and S in conformity to link l1, and the initial interaction takes place. Its label, "a.r", is the name of a conversational interaction, as the interaction name is preceded by the name of the conversation the interaction belongs to.

In the participation model of the supervisor shown in Figure 4, interaction "a.r" is an extension point that can be followed by a number of conversations "v" with reviewers. In the scenario above, supervisor S asks reviewer V to provide a review of the PR and this leads to the pairs of interactions "v.r" and "v.rep" shown in the sequence diagram. Then the PR is approved by supervisor S resulting in interaction "a.r+". This interaction is a monitored one as indicated in the System participation model shown in Figure 5, and therefore it triggers interaction "b.n" between the System and buyer B. The dashed arc connecting interaction "a.r+" and interaction "b.n" emphasizes that "a.r+" is a monitored interaction and "b.n" is a consequence. Buyer B is supposed not to need any additional clarification from the requester and therefore the scenario ends in notification "c.n" sent by B to requester R.

With an orchestration-oriented notation, the sequence diagram for the same scenario becomes more complicated, because interactions between users (from an initiator to a follower) are mapped to pairs of sequential interactions involving the process: the first interaction takes place between the initiator and the process, the second one between the process and the follower.

The orchestration-oriented sequence diagram related to the scenario proposed is shown in Figure 9.

For example, interaction "a.r" from requester R to supervisor S is mapped to interaction "(R) a_r" from R to the process, and to interaction "a_r (S)" from the process to S. The name of the interaction is obtained from that of the corresponding conversational interaction by replacing the dot operator with character "_". In addition, in a user-process interaction, the initiator is indicated between parentheses before the interaction name, while, in a process-user interaction, the follower is indicated between parentheses after the interaction name. The labels of the process-user interactions are shown on the right of the System lifeline, while those of the user-process interactions are shown above the corresponding lines.

The notion of monitored interaction is not needed, as the process is an explicit orchestrator of all the interactions.

A business process defined with an interaction-oriented notation corresponds to a POBPN process that only includes the System participation model, as all the interactions between users are mapped to pairs of interactions involving the process. As an example, the orchestration-oriented version of process PRBP is shown

Figure 8. The conversation-oriented interaction flow for the scenario proposed

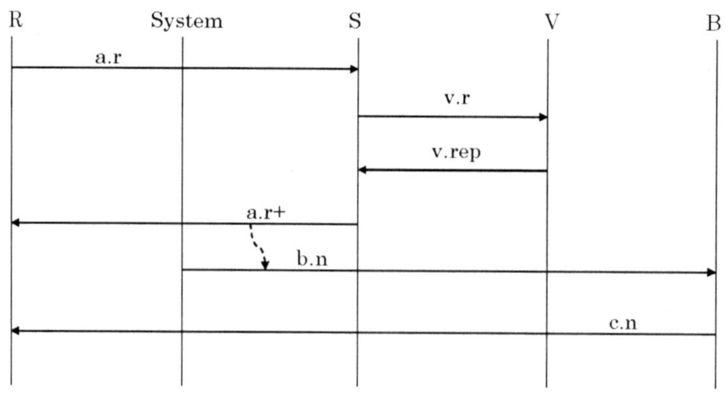

Figure 9. The orchestration-oriented interaction flow for the scenario proposed

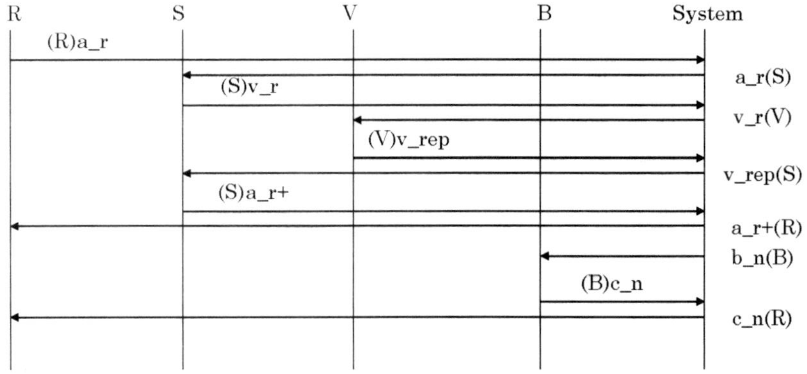

in Figure 10. It is based on the interaction nets introduced in the previous sections, and includes the description of a number of transitions.

In order to reduce the complexity of the model, a number of notational simplifications have been introduced, as follows.

If there are two transitions in series (Murata, 1989), the intermediate place (together with its input arc and its output one) can be replaced with a link that directly connects the two transitions and is labeled with the name and type of the place eliminated. Examples of such links are the one connecting transitions tb1 and tb2 and the one connecting tv4 and tv5.

If a place receives tokens only from a followed interaction and it is connected only to one transition, then it can be eliminated and the followed interaction can directly be connected to the transition: this simplification is carried out with several transitions, e.g. tb1 and tb2.

The third kind of simplification makes use of ε-arcs: an ε-arc links two places of the same type and its effect is that the tokens included in the source place also belong to the destination place and can trigger its output transitions (the vice versa does not hold); if two places, say, p1 and p2, are the source and the destination, respectively, of an ε-arc, p1 is said to be joined to p2.

The interaction labels shown in Figure 10 follow the same convention adopted in Figure 9.

The meaning of the model shown in Figure 10 is as follows. Submitted PRs enter place p1 and then trigger either transition ts1 or transition t1 depending on which precondition is satisfied. The incoming PR is associated with the input token taken from place p1 and the preconditions and the actions of transitions ts1 and t1 use the place name (i.e., p1) to refer to this PR.

Transition ts1 fires in case of an expensive PR, as shown in its precondition: its action consists in initiating interaction "a_r (S)" with the proper supervisor. The

Figure 10. The orchestration-oriented model of process PRBP

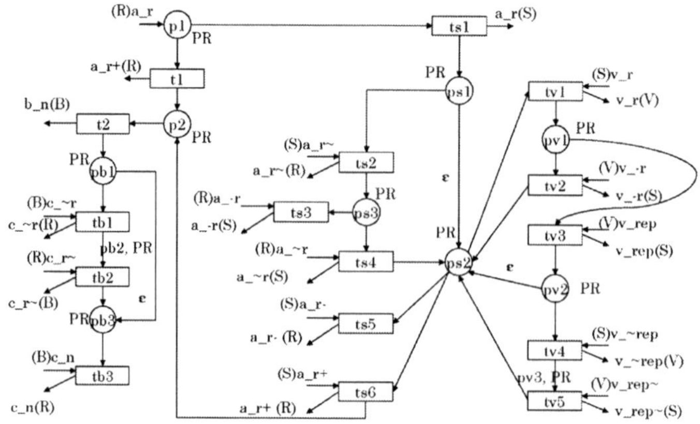

ts1: p: p1.amount > p1.requester.threshold; a: set p1.requester.boss as S.
t1: p: p1.amount <= p1.requester.threshold; a: set p1.requester as R.
tv1: a: set pv1.reviewers.last() as V.
tv2: a: set pv2.requester.boss as S.

follower-selection rules, which, with POBPN, are presented in section "Links" of the top-level process model, with the orchestration-oriented notation must be embedded in transitions. Primitive "set" is used to establish the follower of an initiated interaction. In the action of ts1, the boss of the requester of the input PR is set as "S", because S denotes the follower of interaction "a_r".

Transition ts1 puts the PR into place ps1 and then the process waits for the supervisor's move.

Place ps1 has two outgoing flows. The one on the left handles the case in which the supervisor requests some modifications to the PR: then ts2 fires and puts the PR in place ps3 until the requester makes his/her move, which can be the withdrawal of the PR or the submission of a revised version: these moves cause ts3 or ts4 to fire, respectively. The left path is optional, because ps1 is joined to ps2. Therefore, from place ps2, the supervisor may immediately approve or reject the PR or ask for external support. If the supervisor accepts or rejects the PR, ts6 or ts5 will fire, respectively; the firing of ts6 puts the PR in place p2 where the interaction flow involving a buyer starts.

Transition tv1 fires if the supervisor requests the support of a reviewer and the interaction "v_r" with the reviewer is initiated; the reviewer is the one represented by the last reviewer entity added to the PR, as shown in the action of tv1. The PR is then put in place pv1 where the process waits for the reviewer's move. If the reviewer refuses to review the PR, transition tv2 fires and relays the refusal to the supervisor whose move is waited for by the process in place ps2. If, instead, the reviewer provides the review, transition tv3 fires and relays the review to the supervisor whose next move is one of those associated with transitions tv1, ts5, ts6 or tv4. Transition tv4 fires when the supervisor requests a clarification of the reviewer. Then, the process waits for the clarification from the reviewer and relays it to the supervisor (transition tv5); after that, the process waits in place ps2 for the next move of the supervisor.

Place p2 starts the interaction flow with a buyer. Transition t2 is meant to assign the PR to a buyer. The PR is then put in place pb1, which has two outgoing paths. The path on the left is optional: it enables the buyer to ask some clarification of the requester and ends in place pb3 to which place pb1 is joined. Transition tb3 propagates the confirmation from the buyer to the requester.

CONCLUSION

This chapter has proposed a notation, POBPN, and a conversation-oriented perspective in order to effectively integrate conversations and business processes in an intra-organizational context. The involvement of users in business processes is clearly shown by means of participation building blocks appearing in the top-level representation of a business process. Such participation items can be refined into second-level models which are basically combinations of conversation models.

An example has been presented in order to stress the differences between the orchestration-oriented perspective (followed by most of current notations and languages) and the conversation-oriented one. The former is a centralized approach in which all the interactions are explicitly mediated by the process. If users look at a process description, they cannot immediately identify the interactions they will be involved in, as all user activities are intermingled. In the approach proposed, instead, conversation models come first (from the actualization of standard conversation protocols) and the process model is built upon them. The explicit contribution of the process is restricted to those conversations for which the process itself plays the initiator role or the follower one.

Current work is going on in two directions. One line of research is concerned with the inclusion of inter-organizational conversations. For this reason, the similarities between conversation protocols and B2B collaborations or choreographies need to be thoroughly analyzed.

The other line of research is more pragmatic and addresses the automatic mapping of POBPN models to orchestration-oriented ones; the purpose is to take advantage of current technology while preserving the conceptual strength of the conversation-oriented perspective.

REFERENCES

Austin, J. L. (1976). *How to do things with words*. Oxford, UK: Oxford University Press.

Dietz, J. L. G. (2003). The atoms, molecules and fibers of organizations. *Data & Knowledge Engineering*, *47*(3), 301–325.

Dietz, J. L. G. (2006). The deep structure of business processes. *Communications of the ACM*, *49*(5), 59–64.

Dumas, M., van der Aalst, W. M. P., & ter Hofstede, A. H. M. (2005). *Process-aware Information Systems: Bridging people and software through process technology*. New York, NY: Wiley.

Goldkuhl, G., & Lind, M. (2004). The generics of business interaction - emphasizing dynamic features through the BAT model. In M. Aakhus & M. Lind (Eds.), *9th Conference on the Language-Action Perspective on Communication Modelling*. New Brunswick, NJ.

Kristensen, L. M., Christensen, S., & Jensen, K. (1998). The practitioner's guide to coloured Petri Nets. *International Journal on Software Tools for Technology Transfer*, *2*, 98–132.

Kumaran, S., Liu, R., & Wu, F. Y. (2008). On the duality of information-centric and activity-centric models of business processes. [Berlin, Germany: Springer.]. *Lecture Notes in Computer Science*, *5074*, 32–47.

Künzle, V., & Reichert, M. (2009). Towards object-aware process management systems: Issues, challenges, benefits. In *Lecture Notes in Business Information Processing, 29* (pp. 197–210). Berlin, Germany: Springer.

Lu, R., Sadiq, S., & Governatori, G. (2009). On managing business processes variants. *Data & Knowledge Engineering*, *68*, 642–664.

Medina-Mora, R., Winograd, T., Flores, R., & Flores, F. (1992). The action workflow approach to workflow management technology. In J. Turner & R. Kraut (Eds.), *4th Conference on Computer Supported Cooperative Work*. New York, NY: ACM.

Murata, T. (1989). Petri nets: Properties, analysis and applications. *Proceedings of the IEEE*, *77*(4), 514–580.

Nurcan, S. (2008). *A survey on the flexibility requirements related to business processes and modeling artifacts*. In IEEE 41st Annual Hawaii International Conference on System Sciences. New York, NY: IEEE Press.

OASIS. (2007). *Web services business process execution language*, V.2.0. Retrieved January 18, 2011, from http://docs.oasis-open.org/wsbpel/2.0/OS/wsbpel-v2.0-OS.html

OMG. (2007). *Unified modeling language: Superstructure*, V.2.1.1. Retrieved January 18, 2011, from http://www.omg.org/spec/UML/2.2/

OMG. (2008). *Business process modeling notation*, V.1.1. Retrieved January 18, 2011, from http://www.bpmn.org

Ould, M. (2005). *Business process management: A rigorous approach*. The British Computer Society.

Riss, U. V., Rickayzen, A., Maus, H., & van der Aalst, W. M. P. (2005). Challenges for business process and task management. *Journal of Universal Knowledge Management, 0*(2), 77–100.

Russell, N., ter Hofstede, A. H. M., Edmond, D., & van der Aalst, W. M. P. (2005). Workflow data patterns: Identification, representation and tool support. [Berlin, Germany: Springer.]. *Lecture Notes in Computer Science, 3716*, 353–368.

Russell, N., van der Aalst, W. M. P., ter Hofstede, A. H. M., & Edmond, D. (2005). Workflow resource patterns: Identification, representation and tool support. [Berlin, Germany: Springer.]. *Lecture Notes in Computer Science, 3520*, 216–232.

van der Aalst, W. M. P., Pesic, M., & Schonenberg, H. (2009). Declarative workflows: Balancing between flexibility and support. *Computer Science - Research for Development, 23*, 99–113.

van der Aalst, W. M. P., ter Hofstede, A. H. M., Kiepuszewski, B., & Barros, A. P. (2003). Workflow patterns. *Distributed and Parallel Databases, 14*, 5–51.

van der Aalst, W. M. P., Weske, M., & Grünbauer, D. (2005). Case handling: A new paradigm for business process support. *Data & Knowledge Engineering, 53*(2), 129–162.

Weigand, H. (2006). Two decades of the language-action perspective: Introduction. *Communications of the ACM, 49*(5), 44–46.

Winograd, T. (1987-1988). A language/action perspective on the design of cooperative work. *Human-Computer Interaction, 3*, 3–30.

Winograd, T., & Flores, F. (1986). *Understanding computers and cognition*. Norwood, NJ: Ablex Publishing Corporation.

Chapter 10
Enterprise Information Systems Adoption in Iberian Large Companies: Motivations and Trends

António Trigo
ISCAC – Coimbra Institute of Accounting and Administration, Portugal

João Varajão
UTAD – Universidade de Trás-os-Montes e Alto Douro, Portugal & Centro ALGORITMI, Universidade do Minho, Portugal

João Barroso
GECAD – Grupo de Investigação em Engenharia do Conhecimento e Apoio à Decisão, Instituto Superior de Engenharia do Porto, Portugal

Pedro Soto-Acosta
University of Murcia, Spain

Francisco J. Molina-Castillo
University of Murcia, Spain

Nicolas Gonzalvez-Gallego
University of Murcia, Spain

ABSTRACT

Information Systems (IS) and Technologies assume a wide variety of roles within companies, ranging from operational to strategic support of the company. This fact puts pressure on managers, who are required to manage these investments properly. This chapter presents a study conducted with several Chief Information Officers from large Iberian companies with the purpose of identifying and characterizing the roles

DOI: 10.4018/978-1-60960-529-2.ch010

played by IS and the motivations currently behind their adoption. The findings of this study reveal the reasons why IS and technologies are being adopted by Iberian companies are evolving and that, while the adoption of certain types of systems such as Enterprise Resource Planning systems is now consolidated, the adoption of other systems like Business Intelligence is expected to increase significantly in the near future.

INTRODUCTION

Over the last few decades Information Technologies and Information Systems (IT/IS) have played very different roles within organizations: much has changed from the time when computation surged, where IT/IS were used merely for operational support, to the most recent role of being one of the drivers of an organization's competitiveness (Varajão, Trigo, Figueiredo, Barroso, & Bulas-Cruz, 2009)

Companies currently use multiple solutions of IT/IS to support their activities at all management levels and few of them try to conduct their businesses without seeking to exploit the advantages of IT/IS solutions (Trigo, Varajão, Figueiredo, & Barroso, 2007). Among the systems adopted by companies we can find Enterprise Resource Planning (ERP) systems, Customer Relationship Management (CRM) systems, Business Intelligence (BI) systems and many others.

The great diversity of IT/IS applications implies a great diversity of motivations for their adoption. For instance, the inherent set of motives for the adoption of a CRM system will probably be different from the set of motives for investing in a new version of an operational system. Unlike, the motives for adopting a specific system of BI could be the same as those leading to the acquisition of a particular expert system.

Nevertheless, there is a set of generally inherent motivations to IT/IS adoption that is important to identify and understand in order to conduct investments. These motivations may serve as a guide to maximizing the degree of satisfaction with IT/IS investment initiatives, given the generally significant sums involved in these investments.

In this chapter, we present the results obtained from a study carried out with Chief Information Officers (CIOs) of Iberian companies, namely: current motivations for IT/IS adoption; current implemented systems; current role of IT/IS; and trends for IT/IS adoption.

Next, after a literature review, we present the scope, the research process, the analysis and discussion of the results obtained as well as some conclusions.

BACKGROUND

A common approach to examine the types of IT/IS solutions used within organizations is to categorize their roles at various management levels within the organizational structure (Belle, Eccles, & Nash, 2003; Laudon & Laudon, 2005), according to Robert Anthony's (1965) pyramid of operational control, managerial control and strategic planning.

At the lowest level of the organizational hierarchy we find the transaction processing systems (TPS), which support the day-to-day activities of the business. These applications are normally the first to be computerized and are characterized by large numbers of transactions, updating the corporate database. These systems are usually used by clerical staff, who conduct routine daily business activities such as issuing of invoices, following well-defined business procedures. Low-level managers and supervisors, responsible for monitoring transactions and dealing with any problems that may arise, occupy the next level in the organizational hierarchy. Management Information Systems (MIS) use the data collected by the TPS to assist the operations and line managers with the control of business process activities, usually by means of standard, regular reports. Tactical management occupies the next level in the organizational hierarchy. These managers are responsible for ensuring that plans and targets set by senior management are achieved. They decide on budgets, set targets, identify trends and develop short-term business plans. To achieve this, tactical managers need to have more interactive applications that actually assist them with the decision making process of middle management. These applications are called Decision Support Systems (DSS) and allow managers to request the relevant data, select and apply the appropriate decision model and generate the output report in the required format. At the top of the pyramid, strategic management is responsible for defining the long-term goals and positioning the company within a particular industry. They require an information system that enables them to identify problems that may threaten the organization's competitive position or opportunities and trends that may enhance it. Executive Information Systems (EIS) assist top-level executives with their daily information needs for top management control, as well as their strategic decision-making (Belle, et al., 2003; Laudon & Laudon, 2005).

Knowledge management (KM) embraces all the management levels, since it aims to capture organizational learning and core competencies of the organization from day-to-day operations (Cuffe, 2005). KM is used to achieve better performance due to effective knowledge sharing and organizational learning (Okkonen, Pirttimäki, Lönnqvist, & Hannula, 2002) and tries to prevent the waste of resources by seeking the best practices (Wah, 2000). KM objectives are: to capture, store, retrieve and distribute tangible knowledge assets; to gather, organize and disseminate intangible knowledge; and finally, to create an interactive learning environment where people transfer, and share, their knowledge, and apply it in order to accumulate new knowledge (Wah, 2000). Knowledge Management Systems store information in a repository which is updated during an organization's life cycle and can assist them in reducing their research and development, maintain internal best-practices repositories and reduce the loss of expertise when key individuals depart (Cuffe, 2005). KM is also used to support the strategy process. For example, analyzing employees' competencies can identify organization's core competencies. Sometimes the strategy is formulated around the core competencies. On the other hand, KM activities can be used to implement strategic objectives, such as the decrease in costs by more effective knowledge sharing, or the gain in new know-how among the employees of the organization (Okkonen, et al., 2002).

There is yet another group of IT/IS solutions used by all the management levels, the group of IT/IS solutions that provide an interface for external entities, which include all customers, business partners and third parties. While the majority of IT/IS solutions in the past focused on applications within the boundaries of the enterprise, the focus is gradually shifting outwards, with many managers participating in new IT projects to take advantage of Internet capabilities (Cuffe, 2005), as is the case of, Business-to-Business (B2B), Business-to-Consumer (B2C), Customer-to-Business (C2B), SCM, CRM, etc. Electronic commerce is an emerging trend that streamlines the operations of a business and results in efficiency and profitability (E. Li, Tseng, & Lu, 2007).

IT/IS role in organizations is materialized by the use of diverse IT/IS solutions, such as, Enterprise Resource Planning systems; Customer Relationship Management systems; Supply Chain Management Systems; Business Intelligence; Collaboration and Groupware; and Workflow Management Systems.

Enterprise Resource Planning (ERP) systems are commercial software packages, often transversal to all the management levels of the enterprise, that aim to fulfill all the information system requirements of a business (Belle, et al., 2003) and to integrate all the information flowing through a company (Davenport, 1998). An ERP system is primarily responsible for managing the transactional processing operations of the business in its various areas (e.g., accounting, finance, human resources, marketing, manufacturing, logistics, sales, procurement, etc.) usually supported by a software module (or modules) designed to integrate with the other modules. These packaged modules then need to be configured, and sometimes customized to meet the specific demands of the company implementing the ERP. Since ERP systems consist of different modules, companies only need to purchase the modules they need (Pairat & Jungthirapanich, 2005). Due to the integrated nature of ERP, its modules overcome many of the drawbacks of legacy systems and enable online integration not only within the same function but also within and across the other functions of the business. As a result, ERP systems are considered good candidates for forming a technology platform to support the integration of other intra- and inter-organizational applications such as SCM, CRM, and e-commerce systems.

One of the most visible benefits of ERP systems is the replacement of legacy systems with standardized, cross-functional transaction automation, in which leads to reduced cycle times, improved throughput, customer response times, and delivery speeds (Cotteleer & Bendoly, 2006; McAfee, 2002). All enterprise data is collected once during the initial transaction, stored centrally, and updated in real time. This ensures that all levels of planning are based on the same data and that the resulting plans realistically reflect the prevailing operating conditions of the firm (Hendricks, Singhal, & Stratman, 2007). Taken together, the standardized firm-wide transactions and centrally stored enterprise data, they facilitate the governance of the firm (Scott & Vessey, 2000). ERP reports provide managers with a clear view of the relative performance of the various parts of the enterprise, which can be used to identify needed improvements and take advantage of market opportunities (Hendricks, et al., 2007). These visible benefits are related to the motivations of an organization seeking to adopt an ERP system. For (Oliver & Romm, 2000), there are three categories of factors that determine an organization's initial search for an ERP solution: the need to improve the performance of current operations; the need to integrate data and systems; and, the need to prevent a competitive disadvantage or a business risk from becoming critical. Ross & Vitale(2000) identify six reasons generally cited by enterprises, classifying them into three categories (infrastructure, capacity, and performance) and underscore their overlapping character: the new common systems platform (infrastructure) makes it possible to acquire new capabilities (process improvement, data visibility), which in turn are supposed to allow improvements in organizational performance (cost reduction, strategic decision making, customer responsiveness). Parr(2000) take up the same motives, but give the categories different names: technological (common platform, obsolescence of legacy systems), operational (process improvement, data visibility, operating cost reductions), and strategic (multi-site standardization, customer responsiveness, decision-making improvement, need for efficiencies and integration, business restructuring).

Customer Relationship Management (CRM) is a term used to describe a set of IT/IS solutions that automate customer-facing processes in marketing, sales and service functions of the business. CRM enables an organization to be more customer focused, allowing the analysis and exploitation of customer data (Iriana & Buttle, 2006). One key to managing customer relationships is by providing the same information to everyone within the company so that every product or service need of the customer is met. It provides to individuals within organizations a "Single Customer View". Whether working with a customer from a customer service level, technical support level, or even from a back-office marketing standpoint, all individuals will have a single point of view in understanding the customer. Therefore, with CRM, everyone within the enterprise will be wholly focused on a customer's needs, whether it is for sales or service. The CRM philosophy places the customer rather than the product or process at the centre of the organization in the belief that the development of a close relationship with the customer will enable the organization to determine, fulfill and even predict the needs of the customer (Beckett-Camarata, Camarata, & Barker, 1998). Successful CRM initiatives enable organizations to retain existing customers, increase customer loyalty, acquire new customers and improve the relationship with existing customers (Ryals & Knox, 2001). The main motivations for the adoption of CRM systems are (Elliott, 1997; Kalakota & Robinson, 2000; Ryals & Knox, 2001): to help to identify the most profitable customers; to create customer value; to customize products and services; to receive customer feedback that leads to new and improved products or services; to help to avoid wasting marketing money on ineffective marketing programs; to enable companies to reduce sales inventory costs through better forecasting; to develop stronger relationships with customers and increase customer loyalty and profitability; to faster response to customer inquiries; and to obtain information that can be shared with business partners.

The supply chain encompasses all activities associated with the flow and transformation of goods from the raw materials stage, through to the end user, as well as the associated information flows. Supply Chain Management (SCM) is the integration of these activities through improved supply chain relationships, to achieve a sustainable competitive advantage (Nichols, 1999). In essence, SCM integrates supply and demand management within and across companies, allowing the collaboration and cooperation of firms across the entire supply chain as a whole in order to improve operational efficiency and market competitiveness, via the coordination of all forms of activities, information, and materials from the initial source to the end-user (Stadtler, 2000). SCM software applications provide real-time analytical systems that manage the flow of product and information throughout the supply chain network. They are designed to enhance SCM operations - supplier sourcing, production planning, inventory planning, transportation planning, demand planning, and so on. At present, SCM solutions are fragmented along these functional applications into specific spaces, for example: advanced planning and scheduling for the manufacturing plant, demand planning for the sales group, and transportation planning for the distribution center (Jianbing Wu, 2000).

The primary benefits of SCM systems are better operational and business planning. SCM systems use finite capacity planning algorithms that do not require iterative adjustments to the master schedule, and real-time planning capabilities that allow firms to react quickly to supply and demand changes. Increased revenue, increased productivity, operational cost savings, lower inventory, and reduced order-to-fulfillment cycle time are some of the benefits from SCM system implementations (Hendricks, et al., 2007).

Business intelligence (BI) is a generic term for applications, platforms, tools and technologies that support the process of data exploitation and business data analysis. BI applications provide businesses with the means to collect and prepare data to facilitate the generation of reports, analysis and decision. The purpose of BI systems is to support better business decision-making (Power, 2007). Business intelligence technology has coalesced in the last decade around the use of data warehousing and on-line analytical processing (OLAP). Data warehousing is a systematic approach to collecting relevant business data into a single repository, where it is organized and validated so that it can be analyzed and presented in a form that is useful for business decision-making. The various sources for the relevant business data are referred to as the operational data stores (ODS). The data is extracted, transformed, and loaded (ETL) from the ODS systems into a data mart. An important part of this process is data cleansing in which variation on schemas and data values from disparate ODS systems are resolved. In the data mart, the data is modeled as an OLAP cube (multidimensional model), which supports flexible drill-down and roll-up analyses (Cody, Kreulen, Krishna, & Spangler, 2002). Recent developments in BI include business performance measurement, business activity monitoring, and the expansion of BI from being a staff tool to being used by people throughout the organization (BI for the masses). In the long-term, BI techniques and findings will be embedded into business processes (Negash & Gray, 2008).

Some of the benefits of having a BI system include the ability to access data in a common format from multiple sources, a way to measure goals and analyze cross-departmental data, to see whether customers meet their agreements and to track customer behavior in order to improve services and relationships. These systems can also help tracking specific product sales and distributors to improve supply and production, as well as track external trends to improve processes, track market trends to improve an organization's competitiveness, and fine-tune pricing and marketing policies.

Groupware, also referred to as collaborative software, is a general term for a repertoire of Information Communication and Technology (ICT) applications that support cooperative work between and among groups of people, even though they may not actually be together (Pumareja & Sikkel, 2006), in either time or space (Coleman, 1997). Groupware systems are used to support and carry out the social domains of work, i.e., the aspect of one's job in which interpersonal interaction and cooperative processes take place (Pumareja & Sikkel, 2006). According to Andriessen(2003), groupware systems can be distinguished from other ICT applications by having functions that serve the following human interaction processes: communication; cooperation; coordination; information sharing and learning; and, social interaction.

According to (Coleman, 1997) the primary motivations for the adoption of Groupware systems are: to improve cost control; to increase productivity; to improve customer service; to support for Total Quality Management; to reduce meetings; to automate routine processes; to extend the organization to include both the customer and the supplier; to integrate geographically disparate teams; to increase competitiveness through faster time to market; to achieve better coordination globally; to provide a new service that differentiates the organization; and to leverage professional expertise.

Workflow can be described simply as the movement of documents and tasks through a business process. Workflow can be a sequential progression of work activities or a complex set of processes each taking place concurrently, eventually impacting each other according to a set of rules, routes, and roles (CTG, 1997). Workflow Management Systems allow organizations to define and control the various activities associated with a business process and also the opportunity to measure and analyze the execution of the process so that continuous improvements can be made. Most workflow management systems also integrate with other systems used by the organization, like: document management systems, databases, e-mail, office automation products, Geographic Information Systems, production applications, etc. (CTG, 1997). This integration provides structure to a process, which employs a number of otherwise independent systems (Milutinović & Patricelli, 2002). Some typical features associated with these systems are: a process definition tool; the simulation, prototyping and piloting of a workflow; task initiation and control; document routing; invocation of applications to view and manipulate data; work lists; task automation; event notification; process monitoring; access to information over the World Wide Web; tracking and logging of activities; and administration and security (Milutinović & Patricelli, 2002).

Many benefits can be accrued if the workflow management system is implemented as part of a broader business solution, such as: less intervention to manage business processes; improved communication between employees through notifications and document sharing; improved understanding of the process itself, which can lead to increased collaboration among team members and/or across teams and business units; separation of IT from workflow management, putting the business process immediately and directly under the control of the people using the system; increasing corporate knowledge; and improved security and reliability (CTG, 1997). A workflow management system also eases the costs of developing new enterprise applications and reduces the maintenance of standard enterprise software. From an IT point of view, two important reasons for enterprises to adopt a workflow management system are to ease of software development and reduce risks for overall system development (James et al., 2007).

From the above literature revision we note that there are different motivations that lead to the adoption of diverse IT/IS solutions, such as to reduce operational costs, differentiate products or services in relation to the competitors, improve the quality of products or services, launch new products or services before competition, improve business operations or processes, diversify the line of products or services, identify and occupy new markets, improve customer service, reduce staff costs, establish strategic partnerships, increase the productivity of the employees, improve the communication between the employees, etc.

RESEARCH FOCUS, DESIGN AND METHOD

A survey was conducted to investigate several aspects of the IT/IS situation in large Portuguese and Spanish companies. Specifically for this study, the survey aimed to determine which IT/IS solutions are adopted, the reasons for their adoption, the role played by IT/IS within the company, and which trends influence the adoption of IT/IS.

The general methodology involved a questionnaire that was sent to 1000 Chief Information Officers (CIOs) of large Portuguese and Spanish companies categorized according to their gross revenue. CIOs are responsible for managing the IT department. Therefore, they usually have rich information regarding all aspects concerning IT/IS in their organization.

Subjects

The decision-maker targeted by the survey was normally the person responsible for IT within the company, typically the Chief Information Officer (CIO) or the IT manager. The target population consisted of the 1000 largest companies by gross revenue in Portugal and Spain.

This particular audience was preferred because large organizations are generally leaders in technology use and application (E. Y. Li, McLeod, & Rogers, 2001; Liu & Arnett, 2000; McLeod, 1995) and they need to have a well-structured IT department to manage the overall information system architecture. Therefore, the use of this target group seemed most appropriate.

Questionnaire

A structured questionnaire consisting of close-ended questions was developed from previous studies (CXO Media, 2006, 2007; Varajão, Trigo, Figueiredo, & Barroso, 2007). The questionnaire was divided into several sections, each one with well defined objectives. The formulation and criteria for answering the questionnaire is defined in the Appendix.

The proposed questionnaire was pre-tested with a small sample of CIOs and used in a previous survey (Varajão, Trigo, et al., 2007) to validate its content and readability and to improve some aspects of the questions. The necessary changes were made to the final questionnaire, which was edited in an online survey tool. A briefing letter was subsequently sent to the CIOs regarding the scope and goals of the study, including a link to an Internet home page, which allowed the fulfillment of the questionnaire online. CIOs were asked to answer the questionnaire online. In the first and second rounds, the letter was sent by email and, in the third round, by post.

Data Representativeness

The survey was mailed to a sample group of 500 companies in Portugal and a sample of 500 companies in Spain both from the above mentioned target population in each country during February to October 2008. In order to obtain a representative sample, a casual sample method was used, the stratified sample method, opting for a random sample of 50% of the companies in each group of 100 companies, selected according to their position in the INE list of the 1000 largest national companies in Portugal (INE, 2007b) and the SABI database list of the 1000 largest firms in Spain.

In the first and second rounds, the number of undelivered and returned questionnaires (by email) was 111 from Portuguese firms and 94 from Spanish companies, quite a significant number perhaps due to the email policies of the companies. In the third round, the invitation letter was sent by post and then the number of undelivered and returned questionnaires was 44 and 23 for Portuguese and Spanish firms, respectively. 102 valid responses were obtained (59 responses from Portuguese companies and 43 from Spanish firms), yielding a final response rate of around 10.2%.

This response rate did not come as a surprise as it is comparable with the response rates of others studies conducted in the last few years (Enns, Huff, & Golden, 2001; E. Y. Li, et al., 2001; Lin & Pervan, 2003; Liu & Arnett, 2000; Sohal & Ng, 1998; Trigo, et al., 2007). This may be due to the fact that some subjects are unwilling to respond to unsolicited surveys (E. Y. Li, et al., 2001), or simply had insufficient time (Lin & Pervan, 2003) and many more companies set a policy of rejecting survey questionnaires (E. Y. Li, et al., 2001; Lin & Pervan, 2003).

Tables 1 and 2 show the characteristics of the respondents. The companies of the responding CIOs represent a broad range of companies in terms of their characteristics, which indicates that the results can be used to explain the Iberian IT/IS adoption in large companies. It is important to note that, although it is true that large organizations generally provide leadership in using information technology, differences do exist between small and large businesses (Liu & Arnett, 2000). Therefore,

Table 1. Characteristics of respondents' companies

Characteristics	Portugal	Spain
Total number of employees		
<200	10	7
201-500	21	8
501-2000	21	12
>2000	7	16
Annual sales (million Euros)		
Less than 10	2	0
10 to below 50	14	2
50 to below 250	33	16
Greater than 250	6	22
No answer	4	3
International presence (number of countries)		
1	20	13
2	10	3
3-4	9	2
5-20	7	12
>20	9	11
No answer	4	2

careful use of the results should be made, especially regarding their applicability to small businesses.

According to Table 1, the majority of the sample presented a large number of employees among firms and annual sales above 50 million Euros. In addition, approximately 67% of the surveyed companies demonstrated an international presence in more than one country. (see Table 3)

The majority of CIOs that answer the survey were male (90.2%) in their forties with a Bachelor's degree (60.8%). They have an average tenure within their organization of 10 years and an average tenure in their current position of 8 years.

DATA ANALYSIS AND RESULTS

Nowadays IT/IS have a large variety of applications within businesses and play a fundamental role both at the internal level and at linking companies with their external environment.

Table 2. Activity sectors of participating companies [a]

Sector of activity	Portugal	Spain
Agriculture and agro-industry	4	3
Utilities	3	0
Cellulose and paper	1	0
Commerce	2	2
Car trade	4	2
Building and construction	0	5
Food distribution	3	5
Hotels and restaurants	1	3
Wood, cork and furniture	1	0
Electric and precision equipment	2	0
Metalworking and machinery	4	4
Metallic and non-metallic minerals	3	2
Medical and pharmaceutical products	2	2
Chemistry	2	3
Services	7	7
Telecommunications	1	1
Textiles	1	0
Transports and distribution	4	4
Others	14	0

a) Based on the Portuguese economic activity codes (INE, 2007a)

It has become increasingly self-evident that companies cannot be competitive or profitable without them (Varajão, 2006).

When the scope of IT/IS applications was solely limited to an operational level, the motives behind their selection were reasonably clear and concerned mostly the automation of work with the aim of increasing productivity and implicit cost reduction (Varajão, Ribeiro, Figueiredo, & Barroso, 2007).

As the scope of IT/IS use broadened from company tactics, at first, to strategy later, the range of motivations behind IT/IS adoption also widened, including, for instance, the improvement of the time to market, the establishment of strategic partnerships or the exploration of new markets (Varajão, Ribeiro, et al., 2007)

The great diversity of IT/IS applications entails a great diversity of motivations for their adoption. Nevertheless, there is a group of generally inherent motivations for IT/IS adoption which must be identified and grasped, in order to maximize satisfaction levels with investment initiatives in IT/IS (Varajão, Ribeiro, et al., 2007).

Table 3. Demographic characteristics of respondents' CIOs

Characteristics	Number	%
Gender		
Male	92	90.2
Female	10	9.8
Total	102	100
Age		
Less than 30	5	4.9
31 to 35	15	14.7
36 to 40	21	20.6
41 to 45	22	21.6
More than 45	39	38.2
Total	102	100
Highest degree earned		
High school	9	8.8
Bachelor's	62	60.8
Post-Graduation	12	11.8
MBA	7	6.9
Master's	8	7.8
PhD	1	1
Other	3	2.9
Total	102	100

In the questionnaire for data collection used for this study, we asked the participants to state, in order of importance, the main motivations regarding the adoption of IT/IS in their companies, via an ordinal scale. Twelve motivations were identified in the questionnaire, which the participants were asked to grade from 1 to 12 (in case they were considered important in the specific context of their company).

The prevailing motivations for IT/IS adoption by major Portuguese and Spanish firms are identified by order of importance (average) in Figure 1.

The motivation identified as being currently primary reason for IT/IS adoption in Iberian companies, highlighted at the top of the list with a weighted average of 9.87 (out of a maximum of 12), was "To improve business operations or processes".

In the following three positions, with very similar averages, were the motivation "To improve the quality of products or services", with an average of 9.38, the motivation "To reduce operational costs", with an average of 9.24, the motivation "To Increase the productivity increase of the employees", with an average of 9.09.

Figure 1. Motivations for IT/IS adoption by large Portuguese and Spanish companies

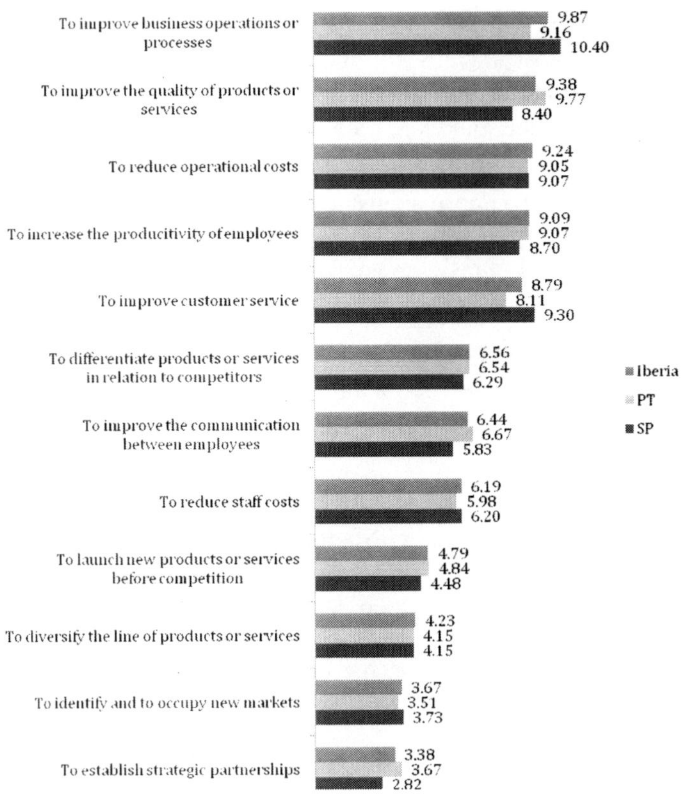

It is worth highlighting that these motives have been frequently identified in the past and that they continue to be of key importance in the present as have been revealed in other studies. In a work conducted in the USA by CIO magazine (CXO Media, 2006) the most widely considered motivation to adopt IT/IS, as identified by respondents, was precisely "To reduce the costs by increasing productivity/ efficiency. Another study conducted in Portugal in 2006 (Varajão, Ribeiro, et al., 2007) also presented "To Increase the productivity of the employees" and "To reduce operational costs" as the two prevailing motivations.

The motivation "To improve customer service" appears in the fifth highest ranked position, with an average of 8.79. It is worth noting that, as will be later stated in this chapter, this motive is probably linked to the prospective growth in the adoption of CRM systems.

At the bottom of the list, are diverse strategic motivations: "To launch new products or services before competition", "To diversify the line of products or services", "To identify and to occupy new markets" and "To establish strategic partnerships", all with a weighted average below 5. On a strategic level, several motives appear in the lower half of the table.

Our study revealed that on the whole, the motivations identified as being the most important continue to be intimately related to operational aspects, similar to those revealed by other studies in recent years (Varajão, Ribeiro, et al., 2007). For example, these type of motivations can be found in the first, third and fourth positions, respectively "To improve business operations or processes", " To reduce operational costs", and "To increase the productivity of the employees". In contrast to other studies in which motivations related to the strategic aspects are clearly emphasized as, for example, in a study conducted by the CIO magazine (CXO Media, 2006), where "To enable innovation in business", "To create/enable competitive advantage", "To improve client satisfaction" appear in the second, third and fourth positions respectively. Our study revealed that these issues, despite their importance, are not the most prevailing.

It can be concluded then, that although the strategic motivations are relevant and considered in the process of IT/IS adoption, the motivations directly related to cost reduction and productivity increase are the primary drivers of investment. Nevertheless, it is important to highlight that for the first time a strategic motivation "To improve the quality of products or services" appears prominently in the top position, which indicates a departure from our findings in previous studies (Varajão, Ribeiro, et al., 2007).

The results obtained concerning motivations are consistent with the role currently played by IT/IS in large Portuguese and Spanish companies. Also, the actual role of the IT/IS in the company was asked, using a Likert scale where 5 stands for very important and 1 for without importance. Figure 2 shows the weighted average of the answers obtained.

In concordance with the current motivations, IT/IS played the most important role in the support of business operations, followed closely by the support of middle level management and top management, to which respondents attributed an average importance of 4.64, 4.21 and 4.10 respectively. This study shows that in large Iberian companies the IT/IS solutions are committed to supporting the business operations and the middle and top management levels, leaving to a second plan: knowledge management and interface with external entities. It should be highlighted that the identified role for IT/IS concerning the three levels of management is currently very similar (with a difference lower than 0.6 in terms of the average importance), revealing that the use of technologies is no longer mainly related to operations, but, on the contrary it is dispersed throughout the diverse levels of management. One of the questions addressed in this study was which IT/IS systems are currently implemented in large Iberian companies. Although the idea that large companies are leaders in the adoption of IT/IS solutions and use them for

Figure 2. Current role of IT/IS in large Portuguese and Spanish companies

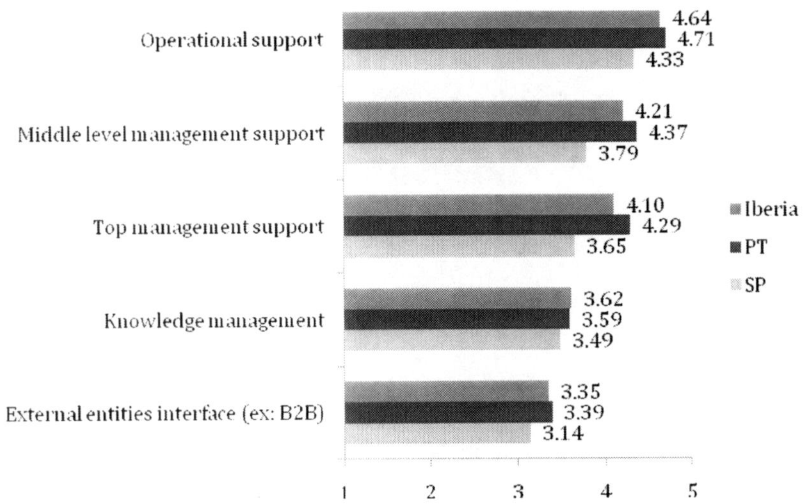

the support of all management levels is usually generalized, this is not always the case and it is of great relevance to identify which systems are currently implemented and which systems companies will intend to develop in the near future. As revealed by previous studies (Trigo, et al., 2007). On the one hand, a high adoption of Enterprise Resource Planning systems was expected to be found, since its adoption is ubiquitous in large companies (Hossain, Patrick, & Rashid, 2002; Norris, Hurley, Hartley, Dunleavy, & Balls, 2000; Rashid, Hossain, & University of Sydney, 2002). On the other hand, high levels concerning the adoption of systems like CRM were not expected, since these kinds of systems in previous studies appeared with a relatively low adoption rate.

To perform this study we started by investigating which systems the companies are more concerned with in a general manner, and, based on previous studies made in North America (CXO Media, 2002, 2006; V. Kumar, 2002) and Europe (Karakostas, Kardaras, & Papathanassiou, 2005; Yvonne van, Jos van, & Eric, 2000), the following systems were identified: Enterprise Resource Planning (ERP), Customer Relationship Management (CRM), Supply Chain Management (SCM), Business Intelligence (BI), Collaboration and Groupware, and Workflow management. This study showed, as presented in Figure 1, that the majority of the companies have already implemented ERP systems, with a current adoption rate superior to that verified two years ago (Trigo, et al., 2007). This was expected considering that ERPs have been around for a long time, since the 1980's, and they are considered the standard backbone of companies' business support (Simchy-Levy, Kaminsky, & Simchy-Levy, 2003). (see Figure 3)

Figure 3. Implemented systems by large Portuguese and Spanish companies

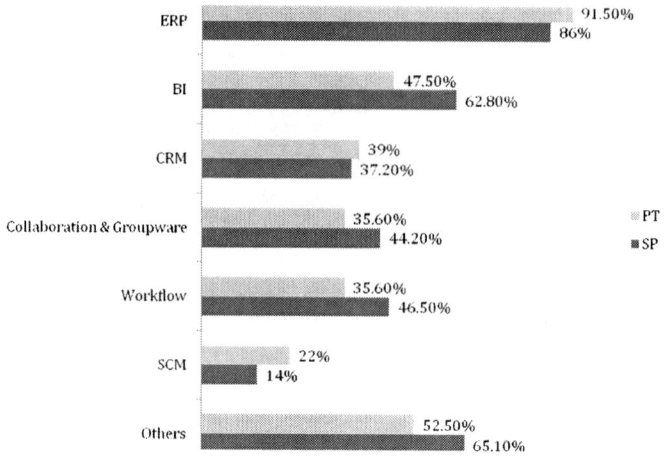

This study revealed that the adoption of CRM, Collaboration, Groupware and Workflow systems continue being low with less than 40% of the respondent companies having these kinds of systems implemented.

Regarding CRM, for instance, a higher rate of adoption would be expected, closer to the adoption of ERP, not only because systems like CRM are easier to be implemented than ERP (Hendricks, et al., 2007) but also due to the fact that these systems can and should be used to improve the competitiveness and strategic positioning of the companies (Trigo, et al., 2007). Furthermore, some open questions were included in the survey to verify if there was another important group of IT/IS solutions. Almost all answers obtained refer to specific business systems.

FUTURE TRENDS

With this study we also intended to identify the future intentions of companies concerning the implementation of new IT/IS solutions.

In Figure 4 it is possible to observe the systems that companies have currently implemented and the systems they will have in the near future.

Practically all the companies are developing IS projects. By 2010 a growth in the implementation of ERP, SCM, and other business specific systems is expected. A slight growth in ERP is perfectly understandable given the high number of companies (about 90%) that already have this type of system in place.

Within those systems, BI and CRM systems appear. It is worth noting that these systems are closely related to two of the motivations which appeared in the top five

Figure 4. Current implemented systems vs. expected implemented systems in Portugal and Spain

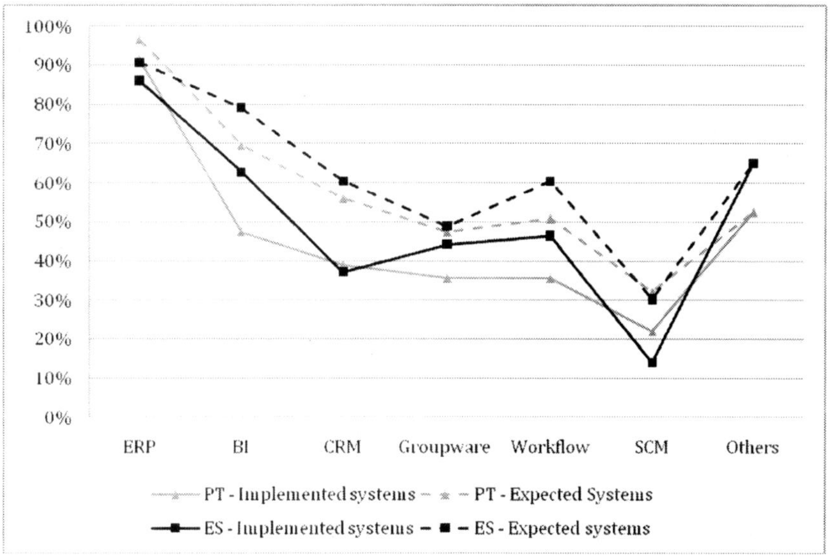

positions in the list of previously identified motivations for the adoption of IT/IS: "To improve the quality of products or services" and "To improve customer service".

CONCLUSION

Companies currently apply a multitude of IT/IS solutions to support and develop their businesses, and their reasons for investing are just as varied as the technologies. Nevertheless, there are several common and prevailing motives, which must be understood so that the process of IT/IS development can be conducted in line with the global aims of the organization.

This study, conducted on large Portuguese and Spanish companies, identified the five most prevalent motivations for the adoption of IT/IS, which are: "To improve business operations or processes", "To improve the quality of products or services", "To reduce operational costs", "To increase the productivity of the employees", and "To improve customer service".

Beyond the importance of the IT/IS operational role, the tactical and strategic approaches being implemented by companies are becoming of great importance.

The IT/IS solutions available to companies are multiple and diverse. Within the systems that companies commonly adopt are: ERP, BI, CRM, Workflow, Collaboration and Groupware, SCM systems, and others.

In large Iberian companies the system mainly adopted and well consolidated is the ERP, similarly to other Europeans countries (Yvonne van, et al., 2000). The adoption of certain types of system, such as CRM systems, essential for enhancing a company's competitiveness, is still below the expected adoption levels. Nevertheless, the adoption of other systems like CRM, Groupware and Workflow, which less than 50% of the companies currently have, is expected to increase in the short-term.

REFERENCES

Andriessen, J. H. E. (2003). *Working with groupware: Understanding and evaluating collaboration technology*. London: Springer.

Anthony, R. N. (1965). *Planning and control systems: A framework for analysis*. Boston, MA: Graduate School of Business Administration, Harvard University Press.

Beckett-Camarata, E. J., Camarata, M. R., & Barker, R. T. (1998). Integrating internal and external customer relationships through relationship management: A strategic response to a changing global environment. *Journal of Business Research, 41*(1), 71–81.

Belle, J.-P. V., Eccles, M., & Nash, J. (2003). *Discovering Information Systems*. Cape Town, South Africa: South African Universities Press.

Cody, W. F., Kreulen, J. T., Krishna, V., & Spangler, W. S. (2002). The integration of business intelligence and knowledge management. *IBM Systems Journal, 41*(4), 697–714.

Coleman, D. (1997). *Groupware: Collaborative strategies for corporate LANs and Intranets*. Prentice Hall.

Cotteleer, M. J., & Bendoly, E. (2006). Order lead-time improvement following enterprise Information Technology implementation: An empirical study. *Management Information Systems Quarterly, 30*(3).

CTG. (1997). *An introduction to workflow management systems*. New York, NY: Center for Technology in Government, University at Albany.

Cuffe, S. S. (2005). Emerging management support systems models for global managers in the new economy. *Journal of Knowledge Management Practice, 6*.

Davenport, T. H. (1998). Putting the enterprise into the enterprise system. *Harvard Business Review, 76*(4), 121–131.

Elliott, C. (1997). Everything wired must converge. *The Journal of Business Strategy, 18*(6), 31–34.

Enns, H. G., Huff, S. L., & Golden, B. R. (2001). How CIOs obtain peer commitment to strategic IS proposals: Barriers and facilitators. *The Journal of Strategic Information Systems, 10*(1), 3–14.

Hendricks, K. B., Singhal, V. R., & Stratman, J. K. (2007). The impact of enterprise systems on corporate performance: A study of ERP, SCM, and CRM system implementations. *Journal of Operations Management, 25*(1), 65–82.

Hossain, L., Patrick, J. D., & Rashid, M. A. (2002). *Enterprise resource planning: Global opportunities and challenges*. Hershey, PA: Idea Group Publishing.

INE. (2007a). *Classificação Portuguesa das actividades económicas, revisão 3* (*Vol. 322*). Instituto Nacional de Estatística.

INE. (2007b). *Lista das 1000 maiores empresas portuguesas. Ficheiro de Unidades Estatísticas - FUE - Base Belém*. Instituto Nacional de Estatística.

Iriana, R., & Buttle, F. (2006). Strategic, operational, and analytical customer relationship management. *Journal of Relationship Marketing, 5*(4), 23–42.

James, C., Joonsoo, B., Qinyi, W., Ling, L., Calton, P., & William, B. R. (2007). Workflow management for enterprise transformation. *Information and Knowledge Systems Management, 6*(1,2), 61-80.

Jianbing Wu, M. U., Cobzaru, M., & Norrie, D. (2000). *Supply chain management systems: State of the art and vision* Paper presented at the The 2000 IEEE International Conference on Management of Innovation and Technology.

Kalakota, R., & Robinson, M. (2000). Customer relationship management: Integrating processes to build relationships. In Kalakota, R., & Robinson, M. (Eds.), *E-business 2.0: Roadmap for success*. Addison Wesley Publishing Company.

Karakostas, B., Kardaras, D., & Papathanassiou, E. (2005). The state of CRM adoption by the financial services in the UK: An empirical investigation. *Information & Management, 42*(6), 853–863.

Kumar, V., Maheshwari, B., & Kumar, U. (2002). Enterprise resource planning systems adoption process: A survey of Canadian organizations. *International Journal of Production Research, 40*(3), 509–523.

Laudon, K. C., & Laudon, J. P. (2005). *Management Information Systems: Managing the digital firm* (9th ed.). Prentice Hall.

Li, E., Tseng, P. T. Y., & Lu, E. (2007). *Measuring the strength of partner relationship in B2B EC: An exploratory research*. Paper presented at the WiCom - International Conference on Wireless Communications, Networking and Mobile Computing, 2007.

Li, E. Y., McLeod, R., & Rogers, J. C. (2001). Marketing Information Systems in Fortune 500 companies: a longitudinal analysis of 1980, 1990, and 2000. *Information & Management, 38*(5), 307–322.

Lin, C., & Pervan, G. (2003). The practice of IS/IT benefits management in large Australian organizations. *Information & Management, 41*(1), 13–24.

Liu, C., & Arnett, K. P. (2000). Exploring the factors associated with Web site success in the context of electronic commerce. *Information & Management, 38*(1), 23–33.

McAfee, A. (2002). The impact of enterprise Information Technology adoption on operational performance: An empirical investigation. *Production and Operations Management, 11*(1), 33–53.

McLeod, R. (1995). Systems theory and information resources management: Integrating key concepts. *Information Resources Management Journal, 18*(2), 5–14.

Media, C. X. O. (2002). *CRM: Are companies buying it?*CIO Magazine.

Media, C. X. O. (2006). The state of the CIO '06. *CIO Magazine*. Retrieved from http://www.cio.com/archive/010106/JAN1SOC.pdf

Media, C. X. O. (2007). *The state of the CIO '07*. CIO Magazine.

Milutinović, V., & Patricelli, F. (2002). *E-business and e-challenges: Emerging communication*. IOS Press.

Negash, S., & Gray, P. (2008). Business intelligence. In Burstein, F., & Holsapple, C. W. (Eds.), *Handbook on decision support systems, 2*. Berlin/Heidelberg, Germany: Springer.

Nichols, E. L., & Handfield, R. B. (1999). *Introduction to supply chain management*. Prentice Hall Press.

Norris, G., Hurley, J. R., Hartley, K. M., Dunleavy, J. R., & Balls, J. D. (2000). *E-business and ERP – Transforming the enterprise*. PricewaterhouseCoopers.

Okkonen, J., Pirttimäki, V., Lönnqvist, A., & Hannula, M. (2002). *Triangle of performance measurement, knowledge management and business intelligence*. Paper presented at the EURAM - 2nd Annual Conference on Innovative Research in Management.

Oliver, D., & Romm, C. (2000). *ERP systems: The route to adoption.* Paper presented at the 6th Americas Conference on Information Systems Association for Information Systems (AMCIS), Long Beach, USA.

Pairat, R., & Jungthirapanich, C. (2005). *A chronological review of ERP research: An analysis of ERP inception, evolution, and direction.* Paper presented at the International Engineering Management Conference (IEMC), Newfoundland, Canada.

Parr, A. N. (2000). *A taxonomy of ERP implementation approaches.* Paper presented at the 33rd Hawaii International Conference on System Sciences.

Power, D. J. (2007). A brief history of decision support systems. Retrieved from http://dssresources.com/history/dsshistory.html

Pumareja, D. T., & Sikkel, K. (2006). Getting used with groupware: A first class experience. *The Journal of Human-Centred Systems, 20*(2), 189–201.

Rashid, M. A., Hossain, L., & Patrick, J. D. (2002). *The evolution of ERP systems: A historical perspective*. Hershey, PA: Idea Group Publishing.

Ross, J. W., & Vitale, M. R. (2000). The ERP revolution: Surviving versus thriving. *Information Systems Frontiers, 2*(2), 233–241.

Ryals, L., & Knox, S. (2001). Cross-functional issues in the implementation of relationship marketing through customer relationship management. *European Management Journal, 19*(5), 534–542.

Scott, J. E., & Vessey, I. (2000). Implementing enterprise resource planning systems: The role of learning from failure. *Information Systems Frontiers, 2*(2), 213–232.

Simchy-Levy, D., Kaminsky, P., & Simchy-Levy, E. (2003). *Designing & managing the supply chain – Concepts, strategies & case studies*. McGraw-Hill.

Sohal, A. S., & Ng, L. (1998). The role and impact of Information Technology in Australian business. *Journal of Information Technology, 13*(3), 201–217.

Stadtler, H. (2000). Supply chain management - An overview. In Kilger, C. (Ed.), *Supply chain management and advanced planning: Concepts, models, software and case studies* (pp. 7–27). Berlin, Germany: Springer-Verlag.

Trigo, A., Varajão, J., Figueiredo, N., & Barroso, J. (2007, 23-26 of June). *Information Systems and Technology adoption by the Portuguese large companies.* Paper presented at the European and Mediterranean Conference on Information Systems (EMCIS), Valence, Spain.

van Everdingen, Y., van Hillegersberg, J., & Waarts, E. (2000). Enterprise resource planning: ERP adoption by European midsize companies. *Communications of the ACM, 43*(4).

Varajão, J. (2006, Jan-Mar). Gestão da função de sistemas de informação. *Dirigir - Revista para chefias e quadros, IEFP,* 3-9.

Varajão, J., Ribeiro, A. T., Figueiredo, N., & Barroso, J. (2007, 12-15 of July). *Motivações inerentes à adopção de Tecnologias e Sistemas de Informação nas grandes empresas portuguesas.* Paper presented at the 6ª Conferência Ibero-Americana em Sistemas, Cibernética e Informática (CISCI), Orlando, EUA.

Varajão, J., Trigo, A., Figueiredo, N., & Barroso, J. (2007, Maio). 2007). TI nas empresas nacionais. *Revista CXO, 2*, 19–23.

Varajão, J., Trigo, A., Figueiredo, N., Barroso, J., & Bulas-Cruz, J. (2009). Information Systems services outsourcing reality in large Portuguese organisations. *International Journal of Business Information Systems, 4*(1), 125–142.

Wah, L. (2000). Behind the buzz: The substance of knowledge management. In Cortada, J., & Woods, J. A. (Eds.), *The knowledge management yearbook 2000-2001* (pp. 307–317). Boston, MA: Butterworth-Heineman.

KEY TERMS AND DEFINITIONS

Chief Information Officer (CIO): Job title for the board level head of IT within an organization.

Enterprise Information Systems: Any kind of computer system that supports enterprise information needs.

IT/IS Role: The functions of IT/IS in companies.

IT/IS Strategy: Long term plan of action designed to align IT/IS with the business goals.

Management Levels: Management hierarchy within an organization.

Motivations for IT/IS Adoption: The driving forces behind the adoption of IT/IS solutions.

Systems Adopted: The IT/IS solutions used by companies.

Trends in IT/IS Adoption: Future directions or changes in IT/IS investments.

APPENDIX

a. Implemented systems in company. Please choose *all* that apply:
☐ ERP (Enterprise Resource Planning)
☐ CRM (Customer Relationship Management)
☐ SCM (Supply Chain Management)
☐ BI (Business Intelligence)
☐ Collaboration & Groupware
☐ Workflow
☐ Business specific
☐ Other: ______________________________

b. What is the actual role of IT/IS solutions (where 1 is without importance and 5 the very important)? Please choose the appropriate response for each item:

	1	2	3	4	5
Operational support	O	O	O	O	O
Middle level management support	O	O	O	O	O
Top management support	O	O	O	O	O
Knowledge management	O	O	O	O	O
External entities interface (ex: B2B)	O	O	O	O	O

c. Systems in developing stage or planned for the near future? Please choose all that apply:
☐ ERP (Enterprise Resource Planning)
☐ CRM (Customer Relationship Management)
☐ SCM (Supply Chain Management)
☐ BI (Business Intelligence)
☐ Collaboration & Groupware
☐ Workflow
☐ Other: ______________________________

d. What are the main motivations behind IT/IS adoption? Please number each box in order of preference from 1 to 12:
☐ To reduce operational costs
☐ To differentiate products or services in relation to the competitors
☐ To improve the quality of products or services
☐ To launch new products or services before competition
☐ To improve business operations or processes
☐ To diversify the line of products or services
☐ To identify and to occupy new markets
☐ To improve customer service

☐ To reduce staff costs
☐ To establish strategic partnerships
☐ To increase the productivity of the employees
☐ To improve the communication between the employees

Compilation of References

Achterkamp, M. C., & Vos, F. J. F. (2006). A framework for making sense of sustainable innovation through stakeholder involvement. *International Journal of Environmental Technology and Management*, *6*(6), 525–538. doi:10.1504/IJETM.2006.011895

Alexandre, S. (2006). A gradual approach for software process improvement in SMEs. *Proceeding of 32nd EUROMICRO Conference on Software, Engineering and Advanced Applications*, (pp. 328–335).

Al-Mudimigh, A., Zairi, M., & Al-Mashari, M. (2001). ERP software implementation: an integrative framework. *European Journal of Information Systems*, *10*(4), 216–226. doi:10.1057/palgrave.ejis.3000406

American Productivity & Quality Center (APQC). (1999). *Creating a knowledge-sharing culture*. Consortium Benchmarking Study -- Best-Practice Report.

American Productivity & Quality Center (APQC). (2000). *Successfully implementing knowledge management*. Consortium Benchmarking Study -- Final Report, 2000.

Amoako-Gyampah, K. K., & Salam, A. F. (2004). An extension of the technology acceptance model in an ERP implementation environment. *Information & Management*, *41*(6), 731–745. doi:10.1016/j.im.2003.08.010

Anderson, P. (1999). Complexity theory and organization science. *Organization Science*, *10*(3), 216–232. doi:10.1287/orsc.10.3.216

Andriessen, J. H. E. (2003). *Working with groupware: Understanding and evaluating collaboration technology*. London: Springer.

Anthony, R. N. (1965). *Planning and control systems: A framework for analysis*. Boston, MA: Graduate School of Business Administration, Harvard University Press.

Ashima, H. (2010). Essence of software process reengineering in SME's: Towards process customization and automation. *Global Journal of Enterprise Information Systems*, *2*, 2.

Ashton, B., & Stacey, G. (2009). Technical intelligence in business: Understanding technology threats and opportunities. *International Journal of Technology Management*, *10*(1), 79–104.

Askenas, L., & Westelius, A. (2003). Five roles of an information system: A social constructionist approach to analyzing the use of ERP systems. *Informing Science*, *4*(3), 105–113.

August, J. H. (1991). *Joint application design: The group session approach to system design*. Englewood Cliffs, NJ: Yourdon Press.

Austin, J. L. (1976). *How to do things with words*. Oxford, UK: Oxford University Press.

Avison, D. E., Lau, F., Myers, M., & Nielsen, P. A. (1999). Action Research. *Communications of the ACM*, *42*(1), 94–97. doi:10.1145/291469.291479

Axelrod, R. (1997). *The complexity of cooperation: Agent-based models of competition and collaboration.* New Jersey: Princeton University Press.

Axelrod, R., & Cohen, M. (1999). *Harnessing complexity: Organizational implications of a scientific frontier*. New York: The Free Press.

Baark, E., & Heeks, R. (1998) "Evaluation of Donor-Funded Information Technology Transfer Projects in China: A Life-Cycle Approach". Retrieved Dec 12, 2007, from http://idpm.man.ac.uk/wp/di/di_wp01.htm.

Bakos, J.Y. and Treacy, M.E. "Information Technology and Corporate Strategy: A Research Perspective," *MIS Quarterly* (1 0:2), June 1986, pp. 107-1 19.

Baltzan, A., & Phillips, P. (2008). *Business driven information systems*. Boston, Mass.: McGraw-Hill.

Barton, C., and Bear, M. (1999) "Information and Communications Technologies: Are they the Key to Viable Business Development Services for Micro and Small Enterprises? Report for USAID as part of the Microenterprise Best Practices Project. March". Retrieved December 12, 2007, from http://www.mip.org/PUBS/MBP/ict.htm.

Baskerville, R., & Pries-Heje, J. (2001, July 27-29). *Racing the e-bomb: How the internet is redefining information systems development methodology.* Proceedings of the IFIP TC8/WG8.2 Working Conference on Realigning Research and Practice in Information Systems Development: The Social and Organizational Perspectice (pp. 49-68). Boise, Idaho.

Beckett-Camarata, E. J., Camarata, M. R., & Barker, R. T. (1998). Integrating internal and external customer relationships through relationship management: A strategic response to a changing global environment. *Journal of Business Research*, *41*(1), 71–81.

Beer, S. (1981). *The Brain of the Firm.* Chichester: Wiley.

Beer, S. (1985). *Diagnosing the System for Organizations*. Chichester: Wiley.

Belle, J.-P. V., Eccles, M., & Nash, J. (2003). *Discovering Information Systems.* Cape Town, South Africa: South African Universities Press.

Besson, P., & Browe, F. (2001). ERP project dynamics and enacted dialogue: Perceived understanding, perceived leeway and the nature of task-related conflicts. *The Data Base for Advances in Information Systems*, *32*(4), 47–66.

Bharati, P., & Chaudhury, A. (2006). Current Status ofTechnology Adoption: Micro, Small and Medium Manufacturing Firms in Boston. *Communications of the ACM*, *49*(10), 88–93. doi:10.1145/1164394.1164400

Bichler, M., Segev, A., & Zhao, J. L. (1998). Component-based e-commerce: Assesment of current practices and future directions. *SIGMOD Record*, *27*(4), 7–14. doi:10.1145/306101.306102

Bingi, P., Sharma, M. K., & Godla, J. K. (1999). Critical issues affecting an ERP implementation. *Information Systems Management*, *16*(3), 7–14. doi:10.1201/1078/43197.16.3.19990601/31310.2

Blili, S., & Raymond, L. (1993). Information technology: threats and opportunities for small and medium-sized enterprises. *International Journal of Information Management*, *13*, 439–448. doi:10.1016/0268-4012(93)90060-H

Boddy, D. (2004). Responding to competing narratives: Lessons for project managers. *International Journal of Project Management*, *22*(3), 225–234. doi:10.1016/j.ijproman.2003.07.001

Boonstra, A. (2003). Structure and analysis of IS decision making processes. *European Journal of Information Systems*, *12*(3), 195–209. doi:10.1057/palgrave.ejis.3000461

Boonstra, A. (2006). Interpreting an ERP implementation from a stakeholder perspective. *International Journal of Project Management*, *24*(1), 38–52. doi:10.1016/j.ijproman.2005.06.003

Braa, J., & Hedberg, C. (2002). The struggle for district-based health information systems in South Africa. *The Information Society*, *18*(2), 113–127. doi:10.1080/01972240290075048

Brady, A., & Voss, B. (1995). Small is as small does. *The Journal of Business Strategy*, *16*(2), 44–52. doi:10.1108/eb039690

Brehm, L., Heinzl, A., & Markus, M. L. (2001). *Tailoring ERP systems: A spectrum of choices and their implications*. Paper presented at the Proceedings of the 34th Hawaii International Conference on System Sciences.

Broadbent, M., Butler, C., & Hansell, A. (1994). A business and technology agenda for Information-Systems executives. *International Journal of Information Management*, *14*(6), 411–426. doi:10.1016/0268-4012(94)90016-7

Brown, D. H., & Lockett, N. (2004). Potential of critical e-applications for engaging SMEs in e-business: a provider perspective. *European Journal of Information Systems*, *13*, 21–34. doi:10.1057/palgrave.ejis.3000480

Bryson, J. M. (2004). What to do when stakeholders matter. Stakeholder identification and analysis techniques. *Public Management Review*, *6*(1), 21–53. doi:10.1080/14719030410001675722

Bukowitz, W., & Williams, R. (1999). *The knowledge management fieldbook*. London: Financial Times Prentice Hall.

Byrd, T. A., Lewis, B. R., & Turner, D. E. (2004). The impact of IT personal skills on IS infrastructure and competitive IS. *Information Resources Management Journal*, *17*(2), 38–62. doi:10.4018/irmj.2004040103

Byrd, T. A., & Turner, D. E. (2000). Measuring the flexibility of information technology infrastructure: Exploratory analysis of a construct. *Journal of Management Information Systems*, *17*(1), 167–208.

Calás, M., & Smircich, L. (1992). Rewriting gender into organizational theorizing: Directions from feminist perspectives. In Reed, M., & Hughes, M. (Eds.), *Rethinking organization: New directions in organizational theory and analysis* (pp. 227–253). London: Sage.

Cameron, N., & Braiden, P. (2004). Using BPR for development of production efficiency in companies making engineered to order products. *International Journal of Production Economics*, *89*, 261–273. doi:10.1016/S0925-5273(02)00448-6

Capon, N. and Glazer, R. "Marketing and Technology: A Strategic Coalignment," *Journal of Marketing* (51:3), July 1987, pp. 1-1 4.

Carr, D., & Johansson, H. (1995). *Best practices in re-engineering*. New York, NY: McGraw Hill.

Carrier, C. (1995). Intrapreneurship in large firms and SMEs. *International Small Business Journal*, (April-June): 54–61.

Cavaye, A. L. M. (1995). User participation in system development revisited. *Information & Management*, *28*(5), 311–326. doi:10.1016/0378-7206(94)00053-L

Cha-Jan Chang, J., & King, W. R. (2005). Measuring the performance of information systems: A functional scorecard. *Journal of Management Information Systems*, *22*(1), 85–115.

Chang, C. J., & King, W. R. (2005). Measuring the performance of information systems: A functional scorecard. *Journal of Management Information Systems*, *22*(1), 85–115.

Chang, L., & Powell, P. (1998). Toward a framework for business process reengineering in SMEs. *Information Systems Journal*, *8*(3), 199–216. doi:10.1046/j.1365-2575.1998.00035.x

Checkland, P. B., & Scholes, J. (1990). *Soft system methodology in action*. Chichester: John Wiley and Sons.

Checkland, P. (1981). *Systems Thinking*. Systems Practice, New York: John Wiley & Sons.

Checkland, P. (1991) "From Framework through Experience to Learning: The Essential Nature of Action Research," in: Nissen, H.-E., Klein, H. and Hirschheim, R. (eds.) Information Systems Research: Contemporary Approaches and Emergent Traditions, North Holland: Elsevier Publishers, 397-403.

Chen, I. J. (2001). Planning for ERP systems: analysis and future trends. *Business Process Management Journal*, *7*(5), 374–386. doi:10.1108/14637150110406768

Churchill, N., & Lewis, V. (1983, May/June). The five stages of small business growth. *Harvard Business Review*, 30–50.

Ciborra, C. (2000). Drifting: From control to drift. In Braa, K., Sorensen, C., & Dahlbom, B. (Eds.), *Planet internet*. Lund: Studentlitteratur.

Clemons, E.K. "Corporate Strategies for Information Technology: A Resource-Based Approach," Computer (24:1 1), November 1991, pp. 23-32.

Clemons, E.K. and Row, M.C. "Sustaining IT Advantage: The Role of Structural Differences," *MIS Quarterly* (1 5:3), September 1991 a, pp. 275-292.

Clemons, E.K. and Row, M.K. "Information Technology at Rosenbluth Travel: Competitive Advantage in a Rapidly Growing Service Company," *Journal of Management Information Systems* (8:2), Fall 1991 b, pp. 53-79.

Cody, W. F., Kreulen, J. T., Krishna, V., & Spangler, W. S. (2002). The integration of business intelligence and knowledge management. *IBM Systems Journal*, *41*(4), 697–714.

Coleman, D. (1997). *Groupware: Collaborative strategies for corporate LANs and Intranets*. Prentice Hall.

Conallen, J. (1999). Modeling web application architectures with UML. *Communications of the ACM*, *42*(10), 63–70. doi:10.1145/317665.317677

Conner, K.R. "A Historical Comparison of Resource-Based Theory and Five Schools of Thought Within Industrial Organization Economics: Do We Have a New Theory of the Firm?" *Journal of Management* (1 7:1), March 1991, pp. 121-1 54.

Copeland, D.G. and McKenney, J.L. "Airline Reservation Systems: Lessons from History," *MIS Quarterly* (12:3), September 1988, pp. 353-370.

Cotteleer, M. J., & Bendoly, E. (2006). Order lead-time improvement following enterprise Information Technology implementation: An empirical study. *Management Information Systems Quarterly*, *30*(3).

Cox, D. F., & Rich, S. U. (1964). Perceived risk and consumer decision-making - the case of the telephone shopping. *JMR, Journal of Marketing Research*, *1*(4), 32–39. doi:10.2307/3150375

Cragg, P. B., & King, M. (1993). Small-Firm Computing: Motivators and Inhibitors. *Management Information Systems Quarterly*, *17*(1), 47–60. doi:10.2307/249509

Craig, J., & Yetton, P. (1992). Business process redesign. *Australian Journal of Management*, *17*(2), 285–306. doi:10.1177/031289629301700207

Craig, J., & Yetton, P. (1997). The real event of re-engineering. In C. Sauer., P. Yetton, & Associates (Eds.), *Steps to the future*. San Francisco, CA: Jossey-Bass.

CTG. (1997). *An introduction to workflow management systems*. New York, NY: Center for Technology in Government, University at Albany.

Cuffe, S. S. (2005). Emerging management support systems models for global managers in the new economy. *Journal of Knowledge Management Practice, 6*.

Cummings, J. L., & Doh, J. P. (2000). Identifying who matters: Mapping key players in multiple environments. *California Management Review*, *42*(2), 83–105.

Cummings, T. G., & Worley, C. G. (2005). *Organization development and change*. Mason, OH: Thomson.

D'Souza, D. F., & Wills, A. C. (1998). *Objects, components, and frameworks with UML: The catalysis approach*. Addison-Wesley.

Dashofy, E. M., Van der Hoek, A., & Taylor, R. N. (2005). A comprehensive approach for the development of modular software architecture description languages. *ACM Transactions on Software Engineering and Methodology*, *14*(2), 199–245. doi:10.1145/1061254.1061258

Davenport, T. H. (1993). Need radical innovation and continuous improvement? *Planning Review*, *21*(3), 6–12.

Davenport, T. H., & Short, J. E. (1990). The new industrial engineering. *Sloan Management Review*, *31*, 4–16.

Davenport, T. H. (1998). Putting the enterprise into the enterprise system. *Harvard Business Review*, *76*(4), 121–131.

Davis, F. D. (1989). Perceived usefulness, perceived ease of use, and user acceptance of information technology. *Management Information Systems Quarterly*, *13*(3), 318–340. doi:10.2307/249008

DeLone, W. H. (1988). Determinants of Success for Computer Usage in Small Business. *Management Information Systems Quarterly*, *12*(1), 51–61. doi:10.2307/248803

Denzin, N. K. (1978). *The research act: A theoretical introduction to sociological methods*. McGraw-Hill.

Dietz, J. L. G. (2003). The atoms, molecules and fibers of organizations. *Data & Knowledge Engineering*, *47*(3), 301–325.

Dietz, J. L. G. (2006). The deep structure of business processes. *Communications of the ACM*, *49*(5), 59–64.

Doherty, N. F., King, M., & Al-Mushayt, O. (2003). The impact of inadequacies in the treatment of organisational issues on Information Systems development projects. *Information & Management*, *41*(1), 49–62. doi:10.1016/S0378-7206(03)00026-0

Dori, D. (2001). Object-process methodology applied to modeling credit card transactions. *Journal of Database Management*, *12*(1), 4. doi:10.4018/jdm.2001010101

Dowling, G. R., & Staelin, R. (1994). A model of perceived risk and intended risk-handling activity. *The Journal of Consumer Research*, *21*(1), 119–135. doi:10.1086/209386

Dumas, M., van der Aalst, W. M. P., & ter Hofstede, A. H. M. (2005). *Process-aware Information Systems: Bridging people and software through process technology*. New York, NY: Wiley.

Duncan, N. B. (1995). Capturing flexibility of information technology infrastructure: A study of resource. *Journal of Management Information Systems*, *12*(2), 37–57.

Duncombe, R., & Heeks, R. (2003). An information systems perspective on ethical trade and self-regulation. *Information Technology for Development*, *10*(2), 123–139. doi:10.1002/itdj.1590100206

Egyed, A., & Medvidovic, N. (1999, Oct). *Extending Architectural Representation in UML with View Integration.* Proceedings of the 2nd International Conference on the Unified Modelling Language (UML), (pp. 2-16). Fort Collins, CO.

Eisenhardt, K. M. (1989). Building theories from case study research. *Academy of Management Review*, *14*(4), 532–550.

Elliott, C. (1997). Everything wired must converge. *The Journal of Business Strategy*, *18*(6), 31–34.

Enns, H. G., Huff, S. L., & Golden, B. R. (2001). How CIOs obtain peer commitment to strategic IS proposals: Barriers and facilitators. *The Journal of Strategic Information Systems*, *10*(1), 3–14.

Epstein, M., & Axtell, R. (1996). *Growing artificial societies: Social science from the bottom up*. Washington, D.C.: The Brookings Institution.

Espejo, R., Schuhmann, W., Schwaninger, M., & Bilello, U. (1996). *Organisational Transformation and Learning*. Chichester: Wiley.

Feeny, D.F. and Ives, B. "In Search of Sustainability: Reaping Long-Term Advantage from Investments in Information Technology," *Journal of Management Information Systems* (7:1), Summer 1990, pp. 27-46.

Fernández, W. D., Lehmann, H., & Underwood, A. (2002, June 6-8). Rigour and relevance in studies of IS innovation: A grounded theory methodology approach. [ECIS]. *Proceedings of the European Conference on Information Systems, 2002*, 110–119.

Ferrell, J. (1996). Help for the other SMEs. *Manufacturing Engineering, 117*(2), 20.

Foong, S.-Y. (1999) Effect of end user personal and systems attributes on computer based information systems success in Malaysian SMEs. *Journal of Small Business Management*, July, **37**(3), 81–87.

Ford, D. (2003). Trust and knowledge management: The seeds of success. In *Handbook on Knowledge Management 1: Knowledge Matters* (pp. 553–575). Heidelberg: Springer-Verlag.

Fowler, A., & Walsh, M. (1999). Conflicting perceptions of success in an information systems project. *International Journal of Project Management, 17*(1), 1–10. doi:10.1016/S0263-7863(97)00063-X

Freeman, R. E. (1984). *Strategic management, a stakeholder approach*. Boston, MA: Pitman.

Fuller, T., & Lewis, F. (2003). Relationships mean everything. *British Journal of Management, 13*, 317–336. doi:10.1111/1467-8551.00249

Fuller, T., Warren, L., & Argyle, P. (2007a). Sustaining Entrepreneurial Business; a complexity perspective on processes that produce emergent practice. *The International Entrepreneurship and Management Journal, 4*(1), 1–17. doi:10.1007/s11365-007-0047-y

Fuller, T., Moran, P., & Argyle, P. (2004). Entrepreneurial foresight; a case in reflexivity, experiments, sensitivity and reorganisation. In Tsoukas, H., & Shepherd, J. (Eds.), *Managing the Future:Foresight in the Knowledge Economy* (pp. 171–178). Oxford: Blackwell.

Fuller, T., & Fewster, R. (2006). *The emergence of Tesco.com: A study of Corporate Entrepreneurship*. Paper presented at the Babson-Kauffman Entrepreneurship Research Conferemce, Kelley Business School, Indiana

Fuller, T., Warren, L., & Welter, F. (2007b, November). *Towards an emergence perspective on entrepreneurship.* Paper presented at RENT XXI, Research in Entrepreneurship and Small Business, Cardiff (pp. 22-23).

Galinac, T. (2009). Empirical evaluation of selected best practices in implementation of software process improvement. *Information and Software Technology, 51*(9), 1351–1364. doi:10.1016/j.infsof.2009.05.002

Galliers, R. D. (1992) "Choosing Information Systems Research Approaches, in: Galliers, R.D. (Ed.) Information Systems Research: Issues, Methods and Practical Guidelines," Henley-on-Thames: Alfred Waller, 144-162.

Garlan, D., & Kompanek, A. J. (2000). *Reconciling the needs of architectural description with object-modeling notations.* Proceedings of the Third International Conference on the Unified Modeling Language - UML 2000, (pp. 498-512). York, UK.

Gebauer, J., & Schober, F. (2006). Information system flexibility and the cost efficiency of business processes. *Journal of the Association for Information Systems*, 7(3), 122–146.

Gibb, A. A., & Scott, M. G. (1985). Strategic Awareness, Personal Commitment and the Process of Planning in the Small Business. *Journal of Management Studies*, *22*(6), 597–625. doi:10.1111/j.1467-6486.1985.tb00014.x

Gibson, K. (2000). The moral basis of stakeholder theory. *Journal of Business Ethics*, *26*(3), 245–257. doi:10.1023/A:1006110106408

Girish, H. (2007). Software quality and IS project performance improvements from software development process maturity and IS implementation strategies. *Journal of Systems and Software*, *80*(4), 616–627. doi:10.1016/j.jss.2006.06.014

Glaser, B. (1978). *Theoretical sensitivity: Advances in the methodology of grounded theory*. Mill Valley: Sociology Press.

Glaser, B., & Strauss, A. L. (1967). *The discovery of grounded theory: Strategies for qualitative research. Chigago*. Aldine.

Goldkuhl, G., & Lind, M. (2004). The generics of business interaction - emphasizing dynamic features through the BAT model. In M. Aakhus & M. Lind (Eds.), *9th Conference on the Language-Action Perspective on Communication Modelling*. New Brunswick, NJ.

Gonzalez, R., & Dahanayake, A. (2007). Responsibility in user participation in information system development. In Khosrow-Pour, M. (Ed.), *Managing worldwide operations and communications with Information Technology* (pp. 849–851). Hershey, PA: IGI Publications.

Greiner, L. E. (1972, July/August). Evolution and Revolution as Organisations Grow. *Harvard Business Review*, 37–46.

Greunz, M., & Stanoevska-Slabeva, K. (2002). *Modeling business media platforms*. 35th Annual Hawaii International Conference on System Sciences, Maui, HI.

Grinter, R. E. (1999). Systems architecture: Product designing and social engineering. *ACM SIGSOFT Software Engineering Notes*, *24*(2), 11–18. doi:10.1145/295666.295668

Grosh, B., & Somolekae, G. (1996). Mighty oaks from little acorns: Can micro-enterprise serve as the seedbed of industrialization? *World Development*, *24*(12), 1879–1890. doi:10.1016/S0305-750X(96)00082-4

Grover, V., Jeong, S. R., Kettinger, W., & Teng, J. T. C. (1995). Implementation of business process re-engineering. *Journal of Management Information Systems*, *12*(1), 109–144.

Håckanson, H. (1989). *Corporate technological behaviour: Co-operation and networks*. London, UK: Routledge.

Hagel, J. (1993). Keeping BPR on track. *The McKinsey Quarterly*, *1*, 59–72.

Hale, A., & Cragg, P. (1996). Business process re-engineering in the small firm. *INFOR*, *34*(1), 15–27.

Hamel, G., & Prahalad, C. K. (1994). *Competing for the future*. Boston: Harvard Business School Press.

Hammer, M. (1990). Re-engineering work: Don't automate, obliterate. *Harvard Business Review*, *68*(4), 104–122.

Hanseth, O., Monteiro, E., & Hatling, M. (1996). Developing information infrastructure: The tension between standardization and flexibility. *Science, Technology & Human Values*, *21*(4), 407–426. doi:10.1177/016224399602100402

Harrison, D. A., Mykytyn, P. P., Jr., and Riemenschneider, C. K. "Executive Decisions About Adoption of Information Technology in Small Business: Theory and Empirical Tests," *Information Systems Research* (8:2), 1997, pp. 171-195.

Hashmi, M. S., & Cuddy, J. (1990) Strategic initiatives for introducing CIM technologies in Irish SMEs. In *Computer Integrated Manufacturing – Proceedings of the Sixth CIM-Europe Annual Conference*, Faria, L. and Van Puymbroeck, W. (eds.) (Springer Verlag, Lisbon).

Hazan, M. (2002) "Virtual South: E-Commerce for unprivileged artisans" Retrieved Dec 12, 2007, from http://www.iicd.org/stories/.

HBSP. (1998). *Harvard Business review on knowledge management*. Cambridge, MA: Harvard Business School Press.

Hendricks, K. B., Singhal, V. R., & Stratman, J. K. (2007). The impact of enterprise systems on corporate performance: A study of ERP, SCM, and CRM system implementations. *Journal of Operations Management*, *25*(1), 65–82.

Hiatt, J. (2006). *ADKAR: A model for change in business, government and our community*. Loveland, Colo.: Prosci.

Hicks, B., Culley, S., McMahon, C., & Powell, P. (2010). Understanding Information Systems infrastructure in engineering SMEs. *Journal of Engineering and Technology Management*, *27*, 52–73. doi:10.1016/j.jengtecman.2010.03.004

Hirschheim, R., & Klein, K. (1989). Four paradigms of information system development. *Communications of the ACM*, *32*(10), 1199–1217. doi:10.1145/67933.67937

Hofmeister, C., Nord, R., & Soni, D. (1999a). *Applied software architecture*. Reading, MA: Addison-Wesley.

Hofmeister, C., Nord, R., & Soni, D. (1999b). *Describing software architecture with UML*. Proceedings of the First Working IFIP Conference on Software Architecture (WICSA1), (pp. 145-160). San Antonio, TX.

Holland, J. (1995). *Hidden order: How adaptation builds complexity*. MA: Perseus Books Reading.

Holland, C. P., Light, B., & Gibson, N. (1999, June 23-25). A critical success factors model for emterprise resource planning implementation. In *Proceedings of the Seventh European Conference on Information Systems*, Copenhagen (pp. 288-301).

Holsapple, C. W. (Ed.). (2003). *Handbook on knowledge management 1: Knowledge matters*. Heidelberg: Springer-Verlag.

Hong, C.-S., & Kim, Y.-G. (2002). The critical success factors for ERP implementation: An organizational fit perspective. *Information & Management*, *40*(1), 25–40. doi:10.1016/S0378-7206(01)00134-3

Honig, B. "What determines success? Examining the human, financial, and social capital of Jamaican microentrepreneurs," *Journal of Business Venturing*, (13:5), 1998, pp.371-94.

Hossain, L., Patrick, J. D., & Rashid, M. A. (2002). *Enterprise resource planning: Global opportunities and challenges*. Hershey, PA: Idea Group Publishing.

Hyman, E.L. and Dearden, K. "Comprehensive impact assessment systems for NGO microenterprise development programs. *World Development*, (26:2), pp. 261-276.

Igbaria, M., Zinatelli, N., Cragg, P. B., and Cavaye, A. L. M. "Personal Computing Acceptance Factors in Small Firms: A Structural Equation Model," *MIS Quarterly* (21:3), 1997, pp. 279-305.

INE. (2007a). *Classificação Portuguesa das actividades económicas, revisão 3* (*Vol. 322*). Instituto Nacional de Estatística.

INE. (2007b). *Lista das 1000 maiores empresas portuguesas. Ficheiro de Unidades Estatísticas - FUE - Base Belém*. Instituto Nacional de Estatística.

Ipe, M. (2003). *The praxis of knowledge sharing in organizations: A case study*. Doctoral dissertation. University Microfilms.

Iriana, R., & Buttle, F. (2006). Strategic, operational, and analytical customer relationship management. *Journal of Relationship Marketing*, *5*(4), 23–42.

Ives, B., & Learmonth, G. P. (1984). The Information Systems as a Competitive weapon. *Communications of the ACM*, *27*(12). doi:10.1145/2135.2137

Ives, W., Torrey, B., & Gordon, C. (2000). Knowledge sharing is human behavior. In *Knowledge management*: *Classic and contemporary works* (pp. 99-129).

Jackson, M. C. (1991). *Systems Methodology for the Management Sciences*. New York: Plenum.

Jackson, M. C. (2000). *Systems Approaches to Management*. New York: Kluwer.

Jacobson, I., Booch, G., & Rumbaugh, J. (1999). *The unified software development process*. New York: Addison-Wesley.

James, C., Joonsoo, B., Qinyi, W., Ling, L., Calton, P., & William, B. R. (2007). Workflow management for enterprise transformation. *Information and Knowledge Systems Management*, *6*(1,2), 61-80.

Janson, R. (1993). Technology – Tomorrows determinate. *The Ohio Journal of Science*, *93*(4), 78–82.

Jianbing Wu, M. U., Cobzaru, M., & Norrie, D. (2000). *Supply chain management systems: State of the art and vision* Paper presented at the The 2000 IEEE International Conference on Management of Innovation and Technology.

Johansson, H. (1993). *BPR: Breakpoint strategies for market dominance*. Chichester, UK: Wiley.

Johnson, P., & Lancaster, A. (2000). *Swarm users guide*. Swarm Development Group.

Jones, M. (1998). *Information Systems and the Double Mangle: Steering a Course Between the Scylla of Embedded Structure and the Charybdis of Strong Symmetry.* IFIP WG8.2/8.6 Joint Working Conference, Helsinki, Finland.

Kalakota, R., & Robinson, M. (2001). *e-Business 2.0: Roadmap for Success*: Addison-Wesley.

Karakostas, B., Kardaras, D., & Papathanassiou, E. (2005). The state of CRM adoption by the financial services in the UK: An empirical investigation. *Information & Management*, *42*(6), 853–863.

Katzenstein, G., & Lerch, F. J. (2000). Beneath the surface of organization processes: A social representation, framework for business process redesign. *ACM Transactions on Information Systems*, *18*(4), 383–422. doi:10.1145/358108.358111

Kazman, R., Klein, M., & Clements, P. (2000). *ATAM: Method for Architecture Evaluation* (Technical report No. CMU/SEI-2000-TR-004): Software Engineering Institute.

Kim, Y.-G., & Everest, G. C. (1994). Building an IS architecture: Collective wisdom from the field. *Information & Management, 26*(1), 1–11. doi:10.1016/0378-7206(94)90002-7

Kinni, T. (1995). Process improvement part 2. *Industry Week, 244*(4), 45–50.

Klein, H. K., & Myers, M. D. (1999, March). A Set of Principles for Conducting and Evaluating Interpretive Field Studies in Information Systems. *Management Information Systems Quarterly, 23*(1), 67–94. doi:10.2307/249410

Knoll, K., & Jarvenpaa, S. L. (1994). *Information technology alignment or "fit" in highly turbulent environment: The concept of flexibility: SIGCPR Computer Personnel*. ACM.

Koontz, C. (2000). Develop a solid e-commerce architecture. *e-Business Advisor*(January).

Kotter, J. (1990). *Force for change: How leadership differs from management*. New York: Free Press (Div. of Simon & Schuster).

Kristensen, L. M., Christensen, S., & Jensen, K. (1998). The practitioner's guide to coloured Petri Nets. *International Journal on Software Tools for Technology Transfer, 2*, 98–132.

Kroenke, D. (1981). *Business computer systems*. Santa Cruz, Calif.: Mitchell Publishing.

Kroenke, D. (2009). *Using MIS* (2nd ed.). New York: Prentice-Hall.

Kuipers, W. (1995). Surviving a system conversion. *Catalog Age, 12*(3), 67.

Kumar, V., Maheshwari, B., & Kumar, U. (2002). Enterprise resource planning systems adoption process: A survey of Canadian organizations. *International Journal of Production Research, 40*(3), 509–523.

Kumaran, S., Liu, R., & Wu, F. Y. (2008). On the duality of information-centric and activity-centric models of business processes. [Berlin, Germany: Springer.]. *Lecture Notes in Computer Science, 5074*, 32–47.

Kuntzmann, A., & Kruchten, P. (2003). The rational unified process—an enabler for higher process maturity. Retrieved April 19, 2007 from http://www-128.ibm.com/developerworks/rational/library/content/03July/0000/0579/Rational_CMM_WhitePaper.pdf.

Künzle, V., & Reichert, M. (2009). Towards object-aware process management systems: Issues, challenges, benefits. In *Lecture Notes in Business Information Processing, 29* (pp. 197–210). Berlin, Germany: Springer.

Kuruppuarachchi, P., Mandal, P., & Smith, R. (2002). IT project implementation strategies for effective changes: A critical review. *Logistics Information Management, 15*(2), 126. doi:10.1108/09576050210414006

Laroche, M., Bergeron, J., & Goutaland, C. (2003). How intangibility affects perceived risk: The moderating role of knowledge and involvement. *Journal of Services Marketing, 17*(2), 122–140. doi:10.1108/08876040310467907

Larsen, M., & Myers, M. (1999). When success turns into failure: A package-driven BPR project in the financial services industry. *The Journal of Strategic Information Systems, 8*, 395–417. doi:10.1016/S0963-8687(00)00025-1

Latchem. C. & Walker, D. (2001) "Telecentres: Case Studies and Key Issues", Vancouver: The Commonwealth of Learning.

Laudon, K. C., & Laudon, J. P. (2005). *Management Information Systems: Managing the digital firm* (9th ed.). Prentice Hall.

Lave, J., & Wenger, E. (1991). *Situated Learning: Legitimate Peripheral Participation*. New York: Cambridge University Press.

Lee, C., & Chen, S. (1992). *The overall environment and the development of Taiwan's SMEs*. Chung-Hua Institution for Economic Research.

Lee, O. (2004, March). A case study of Nevada DMV system. *Journal of the Academy of Business and Economics, 3.*

Lefebvre, L., & Lefebvre, E. (1993). Competitive positioning and innovative efforts in SMEs. *Small Business Economics, 5*, 297–305. doi:10.1007/BF01516250

Lefebvre, L., & Lefebvre, L. A. (1996) "Information and Telecommunication Technologies: The Impact of their Adoption on Small and Medium-sized Enterprises." Retrieved Dec, 12, 2007, from http://web.idrc.ca/en/ev-9303-201-1-DO_TOPIC.html.

Leist, S., & Zellner, G. (2006, April 23-27). *Evaluation of current architecture frameworks.* SAC'06, (pp. 1546-1553). Dijon, France.

Leonard, D., & Straus, S. (1998). Putting your company's whole brain to work. In *Harvard Business Review on Knowledge Management* (pp. 109–136). Boston: Harvard Business School Press.

Levene, R. J., & Braganza, A. (1996). Controlling the work scope in organisational transformation. *International Journal of Project Management, 14*(6), 331–339. doi:10.1016/0263-7863(96)00048-8

Levine, H. G., & Rossmoore, D. (1994). Politics and the function of power in a case study of IT implementation. *Journal of Management Information Systems, 11*(3), 115–134.

Levitt, T. (1960). Marketing myopia. *Harvard Business Review, 82*(7–8), 138.

Levy, M., & Powell, P. (1998). SME flexibility and the role of information systems. *Journal of Small Business Economics, 11*, 183–196. doi:10.1023/A:1007912714741

Levy, M., Powell, P., & Yetton, P. (2002). The Dynamics of SME Information Systems. *Small Business Economics, 19*, 341–354. doi:10.1023/A:1019654030019

Levy, M., P. Powell & P. Yetton. (2001) "SMEs: Aligning IS and the Strategic Context", Journal of Information Technology, forthcoming, Lichtenstein, G.A. and Lyons, T.S. "The entrepreneurial development system: Transforming business talent and community economies," *Economic Development Quarterly*, (15:1), 2001, pp.3-20.

Lewin, K. (1947). Frontiers in group dynamics, Part II-B: Feedback problems of social diagnosis and action. *Human Relations, 1*, 147.

Lewis, B. R., & Byrd, T. A. (2003). Development of a measure for the information technology infrastructure construct. *European Journal of Information Systems, 12*(2), 94–108. doi:10.1057/palgrave.ejis.3000449

Li, E. Y., McLeod, R., & Rogers, J. C. (2001). Marketing Information Systems in Fortune 500 companies: a longitudinal analysis of 1980, 1990, and 2000. *Information & Management, 38*(5), 307–322.

Li, E., Tseng, P. T. Y., & Lu, E. (2007). *Measuring the strength of partner relationship in B2B EC: An exploratory research.* Paper presented at the WiCom - International Conference on Wireless Communications, Networking and Mobile Computing, 2007.

Liao, S., Chang, J., Shih-chieh, C., & Chia-mei, K. (2004). Employee relationship and knowledge sharing: A case study of a Taiwanese finance and securities firm. *Knowledge Management Research & Practice, 2*, 24–34. doi:10.1057/palgrave.kmrp.8500016

Lichtenstein, B. M. B. (2000). Self-organized transitions: A pattern amid the chaos of transformative change. *The Academy of Management Executive, 14*(4), 128–141. doi:10.5465/AME.2000.3979821

Lin, C., & Pervan, G. (2003). The practice of IS/IT benefits management in large Australian organizations. *Information & Management, 41*(1), 13–24.

Liu, C., & Arnett, K. P. (2000). Exploring the factors associated with Web site success in the context of electronic commerce. *Information & Management, 38*(1), 23–33.

Locke, K. (2001). *Grounded theory in management research.* SAGE Publications.

Lu, R., Sadiq, S., & Governatori, G. (2009). On managing business processes variants. *Data & Knowledge Engineering, 68*, 642–664.

Lyytinen, K., Rose, G., & Welke, R. (1998). The brave new world of development in the internetwork computing architecture (InterNCA): Or how distributed computing platforms will change systems development. *Information Systems Journal, 8*(3), 241–253. doi:10.1046/j.1365-2575.1998.00037.x

Lyytinen, K. (1987). A taxonomic perspective of information dystems fevelopment: Theoretical constructs and recommendations. In Boland, R. J. Jr, & Hirschheim, R. A. (Eds.), *Critical issues in information systems research* (pp. 3–41). John Wiley & Sons.

Lyytinen, K., Smolander, K., & Tahvanainen, V.-P. (1989). *Modelling CASE environments in systems development.* Proceedings of CASE'89 the First Nordic Conference on Advanced Systems Engineering, Stockholm.

Mallach, E. (2006). System conversion: Teaching versus reality. *International Journal of Information and Communication Technology Education, 2*(2), 17. doi:10.4018/jicte.2006040102

Mandal, P., & Gunasekaran, A. (2003). Issues in implementing ERP: A case study. *European Journal of Operational Research, 146*, 274. doi:10.1016/S0377-2217(02)00549-0

Mansell, R., & Wehn, U. (1998). *Knowledge Societies: Information Technology for Sustainable Development.* Oxford: Oxford University Press.

Mantzana, V., Themistocleous, M., Irani, Z., & Morabito, V. (2007). Identifying healthcare actors involved in the adoption of Information Systems. *European Journal of Information Systems, 16*(1), 91–102. doi:10.1057/palgrave.ejis.3000660

Markus, M. L., Axline, S., & Petrie, D. (2000). Learning from adopters experiences with ERP: Problems encountered and success achieved. *Journal of Information Technology, 15*(4), 245–265. doi:10.1080/02683960010008944

Markus, M. L., & Mao, J. Y. (2004). Participation in development and implementation—Updating and old, tired concept for today's IS contexts. *Journal of the Association for Information Systems, 5*(11-12), 514–544.

Markus, M. L., Axline, S., Petrie, D., & Tanis, C. (2003). Learning from experiences with ERP: Problems encountered and success achieved. In Shanks, G., Seddon, P. B., & Willcocks, L. P. (Eds.), *Second-wave enterprise resource planning systems* (pp. 23–55). Cambridge: Cambridge University Press.

Markus, M. L., & Tanis, C. (2000). The enterprise systems experience – from adoption to success. In Zmud, R. W. (Ed.), *Framing the Domains of IT Research: Glimpsing the Future through the Past* (pp. 73–207). Cincinnatti, Ohio: Pinnaflex Educational Resources Inc.

Martin, P. Y., & Turner, B. A. (1986). Grounded theory and organizational research. *The Journal of Applied Behavioral Science, 22*(2), 141–157. doi:10.1177/002188638602200207

Matthews, P., "ICT Assimilation and SME Expansion," *Journal of International Development.* (19), 2007, pp. 817–827.

McAfee, A. (2002). The impact of enterprise Information Technology adoption on operational performance: An empirical investigation. *Production and Operations Management, 11*(1), 33–53.

McElroy, B., & Mills, C. (2003). Managing stakeholders. In Turner, R. J. (Ed.), *People in project management* (pp. 99–118). Aldershot, UK: Gower.

McFarlan, F. W., & McKenney, J. L. (1983). *Corporate Information Systems Management.* Homewood, Ill.: Richard D. Irwin.

McFarlan, F.W. "Information Technology Changes the Way You Compete," *Harvard Business Review* (62:3), May June 1984, pp. 98-1 03.

McKeown, I., & Philip, G. (2003). Business transformation, Information Technology and competitive strategies: Learning to fly. *International Journal of Information Management, 23*(1), 3–24. doi:10.1016/S0268-4012(02)00065-8

McLeod, R. (1995). Systems theory and information resources management: Integrating key concepts. *Information Resources Management Journal, 18*(2), 5–14.

McLoughlin, I. (1999). *Creative technological change.* London, UK: Routledge. doi:10.4324/9780203019870

Media, C. X. O. (2002). *CRM: Are companies buying it?* CIO Magazine.

Media, C. X. O. (2007). *The state of the CIO '07.* CIO Magazine.

Media, C. X. O. (2006). The state of the CIO '06. *CIO Magazine.* Retrieved from http://www.cio.com/archive/010106/JAN1SOC.pdf

Medina-Mora, R., Winograd, T., Flores, R., & Flores, F. (1992). The action workflow approach to workflow management technology. In J. Turner & R. Kraut (Eds.), *4th Conference on Computer Supported Cooperative Work.* New York, NY: ACM.

Medvidovic, N., & Taylor, R. N. (2000). A classification and comparison framework for software architecture description languages. *IEEE Transactions on Software Engineering, 26*(1), 70–93. doi:10.1109/32.825767

Medvidovic, N., Egyed, A., & Rosenblum, D. S. (1999). *Round-trip software engineering using UML: From architecture to design and back.* Proceedings of the 2nd Workshop on Object-Oriented Reengineering (WOOR), Toulouse, France, Sept. 1999, 1-8.

Merisalo-Rantanen, H., Tuunanen, T., & Rossi, M. (2005). Is extreme programming just old wine in new bottles: A comparison of two cases. *Journal of Database Management*, *16*(4), 41. doi:10.4018/jdm.2005100103

Meyers, P., Sivakumar, K., & Nakata, C. (1999). Implementation of industrial process innovations: Factors, effects, and marketing. *Journal of Product Innovation Management*, *16*, 295. doi:10.1016/S0737-6782(98)00044-7

Milutinović, V., & Patricelli, F. (2002). *E-business and e-challenges: Emerging communication.* IOS Press.

Minar, N., Burkhar, R., Langton, C., & Askemnazi, M. (1996). *The Swarm Simulation System: A toolkit for building multi-agent simulations*. Retrieved from http://alumni.media.mit.edu/~nelson/research/ swarm/.

Mitchell, R. K., Agle, B. R., & Wood, D. J. (1997). Toward a theory of stakeholder identification and salience: Defining the principle of who and what really counts. *Academy of Management Review*, *22*(4), 853–886.

Moitra, D., & Ganesh, J. (2005). Web services and flexible business processes: Towards the adaptive enterprise. *Information & Management*, *42*(7), 921–933. doi:10.1016/j.im.2004.10.003

Monroe, R. T., Kompanek, A., Melton, R., & Garlan, D. (1997). Architectural styles, design patterns, and objects. *IEEE Software*, *14*(1), 43–52. doi:10.1109/52.566427

Montazemi, A. R. (1988). Factors Affecting Information Satisfaction in the Context of the Small Business Environment. *Management Information Systems Quarterly*, *12*(2), 239–256. doi:10.2307/248849

Montoni, M. (2007). *MPS model and TABA workstation: Implementing software process improvement initiatives in small settings*. 5th International Workshop on Software Quality, (pp. 57-63).

Moore, G. C., & Benbasat, I. (1991). Development of an instrument to measure the perceptions of adopting an information technology innovation. *Information Systems Research*, *2*(3), 192–222. doi:10.1287/isre.2.3.192

Moyi, E. D. (2003). Networks, information and small enterprises: New Technologies and the ambiguity of empowerment. *Information Technology for Development*, *10*, 221–232. doi:10.1002/itdj.1590100402

Müller, R., & Turner, J. R. (2007). Matching the project managers' leadership style to project type. *International Journal of Project Management*, *25*(1), 21–32. doi:10.1016/j.ijproman.2006.04.003

Mumford, E. (2001). Action research: Helping organizations to change. In Trauth, E. (Ed.), *Qualitative research in IS: Issues and trends* (pp. 46–77). Hershey, PA: Idea Group Publishing. doi:10.4018/9781930708068.ch003

Murata, T. (1989). Petri nets: Properties, analysis and applications. *Proceedings of the IEEE*, *77*(4), 514–580.

Murray, S. (2003). *A quantitative examination to determine if knowledge sharing activities, given the appropriate richness lead to knowledge transfer, and if implementation factors influence the use of these knowledge sharing activities*. Doctoral dissertation. University Microfilms.

Muscatello, J., Small, H., & Chen, I. (2003). Implementing enterprise resource planning systems in small and midsize manufacturing firms. *International Journal of Operations & Production Management, 23*(8), 850–871. doi:10.1108/01443570310486329

Nah, F. F. H., Lau, J. L. S., & Kuang, J. (2001). Critical factors for successful implementation of enterprise systems. *Business Process Management Journal, 7*(3), 285–296. doi:10.1108/14637150110392782

Naylor, J., & Williams, J. (1994). Successful Use of IT in SMEs. *European Journal of IS, 3*(1), 48–56.

Negash, S., & Gray, P. (2008). Business intelligence. In Burstein, F., & Holsapple, C. W. (Eds.), *Handbook on decision support systems, 2*. Berlin/Heidelberg, Germany: Springer.

Nichols, E. L., & Handfield, R. B. (1999). *Introduction to supply chain management*. Prentice Hall Press.

Nonaka, I., & Konno, N. (1998). The concept of Ba: Building a foundation for knowledge creation. [Special Issue on Knowledge and the Firm]. *California Management Review, 40*(3), 40–54.

Nonaka, I., & Takeuchi, H. (1995). *The knowledge-creating company: How Japanese companies create the dynamics of innovation*. New York: Oxford University Press.

Norris, G., Hurley, J. R., Hartley, K. M., Dunleavy, J. R., & Balls, J. D. (2000). *E-business and ERP – Transforming the enterprise*. PricewaterhouseCoopers.

Nurcan, S. (2008). *A survey on the flexibility requirements related to business processes and modeling artifacts*. In IEEE 41st Annual Hawaii International Conference on System Sciences. New York, NY: IEEE Press.

O'Dell, C. (2008). *Web 2.0 and knowledge management*. American Productivity & Quality Center (APQC). Retrieved from http://www.apqc.org.

O'Farrell, C., Norrish, P., & Scott, A. (1999) "Information and Communication Technologies (ICTs) for Sustainable Livelihoods." Burton Hall: Intermediate Technology Development Group.

OASIS. (2007). *Web services business process execution language*, V.2.0. Retrieved January 18, 2011, from http://docs.oasis-open.org/wsbpel/2.0/OS/wsbpel-v2.0-OS.html

Object Management Group. (1999). *UML Profile for Enterprise Distributed Object Computing: Request for Proposals (ad/99-03-10)*. OMG.

Object Management Group. (2005). *Unified modeling language: Superstructure version 2.0* (No. formal/05-07-04).

Object Management Group. (2006). *OMG SysML Specification (ptc/06-05-04)*.

Okkonen, J., Pirttimäki, V., Lönnqvist, A., & Hannula, M. (2002). *Triangle of performance measurement, knowledge management and business intelligence*. Paper presented at the EURAM - 2nd Annual Conference on Innovative Research in Management.

Oliver, D., & Romm, C. (2000). *ERP systems: The route to adoption*. Paper presented at the 6th Americas Conference on Information Systems Association for Information Systems (AMCIS), Long Beach, USA.

OMG. (2007). *Unified modeling language: Superstructure*, V.2.1.1. Retrieved January 18, 2011, from http://www.omg.org/spec/UML/2.2/

OMG. (2008). *Business process modeling notation*, V.1.1. Retrieved January 18, 2011, from http://www.bpmn.org

Orlikowski, R. J. (1992). The duality of technology: Rethinking the concepts of technology in organizations. *Organization Science*, *3*(3), 398–427. doi:10.1287/orsc.3.3.398

Ould, M. (2005). *Business process management: A rigorous approach*. The British Computer Society.

Owen, W., & Darkwa, O. (1999). Role of Multipurpose Community Telecentres in Accelerating National Development in Ghana. *First Monday, Vol*, *5*(1), 1–23.

Pairat, R., & Jungthirapanich, C. (2005). *A chronological review of ERP research: An analysis of ERP inception, evolution, and direction*. Paper presented at the International Engineering Management Conference (IEMC), Newfoundland, Canada.

Päivärinta, T., Halttunen, V., & Tyrväinen, P. (2001). A genre-based method for information system planning. In Rossi, M., & Siau, K. (Eds.), *Information modeling in the new millennium* (pp. 70–93). Hershey, PA: Idea Group. doi:10.4018/9781878289773.ch005

Palvia, S., Mallach, E., & Palvia, P. (1991). Strategies for converting from one IT environment to another. *Journal of Systems Management*, *42*(10), 23.

Parr, A. N. (2000). *A taxonomy of ERP implementation approaches*. Paper presented at the 33rd Hawaii International Conference on System Sciences.

Pateli, A. G., & Giaglis, G. M. (2004). A research framework for analyzing eBusiness models. *European Journal of Information Systems*, *13*, 302–314. doi:10.1057/palgrave.ejis.3000513

Pinch, T. J., & Bijker, W. E. (1997). The social construction of facts and artifacts: Or how the sociology of science and the sociology of technology might benefit each other. In Bijker, W. E., Hughes, T. P., & Pinch, T. J. (Eds.), *The social construction of technological systems* (pp. 17–50). Cambridge, MA: MIT Press.

Piscitello, L., & Sgobbi, F. (2004, June). Globalisation, E-Business and SMEs: Evidence from the Italian District of Prato. *Small Business Economics*, *22*(5), 333. doi:10.1023/B:SBEJ.0000022208.34741.55

Poon, S., & Swatman, P. (1999). An exploratory study of small business Internet commerce issues. *Information & Management*, *35*, 9–18. doi:10.1016/S0378-7206(98)00079-2

Porter, M. E. (1980). *Competitive Strategy: Techniques for Analyzing Industries and Competitors*. New York, NY: Free Press.

Porter, M.E. and Millar, V.E. "How Information Gives You Competitive Advantage," *Harvard Business Review* (63:4), July-August 1985, pp. 149-1 60.

Pouloudi, A., & Whitley, E. A. (1997). Stakeholder identification in inter organisational systems: Gaining insights for drug use management systems. *European Journal of Information Systems*, *6*(1), 1–14. doi:10.1057/palgrave.ejis.3000252

Power, D. J. (2007). A brief history of decision support systems. Retrieved from http://dssresources.com/history/dsshistory.html

Pozzebon, M., and Pinsonneault, A. (2005). Challenges in conducting empirical work using structuration theory: Learning from IT research. *Organization Studies (Sage Publications Inc.), 26*(9), 1353-1376.

Prahalad, C. K., & Krishnan, M. S. (2002). The dynamic synchronization of strategy and information technology. *MIT Sloan Management Review, 43*(4), 24–33.

Pumareja, D. T., & Sikkel, K. (2006). Getting used with groupware: A first class experience. *The Journal of Human-Centred Systems, 20*(2), 189–201.

Qiang, C. Z., Clarke, G. R., & Halewood, N. (2006). The Role of ICT. In World Bank (Ed.), *Doing Business Information and Communications for Development—Global Trends and Policies*. Washington, DC: World Bank.

Qureshi, S., Kamal, M., & Wolcott, P. (2008). *Sustainability of Information Technology Therapy on Micro-enterprise Development*. HICSS.

Qureshi, S. "How does Information technology effect Development? Integrating Theory and Practice into a Process Model." *Proceedings of the eleventh Americas Conference on Information Systems*, Omaha, NE, 2005.

Ragsdell, G., & warren, L. (1999). Learning from Beer: Using the Viable System Model for Organisational Design. *OR Insight, 12*(4), 16-23.

Rainer, R. K., & Turban, E. (2009). *Introduction to information systems: Supporting and transforming business* (2nd ed.). Hoboken, N.J.: John Wiley & Sons.

Rashid, M. A., Hossain, L., & Patrick, J. D. (2002). *The evolution of ERP systems: A historical perspective*. Hershey, PA: Idea Group Publishing.

Rational Software Corporation. (2001). Rational Unified Process [Online documentation, Version 2001A.04.00].

Raymond, L. (1988). The Impact of Computer Training on the Attitudes and Usage Behaviour of Small Business Managers. *Journal of Small Business Management, 26*(3), 9–13.

Raymond, L., Bergeron, F., & Blili, S. (2005). The assimilation of E-business in manufacturing SMEs: determinants and effects on growth and internationalization. *Electronic Markets, 15*(2), 106–118. doi:10.1080/10196780500083761

Raymond, L., Bergeron, F., & Rivard, S. (1998). Determinants of BPR success in SMEs. *Journal of Small Business Management, 36*(1), 72–85.

Reddy, S. B., & Reddy, R. (2002). Competitive agility and the challenge of legacy information systems. *Industrial Management & Data Systems, 102*(1), 5–16. doi:10.1108/02635570210414613

Reid, G., & Jacobsen, C. (1988). *The Small Entrepreneurial Firm*. Aberdeen University Press.

Reijers, H., & Mansor, S. (2005). Best practices in business process redesign: An overview and qualitative evaluation of successful redesign heuristics. *Omega, 33*, 282–306. doi:10.1016/j.omega.2004.04.012

Reisman, S., & Dear, R. G. (1998). Managing platform conversion in educational institutions. *International Journal of Educational Management, 12*(5), 225. doi:10.1108/09513549810225934

Ribbler, J. (1996). Delivering solutions for the knowledge economy. *On-line, 20*(5), 12-19.

Riemenschneider, C. Harrison, D. and P. Mykytyn. (2003) "Understanding IT Adoption Decisions in Small Business: Integrating Current Theories" Information and Management, Vol 40.

Riss, U. V., Rickayzen, A., Maus, H., & van der Aalst, W. M. P. (2005). Challenges for business process and task management. *Journal of Universal Knowledge Management*, *0*(2), 77–100.

Robson, C. (2002). *Real world research* (2nd ed.). Blackwell Publishing.

Rockart, J., & Short, J. (1989). IT in the 1990s. *Sloan Management Review*, *30*, 7–17.

Rolland, K. H., & Monteiro, E. (2002). Balancing the local and the global in infrastructural information systems. *The Information Society*, *18*(2), 87–100. doi:10.1080/01972240290075020

Rose, J., & Scheepers, R. (2001). *Structuration theory and information systems development; frameworks for practice.* Paper presented at the Proceedings of the 9th European Conference on Information Systems, Bled, Slovenia.

Ross, J. W., Weill, P., & Robertson, D. C. (2006). *Enterprise architecture as strategy: Creating a foundation for business execution.* Harvard Business School Press.

Ross, J. W., & Vitale, M. R. (2000). The ERP revolution: Surviving versus thriving. *Information Systems Frontiers*, *2*(2), 233–241.

Ross, J. W., Vitale, M. R., & Willcocks, L. P. (2003). The continuing ERP revolution: Sustainable lessons, new modes of delivery. In Shanks, G., Seddon, P. B., & Willcocks, L. P. (Eds.), *Second-wave enterprise resource planning systems* (pp. 102–132). Cambridge: Cambridge University Press.

Rossi, G., & Schwabe, D. (2000). Object-oriented web applications modeling. In Rossi, M., & Siau, K. (Eds.), *Information modelling in the next millennium*. Hershey: IDEA Group Publishing.

Rost, J. (2004). Political reasons for failed software projects. *IEEE Software*, *21*(6), 104–107. doi:10.1109/MS.2004.48

Rumpe, B., Schoenmakers, M., Radermacher, A., & Schürr, A. (1999). *UML + ROOM as a Standard ADL.* Fifth IEEE International Conference on Engineering of Complex Computer Systems, (pp. 43-53).

Russell, N., ter Hofstede, A. H. M., Edmond, D., & van der Aalst, W. M. P. (2005). Workflow data patterns: Identification, representation and tool support. [Berlin, Germany: Springer.]. *Lecture Notes in Computer Science*, *3716*, 353–368.

Russell, N., van der Aalst, W. M. P., ter Hofstede, A. H. M., & Edmond, D. (2005). Workflow resource patterns: Identification, representation and tool support. [Berlin, Germany: Springer.]. *Lecture Notes in Computer Science*, *3520*, 216–232.

Ryals, L., & Knox, S. (2001). Cross-functional issues in the implementation of relationship marketing through customer relationship management. *European Management Journal*, *19*(5), 534–542.

Saaren-Seppälä, K. (1988). *Wall chart technique: The use of wall charts for effective planning*. Helsinki: Kari Saaren-Seppälä Ky.

Saarinen, T. (1996). An expanded instrument for evaluating information system success. *Information & Management*, *31*(2), 103–118. doi:10.1016/S0378-7206(96)01075-0

Sambamurthy, V., Bharadwaj, A., & Grover, V. (2003). Shaping agility through digital options: Reconceptualizing the role of information technology in contemporary firms. *Management Information Systems Quarterly*, *27*(2), 237–263.

Sanders, C.K. "The impact of micro-enterprise assistance programs: A comparative study of program participants, non participants, and other low-wage workers," *Social Service Review*, (76:2), 2002, pp.321-40.

Sauer, C., Southon, G., & Dampney, C. N. G. (1997). *Fit, failure, and the house of horrors: Toward a configurational theory of IS project failure.* Proceedings of the eighteenth international conference on Information systems, (pp. 349-366). Atlanta, Georgia.

SBS. (2003). Retrieved from www.sbs.gov.uk/statistics/smedefs.php

Schein, E. (1990). Organizational culture. *The American Psychologist*, *2*, 109. doi:10.1037/0003-066X.45.2.109

Schreiner, M., & Woller, G. "Micro-enterprise Development Programs in the United States and in the Developing World," *World Development* (31:9), 2003, pp 1567-1580.

Scott, M., & Bruce, R. (1987). Five Stages of Growth in Small Business. *Long Range Planning*, *20*(3), 45–52. doi:10.1016/0024-6301(87)90071-9

Scott, J. E., & Vessey, I. (2000). Implementing enterprise resource planning systems: The role of learning from failure. *Information Systems Frontiers*, *2*(2), 213–232.

Sellers, G. (1997, September). Tools for managing your business process. CMA Magazine, 25-27.

Servon, L. J. and Doshna, J.P. "Microenterprise and the economic development toolkit: A small part of the big picture" *Journal of Developmental Entrepreneurship.* (5:3), 2000, pp. 183.

Sethi, V., & King, W. R. (1994, December). Development of Measures to Assess the Extent to Which an Information Technology Application Provides Competitive Advantage. *Management Science*, *40*(12). doi:10.1287/mnsc.40.12.1601

Shaw, M., & Garlan, D. (1996). *Software architecture: Perspectives on an emerging discipline*. Prentice Hall.

Shenhar, A. J., Levy, O., & Dvir, D. (1997). Mapping the dimensions of project success. *Project Management Journal*, *28*(2), 5–13.

Shin, N., & Edington, B. H. (2007). An integrative framework for contextual factors affecting information technology implementation. *Journal of Information Technology Theory and Application*, *8*(4), 21.

Siau, K., & Cao, Q. (2001). Unified modeling language (UML) — a complexity analysis. *Journal of Database Management*, *12*(1), 26–34. doi:10.4018/jdm.2001010103

Siau, K., Erickson, J., & Lee, L. Y. (2005). Theoretical vs. practical complexity: The case of UML. *Journal of Database Management*, *16*(3), 40–57. doi:10.4018/jdm.2005070103

Silver, M. S. (1991). *Systems that support decision makers: Description and analysis*. Chichester: Wiley & Sons.

Simchy-Levy, D., Kaminsky, P., & Simchy-Levy, E. (2003). *Designing & managing the supply chain – Concepts, strategies & case studies*. McGraw-Hill.

Small, C., & Sage, A. (2006). Knowledge management and knowledge sharing: A review. *Information, Knowledge, and Systems Management*, *5*(3), 153–169.

Small, C. (2006). *An enterprise knowledge-sharing model: A complex adaptive systems perspective on improvement in knowledge sharing*. Doctoral dissertation, George Mason University. University Microfilms.

Smolander, K. (2003, January 6-9,). *The birth of an e-business system architecture: Conflicts, compromises, and gaps in methods*. Hawaii International Conference on System Sciences (HICSS'36), Hilton Waikoloa Village, Big Island, Hawaii.

Smolander, K., & Päivärinta, T. (2002a, May 27-31). *Describing and communicating software architecture in practice: Observations on stakeholders and rationale*. Proceedings of CAiSE'02 - The Fourteenth International Conference on Advanced Information Systems Engineering, (pp. 117-133).Toronto, Canada.

Smolander, K., & Päivärinta, T. (2002b, Aug 25-30). *Practical rationale for describing software architecture: Beyond programming-in-the-large*. Software Architecture: System Design, Development and Maintenance - IFIP 17th World Computer Congress - TC2 Stream / 3rd Working IEEE/IFIP Conference on Software Architecture (WICSA3), (pp. 113-126). Montréal, Québec, Canada.

Smolander, K., Hoikka, K., Isokallio, J., Kataikko, M., & Mäkelä, T. (2002, April, 8-11). *What is included in software architecture? A case study in three software organizations*. Proceedings of 9th annual IEEE International Conference and Workshop on the Engineering of Computer-Based Systems (pp. 131-138). (ECBS) 2002, Lund, Sweden.

Smolander, K., Rossi, M., & Purao, S. (2002, December 18). *Software architecture: Metaphors across contexts*. AIS Theory Development Workshop, Barcelona.

Smolander, K., Rossi, M., & Purao, S. (2005, May 26-28). *Going beyond the blueprint: Unraveling the complex reality of software architectures*. 13th European Conference on Information Systems: Information Systems in a Rapidly Changing Economy, Regensburg, Germany.

Software Engineering Institute (SEI). (1996). *IDEAL^{SM}: A user's guide for software process improvement (Handbook CMU/SEI-96-HB-001)*. Pittsburgh, PA: Software Engineering Institute, Carnegie Mellon University.

Soh, C., Kien, S. S., & Tay-Yap, J. (2000). Cultural fits and misfits: Is ERP a universal solution? *Communications of the ACM*, *43*(4), 47–51. doi:10.1145/332051.332070

Sohal, A. S., & Ng, L. (1998). The role and impact of Information Technology in Australian business. *Journal of Information Technology*, *13*(3), 201–217.

Southwood, R. 2004. ICTs and Small Enterprise: A Motor of Economic Development in Africa, IICD Research Briefs, IICD, The Hague: IICD Research Briefs 9.

Sowa, J. F., & Zachman, J. A. (1992). Extending and formalizing the framework for information systems architecture. *IBM Systems Journal*, *31*(3), 590–616. doi:10.1147/sj.313.0590

Stacey, R. D. (2003). *Strategic Management and Organisational Dynamics, the Challenge of Complexity*. London: FT Prentice Hall.

Stadtler, H. (2000). Supply chain management - An overview. In Kilger, C. (Ed.), *Supply chain management and advanced planning: Concepts, models, software and case studies* (pp. 7–27). Berlin, Germany: Springer-Verlag.

Stair, R., & Reynolds, G. (2008). *Principles of information systems,* Boston, Mass.: Cengage (then Thomson Course Technology).

Star, S. L., & Griesemer, J. R. (1989). Institutional cology, "translations" and boundary objects: Amateurs and professionals in berkeley's museum of vertebrate zoology, 1907-39. *Social Studies of Science*, *19*, 387–420. doi:10.1177/030631289019003001

Stevenson, R. (1993). Strategic business process engineering. In Spurr, K., Layzell, P., Jennison, L., & Richards, N. (Eds.), *Software assistance for business re-engineering*. Chichester, UK: Wiley.

Stigler, G. (1939). Production and distribution in the short run. *The Journal of Political Economy*, *47*(3), 305–327. doi:10.1086/255387

Strauss, A. L., & Corbin, J. (1990). *Basics of qualitative research: Grounded theory procedures and applications*. Newbury Park, CA: Sage Publications.

Street, C. T., & Meister, D. B. (2004). Small Business Growth and Internal Transparency: The Role of Information Systems. *Management Information Systems Quarterly*, *28*(3), 473–506.

Sullivan, B. C. "Economics of Information Technology" *International Journal of Social Economics*. Bradford. (12:1), 1985, pp. 37.

Sutherland, J., & Heuvel, W.-J. d. (2002). Enterprise application integration and complex adaptive systems. *Communications of the ACM*, *45*(10), 59–64. doi:10.1145/570907.570932

Swarm Development Group. (2004). *Chris Langton, Glen Ropella*. Retrieved from http://wiki.swarm.org/.

Talwar, R. (1993). Business re-engineering. *Long Range Planning*, *26*(6), 22–40. doi:10.1016/0024-6301(93)90204-S

Taylor, M. J., McWilliam, J., Forsyth, H., & Wade, S. (2002). Methodologies and website development: A survey of practice. *Information and Software Technology*, *44*(6), 381–391. doi:10.1016/S0950-5849(02)00024-1

Teng, J., Grover, V., & Fiedler, K. (1994). Re-designing business processes using IT. *Long Range Planning*, *27*(1), 95–106. doi:10.1016/0024-6301(94)90010-8

Tersine, R., Harvey, M., & Buckley, M. (1997). Shifting organisational paradigms. *European Management Journal*, *15*(1), 45–57. doi:10.1016/S0263-2373(96)00073-4

Thong, J., Yap, C., & Rahman, K. (1996). Top management support, external expertise and information systems implementation in small businesses. *Information Systems Research*, *7*(2), 248–267. doi:10.1287/isre.7.2.248

Trigo, A., Varajão, J., Figueiredo, N., & Barroso, J. (2007, 23-26 of June). *Information Systems and Technology adoption by the Portuguese large companies.* Paper presented at the European and Mediterranean Conference on Information Systems (EMCIS), Valence, Spain.

Truex, D. P., Baskerville, R., & Kelin, H. (1999). Growing systems in emergent organizations. *Communications of the ACM*, *42*(8), 117–123. doi:10.1145/310930.310984

Trunick, P. A. (1999). ERP: promise or pipe dream. *Transportation and Distribution*, *40*(1), 23–26.

Turner, J. R. (2006). Towards a theory of project management: The nature of the project. *International Journal of Project Management*, *24*(2), 1–3. doi:10.1016/j.ijproman.2005.11.008

Turner, D., & Crawford, M. (1994). Managing Current and Future Competitive Performance: The Role of Competence. In Hamel, G., & Heene, A. (Eds.), *Competence Based Competition*. Chichester: Wiley.

Tyre, M. J., & Orlikowski, J. (1994). Windows of opportunity: Temporal patterns of technological adaptation in organizations. *Organization Science*, *5*(1), 98–119. doi:10.1287/orsc.5.1.98

Ursic, D., Anteric, S., & Mulej, M. (2005). Business process re-engineering in practice - A medium-sized Slovenian company in difficulties. *Systemic Practice and Action Research*, *18*(1), 89–117. doi:10.1007/s11213-005-2461-9

van der Aalst, W. M. P., Pesic, M., & Schonenberg, H. (2009). Declarative workflows: Balancing between flexibility and support. *Computer Science -. Research for Development*, *23*, 99–113.

van der Aalst, W. M. P., ter Hofstede, A. H. M., Kiepuszewski, B., & Barros, A. P. (2003). Workflow patterns. *Distributed and Parallel Databases*, *14*, 5–51.

van der Aalst, W. M. P., Weske, M., & Grünbauer, D. (2005). Case handling: A new paradigm for business process support. *Data & Knowledge Engineering*, *53*(2), 129–162.

van Everdingen, Y., van Hillegersberg, J., & Waarts, E. (2000). Enterprise resource planning: ERP adoption by European midsize companies. *Communications of the ACM*, *43*(4).

Van Stijn, E., & Wensley, A. (2001). Organisational memory and the completeness of process modelling in ERP systems. *Business Process Management Journal*, *7*(3), 181–194. doi:10.1108/14637150110392647

Varajão, J., Trigo, A., Figueiredo, N., & Barroso, J. (2007, Maio). 2007). TI nas empresas nacionais. *Revista CXO*, *2*, 19–23.

Varajão, J., Trigo, A., Figueiredo, N., Barroso, J., & Bulas-Cruz, J. (2009). Information Systems services outsourcing reality in large Portuguese organisations. *International Journal of Business Information Systems*, *4*(1), 125–142.

Varajão, J. (2006, Jan-Mar). Gestão da função de sistemas de informação. *Dirigir - Revista para chefias e quadros, IEFP,* 3-9.

Varajão, J., Ribeiro, A. T., Figueiredo, N., & Barroso, J. (2007, 12-15 of July). *Motivações inerentes à adopção de Tecnologias e Sistemas de Informação nas grandes empresas portuguesas.* Paper presented at the 6ª Conferência Ibero-Americana em Sistemas, Cibernética e Informática (CISCI), Orlando, EUA.

Vos, F. J. J., & Achterkamp, M. C. (2006). Stakeholder identification in innovation projects: Going beyond classification. *European Journal of Innovation Management*, *9*(2), 161–178. doi:10.1108/14601060610663550

Wah, L. (2000). Behind the buzz: The substance of knowledge management. In Cortada, J., & Woods, J. A. (Eds.), *The knowledge management yearbook 2000-2001* (pp. 307–317). Boston, MA: Butterworth-Heineman.

Walsham, G. (1993). *Interpreting Information Systems in organizations*. Chichester, UK: John Wiley & Sons.

Waring, T., & Wainwright, D. (2000). Interpreting integration with respect to information systems in organizations – image, theory and reality. *Journal of Information Technology*, *15*, 131–148. doi:10.1080/026839600344320

Warren, L. (2002). Towards Critical Practice in a Teaching Company Scheme. *OR Insight*, *15*(4), 11–19. doi:10.1057/ori.2002.16

Warren, L. (2003a). Towards Critical Practice in SMEs. *Systemic Practice and Action Research*, *16*(3), 197–212. doi:10.1023/A:1023859805741

Warren, L. (2003b). The crisis of control: a progressive approach towards information systems integration for small companies. *Information Systems and E-business Management*, *1*(4), 353–371.

Warren, L. (2003c). Supporting Knowledge Management through he Viable System Model. *Systemist*, *25*, 156–165.

Warren, L., Fuller, T., Argyle, P., & Welter, F. (2008, September). *A complexity perspective on entrepreneurship: a new methodology for research in high velocity environments*. Paper presented at the British Academy of Management conference, Harrogate, UK.

Wastell, D., White, P., & Kawalek, P. (1994). A methodology for BPR. *The Journal of Strategic Information Systems*, *3*(1), 23–40. doi:10.1016/0963-8687(94)90004-3

Webb, B., & Schlemmer, F. (2006). Resilience as a source of competitive advantage for small IT companies. *Transfer and Diffusion of IT for Organizational Resilience: IFIP*, *206*, 181–197. doi:10.1007/0-387-34410-1_12

Weigand, H. (2006). Two decades of the language-action perspective: Introduction. *Communications of the ACM*, *49*(5), 44–46.

Wind, J., & West, A. (1991). Reinventing the corporation. *Chief Executive*, 72-75.

Winograd, T. (1987-1988). A language/action perspective on the design of cooperative work. *Human-Computer Interaction*, *3*, 3–30.

Winograd, T., & Flores, F. (1986). *Understanding computers and cognition*. Norwood, NJ: Ablex Publishing Corporation.

Wiseman, C. (1988). *Strategic Information Systems*. Homewood, IL: Irwin.

Witherill, J. W., & Kolak, J. (1996). Is corporate re-engineering hurting your employees? *Professional Safety*, *41*(5), 28–32.

Wolcott, P., Qureshi, S., & Kamal, M. "An Information Technology Therapy Approach to Micro-enterprise Adoption of ICTs" *Americas Conference on Information Systems (AMCIS)* 2007

Wolfe, R. A., & Putler, D. S. (2002). How tight are the ties that bind stakeholder groups? *Organization Science*, *13*(1), 64–80. doi:10.1287/orsc.13.1.64.544

Wood-Harper, T. (1985). Research methods in information systems: Using action research. In Mumford, E., Hirschheim, R. A., Fitzgerald, G., & Wood-Harper, T. (Eds.), *Research methods in information systems*. New York: North-Holland Publishers.

Wu, H., & Chou, T. (1992). *Obstacles and reactions of Taiwan's SMEs*. Chung-Hua Institution for Economic Research.

Yap, C. (1989). Computerization problems facing small and medium enterprises: the experience of Singapore, in: *Proceedings of the 20th Annual Meeting of the Midwest Decision Sciences Institute*, Miami University, Miami. *OH. Osteopathic Hospitals*, *19-21*, 128–134.

Yin, R. (1994). *Case study research. Design and methods* (2nd ed.). Newbury Park, CA: Sage.

Yusuf, Y., Gunasekaran, A., & Abthorpe, M. (2004). Enterprise information systems project implementation: A case study of ERP in Rolls-Royce. *International Journal of Production Economics*, *87*, 251. doi:10.1016/j.ijpe.2003.10.004

Yusuf, Y., Gunasekaran, A., & Wu, C. (2006). Implementation of enterprise resource planning in China. *Technovation*, *26*(12), 1324. doi:10.1016/j.technovation.2005.12.003

Yuthas, K., & Dillard, J. F. (1999). Ethical development of advanced technology: A postmodern stakeholder perspective. *Journal of Business Ethics*, *19*(1), 35–49. doi:10.1023/A:1006145805087

Zachman, J. A. (1999). A framework for information systems architecture. *IBM Systems Journal*, *38*(2/3), 454–471. doi:10.1147/sj.382.0454

Zaichkowsky, J. L. (1985). Measuring the involvement construct. *The Journal of Consumer Research*, *12*(3), 341–352. doi:10.1086/208520

Zuber-Skerrit, O. (1991). *Action Research for Change and Development*. Aldershot: Gower Publishing.

About the Contributors

Madjid Tavana is a Professor of Management Information Systems and Decision Sciences and the Lindback Distinguished Chair of Information Systems at La Salle University where he served as Chairman of the Management Department and Director of the Center for Technology and Management. He has been a Distinguished NASA Research Fellow at Kennedy Space Center, Johnson Space Center, Naval Research Laboratory - Stennis Space Center, and Air Force Research Laboratory. He was recently honored with the prestigious Space Act Award by NASA. He holds an MBA, a PMIS, and a PhD in Management Information Systems and received his post-doctoral diploma in strategic information systems from the Wharton School of the University of Pennsylvania. He is the Editor-in-Chief for the *International Journal of Strategic Decision Sciences*, the *International Journal of Enterprise Information Systems*, and the *International Journal of Applied Decision Sciences*. He has published over seventy scholarly research papers in academic journals such as *Decision Sciences, Information Systems, Interfaces, Annals of Operations Research, Omega, Information and Management, Expert Systems with Applications, European Journal of Operational Research, Journal of the Operational Research Society, Computers and Operations Research, Knowledge Management Research and Practice, Computers and Industrial Engineering, Applied Soft Computing, Journal of Advanced Manufacturing Technology, and Advances in Engineering Software*, among others.

* * *

Norita Ahmad is an Assistant Professor of MIS at American University of Sharjah, UAE. She received her PhD in Decision Science Engineering Systems from Rensselaer Polytechnic Institute (RPI), and an MS and a BS in Telecommunications and Network Management and Computer Sciences, respectively, from Syracuse University. Her research interest includes decision analysis, database management systems, and knowledge management. She has presented research internationally and published in a variety of scholarly journals such as International Journal of

Information Technology & Decision Making, Journal of Intelligent Manufacturing, Journal of Business Ethics, and International Journal of Services Operations and Informatics.

Maria Argyropoulou is a doctoral candidate at Brunel University/London. She received her BS and MS in Kapodistriako University of Athens/Greece and Athens University of Economics and Business/Greece respectively. She also holds an MBA from Strathclyde University/Scotland where she works as an Associate Lecturer. She has worked for Greek and international companies for more than 10 years specialising in operations management and ERP systems implementation. Her work has appeared in journals and conference proceedings. Her research interests focus on corporate governance and IT systems implementation and evaluation.

João Barroso, is a Professor at the Department of Engineering of the University of Trás-os-Montes e Alto Douro, where he teaches undergraduate and postgraduate courses on software engineering, image processing, and computer vision. He has been actively involved in the definition and implementation of the Trás-os-Montes Digital project, funded by the Portuguese Government and by the European Community, and focused on the development of the information society in the North-East region of Portugal.

Samo Bobek is a Professor of Information Systems at the School of Economics and Business at University of Maribor. He teaches courses in undergraduate level (Introduction to Information Systems, Information Systems in Finance and Banking), Master of Science program (Information Systems Management, Management Information Systems, Information Systems in Service Organizations) and MBA program (Information Management). Professor Bobek's research areas are strategic Information Systems planning, information management, and banking technology. He has published several books in the Slovene language. His bibliography includes more than 200 articles, conference papers, research reports, et cetera. Professor Bobek is head of Information and Organization Systems Department. Professor Bobek also acts as consultant to several corporations, banks, and insurance firms in Slovenia.

Albert Boonstra is an Associate Professor at the Faculty of Economics and Business at the University of Groningen, The Netherlands, where is director of the graduate programmes in Business Administration. He specializes in the organizational issues that surround the use of advanced Information Technologies, especially in healthcare environments. He has conducted extensive research and consultancy in this field, and has published in International Journal of Information Management, European Journal of Information Systems, International Journal of

Project Management, Journal of Strategic Information Systems. His most recent book is Managing Information Systems, an Organisational Perspective (2009, 3rd edition), with Financial Times/Prentice Hall, Harlow.

Giorgio Bruno is an Associate Professor at Politecnico di Torino, where he teaches courses on software engineering and object-oriented programming. His current interests concern the operational modeling of business processes and collaborative services, and the design of Information Systems and workflow systems. He has authored two books and over 120 technical papers on the above-mentioned subjects.

Jeffrey Chang is Principle Lecturer at London South Bank University where he has been director of the Postgraduate Computing and Information Management Programme for several years. His research and teaching interests are in Information Systems management, the use of IS/IT in SMEs, and organizational change and behaviour. He has had papers published in Information Systems Journal and Knowledge and Process Management and in his South Bank programme has developed and taught modules such as Software Project Management and Strategic Management of Information Systems. Jeffrey received his doctorate from Warwick Business School in 2001. His thesis, entitled "Exploring the links between business process re-engineering (BPR) and small and medium-sized enterprises (SMEs)," involved an empirical investigation into organizational change within the small business domain, with a focus on how Information Technology facilitates business transformation.

Ruey-Shun Chen is an Associate Professor in the Department of Information Management at the China University of Technology in Taiwan. Research interests include IT strategy and planning, enterprise Information Systems, and strategic Information Systems. He has published over 20 papers, which have appeared in several leading journals such as *Information & Management* and *European Journal of Operational Research.*

Maria Manuela Cruz-Cunha is currently an Associate Professor in the School of Technology at the Polytechnic Institute of Cavado and Ave, Portugal. She holds a Dipl. Eng. in the field of Systems and Informatics Engineering, an M.Sci. in the field of Information Society and a Dr.Sci in the field of Virtual Enterprises, all from the University of Minho (Portugal). She teaches subjects related to Information Systems, Information Technologies and Organizational Models to undergraduated and post-graduated studies. She supervises several PhD projects in the domain of Virtual Enterprises and Information Systems and Technologies. She regularly publishes in international peer-reviewed journals and participates on international scientific conferences. She serves as a member of Editorial Board and Associate Editor for several International Journals and for several Scientific Committees of International Conferences. She has authored and edited several books, and her work appears in more than 70 papers published in journals, book chapters, and conference proceedings.

Zdenko Dezelak is research and teaching assistant of Information Systems at the School of Economics and business at the University of Maribor where he studies a Master of Science degree. His research areas e-business solutions and implementation of e-business solutions. His bibliography includes several articles, conference papers, research reports, et cetera. He collaborates in several courses in undergraduate level (E-business, Introduction to Information Systems, E- Finance and E- Banking, Enterprise Resource Planning Solutions, E-Business Information Systems) and several courses in Master of Science program (Business Information Solutions, Strategic Management Issues in E-business). He also cooperates with some companies in Slovenia as a consultant.

Jovan Duduković, Dipl. ing., is a Junior Researcher at the Mihailo Pupin Institute, Belgrade, Serbia. He has received a Dipl. Ing. degree in 2004 at the School of Electrical Engineering, University of Belgrade, Serbia. While working in scientific projects financed by the Serbian Ministry of Science and EU (FP6 and FP7), he took part in the design and implementation of several decision support systems (SARIB), design and implementation of Semantic Web Portal (Web4WeB), and implementation of enterprise applications (SUSDEV). He has experience in enterprise application software development, GIS application development, Web application architecture, and database development. His interests include Semantic Web, knowledge representation and architecture of software systems.

Ted Fuller is Head of Lincoln Business School at the University of Lincoln in the United Kingdom. Formerly, he was Professor of Entrepreneurship and Strategic Foresight and Head of the Centre for Entrepreneurship and SME Development at Teesside Business School, University of Teesside. Prior to that, he was Director of the Foresight Research Centre at Durham Business School. He researches processes of entrepreneurship and the contribution that entrepreneurship makes to the futures of individuals and society. He is member of many boards of academic journals, leads international research programmes, publishes widely, and advises government and corporate organisations.

Jorge Marx Gómez is working as a full-time Professor at the business informatics group at Oldenburg University. His research interests include Very Large Business Applications (VLBA), federated ERP systems, and sustainability reporting.

Angappa Gunasekaran is a Professor and the Chairperson of the department of Decision and Information sciences at the Charlton College of Business, University of Massachusetts, Dartmouth. He has a PhD in industrial engineering and operations research from the Indian Institute of Technology (Bombay). He is teaching undergraduate and graduate courses in operations management and management science. Dr. Gunasekaran has received *Thomas J. Higginson Award for Excellence in Teaching* (2001-2002) within the Charlton College of Business. He has over 200 articles published in 40 different peer-reviewed journals that include *OMEGA, Journal of Operations Management, International Journal of Operations & Production Management, International Journal of Production Research, Production and Inventory Management Journal, European Journal of Operational Research and Computers & Industrial Engineering.* He has presented about 50 papers and published about 50 articles in conferences and given a number of invited more talks in about 20 countries. He has received an *Outstanding Paper Award* from *Managerial Auditing Journal* for the year 2002. Dr. Gunasekaran is on the Editorial Board of over 20 journals. Dr. Gunasekaran edits several journals in operations management and Information Systems. He is currently interested in researching benchmarking, management Information Systems, e-commerce (B2B), Information Technology/Systems evaluation, performance measures and metrics in new economy, logistics, and supply chain management. Dr. Gunasekaran is also the Director of Business Innovation Research Center (BIRC).

Marilyn Helms is the Sesquicentennial Endowed Chair and Professor of Management at Dalton State College in Dalton, Georgia. She holds a doctorate degree from the University of Memphis. She had published extensively on the topics of strategy, quality, and international management and writes a monthly column on management issues for the *Dalton Daily Citizen* newspaper. Her recent research interests include e-commerce, customer service management, and student satisfaction with on-line and hybrid courses.

George Ioannou is an Associate Professor of Operations and Business Processes Management at the Department of Management Science and Technology at AUEB and head of the Operations Management and ERP Systems Research Centre of the Management Sciences Laboratory. He has been Assistant Professor at the Industrial and Systems Engineering Department of Virginia Tech and Head of the Manufacturing Systems Integration Laboratory there. His research focuses on the analysis, design, and optimization of operations systems and business processes, combining advanced network and computational technologies with operational research models and methods. He has graduated from the Mechanical Engineering Faculty at National Technical University of Athens, from the Centre for Robotics and Automated Systems in Imperial College of Science, Technology, and Medicine (scholarship SERC) and from the Computer Integrated Manufacturing Lab of Institute for Systems Research, University of Maryland (scholarship by National Science Foundation).

Valentina Janev, MSc, is a Senior Researcher at the Mihailo Pupin Institute, Belgrade, Serbia. Since 1996 she has participated in design, development, and implementation of many business Information Systems, first as a Software Engineer and later as a Consultant. She is actively involved in scientific projects financed by the Serbian Ministry of Science, as well in EU FP6 and FP7 projects. Her resent interests include Semantic Web, applications of semantic technologies and W3C standards in the knowledge management field, and knowledge management architectures for R&D organizations. She is an author of more than 30 published papers, some of them in international journals and books.

Wen-Jang (Kenny) Jih is a Professor of Computer Information Systems of the Jennings A. Jones College of Business at the Middle Tennessee State University. He obtained his doctorate degree in business computer Information Systems from the University ofNorth Texas in 1985. His recent research interests include: e-commerce, m-commerce, knowledge management, customer relationship management, and innovative instructional methods in Information Systems.

Dimitrios N. Koufopoulos (B.Sc., MBA, PhD MCMI, FIMC) is Senior Lecturer in the Brunel Business School. His work has appeared in the *European Marketing Academy Conference, British Academy of Management and Strategic Management Society Proceedings*, and in various journals like *Long Range Planning Journal, Journal of Strategic Change, Journal of Financial Services Marketing, Corporate Ownership and Control,* and *Corporate Board.* His research interests are on strategic planning systems, top management teams, corporate governance, and corporate strategies.

Ana Lampret has been involved in the IT business solutions since 2003, mostly in ERP, but also CRM. Her professional experience in IT includes Business Solutions Sales Manager at Adacta Software (2003-2007, www.adacta-group.com), and Partner Technology Specialist at Microsoft Slovenia (2007-2008, www.microsoft.com/slovenia/dynamics). Currently she manages the ERP sales in all Balkan markets for SRC group (www.src.si). Her responsibilities have included acquiring new projects, key account management, and project implementation methodology design. Prior to that, Ana worked in the financial industry (1999-2000, sales consultant at Poteza Stock Broking, www.poteza.si; 2000-2003, sales consultant at First Pension Company/Prva pokojninska druzba, www.prva.net), when she was involved in the project of the internal CRM system implementation (custom design). Ana got her B.A. in Politics and Economics at the University of York, UK in 1999 (http://www.york.ac.uk/depts/pep/). She obtained her International Baccalaureate degree (A-level equivalent) at the United World College of the Adriatic, Duino, Italy (www.uwcad.it).

Margi Levy is an Associate Professor in the Enterprise Group at Warwick Business School, University of Warwick. Before becoming an academic she worked as an IS consultant with Coopers and Lybrand in W. Australia, for a number of financial and software development organizations in London. She has published in a number of journals: Information and Management, Journal of Strategic Information Systems, European Journal of Information Systems, Information Resource Management Journal, International Journal of Technology Management, and Small Business Economics. She is the co-author with Philip Powell of the first book to address the study of information strategies for SMEs: Strategies for Growth in SMEs: the role of information and Information Systems, Butterworth Heinemann, 2005. She is currently researching into IS adoption of new and innovative technologies in SMEs and also the role of intermediaries in SME IS adoption.

Daniel Lübke is a Research Assistant at the software group at the Leibniz Universität Hannover. He has worked as software developer and trainer before and is currently researching in the fields Service-Oriented Architecture. Further research interests include Agile Software Development.

Efrem Mallach has taught MIS at the University of Massachusetts Dartmouth since 2003. Prior to that, his career encompassed teaching (Boston College, UMass Lowell, where he served as department chair) and industry (Director of Strategic Planning, Honeywell Information Systems; Division General Manager, General Systems Group; CEO, Kensington Group Inc.). Perhaps because of this varied background, his interests focus on explaining the real world to his students and other audiences. Dr. Mallach has a B.S.E. degree from Princeton University, an MBA from Boston University, and a Ph.D. from the Massachusetts Institute of Technology.

Jaideep Motwani, Ph.D., is a Professor and the Chair of the Management Department at Grand Valley State University. He received his Ph.D. degree in Operations Management from University of North Texas. His research interests include

Information Technology management, enterprise systems, and quality management. He has published in a variety of journals including IEEE Transactions on Engineering Management, Operations Research, Omega, Journal of Operational Research Society, European Journal of Operational Research, International Journal of Operations and Production Management, International Journal of Production Research, and International Journal of Technology Management. Dr. Motwani also serves as a consultant and trainer for a number of organizations in the areas of Information Technology implementation, project management, and total quality management.

Eric W. T. Ngai is an Associate Professor in the Department of Management and Marketing at The Hong Kong Polytechnic University. His research interests are in the areas of e-commerce, decision support systems, supply chain systems, and knowledge management systems. He has published in a number of journals including *IEEE Transactions on Systems, Man and Cybernetics, Journal of Operations Management, Decision Support Systems, Information & Management, Production & Operations Management,* and others. He serves on editorial board of six international journals. Dr Ngai has received the Faculty Award for Outstanding Performance/Achievement in Teaching (2003-2004).

Aidan O'Connor is a Professor of Strategy and International Business at ESCEM Ecole Supérieure de Commerce et de Management, France, and is also Academic Director of the Masters specialization in International Business and Management. He was awarded a Postgraduate Diploma in Statistics and a Master of Science in Economics from Trinity College, University of Dublin, Ireland. He obtained his Doctorate from the Ecole des Hautes Etudes Commerciales, Université de Lausanne, Switzerland. He has extensive experience in management, especially in research and planning and risk management, and academic experience in several European countries. Dr. O'Connor is also Visiting Professor of Strategy at the Universität Osnabrück, Germany. He was also awarded a Fellowship by the Council of Europe. His research interests focus on strategy, industrial organization, and international trade. His book Trade, Investment and Competition in International Banking was recently published by Palgrave and he is the editor of Managing Economies, Trade and International Business to be published by Palgrave in 2009.

Philip Powell is Deputy Dean, Professor of Information Management, and was Director of the Centre for Information Management in the School of Management at the University of Bath. Formerly, he was Professor of Information Systems, University of London, and Director of the Information Systems Research Unit at Warwick Business School. He is the author of seven books on Information Systems and financial modeling. His work has been published in over 90 international journals and over 100 conferences. He is Managing Editor of the Information Systems Journal and associate editor and editorial board member of a number of other journals. He is a past President of the UK Academy for Information Systems. His research concerns the role and use of Information Systems in organizations, especially issues of strategy and evaluation in the context of small firms. More recently he has contributed to research on e-business and knowledge management.

Layth Sliman completed his Diploma in Computer Engineering, then he obtained his Master's and Ph.D. in Information Systems. Since 2003, he underwent many research period and technical training courses in Information and Communication Technologies, mainly in India, and Japan. During the period 2000-2010, he worked as a tele-informatics teacher, in INSA Lyon, visiting researcher in University of the Ryukyus -Japan, a post doctorate at ENIT-Tarbes, France. Presently, he is Assistant Professor at EFREI Engineering School, France.

Simona Sternad is senior lecturer of Information Systems at the School of Economics and business at the University of Maribor where she received a Master of Science degree in 2005. Her research areas are business process reengineering, ERP solutions and e-business solutions, implementation of ERP solutions, and maintenance of ERP solutions. Her bibliography includes more than 50 articles, conference papers, research reports, et cetera. She collaborates in several courses in undergraduate level (E-business, Introduction to Information Systems, E- Finance and E- Banking, Enterprise Resource Planning Solutions, E-Business Information Systems) and several courses in Master of Science program (Business Information Solutions, Strategic Management Issues in E-business). Simona Sternad also cooperates with some companies in Slovenia as a consultant.

Chia-Ming (Jimmy) Sun is the Assistant Professor of the Accounting Department at the National Yunlin University of Science & Technology in Taiwan. He received his Ph.D. in information management from Chiao-Tung University. Research interests include IT strategy and planning and enterprise Information Systems. He has the industrial background that worked as IS manager and consultant in manufacturing companies.

Kathryn Szabat is an Associate Professor of Statistics and Operations Research at LaSalle University. She received her PhD in Statistics, with cognate field in Operations Research, from the Wharton School of University of Pennsylvania. Dr. Szabat provides statistical advice to numerous business, non-business, and academic communities. Her current research interests include collaborative applied research on student performance in education and making statistics more effective in schools of business.

Antonio Trigo, is a PhD candidate in Information Systems at Universidade de Trás-os-Montes e Alto Douro. Currently he teaches at Escola Superior de Gestão e Tecnologia de Oliveira do Hospital of the Instituto Politécnico de Coimbra. His research interests include IS management, IS strategy, IS function, and organizational impacts of IT/IS solutions. António has more than five years experience as a software developer having produced IT/IS solutions for such companies as Portugal Telecom, Cabo Verde Telecom, Meditel and Telesp Celular.

João Varajão is currently a Professor at the Department of Engineering of the University of Trás-os-Montes e Alto Douro, where he teaches undergraduate and postgraduate courses. He supervises several Msc and PhD projects in the domain of Information Systems management, enterprise Information Systems, and electronic business systems. He earned his PhD and MSc from the University of Minho, Portugal. He is the author of several books, refereed publications, and communications at international conferences.

Sanja Vraneš is jointly appointed as a Scientific Director of the Mihailo Pupin Institute and as a Professor of Computer Science at the University of Belgrade. Since 1999 she has been engaged as a United Nations Expert for Information Technologies, and from 2003 as an EU Expert for intelligent content and semantics area. Her research interests include Semantic Web, knowledge management, intelligent agents, e-collaboration, decision support systems, multicriteria analysis algorithms, et cetera. In these areas she has published over 150 scientific papers. She serves as a reviewer of respectable international journals, like IEEE Transaction on Computer, IEEE Intelligent Systems magazine, and also as a reviewer and evaluator of EU FP6 and FP7 projects. She has also served as a project leader and/or principal architect of more than 20 complex software projects. She is a member of IEEE, ACM, and AAAI. She is also a member of Serbian Academy of Engineering Sciences and of National Scientific Council.

Lorraine Warren is Deputy Director of Postgraduate Education, and a Senior Lecturer in Entrepreneurship and Innovation at the School of Management, University of Southampton in the United Kingdom. She researches the processes of high technology/high growth entrepreneurship and innovation in dynamic emergent sectors such as the creative industries in the digital economy. She has presented at international conferences and has published widely in peer reviewed journals. She has worked on a number of funded research projects with universities in the US and Russia, and has advised Russian technology institutes on issues of technology transfer. She is a member of the British Academy of Management and an Associate of the Chartered Management Institute.

Kristi Wenrich has been working in the IT industry for a decade. She has a Master of Software Engineering degree from The Pennsylvania State University School of Graduate Professional Studies and a B.S. in Computer Science from Temple University. Her research interests include software engineering, requirements engineering, ERP systems, and knowledge management.

Index

J

K

L

M

N

O

P

Q

R

S

T

U

V

CPSIA information can be obtained at www.ICGtesting.com
263891BV00004B/1-68/P

9 781609 605292